Jewish Responses
to
Nazi Persecution

Also by Isaiah Trunk

*Judenrat: The Jewish Councils
in Eastern Europe under Nazi Occupation*

Jewish Responses
to
Nazi Persecution

Collective and Individual Behavior
in Extremis

ISAIAH TRUNK

STEIN AND DAY/*Publishers*/New York

A special word of thanks to Joachim Neugroschel for his help in the translation of Part One of this Book.

It is also my pleasant duty to express my hearty thanks to my son Gabriel, who translated Part II of the book, which contains the most difficult material, namely the eyewitness testimonies.

I am most thankful to my wife Celia for her patience and endurance in the tiresome task of proofreading.

My sincere appreciation goes, too, to the YIVO Institute for Jewish Research in New York, whose archives contain the bulk of the source material used in this book.

Copyright © 1979 by Isaiah Trunk
Translation of Part Two
    from the Yiddish, by Gabriel Trunk
All rights reserved.
Designed by Ed Kaplin
Printed in the United States of America
Stein and Day/*Publishers*/Scarborough House,
Briarcliff Manor, N.Y. 10510

Library of Congress Cataloging in Publication Data

Trunk, Isaiah.
    Jewish responses to Nazi persecution.

    Includes index.
        1.   Holocaust, Jewish (1939–1945)   2.   World War,
1939–1945—Personal narratives, Jewish.   I.   Title.
D810.J4T7   940.53'1503'924   78-6378
ISBN   0-8128-2500-4

Maps "The Invasion of Poland, 1939" and "The German Invasion of Russia, 1941" are from *The World at War* by Mark Arnold-Forster. Map "Eastern Europe, 1940" is from *The Battle for Moscow* by Albert Seaton. All are reprinted by permission of the publisher, Stein and Day.

CONTENTS

ILLUSTRATIONS

MAPS

PREFACE

This book focuses on a central aspect of the Holocaust, the *day-to-day life and struggle of the Jewish victims*. The absence of extensive historical research into this important area may be explained by a variety of factors. To begin with, there is a predilection in the general historiography on World War II for investigating the crimes and motives of the criminals while avoiding the experiences of the victims in many instances. While it is understandable that there should be a compelling desire to unravel the evil complexities of the Nazi Reich, the almost exclusive preoccupation with Nazi power has led, on the popular level, to some unsettling consequences. One result of this one-sided concern with the Nazi aspect of the war and the Holocaust is the mistaken notion that, within the immense bureaucracy and technology of genocide, the Jewish victims were passive objects of the "process," and therefore merit far less specialized study.

Until recently, with few laudable exceptions, the Jewish historiography on the Holocaust elaborated its three main concerns, namely, martyrology, resistance, and the Nazi policy and mechanism of extermination. The first of these is the dimension of *martyrology*, which naturally dominates the field and embodies the obligation to preserve and memorialize the tragic events of the war, if only in their bare detail, in their heartrending repetitiveness. The numerous Holocaust memorial books have served both to sanctify the names and martyrs for all time and to catalogue for the world the full nature and scope of the atrocities against the Jewish people. With regard to the second concern of Jewish writing on the Holocaust, that which champions the cause of Jewish *resistance* to the Nazis, there is a more complicated reaction. The external dynamic that has influenced the nature and course of this segment of the literature is, primarily, the above-mentioned disparagement, which posits that Jews went to their death passively, "like sheep to the slaughter." The calumny that Jews were active collaborators in their own destruction has also triggered a strong effort to refute this equally fashionable myth. The whole gamut of writing on Jewish resistance—published memoirs, documentary anthologies, monographic and survey studies alike—has been forced to assume a slightly apologetic air.

At the same time, a stronger inner dynamic was at work, which exerted the prime influence on the direction Jewish Holocaust literature would take. On the one hand, those who had miraculously survived harbored the pressing emotional need to divulge the incidents in their own and other people's lives that would testify to the spiritual will the Jewish nation manifested in its struggle for life. The very telling was a condemnation of Nazi barbarism and a continuation of their struggle against it. Their suppressed feelings of hatred and revenge against the enemy found a meager yet satisfying outlet in the "naming of names," which was the conduit for their subconscious rage against sullying the memory of the dead, by waging the enemy's posthumous battle of distorting the victims' doomed and tragic martyrdom.

To understand the true feelings of outrage of these survivors, one must ask: Why isn't there one recorded instance of armed insurrection by Gentile inmates of a concentration camp, when the conditions for such were more favorable than for the Jews, who rose many times? Why were the children and youth of the Warsaw Ghetto, the pathetically armed remnants of a decimated nation, the first to rise against the Nazis anywhere in Europe?

In trying to resolve its justified anguish, the generation of the Holocaust, bearing its traumatic legacy as a lesson, has turned to a seemingly still hostile and indifferent world. It thus becomes essential that special attention be turned inward to the manifold Jewish experience during the war years. Examination of the daily norms of life under Nazi tyranny, the structures of community activity, the modes of personal and collective struggle, should be intensified and encouraged. Without soundly documented observation, selected aspects of the Holocaust will remain unnecessarily clouded and controversial. We will be deprived of the human face of the victims, their dilemmas in trying to maintain life and integrity under the most trying and tragic conditions known to man. We will lose a facet of the human condition and psyche to generality and mythification.

It must be emphasized anew that Jewish life during the Holocaust covered a complex spectrum of phenomena of which extermination was the last in a torturous series of tragic phases. The annihilation of the Jews in the ghettos and camps was preceded by an intense and relatively long period of struggle for survival, though time in that unprecedented epoch is better measured by the dizzying tempo of calamities and their effects than by chronology. We have an almost visceral interest in knowing how the Jews confronted their daily ordeals. How were the few able to survive those conditions and what were the aftereffects? We are faced with a people who, for the first time in history, were subjected to almost complete eradication in an area where they had been settled for a millennium; who lived day after day within the ever-expanding shadow of death, over a period of several years.

We really know so little about them. The questions are boundless: Was there a dichotomy or an inherent unity in the evolution of Jewish resistance from passivity to activity? What were the developing symptoms, mechanisms of compensation, and long-term effects of the steadily deteriorating physical and mental condition of the Jews in the ghettos and camps? How did Jewish family life survive the decimations and forced "sacrifices" of entire segments of its population, and what changes in the demographic structure of the ghetto populace contributed to the diminution and, at times, to the total disintegration of the family, and consequently to the weakening of the entire social organism? What were the conditions under which Jews eked out their miserable living, and what kind of economic structure and pressures prevailed in the doomed ghettos and camps? What resources could the Jews summon to surmount the unrelenting Nazi terror and psychological warfare used against them, and how were they able to prolong their lives in the disease-ridden and infested ghettos and camps, when Nazi calculations had determined that they should have been dead long ago? How did the Jewish individual and collective interrelate, and how did communal life work for or against the prerequisites for survival? What were the personal and national strengths and liabilities which characterized Jewish reaction to Nazi genocide? Can they be classified into patterns, and if so, are they constant or variable within the period itself and within Jewish history as a whole?

And though this book attempts a more comprehensive survey of the significant manifestations of Jewish life during the Holocaust, it is beyond the scope of this work to thoroughly delineate and analyze in detail all the multiple facets of Jewish life during this period. Such an undertaking will demand a concerted, sustained, and exhaustive research effort. Rather, we wish to direct further interest and inquiry into this area.

For the purposes of presenting both an analytical framework for the diverse problems of internal Jewish life during the Holocaust which concern us in this volume, and a complementary set of documents upon which to base, in part, our discussions and further study, this book has been divided into two separate, yet interrelated sections. Part One offers, in general outline, a picture of Jewish behavior *in extremis* when confronted with the evil, sadism, terror, and murder unleashed by the German and local Gentile enemies. We are concerned specifically with the internal Jewish response to the implementation of the "Final Solution," and with the energies the Jews harnessed in combatting it. During its later stages, this response resulted in the first major armed retaliations against the Nazis in several occupied European countries. Part Two brings to light sixty-two as yet mostly unknown and unpublished eyewitness testimonies of Jewish Holocaust survivors, the *sherit hapleita*, gathered among the ruins of Europe and the still smoldering ashes of Europe's Jews as the war was ending or at its close. These are the experiences of Jewish men, women, and children, who lead us in an abysmal descent through the "seven levels of Gehenna," where their suffering and intimacy with death was matched only by their clinging to life.

Part One

HISTORICAL ANTECEDENTS

Before considering the problem of Jewish responses to Nazi persecution, it will be useful and instructive to review very briefly the historical antecedents. By recalling how in their long history, so full of vicissitudes, the Jews of Europe reacted to persecutions by inimical governments and societies, perhaps we can discover patterns of responses that also have a bearing on Jewish behavior during the Holocaust. We will begin this examination with the Middle Ages.

The Middle Ages

In the Middle Ages the prevailing attitude was one of strict dependence on, and loyalty to, temporal authority. The temporal ruler was the only power who might be able and willing to protect the Jews as his *servi camerae* and as a source of inexhaustible revenues. The Jews, on their part, were interested in the protection of their physical security, their religion, and the inviolability of their property. The economical usefulness of the Jews, and especially of the court Jews, more or less guaranteed the achievement of these modest goals, hence the attitude of loyalty toward the rulers. The messianic hopes of the Jews did not by any means contradict this attitude.

Historical experience had taught the Jews that each upheaval of the social order resulted in a worsening of their status. The crusades, which considerably changed the political and social status of the Jews in Germany and France, supplied a striking example, as did the pattern of behavior of the Jews vis-à-vis the attempts at forced conversion. The then prevailing phenomenon of collective and voluntary martyrdom was unique in their history. However, we find even then a different pattern of behavior, such as armed self-defense, when Jews confronted their assailants, as happened in Mainz, Germany and Shelo, Bohemia during the First Crusade.

In Medieval Jewish chronicles and homilies, we discover justification of the calamity: as a punishment by the hand of God for committed sins—*mipney khatoeynu*. We also encounter in these accounts some sober explanations of the causes of hatred toward Jews: lack of honesty in dealing with Christians, economic competition, and immodest behavior in public. As a result of the Crusades, exclusion from Christian society became the characteristic feature of Jewish life in

3

Western and Central Europe. A similar outcome may be found in the sources relating to the gruesome events during the years of the Black Death (1348–1349). The repeatedly pronounced resolutions of the synods against manifestations of social intercourse between Jews and Christians is matched by rabbinic exhortations against Jews mingling with Christians. Jews were stigmatized as an alien ethnic group and as enemies of Christianity who should be separated from Christians. For the Jews, the Crusades were a deeply felt trauma signaling the end of an epoch of bearable coexistence between them and their surroundings. Their response was an inward withdrawal into their own *dalet amos,* their own secluded ivory tower, as if to say: "You exclude us from your midst, therefore we will make our separation from you even stricter."

The Spanish Catastrophe

The crisis of Spanish Jewry at the end of the fifteenth century presents an entirely different picture compared with the situation of the Jews in Germany and northern France. The Jewish community in Spain, one of the oldest European Jewish communities, achieved a high degree of economic prosperity and social prestige in the provinces under both Islamic and Christian rule. Jewish notables, financiers, physicians, and scholars played an important role in the courts of the rulers. The cultural picture was also different from that of Germany and northern France. The attachment to religion and tradition was somewhat loosened in certain segments of the Jewish population, owing to the influence of Greek philosophy transmitted through Arabic channels. In the confrontation between rationalism and faith, the supernational and mythological elements of the latter fell victim. As time went on, an ever-widening gap separated the naive faith of the masses from the rationalism and skepticism of an influential elite in regard to observing the Torah commandments. Whole segments of the Jewish intelligentsia, the court Jews, and some of the ruling class in the communities freed themselves from the yoke of observing fundamental commandments of the Law, not even shrinking before taking Christian wives or concubines. When in 1391 many Jewish communities, beginning with Seville, had to choose between the Cross and death, the Marranos, forced converts who secretly remained Jews.
thousands chose the Cross and life. Thus was born the problem of
  This phenomenon of mass conversion was repeated during the tragic epilogue of this century of religious persecution and intolerance with the expulsion of the Jews from Spain in 1492 and from Portugal in 1496.

As in Germany during the Crusades, pious and repentant Jews found an explanation for the disaster that befell Spanish Jewry in the weakening of the faith and the abandonment of the traditional way of life. Again God had meted out punishment for the sins committed by the freethinkers. Comparing the behavior of their faithful brethren in Germany and France 400 years earlier with the betrayal by the intelligentsia and the rich and worldly, they arrived at the conclusion that the fault was the deviation from the path prescribed by God's Law. They contrasted the martyrdom or voluntary exile taken upon themselves by the unlearned, especially women, with the unprincipled behavior of many among the upper classes. The conclusion was clear to them: the weakening of the faith by the few was responsible for the apostasy by many.

The Post-Emancipation Period

The period of the Emancipation was a turning point in the Jewish attitude toward Christian society. In Western and Central Europe, where emancipation of the Jews achieved its goals de jure and, more or less, de facto, it was accompanied by a drive for total integration into Christian society, a lessening to a minimum of the differences between Jews and Gentiles. Religious faith was the only acceptable differentiating factor. However, worship was to be drastically reformed so as to acquire the decorum of the church service.

The traditional patterns of behavior—isolation from the outside world and strict adherence to traditional values—were gradually abandoned by large segments of the Jewish population, especially the secularized intelligentsia and the growing working class. The attitude of the emancipated Jew toward the government and society was characterized by gratitude and absolute loyalty, culminating among the most integrated in a strong patriotism and total identification with the interests of the motherland. The post-Emancipation Jews regarded the recourse of appealing to the laws of the country, which bestowed on them equal rights, as the only remedy against certain forms of social discrimination.

Prior to the Emancipation, Jews were as a rule immune to the negative opinions expressed by Gentiles, facing them with contempt and a feeling of superiority. Now, however, the question *Ma yomru hagoyim?* ("What will the Gentiles say?") was a disquieting one for the emancipated Jew and influenced his behavior to a large extent.

In Eastern Europe, the legal emancipation of Jews came much later —in Tsarist Russia after the revolution of 1917, in Poland and the Baltic countries after 1918. Until this time, the methods of struggling against persecution and discrimination were to a large extent a continuation of the traditional ones: intercession with the authorities by Jewish notables on behalf of their coreligionists, circumvention of anti-Jewish decrees, and bribing of officials among the corrupt bureaucracy.

In contrast to the situation in Western and Central Europe, the government was regarded as a hostile power against which one should defend oneself by all means. Thus, the loyalty of the average East European Jew toward his government was only a formal and apparent one, since there were far fewer objective reasons for developing an attitude of identification with the interests of his country.

The Prewar Nazi Period

Among the Jews in Germany, the first ones to be affected by the Nazi onslaught, we find in the beginning a tendency to minimize the ferocity of the anti-Jewish propaganda and measures. There was a widespread belief that with Hitler's ascent to power he would behave like a responsible leader and drop the extravagances of his anti-Jewish program. The leaders of the *Reichsvertretung* (the Representation of the Jews in Germany) and later of the *Reichsvereinigung der Juden in Deutschland* (the National Union of Jews in Germany) hoped to come to terms with Hitler and make life for the Jews somehow bearable.

However, under pressure of the growing tide of persecution—the Nuremberg Laws of 1935, the laws concerning "Aryanization," etc.— the community leadership abandoned the illusion of somehow finding a modus vivendi with the Nazi regime. It now directed its activity along the lines of emigration, *Umschichtung* (abandoning the traditional Jewish trades), and cultural self-sufficiency (the *Kulturbund*). The annexation of Austria and the public humiliation of its Jews during the first few weeks resulted in a psychological breakdown, especially among the Jews in the capital, which manifested itself in an unusually high number of suicides and in hasty mass emigration, particularly after "Crystal Night" in November 1938.

The Boycott Movement

The economic boycott against Nazi Germany began spontaneously in 1933 as an expression of the Jewish response to the first anti-Jewish acts of the Hitler regime. Boycott committees, or boycott actions supported by Jewish organizations, sprang up in the United States. The initiative came from the American Jewish Congress, joined by the Jewish Labor Committee in England, France, Poland, Belgium, Mexico, Canada, and South Africa. During 1934, a central boycott committee of sorts was formed in Geneva.

For three years, the boycott movement was effective, causing Germany economic damage. But for a variety of reasons, both internal Jewish and external ones, the movement declined greatly in 1935, and by 1936, it was finished for all practical purposes as an organized movement. In the United States, two prestigious Jewish organizations were against the boycott from the very start: the American Jewish Committee and the B'nai B'rith Anti-Defamation League. The same position was taken by the Jewish Board of Deputies in England. Their negative attitude was due to their inability to grasp the true nature of Hitlerism. For several years, they hoped that Nazi Germany could be influenced through normal diplomatic channels. They also doubted the success of a boycott, citing the demands of certain German Jewish activists in communal life to halt the boycott as doing more harm than good, since it looked like an indirect confirmation of the Nazi thesis about an international Jewish conspiracy.

One factor intimidating the American Jewish Committee against any assertive action for the benefit of German Jews was the growing American anti-Semitism influenced by Nazi propaganda in the 1930s. The audience for Father Charles E. Coughlin's anti-Semitic radio broadcasts numbered 3½ million listeners, and the polls revealed that half the American population had anti-Jewish feelings. The Jewish organizations therefore decided that the time was not ripe and the social atmosphere not ready for purely Jewish actions. It was not until March 1938 that the American Jewish Committee changed its position. And not until August 1939, when its branches in Germany, Austria, and Czechoslovakia had already been disbanded by the Nazis, did the B'nai B'rith form a boycott committee and instruct its local lodges to become active in the cause.

A main reason for the anti-boycott attitude of these organizations may be sought in the U.S. Department of State's expressed position against a "racist or political boycott" that could mean a loss for American exports.

A second internal factor paralyzing the boycott movement was the so-called "Transfer Agreement" (*Haavarah*), that a Jewish organization, The Trust and Transfer Office, in Tel-Aviv, Palestine, supported by the Anglo-Palestine Bank, had concluded with the German government. This agreement stipulated that every German Jewish emigré to Palestine had the right to take out the equivalent of 1,000 Reichsmarks in cash from his personal assets; the rest would be paid out in the form of German products, which a German exporter of industrial machines would ship to Palestine. This agreement proved to be of economic benefit to both sides. But even Zionists argued about the moral aspect of the agreement, which turned Jewish emigrés into so many exporters of German products. There was a clear internal contradiction between the boycott movement and the "Transfer Agreement."

Meanwhile, after the boycott against Nazi Germany had been endorsed at the second preparatory conference of the Jewish World Congress in September 1933, the Germans promptly began an intensive anti-boycott action. The regime brought pressure to bear on certain governments to liquidate the boycott movement. One such country was Poland, with which Germany concluded a nonaggression pact in January 1934. In June 1935, the Polish government prohibited the activities of the boycott committee in Warsaw and closed its offices. The Lithuanian government similarly outlawed the boycott. In August 1934 the prime minister of South Africa, General James Barry Herzog, appealed to the local Jews to give up the boycott since it harmed the interests of the country. Germany also employed all means to smash the boycott, whose negative results were already palpable. In eight countries that did not interfere with the boycott movement, German exports fell within the six years 1933–1938 from 2.840 million to 1.760 million Reichsmarks. A German economist, Albrecht Fortsmann, admitted that the reason for this decline was the effective boycott action in the United States, South Africa, Holland, Poland, and the Baltic countries.[1]

The boycott movement weakened greatly as a result of the political pressure from the governments involved and the lack of a united Jewish boycott front. By the end of 1936, the boycott had collapsed. The failure of the first organized Jewish attempt at a defensive struggle against Nazi Germany did not bode well for the future.

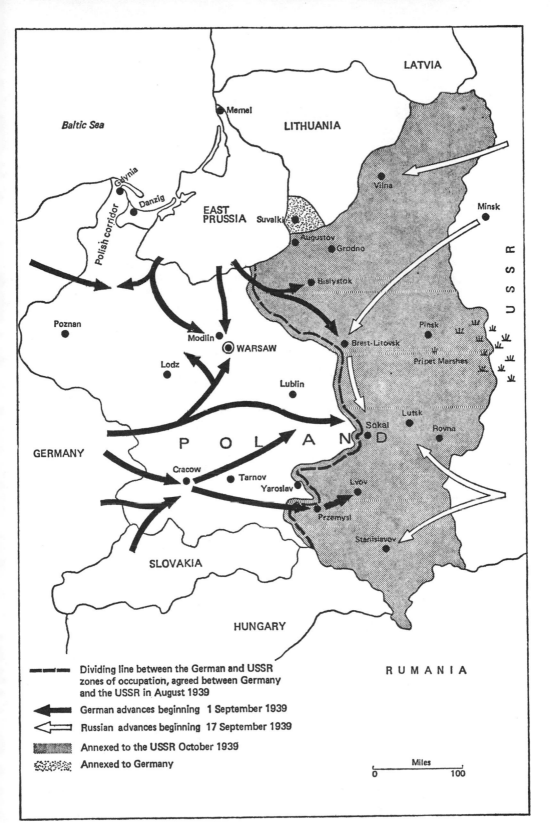

The Invasion of Poland, 1939

RESPONSES TO THE NAZIS

After the Outbreak of the War

When the war broke out, the Jews in Occupied Europe were confronted with a unique enemy. For the first time in Jewish history they faced a government that did not recognize any legal or moral considerations in regard to Jews. Their historical experience had not prepared them for confrontation with such an enemy. Recollections of relatively civilized German behavior in the occupied territories of Eastern Europe during World War I were still alive among the older generation. The traditional Jewish leadership there entertained the illusion that the old defense remedies that had served the Jews well in the past—intercession, bribes, economic usefulness to the authorities and the army—would also be effective in the new situation. The paramount importance of the Jewish factor in the theory and practical implementation of the overall Nazi strategy of world domination was generally underestimated, as was the Nazis' fierce determination to destroy the Jewish people. Therefore, the traditional methods of self-defense were entirely inadequate in the radically changed situation. They sometimes brought a short respite, a postponement of the inevitable doom, but they couldn't change the final course of events.

The Tools of Self-Defense

In time, with the intensification of the systematic persecution, the Jews developed other, more fitting clandestine tools of moral, economic, cultural, and political self-defense against the Nazis. In order to understand them, we must first analyze the reactions of the Jews incarcerated in the ghettos. And here, some questions are in order: What were the personal and collective strengths and weaknesses of the Jewish reactions to the relentless persecution and, in the last phase, to genocide? Can those reactions be classified into patterns, and if so are some patterns characteristic of certain segments of the ghetto population? Is there a connection between the various forms of response and such criteria as the victims' geographical origin (Eastern or Western Europe), ideology (religious or secular), social background (middle, lower, or working class), age, or political affiliation?

Patterns of reaction do become apparent. Jews of Eastern Europe did, by and large, respond differently from Central and Western European Jews. A chapter from the history of the Łódź Ghetto illustrates this in part. In autumn 1941, approximately 20,000 Jews were expelled from Berlin and other German cities and from Vienna, Prague, and Luxemburg and brought into the Łódź Ghetto.

A contemporary source observes the attitudes and behavior of the expellees:

> Almost all maintained a passive attitude toward life and the conditions they faced in their new environment, where bitter fate now forced them to live. The expellees' adjustment to ghetto conditions met with hard, often insurmountable difficulties. They were profoundly disappointed on arriving in the ghetto.
>
> They had been told that they were being taken to work either in industrial towns or in agricultural colonies. They had not lived in ghettos before their expulsion.
>
> Their economic situation had been in the main bearable, and therefore, the sudden change was the more shocking, leading to alienation and hate.
>
> Symptomatic is their attitude toward the native ghetto inmates. Instinctively they defended themselves against identification with the indigenous Łódź Jews, trying to separate by all means from the natives in the belief that this might save them from submerging into the mass of the ghetto population.[2]

"They were not so much sorry for being dragged into the ghetto, as for being equated with the Polish Jews,"[3] commented a survivor on the feeling of the expellees driven there from the Reich and Protectorate (Bohemia and Moravia, former provinces of Czechoslovakia, under Nazi rule) to Zamość.

The legalistic mentality of the German Jews and their apparent loyalty to the German ghetto administration contributed to their mistrust by the Polish Jews. The German Jews were open to suspicion because they looked for favors from the Gestapo and because of the apprehension that some of them might be undercover agents or informers. An additional factor contributing to mutual bitterness was the relatively large number of Catholics and Protestants of Jewish origin among the expellees. The situation became even more acute during the deportations from Łódź in May 1942 and again from June to August 1944. Central European Jews went obediently and in orderly fashion to the assembly places, still nourishing the illusion that they would eventually return to their former homes, where they hoped conditions would be more "favorable for survival."[4]

We find similar observations of the attitudes of the German Jewish expellees in the chronicles of the Riga and Zamość ghettos.

Social background also seems to have been a differentiating factor influencing reactions to the anti-Jewish measures. There is some evidence that lower- and working-class people responded in ways somewhat unlike those of the middle class. A number of the former reacted defiantly, even risking their lives.

The Jews in Wilno, for example, were allowed to carry into the ghetto only bundles of belongings, and no more than 300 Soviet rubles (30 Reichsmarks) in cash. Gold and other valuables had to be surrendered directly before entering the ghetto. Fearing dreadful consequences—the first slaughters had already occurred in Ponary— the majority of people, for the most part middle class and professionals, complied with the order. Others, however, took a chance and carried into the ghetto cash and valuables hidden in their clothes. These intrepid people were mostly the teamsters, coachmen, porters, black market dealers, and underworld operators.

It was from this segment of the Jewish population that the smugglers mainly emerged. Some of them even entertained close contacts with bribed German and Polish policemen. Those people were already familiar with hard conditions of life before the war; the transition to ghetto life was for them not so great a shock as for the middle class. The latter immediately lost the basis of their sustenance, and broke down rapidly. The workers, especially the skilled ones, had the temporary opportunity to be employed in the ghetto shops which worked for the Germans. Many were able to eke out, often by illegal means, a meager living.

Jewish workers employed outside the ghettos also had an opportunity to engage in risky barter with Christians, to work clandestinely for the internal needs of the ghetto, and to convert production in German shops for the benefit of the ghetto population.

The middle class, in contrast, could not easily adjust to the radically changed conditions; after exhausting their saved prewar resources, most fell to the nadir of utter destitution and misery.

What was the general attitude of Polish Jewry toward the Nazis? We read in a contemporary document the following analysis:

> The attitude on the part of the Jewish masses toward the Nazis is like [that toward] a ferocious beast; there is a fear of the beast, she may kill, she bites, tears pieces out of the human body, one feels pain, but there is not a feeling of being insulted and morally denigrated by the beast. Not being aware of the character of the Polish Jews, the Nazis expected that the persecutions would cause a moral collapse. Their expectations did not materialize. They could not comprehend the Jewish reactions and were often confused. When they introduced the yellow

badge they were sure that the Jews would be ashamed to appear in the streets, but they were astonished by the behavior of the Jews in regard to this evil decree. The Germans call the yellow badge the badge of shame, but the Jews have no feeling of shame.[5]

We will now briefly examine the different kinds of responses and reactions of the Jews shut up in the ghettos. Before dealing with this, however, one must first analyze the physical and mental condition of the Eastern European Jews who were incarcerated in the ghettos.

The Physical and Mental Condition of the Ghetto Jews

The condition of the Jews in the ghettos can be illuminated by recourse to observations made by competent psychologists and sociologists about the physical and mental state of the inmates of German concentration camps. Even though ghetto conditions were not identical with those in Nazi concentration camps, one can nevertheless apply some of the observations made in concentration camps to the Jews locked up in ghettos. In practice, the ghetto, especially the closed ghetto, was something like a camp with a milder administration.

A number of constant factors characteristic of the living conditions in the camps and the influence of those factors on the mental state of the inmates are also typical of the climate in the ghettos. These were, first of all, starvation, human degradation, terror, and insecurity about the future.

Starvation The official food ration provided, at best, 46 to barely 60 percent of the number of calories required daily for human survival.[6] This diet greatly weakened the physical and mental resistance of the ghetto Jews, giving rise to such phenomena as apathy, self-neglect, resignation, and despair.

The daily bulletin of the *Chronicle* of the Łódź Ghetto of April 16, 1943, states: "The people drag like shadows through the streets, they all complain of terrible feebleness in their legs. . . . It's mainly potatoes that the bones lack. . . . In contrast to last year, we see fewer people swollen with hunger, but there are a conspicuous number of emaciated faces like those typical of TB." In the bulletin of February 13, 1943, we read: "A year ago at this time, there were many cases of hunger swellings in the ghetto population. . . . Now, in contrast, we often find decalcification of the bones as well as muscular atrophy—caused by a deficiency of vitamins and fat."[7]

The results of starvation in the Nazi concentration camps were mental regression and a return to a primitive animalism. The prisoner's sole thought was to stay alive. Unsatisfied hunger undermined normal moral standards: egotism, indifference to other prisoners, and ruthlessness became common characteristics. "We prisoners had only one standard: Anything that helped survival was good, anything that threatened survival was bad and had to be avoided."[8] In the ghettos, the situation did not assume such a dramatic form because it was softened by other factors, which are discussed below. However, the socially negative results of unsatisfied hunger were more than perceptible.

Degradation The Nazis employed a brutal and sometimes cunning system of moral degradation in the ghettos; its goal was to destroy the Jew's sense of his own human dignity. Similar methods of dehumanization were used more intensively by the SS in the concentration camps. The reports on those camps evidence that systematic process of degradation and the effect of the camp hierarchy's refusal to acknowledge the value of human life. The prisoners did begin to feel inferior; they felt their own worth depreciated. If the prisoner didn't make some effort to defend himself against the authorities' methods, he gradually reached a level where he no longer felt that he was human.

In the ghettos, however, the Nazi methods of dehumanization did not achieve the desired results. The ghetto population created an effective armor against degradation of their humanity and Jewishness. The ghetto inmate protected himself through a recourse to his historical tradition of belittling negative Gentile attitudes toward Jews, and by deliberately creating defense mechanisms adjusted to the new, radically different conditions.

Terror One of the most powerful weapons the Nazis used to control and subjugate the civilian population in occupied countries was the specter of terror. With terror, they planned to break the desire for resistance and transform these areas into quiet, passive objects of rule.

Sharp repressions of the local populace together with promiscuous executions of individuals and whole groups accompanied the marching German armies from the very first days of the war, especially in Poland and later in the Soviet Union. From the beginning, the Jews were declared outlaws and physical terror as a means of intimidation was employed with all its harshness against them. The terror against Jews was often amplified with public spectacles ridiculing the victims' human and religious feelings. With the greatest cruelty, the Nazis applied the principle of collective responsibility for the deeds of individuals. The means of terror varied: public executions of alleged Jewish culprits as in Łódź in 1940 and other towns in "Wartheland" in 1942, and public shootings of Jews seized on the "Aryan" side as in Warsaw in November 1941.

The Nazi terror was effective as an intimidating and paralyzing instrument. Jewish tradition had always regarded human life as the highest and holiest value; now it collided with the "Valhalla cult," a system that placed little value on human life. The Nazi ideology worshiped heroic death as the highest moral attainment of the human race. In the camps, where the permanent atmosphere of terror created such a dreadful mental climate that death lost its intimidating effect, prisoners became almost indifferent to dying. As a daily experience, it could seem rather normal.

The Nazi terror worked parallel destructive influence in the ghettos, but most Jews held fast to life there. They did not believe that the Germans would ultimately win, and the will to survive the war was very strong. A Jewish religious thinker in the Warsaw Ghetto, Rabbi Yitzhak Nisnboim, offered the slogan of *kiddush ha-chaim* ("sanctification of life") in contrast to the traditional *kiddush hashem* ("sanctification of the Name of God") and the martyrdom that sometimes required. This does not refute what I said several paragraphs ago. In the Middle Ages, Christianity tried to deprive the Jew of his soul by forcing his conversion, and the reaction had been martyrdom. The Nazis wanted to destroy the Jewish body, so the answer had to be the sanctification of physical life.[9] This heightened will to live explains why no suicide *epidemic* ever broke out in the Eastern European ghettos. The Nazis hoped for and expected a wave of suicides after their experiences with German and Austrian Jews. Indeed, there had been relatively numerous suicides after the Austrian *Anschluss*, after Crystal Night in November 1938, and just before the deportations to Eastern Europe.

Besides the heightened will to live, two other factors helped keep East European ghetto suicides to a low number. First, there were religious sanctions against suicide. Second, death had become so familiar a daily occurrence in the ghettos that little or no personal drama could be linked to a suicide. Death was such a commonplace that to lose one's life in the ghetto, one didn't have to lay hands on himself. All a Jew had to do was give up the struggle for survival and death would come quickly, of its own accord. Similar observations were made in the concentration camps; no epidemics of suicide ever broke out there either.[10]

On the other hand, the terror led to apathy and resignation in part of the starving ghetto population. Some of those who were physically enfeebled, who lived in contant fear, and who saw helplessness in their situation, made peace with fate. A witness tells of the following experience in a courtyard in the ghetto of Częstochowa, where a group of Jews was waiting for "resettlement": "The people were sitting there, each in his own corner, motionless and bored. Their tragic condition was so familiar, so daily and normal, that it was no longer a cause of tension."[11]

Countless sources tell us that the fear of having large numbers of other Jews held collectively responsible helped to paralyze the will to raise an active resistance. That concern restrained even those who were ideologically and organizationally prepared to take such a step. These Jews simply could not convince themselves to be party to the sacrifice of the lives of the majority of the ghetto inhabitants, who were neither physically nor mentally prepared for any resistance.

That same sense of responsibility for the community prevented spontaneous individual acts of revenge against Nazis. Those who would have carried them out had to anticipate serious reprisals against the collective. The same phenomenon occurred in the camps, where the tortured prisoners very seldom revolted; they feared that the SS guards would employ the harshest reprisals against the many as a punishment for the desperate deeds of the few.[12]

Methods of Economic Self-Defense

The Nazi strategy of economic warfare against the Jews—expropriation, elimination, and isolation from the general economic framework and the exploitation of Jewish labor, among others—might have been expected by itself to produce impoverishment of the Jews, starvation, and outbreaks of epidemics and high mortality rates, resulting in a rapid decrease in the Jewish population, and perhaps, its ultimate disappearance. However, many Jews resisted this design of extermination by economic means, resorting to such defensive measures as smuggling food and raw materials into the ghettos, illegal barter with Christians, illegal underground industrial production, converting the output of shops working for the Nazis to the benefit of the ghetto population, and last but not least, dealings with corrupt Nazi officials.

An overall goal of the German economic policy in the lands under their rule was to completely uproot the Jews from the economy. Jews were allowed to work only so long as it benefited German civil and military interests. However, urged on by vitality, armed with ingenuity and skills, and driven by their natural will to live, the Jews succeeded, in many ghettos, in adjusting themselves to the dire conditions. This response to their calculated oppression was a surprise to the Nazis, who had expected that economic measures resulting in continuous hunger and ever-growing mortality, along with emaciating hard labor, would bring about the results they desired. One may wonder if the "poor results" of their slow-death policy did not play a role in the Nazis' decision to turn to methods that would speed up the mass murder.

Emanuel Ringelblum describes the economic conditions and the defense methods of Jews in the Warsaw ghetto as follows:

By creating a ghetto, the Germans intended, first of all, to isolate the Jews completely and cut them off absolutely from the Aryan population. The isolated ghetto had to be brought to such a state that the Jews would lack air to breathe and would starve to death. The process of excluding the Jews from the economic and cultural life of the country began the instant the Germans marched in. The Jews were expelled from all positions in the national, municipal, and public legal institutions and enterprises. Aryan firms were prohibited from employing Jewish blue-collar or white-collar workers. Jews were not allowed into public or private libraries, theaters, movie houses, etc. They were not permitted to use any national or local transportation (railroads, suburban trains, buses, trolleys). Jewish youth could not go to public schools or—obviously—private Aryan schools. Any economic or cultural contact between Jews and Aryans had to be completely broken off. Theoretically, Christians could have no social intercourse with Jews. Even though such a directive was never issued, it was carried out in practice. The ghetto would be the acme and end of this process of isolating the Jews. From now on the Jew could communicate with the world only by permission of the power organs, who had to check and control such economic contacts. The ghetto had to be hermetically sealed. The Aryan world, according to the official terminology, was an *Umwelt*, a surrounding world, a kind of foreign state, separated from the ghetto by a toll border. Trading took place between the two states on the basis of a clearing house. This clearing institution was the especially created "transfer point" (*Transferstelle*). The ghetto had to receive as much food as it earned by working. At the time of the creation of the ghetto, there were other plans as well, which, had they been carried out, would speedily have led to a catastrophe. The ghetto would have had to pay for the food items with cash, jewelry, and gold. Fortunately, both plans were dropped. For some reason or other, the commissioner for the Jewish region, Auerswald, could not deal effectively with the problem, and he let the matter take its natural course. In reality, the ghetto was a kind of autonomous area with a local municipal administration, with its own facilities for maintaining public order, its own postal system, jail—and even an office of weights and measures. The Jews called the ghetto a concentration camp, surrounded by a wall and barbed wire, with the distinction that inhabitants of the ghetto had to support themselves.

The creation of the ghetto aroused terrible anxieties in the Jewish community. It was calculated that within a year at the most, the ghetto would be left without any means of payment, which would halt all flow to the other side to pay for food. The official food rations would suffice at best for a few days per month. The remaining days would have to be provided for through smuggling. They would soon see how "gray" theory was, and how different the "tree of life." The Germans wanted to wedge the ghetto into the Procrustean bed of production for the *Wehrmacht*. And yet, despite the special service guarding the ghetto from the outside, despite the gendarmerie and Polish police, despite the SS and the security service, despite the "transfer point" and the Jewish ghetto police—despite all this, the tensions of Jewish life, the energy and enterprise of Jews, their professional knowledge and traditions of generations, the will to live of 400,000 Jews, worked miracles. And the ghetto proved to be capable of a self-sufficient economic life. A year later, when they tried to draw an annual balance, even the most stubborn pessimists, who had uttered the darkest prophecies (exhaustion of ghetto finances and universal famine for the Jewish population), were obliged to admit that their forecasts had been wrong. Their chief error was the assumption that trade between the ghetto and the Aryan world would pass only through the official route, i.e., through the specially created "transfer point." In practice, however, it turned out that the proportion of official import to nonofficial import was the same as the proportion of official rations to real ones. It turned out that the ghetto kept up live economic relations with the Aryan side, that the economic ties dating back to long before the war did not break off despite the growing walls that cut the ghetto off from the Aryan world. Parallel to the official production for German military needs and generally for German market needs, the ghetto continued producing for the Polish export market, using the raw materials that were smuggled into the ghetto. These were obtained from the caretakers imposed upon Jewish firms in Tomaszów Mazowiecki, Częstochowa, Łódź, etc. Of course, they were obtained *illegally*, from the raw materials allotted to the firms. Jewish industrialists and craftsmen proved to be extraordinarily resourceful in finding surrogates for missing raw materials. They produced everything for the Aryan market as before the war. The weaving mills manufactured excellent textiles from wool stolen from the factories of Częstochowa, the Warsaw "Wola" factory, and other places. They would dye prayer-shawls and convert them into scarves, knitted jackets. They developed a manufacture of ladies' scarves, knitted jackets, peasant jackets, etc. These were processed from old clothes bought in masses on the enormous square on Gęsia Street, where there was a huge sale by the Jewish population, who were growing poorer from day to day. Special agents of various firms, day after day, bought thousands of kilograms of old sheets and all kinds of rags over there.[13]

A vivid description of the resourceful techniques of smuggling into the ghetto of Warsaw is preserved in a contemporary document emanating from the Ringelblum archives.[14]

Moral and Religious Resistance

Nazi propaganda did everything it could to present the Jews as racially inferior offal, the dregs of humanity, subhuman, absolutely immoral, and asocial. A gigantic literature was written to prove these allegations. Day after day, the press, the radio, exhibits, wall newspapers, and other media hammered the message into German and non-German ears: *Judah, der Weltverbrecher* ("Judah, the international criminal"). The Jew was beneath the definition of a human being.

Historically, Jews were relatively immune to Christians' negative opinions of them. Their tragic experiences of the ritual blood slanders reinforced Jewish emotional armor. Traditional Jews, in fact, even felt contempt toward the Christian world. With Emancipation, this attitude was deeply shaken. Emancipated and assimilated Jews actually became hypersensitive to Gentile notions about Jews. Jews produced a monumental apologetic literature which was still coming out at the start of the Nazi takeover; the defensive works of Chaim Bloch in Vienna are examples. The Nazi Occupation confronted Jews not with mere theoretical accusations and slanders, but with a political system that transformed the Nazi theories about Jews into persecutions in everyday life. Jews were cast beyond the pale of the law. Jewish life, Jewish property were at any Aryan's mercy. And all this was amplified with degrading directives requiring each Jew to doff his hat to every passing German, to walk in the street rather than on the sidewalk. Then followed incarceration in ghettos and other indignities.

The moral standard in the ghettos was threatened by a further danger—an internal one. The impossible living conditions in many ghettos caused an internal demoralization. The daily struggle for sheer physical existence corrupted many people. Those who bent every effort for self-preservation were not picky about their methods. Often, a Jew tried to save himself at the expense of a fellow sufferer—to whose woes he had grown indifferent. Corruption was not infrequent in the *Judenräte,* the community "self-government" councils imposed upon the Jews by the Nazi authorities.

Contemporary statements on these phenomena are offered here on the basis of a questionnaire that was sent to a number of Jewish intellectuals in the Warsaw Ghetto during 1941. The questionnaire was circulated by the secret ghetto archive, known as *Oneg Shabbes.* The answers survived and were published after the war. Shmuel Stupnicki, a well-known journalist, replied as follows:

> My answer may sound like a paradox—but I regard it as a positive thing. It's a miracle that people aren't crushed, broken by these macabre

street scenes, that they never lose their sense of balance at seeing hosts
of naked, barefoot children starving to death in the streets. If it weren't
for this cruel indifference, such scenes could paralyze our entire life
process, driving the people into such a state of depression that they
would fall into resignation and decline. I therefore regard it as positive
that people have become so hard and stony. . . . And they keep on fighting for their lives.[15]

The writer Aron Einhorn, who contributed to *Haint*, a daily newspaper, answered:

It's hard to say whether our moral slough in the ghetto is a result of
the abnormal conditions, or whether the ghetto has merely uncovered
things that were previously concealed, disguised. It's possible that another nation in a crisis would have fallen even deeper. But let's have
the courage to tell the truth: Morally, we have sunk to the depths of
the abyss. Never has there been so much stealing among Jews as now.
Cruelty is blatant everywhere. We walk indifferently past scenes that
would elsewhere arouse the greatest astonishment. . . .[16]

The well-known writer Hillel Zeitlin replied:

Unfortunately we have to admit that Jews proved much weaker, much
less resistant than one would have thought. The Jews have turned out
to be incapable of resisting the slightest temptation. . . . The corruption,
demoralization, thievery in the ghetto are dreadful. The reason: the
extraordinary difficulties. All vices and low instincts have manifested
themselves naked. But if 400,000 Christians were locked up in a ghetto
like Warsaw's, who can say whether the picture would be any worse.
They would probably simply slaughter one another.[17]

Dr. Yisroel Milejkowski, the chairman of the health department
of the *Judenrat*, wrote in his reply:

People complain that our ghetto smells worse than other places. That
is certainly true. But it comes from the fact that our substance is nobler,
more delicate, and thus decays faster. . . . The fault lies in the conditions
we live in. These conditions trigger the corruption, and the fight against
corruption is a very hard one. . . . Hopeless. Fighting against corruption
means fighting against the ghetto. Our vegetating is accursed between
the ghetto walls. . . . The ghetto demoralizes. Something that is a bless-
ing for the ghetto—for instance, smuggling—is a curse from a broad
national viewpoint. What kind of a generation will grow up from the
smugglers, from these lawless boys? Isn't it a curse? . . . The dregs are
floating up to the surface of our life: Extortionists, blackmailers, in-

formers, bribers of all kinds, people with pull. . . . There is always such
an underworld in every society. Such people grow stronger and multiply
in wartime. . . . The authorities demand dirty work from us, it has to
be done under their pressure. Not everyone is capable of doing it, and,
willing or not, we have to turn to the underworld. That is how I see
the positive role played by these elements in the life of the collective.[18]

Judenrat member H. Rosen, an engineer, said:

When we look at the moral physiognomy of the ghetto, we find
enormous contrasts. On the one hand, we see a marvelous discipline in
the Jewish masses. Despite all the oppressions, all the dreadful cruelty,
the cynical sadism, there has not been a single case of irresponsible
transgression or action. And there was no lack of opportunity for such
things either. . . . Such a wonderful sense of responsibility, such discipline are hard to find. The demoralization in the ghetto is due to the
fact that everything is prohibited for Jews. Hence, all the excesses. . . .
Every Jew is forced to break the law, and this is also a fine training
for outrages against morals between individuals, or between the indi
vidual and the society. . . . We therefore have to emphasize all the more
strongly the moral discipline of the impoverished and hungering Jewish
masses. The police chronicles cannot record any mass robberies, lootings,
muggings.[19]

How did religious Jews react to the Nazi persecutions of the religion itself? In the occupied territories, the Nazis, from the very
start, waged a bloody campaign against such religious practices as
ritual slaughter. The first anti-Jewish decree issued by Hans Frank,
governor general of the major part of occupied Poland, was the
prohibition of kosher slaughter, October 26, 1939. Similarly, the Germans outlawed beards and earlocks, prayers in general, ritual baths,
the study of the Torah as well as other religious books, and more.
Some of the vilest acts were taken against Jews who wore beards
and earlocks. With dull instruments, the Germans cut that hair from
pious Jews; they tore out tufts of a beard from a Jew's face, or set
fire to the hair, beating the man mercilessly, and put on mock "gym-
nastic spectacles." The Nazis even photographed such outrages. Devout Jews were faced with a terrible ordeal.

A contemporary source relates that the rabbi of Rawa Mazowiecka,
a small hamlet in the area of Łódź, attempted, through the mediation
of the local priest, to obtain the permission of the Gestapo chief to
continue wearing his beard. The German gave the rabbi the choice
of buying this right in exchange for a hundred lashes. The rabbi
accepted the heavy sentence. At the tenth stroke, the rabbi fainted.
He had to be taken to the hospital, where he spent two weeks. But

his "payment" saved his beard.[20] Still, this case was an exception. In order to avoid vexations and torments, as well as spectacles of public ridicule, devout Jews themselves cut off their beards and earlocks.

The sources also tell of Jews who tried to enter burning synagogues and houses of study to save the Torah scrolls, even though the Germans shot at them. Many of these rescuers died in the flames. The close of the ritual baths was a severe blow for pious Jewish women. Although a decree in Warsaw provided for punishments of from ten years in prison to death for anyone visiting a ritual bath, Jewish women risked their lives and found various ways to sidestep the draconian regulations. Some went to nearby small towns where the baths had not yet been closed, and some paid large bribes in order to fulfill the commandment of purification by immersion. Similar tactics were taken to continue ritual slaughter. Jewish butchers risked their lives to provide Jews with kosher meat; their efforts often involved smuggling.[21]

Devout Jews preferred to starve rather than eat the unkosher meals served in public kitchens, since the only kind of meat that the authorities doled out in ghettos was horsemeat. Jews formed secret *minyens,* keeping someone on watch. They left work to sneak into a *minyen,* on holidays, and Yeshiva students met in basements and attics to study the Talmud. There were even cases of nonreligious Jews who became devout in the ghettos. Religion, for them, was the only remaining internal manifestation of Jewish identification.[22]

In some ghettos, such as Łódź, Warsaw, and Kaunas, rabbis took the extraordinary times into account and adapted the strict religious laws, permitting things that would have been prohibited in normal times. Thus, women in childbed, the sick, and the feeble were allowed to eat unkosher meat,[23] and food was used at Passover that normally would not have been permitted because of the suspicion of leaven.[24] Also allowed were cooking on the Sabbath for the Jewish forced laborers and working for the Germans on the Sabbath, even on Yom Kippur. In the Kaunas Ghetto, doctors were allowed to perform abortions on women threatened with capital punishment, since in the Commissariat General of Lithuania, Jewish women were not allowed to have children.[25]

The rabbis were faced with the task of reconciling the severe demands of Jewish law with the ruthless facts of the ghetto reality. But Jewish law did permit any transgression in order to save a life. In many ghettos, the rabbis liberally applied the rule of saving a life and tended toward leniency.

By way of analogy, we should look at the role of religion in the concentration camps. Victor Frankl, who passed through many camps, observed the following:

Smuggling in the Warsaw Ghetto.

A pious Jew who has covered his beard, forcibly cut by the Nazis.

Humiliation of Jews in the town of Łuków, Lublin district.

The religious interest of the prisoners as far and as soon as it developed, was the most sincere imaginable. The depth and vigor of religious belief often surprised and moved a new arrival. Most impressive in this connection were improvised prayers or services in the corner of a hut, or in the darkness of the locked cattle truck in which we were brought back from a distant work site, tired, hungry and frozen in our ragged clothing.[26]

Eyewitness Testimony 25 affords a description by a camp inmate of an episode in the Jewish barracks in Auschwitz:

I remember the *Blokowa* of Barrack No. 19, where I stayed, especially— she was a Jewish woman from Czechoslovakia. *Erev* Yom Kippur, 1944, this woman put a white tablecloth over the barrack oven, lit some candles, and told all the Jewish women to walk up and pray in front of the candles. All of us went up and the barrack was filled with an unbearable wailing. The women again saw their annihilated homes. *Froh* Rotshtat, the famous violinist from Łódź, was also kept in our barracks. The *Blokowa* brought in a fiddle and asked *Froh* Rotshtat to play *Kol Nidre*. She refused, saying she couldn't play because her heart was bursting. The *Blokowa* threatened to beat her, to put her on punishment details, if she didn't play. When *Froh* Rotshtat began playing, the Jewish *Blokowa* suddenly lost control and started pushing us away and clubbing the Jewish women, yelling: "Enough! You've had enough pleasure!"

What was the reason for the Jewish *Blokowa's* sudden change of mind? One can only guess that, fearing the inmates would see how she was overcome with emotion by the solemn tones of *Kol Nidre*, she would thus be seen in a state of weakness and would consequently lose the firm grip she had on them.

In this time of dreadful ordeals, many deeply religious Jews became even more pious, detecting the hand of God punishing the Jews for their sins. Why was God punishing only the Jews? A religious Jew in the Warsaw Ghetto had one answer: "Providence has always made greater demands on Jews than on other nations, whether or not we like it. A nation of prophets, a nation that produced a Moses, created a Bible, can have greater moral and ethical demands made upon it than other nations, and hence we are punished harder than other nations." Other religious Jews saw the sufferings as presaging the advent of the Messiah: "Jews will ultimately come through this ordeal of fire and be purified, and they shall once again attain the level of the People of the Spirit."[27]

Devout, mystically oriented Jews saw the sufferings as "the Dawn of Redemption," and the concentration of Jews from faraway places as "the Ingathering of the Exiles."[28]

On the other hand, there were quite different reactions. Some pious Jews lost their faith and began eating unkosher food and violating the Sabbath—a kind of rebellion against God, who was deserting his Chosen people. In one small ghetto in the Kalisz area (German name Heidemühle), a trial was held with God as the accused.[29]

Hillel Zeitlin, in his answer to the *Oneg Shabbes* questionnaire, remarked in regard to the religious life:

> Unfortunately, we must admit that the Jews have turned out to be much weaker, much less resistant, than we thought. They are unable to endure even the slightest temptation, as we saw even before the war in the struggle against the slaughter prohibition and for kosher food. They ate unkosher meat even when the difference in price was negligible. And we saw the same thing in the fight for Sabbath repose. . . .
>
> The provincial Jews have proven to be better. They have not yet had their old Jewish sense of compassion torn out of them.
>
> Provincial Jews are willing to sacrifice their own lives, they give away their last crust of bread to send packages to relatives, friends, even strangers in Warsaw.
>
> It is also sad that there are no Messianic dreams in the ghetto. No dreams of redemption, I mean redemption in a higher, spiritual sense. People think in purely materialistic terms. Redemption means going back to an easy life, the fleshpots of Egypt. There is, of course, a feeling that these sufferings herald the coming of the Messiah, but no one wishes to draw the proper inferences, and so we do not see them preparing themselves, girding themselves for the higher spiritual Messianic Redemption.[30]

The Reactions of Secular Jews

While many religious Jews armored themselves with their faith against the Nazi persecutions and degradations, for secular Jews, nonbelievers, this faith was often replaced by a national consciousness, which had reached a high stage of development during the first decades of the century in Eastern Europe. The national and social movements gave the Jewish masses a clearly formed consciousness of national uniqueness and human dignity. These movements fashioned a national cultural mass of several million Jews, who were fully cognizant of their civil and national rights and their impressive cultural achievements: a Jewish literature and press in both Yiddish and Hebrew, a vast publishing industry, a network of Jewish schools, cultural

and athletic institutions, and theaters. It was a healthy national organism which continually hardened in its difficult struggle for civil and
national rights against generally anti-Semitic governments and an
anti-Semitic Christian society in Eastern Europe.

Among them were still alive old and new traditions of armed self-
defense during the pogroms in Tsarist Russia in the Ukraine and
Poland.

The average and even the higher Nazi bureaucrat in the occupied
territories of Eastern Europe had a false notion of the Jewish population there. He came with fixed ideas about Jews as businessmen,
financiers, and professionals—strata represented as parasitical in the
Nazis' anti-Semitic propaganda. To a great extent, this social-eco-
nomic structure did exist among the Jews they encountered in Germany, Austria, and parts of Czechoslovakia. But in the occupied areas
of Eastern Europe, the Nazis came upon a large stratum of Jewish
workers, many of them highly skilled. According to the census of 1931,
more than 45 percent of the Jewish population in Poland were craftsmen or industrial workers; in Lithuania, according to statistical data
of 1936, about a third. These Jews, mostly poor, played a major part in
the economy of these countries.

Some Nazis, not blinded by their own propaganda, were surprised
by this "discovery." They were also amazed at the vitality of the Jews,
their strong will to live, and their faculty of adjusting to the worst
living conditions.

The reactions of the nonreligious secular Jewish strata were expressed in modern forms adjusted to the radically different living conditions. Much of this expression took form in the domain of culture.

Reactions in the Cultural Domain

The nationally conscious groups in the ghettos reacted to the Nazi
methods of dehumanization by preserving and even strengthening
cultural life. In the Government General, the central Polish territory
under German rule, Governor General Hans Frank had eventually
permitted elementary schools under the aegis of the *Judenräte* (Councils of Jewish Elders) on August 31, 1940. But opening the officially
authorized schools involved great difficulties, as the local authorities
often sabotaged Frank's decree. Jews were not permitted to attend the
public "Aryan" schools. In many ghettos, where the *Judenrat* either
made no effort or was unable, because of difficult local conditions, to
open a Jewish school, or where the authorities did not grant authorization, some elementary instruction was organized within the framework of the social protection of children, in the children's homes and
orphan asylums and at food distribution points.

In an old-age home in the Łódź Ghetto.

Members of a sports club in the Łódź Ghetto.

The difficult problems of organizing schools in the ghettos gave rise to the secret arrangement known as the *Komplety* mostly through the initiative of Jewish teachers. These *Komplets* comprised small groups of about six to twenty pupils, and the lessons were given in the private apartments of the pupils or teachers. Some *Komplets* had a complete high school program—with the exception of the more complicated technical subjects. (High school education was generally forbidden for both the Jewish and Christian populations.) According to statistics collected in the Warsaw Ghetto by a group of teachers, some 20 percent of the former Jewish high school students were studying in the *Komplets,* and these secret gatherings numbered as many as several hundred by 1941. They also existed in other ghettos, in Lublin, for instance, where they were carried on in an atmosphere of resourceful conspiracy, and in constant danger of being discovered in the course of frequent German visits to Jewish homes.[31] Secret student groups were also created by underground political parties and cultural and educational institutions that had been shut down.

Permission to give technical courses was granted more readily by the authorities, since such instruction would prepare a future Jewish labor force for German exploitation. This permission was connected in some ghettos, such as Warsaw, Wilno, and Kaunas, with general and even higher theoretical subjects. In the Warsaw Ghetto, and briefly in Łódź, Jews went even further. Despite the extraordinary obstacles and the danger of discovery by the Germans, courses were given at the university level in medicine, technology, and the humanities, as well as Judaic studies. Jews in the Warsaw Ghetto also did secret scientific research. We know of the clinical investigations carried out by a group of Jewish doctors about hunger-related diseases. The results were preserved, and then published after the war: the original Polish and a French translation in Warsaw.[32]

The clearest and most intense expression of cultural activity took place in the Wilno Ghetto. There, a cultural tradition that had been deeply rooted for generations was able to manifest itself in the most extreme conditions. This tradition, upheld by the remnants of a decimated community of those who survived the massacres in the Ponary woods, was an official and important part of the activities of the *Judenrat.* Reading the relative wealth of preserved documents about the cultural life in the Wilno Ghetto, one can scarcely believe that this colorful, almost "normal" cultural activity was going on in a ghetto that had received the survivors of a murdered community living under a Damoclean sword of death.

Two contradictory tendencies can be observed among secular Jews, especially in the larger ghettos. On the one hand, there was a stronger interest in and need for universalist cultural and aesthetic experiences as well as an aroused interest in Jewish culture in particular. Contem-

Mordecai Chaim Rumkowski, chairman of the Council of Elders (*Judenrat*) of the Łódź Ghetto, among children at a kindergarten.

Embroidery class at an orphanage headed by Janusz Korczak in the Warsaw Ghetto.

porary sources in the ghettos of Wilno, Warsaw, Łódź, and other
places tell of Jewish music, Jewish theater, and a "thirst for a Jewish
book" among many ghetto inhabitants. There is no doubt that escap-
ism helped to dictate some of these needs; "intoxication with a book"
was good mental compensation against a sense of inferiority that the
Nazis tried to force upon the ghetto Jew. Frequently there was also a
real effort to get to know the literature about the past sufferings of the
Jewish nation, an attempt to find an answer and solace for the ongoing sufferings. This was especially manifest in the socially oriented
young people.

The countervailing drive to assimilate into the surrounding Christian population possessed not only some of the professionals and intellectuals, who before the war were linguistically and in part
culturally assimilated, but other strata of the Jewish community as
well. Stupnicki tries to explain this phenomenon with practical reasons: "Jews tried to pretend they didn't understand German. . . . They
began speaking Polish, so that when a German addressed them, they
could reply: *Nie rozumiem* (Polish for 'I don't understand')." But
there were also intellectual reasons: "The Jews are squeezed into a
ghetto. They are seeking contact with the outside world . . . and they
are clutching at the foreign tongue as if it were a rescue plank. They
imagine they can thereby take up contact with the world on the other
side of the wall."[33]

The wish for assimilation among some ghetto Jews was doubtless
influenced by the fact that groups of assimilated intellectuals were
locked up behind the ghetto walls, as were converts to Christianity.
In the Warsaw Ghetto, due to their leading positions in the apparatus
of the *Judenrat* and its institutions, as well in the ghetto police, they
exerted an evident influence on the intellectual climate of the ghetto.

The bitter fate of the Jews had an adverse effect on those who had
less of a national or cultural awareness. Theirs was an urge to escape
from the community suffering that fate. In a time when being a Jew
held such enormous dangers, conditions were created for a "national
mimicry." This urge was probably fed by the widespread dream of
saving oneself by escaping to the "Aryan side," where one had a
chance to survive only as a non-Jew.

In sum, then, the cultural life in the ghettos, as a reaction to the Nazi
methods of human and national degradation of the ghetto Jew, played
an important role. On the one hand, the cultural activities were an
attempt to immunize, with more or less success, the conscious and
sensitive segments of the ghetto population, especially the youth,
against the inevitable demoralization of ghetto life. This cultural
work created a spiritual support in the atmosphere of naked, often
brutal materialism that permeated many of the ghettos. On the other
hand, the culture strengthened the ghetto Jew in his sense of self-

A kiosk with posters advertising social activities in the Warsaw Ghetto.

Child street vendors selling books in the Warsaw Ghetto.

esteem and dignity. These efforts bore the clear stamp of spiritual and intellectual resistance.

Political Responses

For the most part, the political activists had disappeared from the Jewish communities. Feeling themselves endangered by the oncoming German army, they were among the first to flee eastward in the opening days of the war, and after September 17, 1939, found themselves in the part of Polish territory occupied by the Red Army, in accordance with the Russo-German nonaggression pact of August 28, 1939. Few of them returned. Some, especially the labor activists, were arrested by the Soviet authorities. Some succeeded in securing a legal means for escape by a westward route (Italy, Spain) or by an eastward one (Soviet Union, the Far East).

Early in the first weeks of the Occupation, the Gestapo arrested many remaining known political activists from among both the Jewish and Polish populations. The majority of them were deported to concentration camps or even executed immediately. This happened in Łódź, Radom, Częstochowa, Kielce, Piotrków, Włocławek, and many other cities.

Of those activists who remained in their areas and who were spared the initial persecutions, not all could, or wanted to, adapt to the radically changed circumstances. Because of the fear of repressions against former political activists, some of them withdrew from political life, hid behind aliases, or fled to larger population centers. Indeed, acts of terror against remaining political activists, especially of the labor parties, continued with the creation of the ghettos.

Generally speaking, then, a new, younger generation of activists emerged in Jewish community life under German Occupation. They were recruited for the most part from the youth movements of the political parties. This youthful element was better suited for political activity in circumstances of illegal conspiracy. It was more militant and daring, and bound less tightly to the structures and traditions of political activity that existed before the war. Lacking family ties, for the most part, and exhilarated by the risky situations they faced, the young militants dared to establish contacts among practically isolated ghettos, gather news and information, spread illegal periodicals, smuggle arms, and engage in similar ventures. "Only our people could come and go in the ghettos, crawl through walls and climb over barbed wire," noted Mordecai Tenenbaum-Tamaroff, a leader of the Zionist youth movement *Dror,* in his diary.[34] The same can be said of other political movements. The activists of the underground movement and the fighters in the ghettos and camps were recruited from this youthful element.

New people emerged in almost all political movements active in the ghettos, people who had been little known, of the second and third political rank, so to speak. The young political activists who grew and matured during the war years were still adolescents at the start of the war, still attending schools and participating in the youth movements of their respective political parties.

Under the impact of the profound blow suffered because of the German occupation, the remaining Jewish political activists were preoccupied first of all with the preservation of the sparse party cadres. They concentrated largely on the effort to assist destitute party members, to intervene at the Jewish councils on their behalf, and to get in touch with the central party committees in the capital. Soup kitchens for party members were initiated with funds received from the councils or from party headquarters. The kitchens often served as clandestine meeting places for disguised political and cultural activists and activities.

Because travel by Jews was outlawed, contacts with the central party committees in Warsaw were severely curtailed. Communication channels, such as they were, were only made possible thanks to the devotion and daring of the liaison personnel. The majority of these were youthful couriers, among whom girls prevailed. The emissaries of the American Jewish Joint Distribution Committee (popularly known as the "Joint") in Poland also helped for as long as that organization was permitted to conduct relief work—until December 1941.

One of the earliest and most complicated problems that the political parties faced was what attitude they should assume toward the Jewish Councils, or the Councils of Elders (*Judenräte*), which the Germans ordered to be established in the fall of 1939. Most acute was the problem of whether to participate in the activities and, if so, in what form, or whether to oppose the *Judenräte* from the start. This dilemma caused heated discussions at the local and central party levels. Depending on local conditions, the policies varied, with modifications of both alternatives.

The form of political activities was determined by the need to work clandestinely. Membership was divided into small groups of five or seven individuals, with only proven and trustworthy persons admitted. They usually met in the private homes of comrades, or in cemeteries, at the soup kitchens, and other places considered secure. In Warsaw, Cracow, Wilno and Białystok, some of the parties such as the *Bund, Poale Zion, Hashomer Hatzair*, and the Communists, used apartments occupied by their party comrades in the "Aryan" side to meet in secret. In some of the larger ghettos, the activities of the political parties were quite lively. Ringelblum noted in his diary on May 7, 1942:

> Until the famous Friday of April 18, 1942,[35] the era can be considered as one of legal conspiracy [in Warsaw]. All political parties were rather semilegal. Publications mushroomed. . . . Things went so far that a certain faction issued its publication twice in a single week. Distribution was made freely, and the leaflets and releases were read in the offices and shops. Meetings of various political parties were held almost openly in the locales of the existing ghetto institutions. Large public celebrations were also arranged. During one such meeting, the speaker talked of active resistance to the 150 people who were assembled. I have attended a celebration arranged for 500 youths by a certain political group. It was no secret who the authors of articles in the [underground] papers were. The articles were discussed and invectives exchanged, as was the habit in the good prewar years. One believed that everything was permitted . . . that it was all the same to the Germans what the Jews thought or did. The prevailing opinion was that they were only interested in uncovering Jewish goods, cash, currency, and that spiritual problems were of no concern to them.[36]

According to incomplete information, approximately fifty underground publications in Yiddish, Polish, and Hebrew, representing almost all of the political parties, were issued in Warsaw between 1940 and April 1943.[37] Even pamphlets entitled *Martyrdom and Heroism* and *The Paris Commune* were published. An incomplete list of Bund publications alone contains thirteen titles with a total of 180,000 typewritten pages. Illegal literature of varied character and form, such as hectographed wall newsletters, proclamations, and leaflets, were also issued in other, smaller ghettos.

Underground activists in the Częstochowa Ghetto, who grouped themselves around the TOZ (Society to Protect the Health of Jews), periodically issued an illegal hectographed publication called *RASTA* (shortened from *Rada Starszych*—Council of Elders), which included an illustrated section of caricatures. The life of the Jews under the German Occupation, the gruesome activities of the Gestapo, security police, and mayoralty, as well as the tragic role of the Jewish Council and the Jewish Police, were mirrored in *RASTA*. The dissemination of *RASTA* was even aided by two Poles. When in the so-called "small ghetto" of Częstochowa a unified command of almost all political movements was established for an eventual uprising, it issued bulletins and proclamations. The bulletins consisted of informative material drawn from news picked up on a secret radio.[38]

During a long period in the Łódź Ghetto, a mimeographed and illustrated *Byuletin fun Bund* with radio news and critical notes on

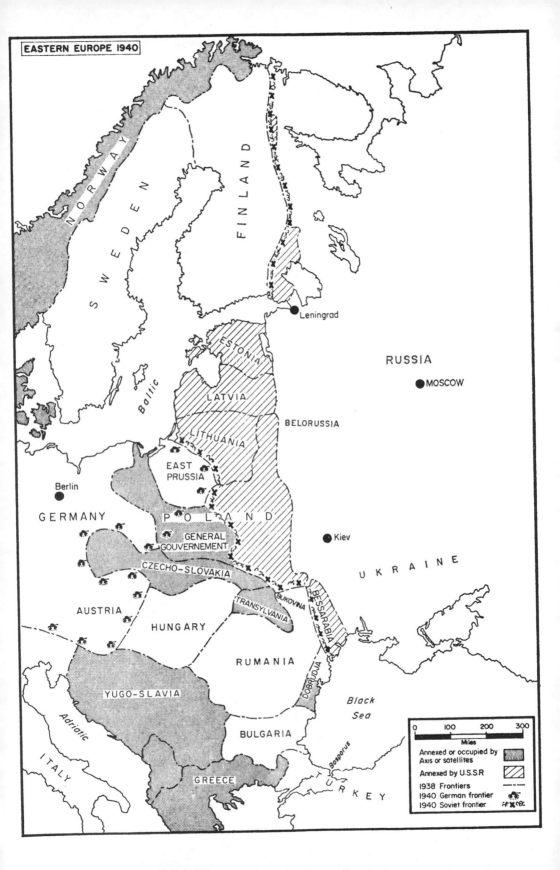

EASTERN EUROPE 1940

NORWAY

SWEDEN

FINLAND

RUSSIA

• Leningrad

• MOSCOW

ESTONIA

LATVIA

BELORUSSIA

LITHUANIA

Baltic

EAST
PRUSSIA

Berlin
•

GERMANY

P O L A N D

• Kiev

GENERAL
GOUVERNEMENT

U K R A I N E

CZECHO–SLOVAKIA

BUKOVINA

BESSARABIA

AUSTRIA

TRANSYLVANIA

HUNGARY

RUMANIA

YUGO–SLAVIA

DOBRUDJA

Black
Sea

Adriatic

BULGARIA

ITALY

GREECE

Bosporus

T U R K E Y

0	100	200	300

Miles

Annexed or occupied by
Axis or satellites

Annexed by U.S.S.R

1938 Frontiers

1940 German frontier

1940 Soviet frontier

the activities of the Rumkowski ghetto administration was issued. It appeared every three to four weeks in 1941. Besides this, an Orthodox prewar journalist issued a written pamphlet in Hebrew called *Hamsaper* with a literary section, *"Min Hamaytser,"* where he chronicled ghetto life and published articles, contemporary ghetto songs, and ghetto humoresques in Yiddish on his own initiative for almost three years. It's not known how widely this pamphlet circulated in the ghetto. During the stormy periods in ghetto life, as during the August demonstrations of 1940 against the Rumkowski regime, the political movements that engaged in the struggle issued written proclamations and leaflets.[39]

In the second half of 1942, the Zionist youth groups in Cracow— Hashomer Hatzair, Bney Akiba, Hechalutz, and others—began to issue an illegal pamphlet called *Hechalutz Halochem* ("The Fighting Pioneer"). Written in Polish—only the title was in Hebrew—it had a circulation of about 250 copies.[40] In the Wilno Ghetto, a *Bulletin of Radio News* from the United Partisan Organization periodically appeared.[41] In other ghettos, news was disseminated through handwritten or hectographed illegal proclamations posted on walls. In them, various party groups and underground resistance organizations took positions concerning unusual events in the ghetto, such as strikes, demonstrations against the ghetto administration, and German "actions."

Though the output of the illegal press was limited due to understandable factors, its moral and political significance was remarkable. It was striking proof that despite hermetic isolation in inhuman conditions, political thought among the socially active segments of the Jewish population could not be stifled. The press was a source of information about the political and strategic condition of the world. It was information that was not falsified or censored by Nazi propaganda, and it served as a source of encouragement and inspiration.

With the aid of couriers willing to take the risk, the provincial ghettos received illegal literature from the central committees of the respective parties. Naturally, failures occurred which occasioned gruesome consequences at the hands of the Gestapo. Such a failure took place at the beginning of June 1941 when the arrest of a female Polish underground courier carrying illegal Bundist literature led to the arrest and deportation to concentration camps of Bundists in many ghettos, such as Piotrków, Radom, Częstochowa, and Tomaszów Mazowiecki.[42]

Activists of the political parties and editors, printers, and publishers of the illegal press were the main targets of bloody political acts of terror that occurred in many ghettos during the months of February and April 1942. In spite of the April massacres the illegal press was not interrupted, but the political activity "developed into a real conspiracy, digging deeper underground."[43]

Another activity of political groups in the ghettos was the listening to secretly constructed radio receivers to breach their isolation from the outside world.

During the first few months of occupation, the population was directed to surrender all their radios to the authorities; severe punishments were threatened for those who did not comply. That threat notwithstanding, people continued to listen to foreign radio broadcasts on hidden or secretly constructed, often primitive, shortwave sets in many ghettos. In the Warsaw Ghetto, the communiqués of the BBC were widely distributed until the tragic day of April 18. Ringelblum adds that "some people earned their livelihood this way."

In the Łódź Ghetto, the group of Bundists, Zionists, and others who organized the secret radio listening met a tragic end. Betrayed by an unknown informer, all but one were arrested between July 6 and 8, 1944. The remaining member, a Zionist activist, committed suicide so that he would not fall into the hands of the Gestapo.[44]

Radios were also listened to secretly in Częstochowa, Białystok, Wilno, and in smaller ghettos. The radio listening in the ghettos had a moral and political significance comparable to that of the illegal press. It made possible a daily orientation to the actual strategic situation at the fronts, which German propaganda portrayed in a false and tendentious light. The foreign radio reports also strengthened the pride, will, and hope of the suffering inmates. To quote an entry dated May 8, 1944, from a diary found in the Łódź Ghetto: "The little news that reaches the ghetto is a lifesaver which prevents the people from giving up all hope."

Some traditional party holidays and memorial days continued to be celebrated in the ghettos. In Łódź, for example, May Day celebrations were held in those workshops where the official, and later the secret, delegates were Socialists. Notes were passed secretly among the workers reminding them of the date, and asking them to stop work for a while and sing revolutionary songs. In many ghettos, during May Day or other party celebrations, people gathered in small groups in private apartments to eat "holiday banquets" at poor and meager ghetto tables.[45] In the Wilno Ghetto, May Day celebrations were held under the guise of Festivals of Spring, and hundreds of people participated in them. The twentieth of Tamuz was celebrated by Zionist groups with commemorations of Theodor Herzl and Hayyim Bialik. On May 20, after Vladimir Jabotinsky's death in the summer of 1940, the Zionist Revisionists held a memorial celebration in the Łódź Ghetto quarter of Maryshin. The Zionist youth movements and the Bund youth organization Tsukunft ("Future") maintained their kibbutzim and seminars in the ghettos of Warsaw, Łódź, Wilno, Cracow, Białystok, Częstochowa, Sosnowiec, the Kielce region, and others. The seminars continued until the final deportation period.

The underground political activities in the ghettos and camps laid the foundation for the armed resistance that finally erupted in several of them. The ghetto and camp uprisings did not come about in a social vacuum. They gradually matured and grew from the soil in which kernels of resistance had been sown long before.

The Host Peoples

By segregating the Jews in ghettos in the areas under their occupation, the Nazis hoped to isolate them from the Christian population and prevent them from obtaining aid from outside. This policy succeeded to a large extent—but not entirely. In several large ghettos Jews were able to penetrate the wall of political isolation—as well as that of economic isolation. Some contacts were established with illegal political movements on the Christian side.

The facility with which these contacts could be created depended on several factors rooted in the ethnic and political attitudes of the peoples who lived outside the ghetto walls. In practice, the contacts were dependent on the political orientation (pro- or anti-Nazi) of the leading political movements of the respective nations, the depth of anti-Semitic feeling in the different ethnic and social groups, the historical background, and whether or not satisfactory Jewish-Gentile relationships had existed during the interbellum period.

Among such nationalities as the Lithuanians, Latvians, Ukrainians, and some of the White Russians, who populated the areas surrounding the ghettos in Eastern Europe, a pro-German orientation was dominant, and the anti-Semitic attitudes of the overwhelming majority of the population were strong and deep-rooted. Indeed, these anti-Jewish feelings were highly intensified during the short period of Soviet occupation of these lands from 1939 until July 1941. Thus, political contacts or offers of aid for the oppressed Jewish population were almost always limited and perfunctory. In fact, some political groups and circles in those nations not only enthusiastically supported the German extermination policy against the Jews; they also participated in its implementation. One needs only mention the Lithuanian "Partisans," the Latvian *Perkonkrusts* (Thunder-Cross), and the Organization of Ukrainian Nationalists (OUN) with its paramilitary partisan units Ukrainska Powstanska Armia (UPA) led by Andrei Melnik and Stepan Bandera. Aside from the sporadic intercessions made by Jewish community leaders with Gentile former politicians and well-known personalities, such as those which took place in Lwów and Kaunas, little could be accomplished.

Large segments of the Jewish population in Lithuania were murdered by the "Partisans" soon after the withdrawal of the Soviet army and prior to the establishment of the German Occupation regime. On a smaller scale, the same thing happened when the German army entered Latvia, eastern Galicia, and Volhynia. An August 16, 1941, report by Trampeldach, chief of the political department of the *Reichskommissariat Ostland,* dealt with the political situation in Latvia. In it we read of the *Perkonkrusts* units that, "with regard to the extermination of Bolsheviks and Jews, they were reliable and invaluable from the start."

The pro-Nazi elements in Ukrainian society, who looked for favors from the occupation authorities, achieved positions of influence and power everywhere in the occupied territories. They instigated a campaign of slander, claiming that the Jews had been the real rulers of eastern Galicia and Volhynia during the Soviet occupation. They maintained that Jews had informed to the NKVD on Ukrainian anti-Soviet activists who were subsequently executed in Soviet prisons prior to the German invasion. These charges were disseminated in the Ukrainian press and in leaflets distributed by local committees until it was widely believed that the Jews had actually been party to the Soviet atrocities (see Eyewitness Testimony 18).

The Nazis' virulent anti-Jewish propaganda found a welcome forum in the columns of the collaborationist press in the Ukraine, in the incorporated territories, and in Czechoslovakia. The invasion of the Ukraine by the German army was accompanied in many localities by a wave of anti-Jewish pogroms. On several occasions, the Ukrainians took the initiative in establishing concentration camps for Jews. In a number of places, Ukrainian civil officials charged with the administration of Jewish affairs issued a series of anti-Jewish decrees. Ukrainian committees drew up plans for "actions" against Jews, submitted them to the German authorities for approval, and then carried them out. The participation of the Ukrainian auxiliary policy (*Hilfpolizei*) in the persecutions and massacres of Jews in the Ukraine, and even beyond its borders, is well documented.[46] In a secret report of June 1943, compiled by a high German official, on the situation in the former Soviet Ukraine, he states that during his journey through the region, he encountered only four Jews interned in a penal camp, and that the Ukrainians reacted with indifference to the execution of Jews.[47]

To be sure, there were more cases of assistance and sympathy toward the persecuted Jews in the Ukrainian districts that had belonged to Poland until September 1939 than in the Soviet Ukraine. It suffices to cite the February 1942 letter to Heinrich Himmler of Metropolitan Andrei Sheptitsky and his pastoral letter to the priests protesting the murder of Jews and the use of Ukrainian militia in carrying out the executions. Mention should also be made of the rescue of Jews undertaken by the Greek Catholic (Uniate) monasteries, as by Sheptitsky himself, and of individual rescues of Jews which Friedman cites in his study of Jewish-Ukrainian relations during World War II.[48] Instances of hiding and aiding Jews are brought to light in Part Two of this book.

It should be stressed, however, that no Slavic nation under Nazi rule manifested such active and zealous participation in the extermination of the Jews as did the Ukrainians, both on their own territory and beyond (e.g., Treblinka and elsewhere). The combination of an ingrained anti-Semitism, which had its roots in ancient history, with the Nazis' own hatred of the Jews bore the bloodiest fruits possible upon Ukrainian soil.

The minor exceptions to the terrible rule in the relations between the Jews and the surrounding nationalities were the voices of individual and, regrettably, belated protest arising from small groups disillusioned with Nazism. A proclamation of the "Ukrainian Committee in Volhynia" (no date given, probably the end of 1943 or beginning of 1944) denounced the murder of Poles and the participation of the Ukrainians in the annihilation of the Jewish population, and a leaflet of May 1943 of the "Lithuanian Liberation Union" (an anti-Nazi Communist group?) condemned the murder of Jews and appealed to the Lithuanians not to participate in those acts.

In Byelorussia, a conspicuous difference is evidenced between the old Soviet part of the region and the area that had previously belonged to Poland and was under Soviet rule from September 1939 to June 1941. Nazi anti-Jewish propaganda drew a weak response in the former Soviet Byelorussia: we encounter complaints in Nazi documents that, "it's extremely hard to incite the local populace to pogroms because of the backwardness of the Byelorussian peasants with regard to racial consciousness."[49] Anti-Jewish feeling in the former Polish part of Byelorussia, however, was far stronger.

We read the following in an August 1942 secret memorandum by a Byelorussian collaborator to the *Wehrmacht Befehlshaber* (Chief of the German Army) *in Ostland*: "There is no Jewish problem for the Byelorussian people. For them, this is a purely German matter. This derives from Soviet education which has negated racial difference.... The Byelorussians sympathize with, and have compassion for the Jews, and regard the Germans as barbarians and the hangmen of the Jews, whom they consider human beings equal to themselves.... This mob is clearly indifferent to German propaganda.... The appeal to join the volunteer Byelorussian [auxiliary police] units found no response."[50] It is symptomatic that in an appeal to the partisans issued on March 13, 1944, by the "Central Byelorussian Council" in Minsk, exhorting them to return from the woods under pardon, no mention is made of the Jews, though their participation in the Byelorussian partisan movement was highly visible both in the

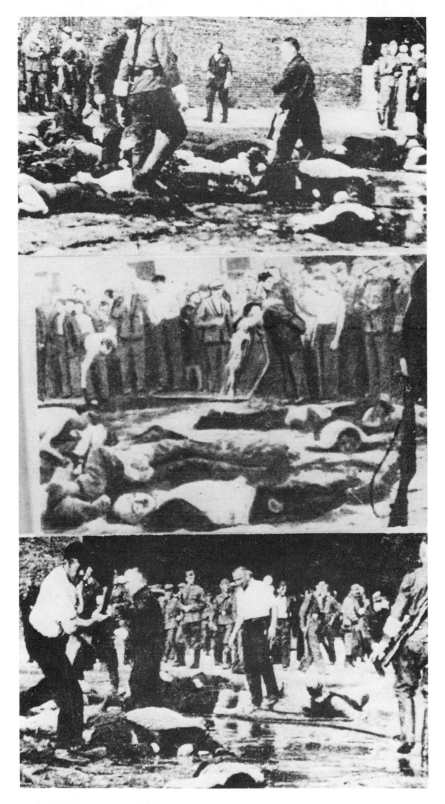

Lithuanians murdering Jews in the streets of Kaunas, June 1941.

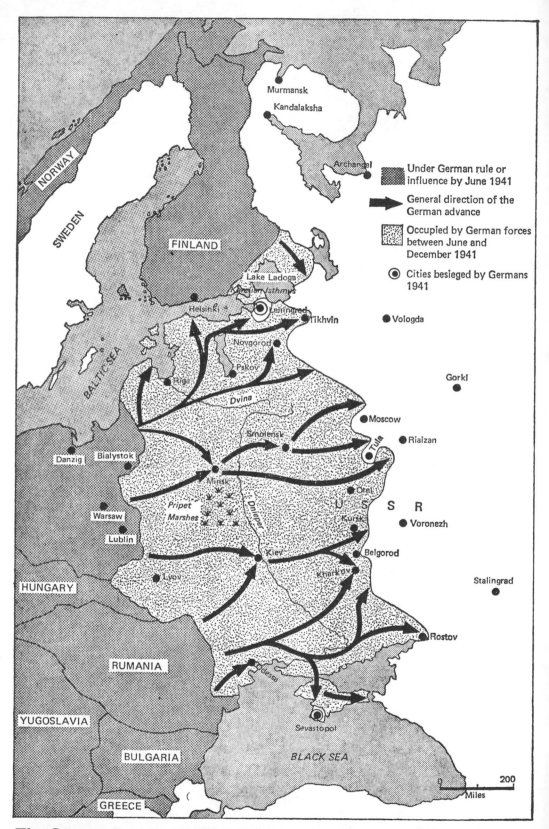

The German Invasion of Russia, 1941

ranks of "integrated" units and within the several separate Jewish units.[51]

In the formerly Polish part of Byelorussia, the approximately two years of Soviet occupation strengthened the anti-Jewish mood among the local Byelorussian populace to a large extent. Nazi anti-Soviet propaganda which pointed out Jewish participation in the Soviet occupation apparatus had the desired poisoning effect. Here there was collaboration with the German occupiers by large segments of the Byelorussian population, especially in the urban areas. These collaborators joined the auxiliary police, and often participated in executions, persecution of Jews in hiding, and similar activities.

Among political groups, only the *Byeloruskaya Narodnaya Respublika* (founded in 1918), which consisted mainly of refugees from Soviet Russia, was more or less pro-Nazi. It had a very low opinion of other political groups such as the *Vosvishentsy* ("Awakeners"), and the *Natzdemis* (National Democrats), in which remnants of the "nationalistic deviants" purged by Stalin found refuge. The latter two groups regarded anyone who identified with the Germans, and who thereby lost contact with the Byelorussian masses, as a traitor.

One can assume, then, that the very large-scale Jewish participation in the partisan movement in Byelorussia, including the unique "Jewish family enclaves" in the woods, was made possible by the relatively low degree of Byelorussian anti-Jewish sentiment, especially in the former Soviet territory.

However, it is important to understand that the duration of the ghettos in the Baltic lands, in White Russia, and in the Ukraine was such a short one that by the time some political segments of those populations (the Lithuanian Christian Democrats, Melnyk's and Bandera's groups of the OUN, and others) started on the road to sobriety and disillusionment with their earlier pro-Nazi position, almost no Jews remained alive in those territories. Moreover, the professed anti-Nazism of the Ukrainians was coupled with a merciless hatred of Jews. "Ukraine free of Germans, Poles, and Jews" became their slogan after the crushing of their hopes to create an independent Ukrainian government with German aid.

Only with the growth of the Soviet and pro-Soviet partisan movement in these areas was it possible for the remaining ghettos, such as Wilno, Kaunas, and Białystok, to establish contact with a political movement which, theoretically at least, was not anti-Jewish. The Soviet partisan movement, in fact, was not free of anti-Semitic feelings, which here and there were acted out aggressively.

Relationships with underground political groups in occupied Poland evolved in a more complicated manner. Anti-German feeling was very strong among the Poles, but broad segments of the Polish population were strongly anti-Semitic too.

Symptomatic of the intensity of the Polish hatred of the Germans was the virtual disappearance of surface anti-Semitic feelings during the first embattled month of the war. It seemed almost a second period of Polish-Jewish brotherhood, similar to that which had existed during the short period before the uprising of 1863. But this buried anti-Semitism soon surfaced again. The resurgence of open anti-Semitism came about mainly because of exaggerated and tendentious reports about the behavior of Jews in the eastern part of Poland occupied by the Soviets. At the time of the Soviet annexation, some Jewish Communists had behaved in a tactless and even treacherous manner, indulging in triumphant greetings, infiltration into the Soviet occupation apparatus, and informing to the NKVD on regional Polish and Jewish bourgeois and Socialist leaders. In addition, the Jewish population generally welcomed the Soviet occupation, which temporarily saved it from the danger of falling under Nazi rule. These facts were portrayed to the Polish population by returning refugees and by the anti-Semitic, pro-Nazi, and right-wing underground press as a collective betrayal by the Polish Jews, and as proof of the old anti-Semitic slogan about *Żydo-Komuna* ("Jewish Bolsheviks").

After the outbreak of the German-Soviet war, Nazi propaganda and the collaborationist legal Polish press naturally employed these reports to arouse hatred against the Jew.

With few exceptions, the prewar attitudes of the Polish political movements toward the Jews remained intact during the entire occupation period. The rightist camp, with the *Narodowa Demokracja* (Endeks) at its head, remained anti-Semitic (we exclude instances of individual metamorphosis), and silently witnessed with satisfaction Hitler's radical "solution" of the Jewish question in Poland, though officially it condemned his methods as barbaric.

The extreme right wing group *Oboz Narodwo-Radykalny* (ONR), the "Falanga," which had carried out an aggresive anti-Semitic policy before the war, was enthusiastic about Hitlerism, and actually justified the massacres with the argument that the Jews had earned the punishment. They often placed the victims on the same moral level as their murderers. They were not satisfied with preaching anti-Semitism, they were active. Pogroms took place in those parts of Poland where their influence was strong. In the town of Goniądz in the Grodno region, on the night of July 20, 1941, a gang of armed Polish ruffians took advantage of the short interregnum (the Soviets were gone and the Germans had not yet arrived) and killed approximately twenty Jews, including five entire families. A witness to this massacre related ironically that the terrorized local Jews "started to feel relieved when a unit of the German field gendarmerie entered the town from the nearby fortress Ossowiec on the next day and arrested seven Polish bandits."[52]

Ukrainians beating up Jews in the streets of Lwów in July 1941.

Physical assaults against Jews, accompanied by pillage of Jewish property, took place in Zamość, Krasnystaw, and in other parts of the Lublin district in the first month of the German invasion of Poland.[53]

On the other hand, the Polish Socialist Party (PPS), especially its left wing (PS), the Polish Socialist Labor Party (RPPS), and in March 1942, the reorganized Communist party (the Polish Labor Party—PPR) openly condemned the Nazi war of extermination against the Jewish population in their illegal publications, actively participated in relief actions, and appealed to the Poles for a show of aid for the persecuted. The Democratic Party took a similar position. In its official pronouncements the once strong Sanacja Party did not take a uniform stand. It generally took the same position as the Polish government-in-exile.

Following the pattern of the unification that had occurred at the beginning of 1940 between the parties of the government-in-exile in London, the Polish underground movements, with the exception of the Communists, eventually united. The *Delegatura* (Delegation) of the Polish government-in-exile was entrusted in Poland with all the political and administrative matters of an underground government. It was also the highest ranking underground governmental body for the Jewish population.

Even before the creation of the *Delegatura,* the Bund, which was the only Jewish group besides the Communists to maintain a long tradition of cooperation with the Polish Socialist Party (PPS), attempted to maintain prewar contracts with the Polish Socialist movement in the ghettos of Warsaw, Cracow, Tarnów, Włocławek, Piotrków, and other cities.

In its report of March 16, 1942, to the American representatives of the Bund, the Central Committee of the underground Bund in the Warsaw Ghetto wrote:

> Until mid-1941 we maintained contact with WRN (code name of the PPS) and with the group *Wolnocs* ("Freedom"). The contact was loose and somewhat cold through no fault of our own. . . . In the second half of 1941 we started relationships with another group, from which the organization of Polish Socialists was later formed. . . . It absorbs all former oppositional and leftist elements of the party. The contact with the Polish Socialists kept becoming closer. It became clear that they responded to the principal questions as we did. This is expressed in their publications . . . we aid each other in several ways. We continue to meet with the WRN and don't conceal our relationships with the Polish Socialists from them.

Thanks to the Polish Socialists, an opportunity arose during the period of preparations for the ghetto uprising for the engineer

Mikhal Klepfisch, a leading member of the Jewish Resistance Organization, to learn how to make grenades, other explosives, and arms on the "Aryan" side.[54]

The Jewish Communists also maintained a lively contact with the PPR on the other side of the wall. Messengers of the ghetto underground met with representatives of the newly organized Polish Communist party—"Polska Partia Robotnicza" (PPR), and both the PPR and RPPS aided the ghetto from their own meager resources. They supplied arms and conducted diversion tactics on the eve of and during the ghetto uprising in Warsaw, and led fighters who were still alive out of the destroyed ghetto.

Other parties maintained weak contacts with certain Polish political groups, generally on an individual basis. The *Hashomer Hatzair*, for example, thanks to the enthusiasm of two of its sympathizers in the Polish Scout Movement (*Harcerz Polski*), benefited from support and aid from the latter's ranks. One of these exceptional women, Irena Adamowicz, faithfully served the group as a courier on the dangerous trips from ghetto to ghetto.[55]

The Revisionists in the Warsaw Ghetto received aid from an established contact within a conspiratorial organization headed by Major Henryk Iwinski, whose *nom de guerre* was "Bystry." That group stood outside the ranks of the Polish underground national army. "Bystry" helped to organize and to purchase arms for the Revisionists' fighting unit, *Żydowski Związek Wojskowy* ("Jewish Military Union").[56]

The Jewish National Committee and the two representatives of the Jewish Coordination Commission (one person representing the Bund and one representing the Zionist groups which were united in the Jewish National Committee) in the ghetto were in constant contact with both the civil and the military sectors of the *Delegatura* in Warsaw. Thanks to the *Delegatura* and its couriers, starting in the fall of 1942 the above-mentioned Jewish parties and bodies could contact Jewish parties and organizations in the free world, send them coded telegrams and reports, and receive moral and financial help from them.

The leadership of the underground armed forces (ZWZ—"Union for Armed Struggle"), later called the *Armia Krajowa* (AK—"Home Army"), generally took a negative position in regard to the question of supplying the ghetto (which was preparing for an uprising) with a large amount of arms. In a telegram sent by the commandant of ZWZ (pseudonym "Kalina") to London on January 7, 1943, we read: "Jews of various groups, including Communists, approach us post factum about arms as if we had full caches. As an experiment, I gave several pistols to them, but I doubt they will use them. I will issue no more arms, because as you know, we have none ourselves and are awaiting them. . . .[57]

Only after the deportation action of January 1943, during which the first armed encounters between groups of the Jewish Fighters Organization (JFO) and German gendarmes occurred, did the underground military sector supply the ghetto with fifty pistols, fifty grenades, and four kilograms of explosive material, which, compared to the needs of an organized armed uprising, was like a drop in the ocean. This was the second and last time that the official Polish underground aided the Warsaw Ghetto during the period of preparations for the uprising. Later, when the uprising broke out, all calls for aid by the representatives of the "Coordination Commission" and the JFO went unanswered.

The military leadership in the occupied country held firmly to this policy of not aiding the Jewish underground with arms, ignoring a specific instruction of General Władysław Sikorski's staff in London to the commandant of the AK on July 27, 1943, which orders him "to give them [the Jews] whatever aid is possible, supplying them with arms and military supplies from the existing caches."[58] One of the reasons for this policy was the general position of the official leadership of the Polish underground during this period, which was to avoid mass armed encounters with the German occupier at any price, its motto being "Wait with your gun at your side." It was afraid that an organized Jewish uprising in the ghetto would spread and involve the urban Polish population. Secondly, the ghetto had the reputation in these circles of being a nest of Communist infiltration, and it was feared that arming the ghetto would be tantamount to arming Communist groups.

There was also a third reason: the growing influence of reactionary and anti-Semitic circles in the Polish underground movement as the German-Soviet front began to move into Polish territory. This strengthened anti-Soviet attitude was clearly expressed, after the Germans raised charges in 1943 of the Katyn Forest massacre, and the breaking off of Soviet-Polish diplomatic relations in the summer of 1943.

The way was now paved for reconciliation between the Polish parties, including even Fascist groups such as the ONR. In March 1944 the military underground organization of this group, *Narodowe Siły Zbrojne* (NSZ—"National Armed Forces") officially joined the AK. In their bestial anti-Semitism, the NSZ bands did not shrink from murdering Jewish partisans in the woods, as well as Jews who escaped from the slaughters in the ghettos and camps.[59]

Anti-Jewish feelings on the part of the Polish population and the underground were sharpened by the much-exaggerated reports of confiscations of food, clothing, and other supplies which some Jewish partisan groups carried out among landlords and peasants in the countryside in order to feed and clothe themselves. This was commonly done by non-Jewish partisan units, too. The *Delegatura* did not officially recognize the Jewish partisans as a part of the general partisan movement. It refused to support them and took a generally negative position in regard to their very existence. The news of the desertion of Jewish soldiers from General Władisław Anders' corps that was fighting with the Allies in the Middle East—caused by anti-Semitic excesses committed against them—also served as grist for the mill.[60]

The relations became tense, and suffused with mutual distrust. Of all Polish parties active in the Polish underground, the Communist PPR was the only one employing the tactic of engaging in an immediate armed struggle with the Nazi occupiers. The PPR was actually a diversion group of the Red Army in Poland, and was considered as such by the Polish underground. Because of this strategy of immediate struggle, the PPR became the natural ally of the Jewish Fighters Organization. The JFO dared not be so selective in choosing allies otherwise it might risk losing what might well be its last chance to fight for the rescue of the still living remnants of the destroyed Jewish community.

In other larger provincial ghettos, the situation was the same, if not worse. In the Białystok Ghetto, for instance, Mordecai Tenenbaum-Tamaroff, one of the leaders of the Jewish Resistance Movement, requested weapons aid in a letter dated April 2, 1943, addressed to the leadership of the Polish "Civil Struggle." According to all sources except an uncorroborated one, the Jewish Fighters Organization there received no such aid.[61]

The remnants of annihilated Polish Jewry also had contacts with Polish society through the *Rada Pomocy Żydom przy Delegaturze Rzadu*, an affiliate of the *Delegatura*. This "Council to Aid Jews" was finally organized at the end of November and the beginning of December, 1942. Participating in the council were the *Delegatura* official in charge of Jewish matters and representatives of the Polish Socialist Party, the two democratic parties, and the peasant party.

For a time, until July 1943, when anti-Semitic feelings in the Polish population increased sharply, a representative of the "Catholic Front for a New Poland" participated. When the Catholic deputy left the council, his place was filled by a representative of the second Socialist Party, the RPPS. Two Jewish members were also on the council; its vice-president was a representative of the Bund and its General Secretary was a member of the Jewish National Committee.

In April 1943, a branch of the council was set up in Cracow for that city and the surrounding district, and later in Lwów for that city and its entire district, with a party makeup analogous to Warsaw's. A Jewish member also participated in the Cracow branch.

The main function of the "Council to Aid Jews" was to assist the thousands of Jews who lived like Marranos on the "Aryan" side. This aid consisted of false "Aryan" documents, distributions of monthly financial support for the hidden Jews, assistance in finding living quarters for them, secret medical aid, the placement of Jewish children in Christian children's homes and so forth. The council made an energetic effort to combat the criminal blackmail epidemic waged against hidden Jews which caused thousands of them to fall into the hands of the Gestapo. Upon the intervention of the council, the *Delegatura* published a semiofficial appeal in the Polish underground press threatening the blackmailers and their accomplices with the death penalty by order of a special civil court. The council asked that this warning be posted in public. In addition, the council distributed leaflets in Warsaw condemning the blackmailers as criminals. The leaflets exhorted Poles to aid the Jews and to fight against the blackmail evil.[62]

The Polish underground press, which did not reach the broad masses, announced thirteen death sentences against Poles for blackmail and for informing on Jews to the Gestapo.[63] Among them were a priest and a sergeant in the Polish police. Generally, however, the effect of the campaign against blackmail was minimal, from August 1943 until September 1944, because of the *Delegatura's* cautious position on the question of Polish complicity in the persecution of the Jews. Indeed, the strong anti-Semitism among the majority of the Polish population made the *Delegatura* reluctant to take too strong a pro-Jewish position.

Individual cases of negative and positive attitudes toward the persecuted Jews by their Gentile neighbors will be dealt with in Part Two of this book.

Behavior During the "Resettlement Actions"

A decisive factor that must be taken into account in analyzing the problem of Jewish behavior during the "resettlement actions" is the question of whether or not the Jews understood the true significance of these events. Until the start of the period of mass murder in the first three months of 1942, the Jewish population hoped that the majority would somehow survive. "We'll outlive them" was a popular saying in the ghettos and camps. Of course, there had already been countless victims of individual murder, of ghettoization, starvation, labor camps, diseases, and epidemics. The Jews realized that many of their number would not live to see the end of the war. But even the greatest pessimists in their darkest fantasies could not imagine that the "final solution of the Jewish problem in Europe" meant the total physical extermination of all Jews regardless of sex or age. That would have been a crime without precedent in the history of mankind, and sane and reasonable people were incapable of conceiving of such a possibility. A few rare individuals had managed to escape from the death camps in Chełmno, Treblinka, or Auschwitz, or, barely alive, from under the piles of corpses from mass murders in the woods. But when they told of their experiences, they encountered disbelief from people who listened sympathetically but who treated the stories as products of sick imaginations and disturbed minds.[64]

The Western world in general also received with skepticism these tales of mass murder. The BBC and other radio reports on massacres in the East were regarded by most as exaggerated anti-Nazi propaganda.

The Nazis' system of *gradual* liquidation of the ghettos also contributed to this false appraisal of the "final solution." Wherever "resettlements" occurred, the Nazis left behind a part of the ghetto population—in some places just a few, even very few, Jews, but in others, tens of thousands, as in Warsaw, Łódź, Będzin, or Sosnowiec. This was seized upon as proof that total annihilation wasn't intended. Thus, one way of attempting to save oneself was to flee from one ghetto where no "actions" had taken place to another ghetto which had already experienced such an "action." Many people took this step, only to quickly realize their mistake in not appreciating the full scope of the annihilation plan: *all* Jews were meant, with no exception.

A second factor in misleading the Jews was the effectiveness with which the ghettos were sealed off. The Nazis were so thorough that the inhabitants of city and town ghettos far from death camps such as Treblinka, Bełżec, or Auschwitz never even heard rumors of the existence of those places.

Communications between ghettos were also enormously difficult, especially since leaving a ghetto was punishable by death. Similarly, contacts with the Christian population were severely prohibited. As a result, the Jews had only imprecise information about what was happening in even neighboring ghettos. They had to make do with rumors.

A third factor which restricted the awareness of the victims and which prevented them from even imagining their impending doom was the cunning Nazi system of lies and deceit. Hundreds of instances have been documented.[65] The deceptive direction signs in railroad stations, fake bathing facilities, and the like kept the victims from knowing, until the very last moment, what was in store for them in the extermination camps.

A fourth factor contributing to the disorientation of the "resettled"

Jews was the secrecy in which the "final solution" was wrapped. The extermination camps were located in isolated places, and the native populace was evacuated from the immediate area. Specially built railroads led to these camps, and the camps themselves were artfully concealed from all outside eyes. Non-German railroad workers had to leave the transports before arrival. All the SS men in the camps had to swear a military oath that they would keep their macabre activities a secret even after leaving the service.

The refusal to believe, the very rejection of any thought of inevitable death, were also enhanced by the normal human instinct of self-preservation which grabs at any illusion, any fantastic hope of salvation. The Jews knew that there were labor camps enslaving tens of thousands of their brothers, and so virtually every ghetto Jew thought that he would be among the "lucky" ones who would be sent to such a place during a "selection."

It is indisputable that most Jews did not know exactly what ultimate fate the Nazis were preparing for them. At best, more sensitive and logical individuals—and logical thought was not easy in those unprecedented times—had an inkling that the "resettlements" were linked to physical danger greater than the persecutions they'd so far experienced. But that they spelled the absolute physical annihilation of all Jews without exception—that was one thing they could not imagine, or rather, they drove away such a thought as an improbable nightmare. Thus Ringelblum, in his comprehensive treatment of Jewish-Polish relations during the war, noted that the attempts by the ghetto underground to make the other ghetto Jews understand the true meaning of the "resettlements" were regarded as Nazi-inspired provocations to trigger a Jewish resistance.[66] In his entry of December 5, 1942, we read: "I am convinced that even today, when Treblinka is known to the few Jewish remnants still in Warsaw [after the summer "resettlements"], there are still hundreds and even thousands of people who still believe the false reports about the children's camps [that the Nazi propaganda has spread among Jewish workers in the factories, who were asked to go voluntarily to the labor camps in the Lublin area]." In regard to the West European Jews deported to Treblinka, he says: "They do not know what Treblinka is, they think it's a labor colony, and on the railroad they ask the distance to the industrial factory of Treblinka. . . . If they knew they were going to their deaths, they would certainly put up a resistance."[67]

In regard to the more than 34,000 victims of Babi-Yar, the murderers themselves testified that "until the very last moment before the execution, they believed they were going to be transported somewhere else—thanks to the marvelously intelligent organization."[68]

Contemporary sources tell of the same mood among the Jews deported from Greece, Holland, France, and other countries. Even in Hungary, where the deportations began very late, in May 1944, only the official Jewish leadership knew something of the full scope of the Jewish catastrophe in Europe. But in the ghettos, nearly everyone was convinced that the transports would not go beyond Hungary's borders.[69]

There is a widespread opinion, even among Holocaust historians, that the Jews went "like sheep to the slaughter." At most, it is granted that there were individual but infrequent exceptions. What are the facts?

First of all, we have to establish that Jews were everywhere brutally forced into the transports. During the "resettlements," the SS created an atmosphere of ferocious terror in the ghettos in order to break the victims' will to resist. In many instances, the deportations began with wild shooting sprees. In regard to the "action" in Słuck, White Russia, the territorial commissioner Karol reported to his superior: "The appearance of the town was shattering. The German police and Lithuanian partisans [auxiliary police] drove the Jews out of their homes with a cruelty and brutality that are indescribable. Echoes of shooting came from all parts of the city, and heaps of Jewish corpses lay about everywhere."[70] The doors to Jewish homes were broken down with axes and rifle butts, and when that didn't help, and the Jews still refused to come out, the doors were blasted by hand grenades, as in Rowne in Volhynia.[71]

The official announcements of "resettlements" contained a warning that any Jew trying to hide would be shot on the spot when discovered. In many cases, the Jews were kept at the gathering points for many days without even a drop of water, under a burning sun, or in pouring rain or snow, or else locked up in schools, synagogues, and churches, where they fainted and even died because of the crowding, the heat, hunger, or thirst. The terror made the Jews "more fearful of the Germans than of death itself," which often came as a savior.[72]

The realities of these "resettlements" can be seen from the following brief excerpts from two testimonies from two ghettos, Stanisławów in Eastern Galicia, and Sarny in White Russia. The first is from Eyewitness Testimony 18; the second, from Eyewitness Testimony 19.

On September 13, 1941, thousands of Jewish families from the neighboring towns were deported into the center of the city. People were herded in from Drohobycz, Stryj, Sambor, Kałusz, Tłumacz, Bohorodczany, Nadwórna, and around 22,000 Jews from Carpatho-Rus. Thousands of Hungarian Jews were also transported into the city. There was no ghetto in Stanisławów. Again there were huge numbers of Jews in the city, packed into every section of town. Thousands of families milled around in the streets and courtyards, until the next *aktsye* cleared them away.

Six weeks later, the Nazis began the final extermination of the Jews. All the people who'd been shipped into the city were now herded together and shot en masse, the same way it happened the first time.

Every two or three weeks, they simply murdered Jews at random. The Germans stormed into homes, heaving grenades and shooting up the people who tried escaping through the windows.

A moment later, a cry that pierced the heart rose from the 15,000 people and filled the skies: "Run, they're killing us!" The Germans and the police converged on the square. Shots rang out from behind the windows. I don't know how I reacted. I only remember this enormous weight suddenly falling on me. I started twisting and squirming and finally crawled free from under the dozens of bodies on top of me. I couldn't see where my mother and child lay. The bullets whistled past me. My dress was drenched with blood. I felt I was hit! No—someone had fallen on me. Whether they were dead or wounded I'll never know. The square was completely covered with bodies: some dead, others were wounded, and many were in shock and paralyzed with fear. Wild screams pierced the air. I couldn't get up anymore, there were people falling all over me. Slowly, I regained my senses. Death was staring me in the face. God! What do I do?! Where's my *mameh*?! My child?! I thought of getting up and running home. Maybe my mama and child were already there. But it was impossible to move. I started crawling over the bodies. Our house was nearby. But I saw policemen shooting from the staircase. I was afraid to crawl any further because they were right in front of me. I felt my heart stop beating.

Despite the atmosphere of terror and threats of death for disobedience, some Jews tried to avoid going to the gathering-places. The number of Jews shot during the "resettlements" bears witness to this fact. Many who refused to cooperate were captured in hiding-places. According to official German reports, during the deportations from Warsaw, July 22–September 21, 1942, 5,394 Jews were shot; in other words, approximately that many people refused to go to the "transfer point" and were killed on the spot. In the Lublin ghetto "resettlement" action in the second half of March 1942, several hundred Jews were shot in hiding places.[73]

We have a laconic statement from a German source about a "mutiny" that broke out among the approximately 2,000 Jews in the small Lithuanian town of Žagaré when they were being taken to the execution point on October 2, 1941. The terse report of *Einsatzkommando 3* ends with the matter-of-fact information that during the suppression of the uprising, 150 Jews were shot on the spot

and seven Lithuanian "partisans" were wounded.[74] We also know
of individuals who, standing at the execution point, threw themselves
upon the SS men with their bare hands. One Jew even crawled out
of the grave and dug his teeth into the throat of an SS man, acting
according to the biblical verse: "Let us die with the Philistines."[75]

There was a widespread construction of camouflaged hiding places,
so-called "bunkers," in which people hid during the "actions." A
German woman living in Warsaw during the ghetto uprising left an
account of the complex system of underground bunkers in the ghetto.
She wrote: "The ghetto action carried through by the SS and prepared one day earlier in top secrecy was betrayed. When the SS
marched into [the ghetto] with light military vehicles, they encountered gunfire on all sides. Clearing out the ghetto, which by earlier
calculations should have taken three or four days, actually lasted
five weeks. . . . The labyrinths under the ghetto buildings, which one
could scarcely squeeze through, the underground passages from
house to house, and the extraordinarily well-camouflaged bunkers
and exits through the sewers [which lead] to the Vistula in the Polish part of the city. In order to terminate [the Ghetto uprising], the
Brandkommandos [conflagration squads] had to set fire to house
after house, destroying an enormous amount of property."[76]

We also have information in regard to well-camouflaged underground hiding places, from such places as the ghettos of Białystok,
Wilno, Kaunas, Łódź, Lwów, and Brody. Both Jurgen Stroop, the
suppressor of the Warsaw Ghetto Uprising, and Fritz Katzman, who
led the annihilation action against Jews in eastern Galicia, aded photographs of discovered bunkers to their reports in order to show how
skillfully the Jews managed to build their hiding places in order to
avoid the "resettlements."[77]

There is perhaps a further moral and psychological element ex-
plaining why most of the victims went quietly and passively to their
death: a possible refusal to show the murderers any panic or hysteria
that might have given additional pleasure to the sadists among
them. The victims preferred dying with dignity and with scorn
toward the killers. The Jews might also have actually wondered
whether it was worth fighting for one's life in a world where the
human beast could rule undisturbed amid the passive silence of the
entire civilized world. And if you find this unconvincing, read the
reports below.

The same German witness to the slaughter in Rowne wrote that
when the victims were driven together near mass graves, he noticed
"a father holding the hand of a boy of about ten and talking to him.
The boy could scarcely keep from crying. The father pointed at the
sky, caressed his head, and tried to explain something to him." One
can imagine what the father was saying to the boy at that time.

An important source for understanding the spiritual state and psychological reactions of the Jews preparing themselves for the imminent and inevitable "resettlement" was the mass of mail sent from the provincial towns to relatives and friends in Warsaw and preserved in the Ringelblum Archives. These thousands of items, mostly postcards, were written by all sorts of people: adults and children, men and women, simple people and educated people, religious and nonreligious, people of different professions and political affiliations. These documents record resignation and desperate calls for help, faith in divine providence and utter atheism, apathy and feverish efforts to find some kind of rescue, natural optimism and unlimited despair, a clear sense of what was in store and completely unfounded illusions. The letters tell us how diversely different people reacted to the same events. We can also see the same people in various situations: in a tortured period of waiting for the "resettlement," during the "resettlement" (letters written with trembling hands and stained with tears), and afterwards when a minuscule remnant had miraculously succeeded in saving themselves.[78]

We also have records of the behavior of the victims during the selections and on the threshold of the gas chambers in death camps such as Auschwitz, Sobibór, and Treblinka. A tremendous shock was the division of families into two groups: for definite, immediate gassing (the women with children, old and weak people), who were to be gassed immediately, and the strong and the young, who were to perform labor in the camp. During this procedure, husbands often broke from the ranks and ran to their families in the first group, despite the fate in store for them if they did so. Families tried to stick together at any price. Special concern was given to the children, and people tried to ease their final minutes.

Rudolf Hoess, the *Kommandant* of Auschwitz, describes in his autobiography, which he wrote in a Polish prison, how a mother, who knew what lay ahead, managed to gather the strength to joke with her children, despite the mortal terror gaping from her eyes. And he tells of a young woman who drew his attention because she kept running back and forth, helping small children and elderly women undress and keep calm. Her own two children had already been taken. As she stood at the gas chamber, she called out to him: "I knew all the time that we were being taken to Auschwitz to be gassed, and I deliberately avoided being chosen for labor because I wanted to take care of my children and go through all this in the full awareness of what was happening. I hope it won't take long."

But there were also less controlled and less tranquil reactions. Some women, while undressing, would scream dreadfully, tear out their hair, and become hysterical. They were instantly taken behind the gas chambers and shot. This was generally what happened to all those who did not remain calm. Sometimes, the victims became defiant, especially children. They refused to enter the gas chamber. In such cases, the Germans had to resort to violence and drag them in. Hoess tells of a Jew who, walking past him, hissed: "Germany will pay a heavy penalty for the mass murder of the Jews." In his autobiography, the *Kommandant* also noted other reactions, ethically negative ones. For instance, he tells about a Dutch Jew who, undressing prior to entering the gas chamber, gave him a list of Dutch families concealing Jews, and he wonders why the Jew has done this. Was this an act of personal revenge against the Dutch families who refused to take him in, or an expression of envy to let the hidden Jews be saved while he died?[79]

In Eyewitness Testimony 48, an adolescent in the Jewish labor squad at the death camp of Sobibór describes the behavior of people about to be gassed. The sources also tell of how religious Jews went to their death. They would look upon their final road in terms of historical martyrdoms. We know of a rabbi in Kelmė, Lithuania, who walked at the head of the Jewish community as they went to the execution point. He asked the SS man for permission to say a few words to the gathered Jews, and, obtaining this permission, he encouraged them, saying they had the rare opportunity of fulfilling the commandment of martyrdom for the faith. The SS man interrupted him for talking too long. The rabbi said to him: "I'm done. Now you can do your job."[80]

From a few ghettos, we have heard that pious Jews walked to the execution point in their prayer shawls and phylacteries, loudly reciting confession of sins, Psalms, or *Kaddish*, as for instance in Rubieże-wicze, White Russia.[81]

Pious Jews would prepare for death with meditation, a spiritual stocktaking. In a letter from a small town in Central Poland, when it was clear what lay ahead (the deportation to the extermination camp of Chełmno began in Wartheland around the middle of December 1941), a pious Jew wrote that he was "not broken, thank God, for everything comes from the hands of the Creator. I pray that I have no doubts in the last minute. I ask you all for forgiveness."[82]

Part Two

INTRODUCTION

The eyewitness testimonies of Holocaust survivors are at once both individual narratives of personal trauma and a more general source for the understanding of the "Final Solution" in all its tragic dimensions. The interviews with Jewish survivors included here are fraught with nightmarish images from the ghettos and death camps, from the holes used to hide in on the so-called "Aryan" side, from cellars and bunkers and the forests where Jews lived the lives of trapped animals. The witnesses volunteered this evidence with a view to indicting the Nazi criminals and the unparalleled sadism and atrocities these Nazis practiced against the survivors personally and the Jewish people as a whole. The accounts are frequently interrupted by tears, incoherent muttering, and silence as the survivors relive their own and others' tortures. At the same time, the narratives reveal the various means of resistance the victims honed in extremity in order to withstand first the onslaught of satanic Hitlerian deception, then the final and elaborate regimes of death. Here, as well, are tales of miraculous rescues, descriptions of the torments of daily survival, of the deteriorated conditions in the ghettos and camps, attempts at an analysis of the relations between the different social strata and the activities and role of the Jewish guardians and intermediaries—the *Judenräte*, the ghetto police, the camp *Kapos*, and the like—all within the context of Nazi terror.

Through these documents runs, in addition, the recurrent proof that the Jews were faced with an endless number of external enemies besides the Germans, surrounded as they were on all sides by hostile indigenous populations. Though the accounts recall scattered instances of help from Gentiles, the oppressive majority of the testimonies cries out against the complicity of large segments of the local populace of Eastern Europe in the genocide of the Jewish people. Within the conclusive evidence presented here, there is much which sheds light generally on the tragic dialectic of "Israel among the nations."

Eyewitness documents of the Holocaust are particularly valuable in bringing to light a wide range of Holocaust phenomena for which they are the major, and frequently the *only*, authentic source. These phenomena include the psychological extremes caused in the victims by the unspeakable horrors of German degeneracy and bloodlust and the indelible scars these left upon their psyches; the personal and national reckoning made by the Jewish individual and mass come

61

face to face with imminent annihilation; the resilience, tenacity, and ingenuity displayed by the Jews in combatting the Nazi attempts to dehumanize and humiliate them; the intense yet doomed actions of Jewish social activists and agencies to counter the accelerated deterioration in the ghettos and camps; the evolution of the varied means of resistance created by the Jewish individual and collective in the struggle for daily survival, dignity, and freedom; the psychic shift which occurred in the Jewish people during the war that led to the armed Jewish uprisings in occupied Europe and marked their subsequent course of national self-defense and liberation; the subterranean, Marrano-like existence endured by Jews in hiding on the "Aryan" side; and the interrelations among the various Jewish Diasporas "ingathered" by murderous premeditation in one common vale of tears. All these starkly personal and collective ordeals find expression in the painstakingly detailed testimonies of the living survivors who experienced these events firsthand.

The majority of these interviews were conducted at a time when large-scale proceedings were being initiated against Nazi war criminals and their collaborators. Therefore, they contain an abundance of substantiated charges and evidence against both the SS and their Slavic and Baltic underlings, as well as those Jewish accomplices who assumed active roles in the persecution of their brethren, deluded into thinking that this would ensure their personal survival or, in some instances help in rescuing a segment of their condemned people. The accounts span a wide geographic area, from partisan activity near Moscow to detention camps in southern France, and uncover new facts about German genocide in the major killing centers of Poland. They also reveal the chronologies and characteristics of the demise of a significant number of smaller Jewish settlements about which information until now has been scant, and extant only in the memories of their survivors. The witnesses are thus able to rescue many facets of the Jewish national calamity from oblivion.

The nature and scope of the eyewitness testimonies is, understandably, varied. Meticulous memoirs covering tens of pages, fully detailed and chronologically complete, often revealing deep insight and thorough recall of the events described, contrast sharply with fragmentary episodes consisting of no more than a few pages, which outline only in bare detail the wartime experiences of the witness. The fate of the Jews under Nazi Occupation was sealed with such uniform devastation, however, that even expressly personal and limited experiences reveal much of that common destiny.

The accounts were purposely not arranged along strict thematic lines that would have grouped together, for example, descriptions mainly of life and death in the concentration camps, or of hiding in the forests. Experiences of this kind occurred throughout the course of the war and under varying degrees and circumstances. Nor were the underlying leitmotifs of the testimonies such as resistance or the breakdown in normal human relations readily segregable or even tangibly definable in the maze of suffering and conflict endured by the witnesses. To have divided up these structural contexts, so to speak, of the survivors' tribulations would have been to destroy, in a sense, the organic inevitability of these experiences as they were endured from the beginning of September 1939, in most instances, until Liberation in the summer of 1944 or spring of 1945. Though such a thematic categorization could have been theoretically justified, we did not wish to fragmentize the accounts or undermine their documentary and emotional value. We proceeded, therefore, to arrange the interviews along loosely chronological lines in order to mirror the progression of the witnesses' own perceptions of the events and the ways they reacted to them. The thrust of each Eyewitness Testimony consequently assumes its place in a continuity that embraces both the general stages of the war and the specific behavior of Jews who were assaulted with such murderous abandon as to become paralyzed. The tragic tension that develops in these accounts as the victims contend with the known and unknown elements of the Nazi plan to destroy them, can give us an insight into the individual's behavior under prolonged terror as well as an idea of the general mentality of the Jews in the catastrophe they lived through. Descriptive headings, however, have been added to each document number to suggest the topical emphasis in which the events took place.

Each interview was chosen for its graphic and poignant nature and for the way it illustrates a central problem of the Holocaust. The four basic areas with which these accounts deal are:

1. Resistance to the Nazis in all its forms—individual and collective, spontaneous and planned. The accounts range from exact and prolonged descriptions of the strategies and battles of Jewish partisans in the Byelorussian forests (Eyewitness Testimony 41), or of the successful rebellion in the Treblinka death camp (Eyewitness Testimony 47), to short, almost caustic reports on the fate of Jewish combatants in the Polish Uprising in Warsaw of August–September 1944 (Eyewitness Testimonies 49, 50). You will see that these informants develop the theme of *physical* resistance with much greater frequency than they do passive resistance. This is not the place to dwell on the reasons for this development, nor does it denigrate, by contrast, the other, nonviolent forms of resistance. Indeed, this entire phenomenon demands a thorough and profound analysis, which must take into account the tragic nature of all resistance to systematic Nazi evil and murder. But what these documents do suggest is not that the victims survived as a result of having fought with arms, but that armed

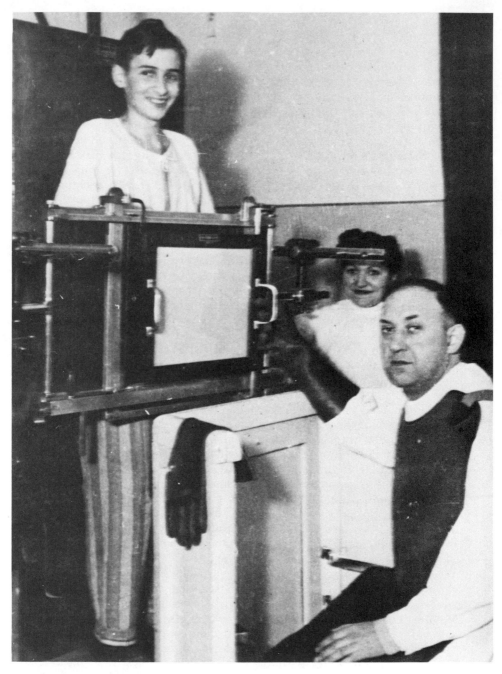

An infirmary in the Łódź Ghetto manned by Dr. Daniel Weiskopf.

A new trade: selling Jewish armbands in the Warsaw Ghetto.

A soup kitchen in the Żelechów Ghetto.

resistance—whether it ended in life or death—was finally perceived as the only possible way of breaking out of the doomed cycle of death the Nazis had imposed on the Jews. Up to that point, the means generally employed to resist the Nazis—and these have been overlooked with the consequence being the paradoxical notion that the Jews were resigned to their fate—were constant through all areas of Jewish life and included cultural, moral, religious, economic, hygienic, political, and personal elements. Jewish history had sharpened the survival instincts the Jews needed in the face of long and trying ordeals, though nothing had prepared them for the dimensions of Nazism. Yet the tradition of resistance was instinctive—one could almost say, subconscious—and out of this process of brute suffering and degradation, the Jews were still able to manifest a spirit of defiance and to initiate operations of armed resistance that remain unparalleled, especially when we consider the immeasurable difficult conditions under which they arose.

2. The second major group of Eyewitness Testimonies deals in some measure with the attitude and behavior of the non-Jewish natives when they became witnesses to or participants in the wholesale murder of the Jews in their lands. The accounts speak of the different kinds of complicity and betrayal practiced by Gentiles against the Jews, and the various shades of relations that existed between these two groups. The interviews do reveal, however, a number of courageous attempts to help the victims by Christian people who risked and sometimes paid with their lives for these acts.

We won't deal here with the various motives for overt betrayal and murder the Gentiles harbored against the Jews, which also find their place in these accounts over and over again. The age-old, almost atavistic hatred of the Jews wherever they have lived unprotected—modern anti-Zionism can also be seen mostly as an inverse variation of this hatred—is such a familiar phenomenon that it needs no elaboration here; it has both exhausted and been ignored by its primary victims even to this day. What is more readily evident, especially in these documents, are the reasons for the positive actions, temporary or prolonged, taken on behalf of Jews.

In most instances where Jews were taken into hiding by Gentiles, huge material compensation was exacted from them in the form of outlandish sums of money, jewelry, mortgages, and so on. Jews finding shelter among Christians had frequently to cover not only their own and their family's living expenses, but those of the person or family hiding them out (see Eyewitness Testimony 15). Though some Gentiles assisted Jews out of a purely human impulse with no thought to financial reward (Eyewitness Testimonies 25, 29, 56, etc.), others did so simply as a way of retaliating against the despised German occupiers (Eyewitness Testimony 6). There are inspiring stories of peasants sometimes sharing their meager food rations and only bed with Jews who had escaped from death camps and transports (Eyewitness Testimonies 17, 38), as well as acts of kindness performed as expressions of political solidarity (Eyewitness Testimony 9). There is a case here, too, of the dangers involved in rescuing Jews serving as the circumstantial stimulant for a Gentile man falling in love with a Jewish girl and risking his life to save her and her loved ones (Eyewitness Testimony 26).

Most often, the Gentile benefactors couldn't withstand the grave psychological pressure of living under constant threat of exposure, and finally forced the Jews from their homes. There were also the oft-recurring betrayals by opportunists and criminals, who, wishing to rid themselves of Jews from whom they had no further material benefit—having already deprived them of everything they had—turned them over to the Germans, or, as happened at times, murdered them themselves. Informers, extortionists, even partisans and guerrillas, as well as ordinary civilians, all of them in varying degrees of villainy, were the scourge of Jews in hiding in the Gentile world.

The treatment of the Jews by the indigenous population was noticeably different in Western Europe, where assisting the Jews in their hour of need was not the rare occurrence it was in Eastern Europe. In Holland, Belgium, France, and Italy, large segments of the non-Jewish populace, including at times even police authorities who were frequently charged by the Nazis with carrying out anti-Jewish persecution and deportation measures, sympathized to varying degrees with the condemned Jews and translated this attitude into attempts at rescue and thwarting of final-death decrees. To illustrate this, we've included three Eyewitness Testimonies from Western Europe—Italy (34), Holland (35), and Belgium (36).

Absolutely no statistical conclusions are to be drawn from the disproportionately large number of Eyewitness Testimonies published here that shed a positive light on the behavior of Gentiles during the annihilation of Europe's Jews. The relatively few instances where aid and protection were extended to the persecuted are, in view of all the accumulated damaging evidence we possess in this area, but a solitary ray in a world steeped in the darkness of anti-Semitism and fratricide. But these compassionate acts of people who were not swept away by the traditional tide of Jew hatred deserve to be brought into the open. Somehow, despite the relentless psychological pressure from their environment, and despite their own fear of death, they found the strength and courage to stand beside a people driven and hounded beyond endurance. The witnesses have paid special recognition in these interviews to the Gentile rescuers who paid with their own lives for attempting to maintain their "likeness of God" (Eyewitness Testimonies 38, 48).

The testimonies revealed that even among the Germans were people who showed compassion for the persecuted Jews. (Eyewitness Testimonies 10, 13, 18, 61.)

3. The third realm of experience during the Holocaust that is often described in these interviews is the life, suffering, and martyrdom of Jewish children and youth who were forced through a special hell by the Nazis.

The Nazis conceived a plan of denying life to the Jewish child from the very beginning and meticulously mapped the implementation of this process. By subdividing the Jewish population into categories of "useful" laborers, who were temporarily reprieved from death, and nonlaborers, the so-called "pernicious elements," who were either slaughtered outright or deported for eventual extermination, they assured that the Jewish child would fill the ranks of the second category. The pronounced motive for the systematic extermination of the Jewish children by the Nazis and their confederates was the desire to sever the biological roots of the Jewish people, depriving even a remnant handful of survivors of the remotest possibility of regeneration. This dementia, unprecedented in the annals of mankind, whether seen as an ideological disease or an obsessive bloodletting, has yet to be adequately fathomed and must be consigned to the area of psychopathology dealing with the contemporary German character, something which still demands further attention and study. We have confined ourselves here to the life-and-death struggles of the victims, the children.

There are German documents of the day that express amazement and frustration at the obstinacy, endurance, and moral and physical courage of the Jews in face of all manner of means to degrade and humiliate them. This is especially true with regard to the Jewish children, who, as is known, were a significant lifeline for the ghettos and even for the camps as they smuggled, stole, and thwarted the Nazi regime in any way they could, procuring food and economic necessities for themselves and their families. The Eyewitness Testimonies in this volume reveal time and again how the simplest act of integrity, human solidarity, and defiance on the part of the Jews produced the most violent and aberrant acts of retribution against them by the Nazi murderers and oppressors. This wretched German battle aimed against the Jewish spirit, against parents trying to save their children and against these children themselves, was often met by a steadfastness and by acts of sacrifice that belied those abject "victories" Nazi nihilism was able to claim over its victims' humanity.

It was the Jewish child of the Nazi period who most remarkably displayed this vitality and fight for life. Condemned to be the first to die, hounded, their parents ravaged by massacres, hunger, deportations, and disease, abandoned sometimes by the callous self-preoc-

A child street vendor of artificial candy in the Warsaw Ghetto.

cupation of adults themselves struggling to survive, Jewish children had to fend for themselves in a world so base no prior experience could have prepared them for it. Adults had various spiritual and self-deluding ways to insulate themselves, but children had to create their life anew from chaos or perish—if not directly by the enemy's hand, then by succumbing in the pathetic contest of child against the monstrous, all-pervading evil. The brutalization the children withstood, and the heroism they displayed, exemplify their will to adhere to decent rules of life. This is shown in the account included here of the eleven-year-old child at the outbreak of the war, who tells how he volunteered to work in a slave labor camp because he "wanted to save my father," meaning he stood in for his father at slave labor (Eyewitness Testimony 27). Another child of the same age also volunteered for hard labor, and was put to work in a glass factory. While he was struggling at the various jobs that were designed to kill him slowly, both his parents were deported to their deaths, and he subsequently had to endure a great many atrocities and vicissitudes on his own in German concentration camps (Eyewitness Testimony 21).

Children were occasionally able to have their "life" documents (*Lebensschein*) forged, making them out to be much older than the age that would have targeted them for deportation, so that they were "entitled" temporarily to "life through labor." Needless to say, if they survived the period of this exemption, their death sentence was still sealed for the next phase—deportation and extermination (Eyewitness Testimony 13).

There is an account here by a child who, as a nine-year-old, was part of a group of children aged nine to eleven who'd been separated from their parents during a massacre and escaped the ghetto by their own devices, finally reaching a forest where some of them hid. They were integrated into a families unit of Jewish partisans and saw action in the Byelorussian woods (Eyewitness Testimony 55). There are also descriptions of horrors by Jewish children who saved themselves by taking refuge in deep latrines and under outhouses (Eyewitness Testimonies 13, 55).

Some older children were able to escape to the "Aryan" side by themselves or through the help of underground networks. Leading concealed lives, they were constantly threatened by enemies in all uniforms as well as in civilian clothes, and were always in flight from betrayers and blackmailers (Eyewitness Testimony 26). Jewish children who escaped the ghettos were sometimes able to hire themselves out to heartless peasants as laborers in the countryside, and had to perform all kinds of menial and backbreaking work just to receive a meager piece of bread. Children who were torn away from their parents during selections and at other instances were occasionally

left in strange Gentile homes or deposited in convents, where the
chances for survival were by no means assured (Eyewitness Testimony 36, etc.). One long tragic odyssey included here is of a child,
eleven at the start of the war, who endured the very depths of Nazi
hell inside the Sobibór death camp (Eyewitness Testimony 48).

The infanticide practiced by the Germans and their helpers sur-
passes in brutality and sadism the most heinous of other Nazi crimes.
The Eyewitness Testimonies abound with descriptions of German
and Ukrainian ghouls throwing live children into fires or garbage
pits (Eyewitness Testimony 48), assaulting them with hand grenades
(Eyewitness Testimony 14), grabbing them by their little feet and
smashing them head first into walls (Eyewitness Testimony 17),
and other unspeakable atrocities. The percentage of Jewish children
who survived this German infanticide is the lowest of any age group
to have come out of the Holocaust alive.

4. The fourth and last major subject central to these eyewitness
accounts is the internal conditions among the Jews imprisoned in
ghettos and camps. The events described as part of the day-to-day
struggle for life in these zones of horror include the expulsion of an
entire Jewish community from the historic town of Auschwitz and
their subsequent accommodation by the fraternal and supportive
Jewish communities among whom they were scattered (Eyewitness
Testimony 24); the life and suffering in the Łódź Ghetto of the exiled
Jews of Prague, who were totally shocked and unprepared for the
ordeal but who shared the common misery with their local brothers
(Eyewitness Testimony 10); the functioning and role of the ghettos
and the *Judenrat*, or Jewish Councils, describing various retribution
measures, including the collecting of ransom monies and tribute for
the German SS (Eyewitness Testimones 1, 5, 64, etc.); the conditions
in and escapes from the Łódź Ghetto prison (Eyewitness Testimony
9) and the life lived within its walls by the last remnants of Jews
driven to their final destination after the liquidation of their provincial ghettos (Eyewitness Testimony 7); the opposition mounted
by the Bund and other political parties to the administration of
Mordecai Rumkowski (Eyewitness Testimony 40), and more.

A second group of these Eyewitness Testimonies portrays the nightmarish existence of the Jewish camp inmates. There is the macabre
scene of a Kol Nidre night in Auschwitz and the hysterical behavior
of a Jewish female *Kapo* (Eyewitness Testimony 20), an account of
the mortally dangerous labor involved in the construction of the V-1
rocket and other lethal weapons of mass destruction (Eyewitness
Testimonies 9, 58), testimony by and about Jewish women, who were
treated with such brutality and perversity in Auschwitz (Eyewitness
Testimony 20, etc.), and a description of the horrors of the "medical
experiments" (castration) performed on the men in the camps (Eye-

witness Testimony 25). You'll read of the ordeal of the concentration camp set up in the devastated Jewish section of Warsaw in which Greek, Hungarian, and Polish Jews were enslaved at the torturous labor of razing and clearing away the mass of rubble and refuse left from the burned-out Warsaw Ghetto (Eyewitness Testimony 58), and the tale of terror of Jews trapped in a bunker living out their grotesque existence under the ruins of Warsaw, yet who endured, to be liberated (Eyewitness Testimony 57). And there are the reminiscences of those who survived the indescribable death marches designed to bring about the deaths of the inmates the camps could no longer "accommodate" in the last stages of the war (Eyewitness Testimonies 57, 60, 62, etc.)

Another characteristic of these documents is that they comprise only isolated details and fragments from the overwhelming Jewish catastrophe. They are like projectiles cast out from the frothing volcano that engulfed the Jewish nation in Europe.

This feeling of fracture, of being subjected to things incomprehensible and unutterable, was felt by the witnesses themselves as they recounted their suffering. A Jewish woman expressed herself in her Eyewitness Testimony this way: "Everything I'm telling you now is like a grain of sand by the sea—absolutely nothing compared to what happened" (Eyewitness Testimony 18). Another Jewish woman, who was deported from Prague into the Łódź Ghetto and then later, to Auschwitz, ended her Eyewitness Testimony with these words: "Not all of it can be described. There are things we lived through, we witnessed, that we can't begin to talk about. Such things that have no equivalent in words. It remains inside us as our deepest part—we, who saw with our own eyes what the Germans are capable of" (Eyewitness Testimony 10).

There was to be no limit to Jewish suffering and humiliation under Nazi tyranny, as the destruction process was so unrelenting and subject to such arbitrariness and "improvisation" that death, through rebellion and, infrequently, suicide, was viewed as the lone escape from the all-pervasive torture of living. The abysses men sank to were so deep that Jewish resources were tried beyond endurance in coping with the satanism of the annihilation process. As profound as the evil was on one level, there still opened under it a deeper one, where Nazi venality sank still further into the unplummetable depths. It's understandable that this sensitive Jewish woman from Prague should draw back into emotional self-protection when confronting recollections of the extremes of human degradation.

The methodological question will inevitably arise as to how reliable these Eyewitness Testimonies are as historical sources. It's evident that the reliability of a statement taken down some time after the events occurred is susceptible to the obscuring influences of imperfect memory. This is especially true when the witnesses have emerged from such traumas as these to be confronted with a consternation and even controversiality which might further alter their original perceptions. These variable factors, however, can in no way disqualify the Eyewitness Testimonies published here from being considered incontestable documentations of fact. The witness may, and occasionally does, err about the date, name, number, and other, so to speak, formal elements of the events and their sequence. But the essential truth about the fact itself remains unchanged, more so since the witnesses have emerged from their scathing experiences in relatively stable psychological condition and, more remarkably, evidence objectivity and conscientiousness in their testimony. The overwrought emotional state brought about by the recounting of their ordeals can certainly lead the Holocaust survivors into exaggerations and even modifications of circumstances pertaining to their own roles in the events, or the roles of others by whom they were either positively or negatively affected, and this emotional factor must be taken into consideration by the reader. But the further away the witnesses travel in time and place from these experiences and from the entire period, the greater is the chance that they may yet be able to confront these horrors with the modicum of sufferance and historical perspective that was impossible in the turbulent days after Liberation.

Naturally, the degree by which we can assess the objective validity of the account rises when its contents can be compared to that of another account covering the same event. We've illustrated this by including two Eyewitness Testimonies—33 and 41—both of which relate identical facts and impressions about the freeing of Jewish slave laborers from the camp in Świerzeń Nowy (Nowogródek District). We learn that, apart from certain details about the exact number liberated and some known identities of those accompanying the leader of the escape, Hershl Posesorski, both accounts overlap almost perfectly in their description of the event itself and its significant components.

This is also true when we examine Eyewitness Testimony 47 about the uprising in Treblinka. It's clearly in accord with the well-known published version by one of the participants in the Revolt, Yankl Viernik, which was issued clandestinely in Warsaw in 1944, a year after the outbreak of the successful rebellion in the death camp. There is also significant correlation between the widely disseminated published version of the uprising in the Sobibór death camp by the Jewish Soviet lieutenant, A. Petchorski, who was among the organizers of the uprising, and the account in Eyewitness Testimony 48 included here.

To this day, many survivors refuse or are unable, in many instances, to escape from under the burden of memory, which still tortures them in their dreams with visions of the ghettos and camps. Coursing through these Eyewitness Testimonies is an undercurrent of misery and pain that can only transport the sensitive reader into a realm that is as tragic in its scope as it is horrific in its detail. It thus becomes encumbent on the reader to try to develop a deeper awareness of what is implied in these annals of suffering and humanism through intensified study, psychological empathy, and, in the case of the Jewish reader, heightened national consciousness.

The reader will notice immediately that although we have attempted to arrange the themes of the interviews along chronological lines, the Eyewitness Testimonies occasionally overlap, anticipate later events, or reverse ordered time sequences. This was done to let the informants develop their themes in relation to the general contexts of the war and the major stages in the destruction of the Jews of Europe. It enables the reader to progress through a wide range of experiences in a thematically sequential rendering of the Holocaust. An insignificant number of brief deletions were made for the sake of conciseness and continuity. Minor clarifications were inserted in a few spots. For reasons of discretion, the names of the witnesses are given only by initials. The language and style of the informants has been preserved almost intact in a translation that attempts to render the original idiom into an English that is prevalent, in most cases, among the witnesses themselves. This was done in order to convey a sense of the raw immediacy apparent in the Yiddish, and to provide a kind of environmental baggage for the crossover to the English. The Glossary that precedes the Notes section provides translations from the Yiddish, as well as from German, Russian, and Hebrew.

These interviews were dictated—the bulk of them in Yiddish—by the eyewitnesses themselves and recorded on the spot by field workers of the YIVO Institute for Jewish Research and others immediately after Liberation in the freed camps, hospitals, Displaced Persons camps, urban barracks, and wherever a survivor was to be found. Some of the interviews were recorded a number of years after the end of the war when both the informants and the interviewers had left the graveyard of Europe. This broad, representative cross-section of Eyewitness Testimonies forms part of the Eyewitness Testimonies Collection of the YIVO, which numbers over 3,000 interviews with survivors of the Holocaust. The great majority of these testimonies, as well as the ones included in this book, are from people not prominent in Jewish affairs, and represent the experiences of *folksmentshn* —people of the masses—who endured the daily struggle against the Hitler beast in the hope they would be part of a physical and spiritual rebirth of their nation.

EYEWITNESS TESTIMONIES

Eyewitness Testimony 1. Fifteen Lashes for Each *Judenratler!*

M.M. Lived in Sokoły, Białystok District. Recorded a few months after Liberation, in Białystok, May 14, 1945.

At the start of *Khol-hamoyed Paysekh*—this was in 1942—the Sokoły *Judenrat* was handed an order from the newly appointed *Amtskommissar* to have all able bodied men, regardless of age, lined up at 11 A.M. sharp in front of the *Judenrat* building.

The news started a panic in the *shtetl*. We were still in shock from the massacres in the surrounding villages, so whenever we heard about sudden lineups, we knew they always ended either in complete slaughter or deportation to be exterminated somewhere else. Even though we were terrified and ready to run, we listened to the "optimists," who tried convincing us that if the *Amtskommissar* wanted to deport us, he'd make no distinction between men, women, and children, but order everyone out, like he did in Tiktin, Dvokeh, and other places.[1] We had to hope this cruel argument was true. But we still wouldn't trust him—*"Poter biloy klum yiefshar."*[2] This had to be a kind of final decree because if the Germans wanted to impose some minor penalty, they usually let the *Judenrat* do it alone.

By late morning, a crowd of a few hundred men had gathered in the street in front of the *Judenrat,* but it was plain that over half the men in the *shtetl* hadn't come. At exactly eleven, the "blond beast" appeared. It was the *Amtskommissar*—his sinister eye magnified through the monocle he wore—like the Angel of Death, himself. His escort was this sadistic-looking German official—a monster of a man. The *Präses* of the *Judenrat* leaped forward, removed his hat, and bowed from the hip ceremonially. But the *Amtskommissar* only shouted at him: *"Varum hat sich da so ein kleines Publikum versammelt?"*[3] The *Präses* replied he had sent word to every household and threatened severe consequences for anyone not complying. Why the others hadn't shown up—he didn't know. "We have no police, you see. To drag everyone out by force . . ." The *Amtskommissar* went wild, cutting him off and slapping his head and face. He snapped open his pocket watch and screamed: *"Im Verlaufe einer halben Stunde sollen alle hier versammelt sein! Sonst wird der Judenrat bald erschossen!"*[4] This sent a new shock through the *Judenrat*. Suddenly, they were changed men. All twelve of them along with their aides and assistants rushed through the streets of the *shtetl*, going from house to house and dragging everyone out, big and small. No one could stop them. Then they lined everyone up in rows. If any "malingerers" didn't show up, they said, that *Ashmedai* would execute the whole *Judenrat!* In fifteen minutes, the street was jammed with people, and the *Judenrat* marched them off in double file.

Fifteen minutes later—a half hour to the minute—the *Amtskommissar* and his cohort were back. He shouted at the *Judenrat* to move over where he was and take their place at the head of the column. The twelve stepped up and he reviewed the entire line, like he was counting them off. Then he ordered the *Präses* to bring him a footstool and went along himself to make sure it was the kind he wanted. They came back in a few minutes, with the *Präses* carrying a metal grate used to scrape the mud off boots. The *Amtskommissar* then ordered the *Präses*, Alter Ginzburg, the so-called "Jewish Prime Minister," to stretch himself out on it and raise up his coattails over his behind. The accomplice, that fat brute, walked up and lashed out fifteen full strokes with a whip. He also clubbed him a few times over the head "for good measure." Next, he ordered the "Minister of Finance," the proud and aristocratic Yoyne Ginzburg, to bend down over the grate. He also got fifteen hard swishes across the backside and had his head beaten. The third one in line stepped up—Yisroel Maik, the wealthy jeweler and watchmaker. He got the same punishment. Then the "Labor Ministers" came up—Yanov, Khaskele Tservanets, and Zeydl Ratchkovski. Next, it was Yankl the shoemaker's turn. He started pleading with that hangman: "*Ikh bin der barimter Schumacher, makh dokh fir die daytshn gute Schuche, gute Schtiefel?!*"[5] It was no use. He had to bend down over the grate and got his share of lashes. The shoemaker yelled out: "*Shoyn genug!*"[6] By now, the executioner was exhausted, dripping with sweat, and he started cutting down on the number of strokes. Some of the older *Jundenrat* members, like Aren Zholte, Leybl Okan, Lazer Rozenovitch, and the builder, the *Amtskommissar* passed over, and they weren't beaten. Dr. Makovski was publicly humiliated by the "blond devil" because he prescribed too many medicines to the sick. He was whipped a couple of times, too, and banished from Sokoły and the whole region. He was given three days to get out.

The *Amtskommissar* then started a tirade on why he had whipped the *Judenrat:* "You don't carry out the express orders of the authorities! You hoard goods in secret places and won't turn them over to the regime! Laborers escape from the work gangs every day! When you're told to assemble, you don't show up! All this is the fault of the *Judenrat!* The longer the war lasts, the more our laws will strangle you! Every act of disobedience is an act of sabotage and will be met with death by firing squad! This time, I'm letting you off lightly. Next time, I'll give you no warning and shoot you on sight!"

When he had finished the floggings, the *Amtskommissar* ordered everyone who had been whipped to line up in a double row, and he marched them off to prison and had them all locked up. We were outraged. People cried out: "Isn't it enough that they humiliated the *Judenrat* like animals, tortured the Jewish representatives publicly, before the eyes of the *goyim*?! Did they also have to lock the eight men away?! What cruelty! God knows what else they'll do to them!"

On that first day, we still had hope they'd be released. When another day passed and they still hadn't returned, their families became wild from worry. The next day, that monster came into their cells and flogged every one of them all over again. He also beat up old Leybl Kogan,[7] who was spared the first day because he was old and very sick.

The families of the hostages went hysterical and ran from one place to the other trying to find some way out of this. The four members of the *Judenrat* who weren't tortured refused to speak up to the *Amtskommissar* because they were afraid the mad dog would throw them into prison, too. The first one who tried to intervene was Yoyne Ginzburg's wife—she was the former teacher at the Polish public school. Her younger sister, Lotke, was very coquettish and spoke German beautifully, with a real Prussian accent. She had met all the ranking, influential German officers before. So Celina—Ginzburg's wife—and her younger sister went to the brute, who was actually promoted over the *Amtskommissar* for his cruelty. They brought him very expensive gifts. The sadist pocketed the presents, released Yoyne Ginzburg the next day, but kept the others in prison. The families of the wealthy arrestees now lost all patience and had Lotke take over a wagonload of gifts to win over that criminal. After a third day passed, the remaining members of the Sokoły *Judenrat* were set free.

Eyewitness Testimony 2. The Rambam Said, "Resist!"[1]

Ebelsberg,[2] June 24, 1948

SWORN TESTIMONY

I, Noach Denenburg, born in Węgrów, Warsaw District, on January 18, 1893, currently staying in Ebelsberg, Block 3/214, do solemnly swear . . . and give the following testimony:

Jadowa[3] during the German Occupation

During the German Occupation, the Tluszcz Rabbi resided in the town of Jadowa, three kilometers from the Urle[4] train station on the Białystok-Warsaw line. Because the learned rabbi had preached to the Jews of Jadowa that the moral obligation of our people was to resist with courage and commitment, the Gestapo called for his immediate surrender to the authorities. The alternative offered was the taking hostage of ten Jews in place of the rabbi. The *Judenrat* reached a decision immediately and took steps to detain the ten. After praying and meditating, the rabbi came into the *Judenrat* and protested this decision with all his conviction. He put on his *yontiv* clothes, walked over to Gestapo Headquarters, and turned himself in. Before his execution, he spoke his last words and told the murderers to their face exactly what he thought of them. But he was shot dead before he could finish. Later, his body was given up to the *Judenrat* and he was brought to his eternal rest in the Jadowa Jewish cemetery.

[signed] Noach Denenburg

The signature of Noach Denenberg, written by his own hand, is hereby verified. [Court statement and seal]

Eyewitness Testimony 3. ". . . to Its Logical Conclusion"—Borysław

Anonymous. Recorded by Duvid Graysdorf in a DP camp in 1947.

Before the war, there were 14,000 Jews living in Borysław: storekeepers, craftsmen, and also workers in the oil fields and wax refineries. Maybe 400 of them survived the Nazi Holocaust: about 300 went through the hell of the camps and close to 100 went into hiding in the forests or with Gentile acquaintances.

On the fifteenth of September 1939, Borysław was annexed by the Russians, who stayed on in the city till July 1, 1941. During this period, Borysław was relatively calm.

On the first day in July 1941, the Germans overran Borysław. Three days later, the Ukrainian mayor, Dr. Tarletski—now imprisoned in Dachau—gave the signal to the Ukrainian nationalist militias to make the first pogrom on the Jews, which took the lives of over 800 people. Two weeks after the start of the German Occupation, all Jews were ordered to wear white armbands with the blue *mugen duvid*. Heavy ransoms were imposed on the *Kehileh* and on certain individuals, and the general confiscation of all Jewish property was put into effect. Very soon afterwards, two new terrible pogroms were unleashed against us.

On November 28, 1941, 900 Jews were taken into the surrounding forests—half to the Mikolaya Woods and the other half to Pionar. They were stripped naked and shot. Some were buried alive. The organizer of the pogrom was a Viennese German named Niemetz. He was Chief of the Ukrainian Police—today, he's in Dachau.

On the seventh of August 1942, the third pogrom started. The German *Schutzpolizei* officers—Gouldon, Neumayer, Schuch, Niemetz, Weigel, Wiefel, Genosse, and Pohl—led the roundup of over 5,000 Jews who were loaded into cattle cars coated with lye and hauled off to the Bełżec crematoria.

By the end of August 1942, two open ghettos had been designated for Borysław. As soon as the areas were ready, over 2,000 Jews were "resettled" from the surrounding villages into the ghettos. On October 20, 1942, the second German *aktsye* was put into operation and went on for three full days. The German police themselves rounded up over 2,000 Jews then and transported them to Bełżec. Again, on the fifth of November, a new *aktsye* took place. This time, the Germans ordered the *Judenräte* to assemble over 600 Jews, mostly women and children, who were shipped off to the Bełżec crematorium like the rest.

On February 15, 1943, a new kind of *aktsye* befell us. The German police surrounded the ghettos, then charged in and dragged over 600 Jews off to the local slaughterhouse. Inside, they were forced to strip and tie their clothes into bundles. Still holding onto their rags, these naked victims were made to run for another 200 meters to the edge of a mass grave. They had to mount a board, which spanned the pit, in groups of five, and were shot at midpoint so they dropped right to the bottom. This was the first public execution in Borysław which was carried out before a group of Ukrainians, Poles, and Jews. The executioners were *Schutzpolizeihauptmann* Wiepert, Milos, Pohl, Neumayer, Niaw,[1] Gouldon, Schuch, Wiegel, and the others. They were backed up and assisted by the *Reiterzugpolizei* and the Ukrainian police cavalry.

When this *aktsye* was finished, the ghettos were liquidated. Some of the Jewish laborers were relocated into a new ghetto on Petramogila Street. Only those workers stamped "R" were included. The people in the Petramogila Ghetto lived in terrible overcrowding— over twenty to a small room. There, the living envied the dead.

This is the way we lived until April 1943—*Khol-hamoyed Paysekh*. The seventh *aktsye* started then and most of the remaining Jews were taken to Drohobycz[2] and put into the concentration camp there. The camp commandant was *Obersturmführer* Hildebrand. The camp was soon dissolved, though. A remnant were taken to Pastemita,[3] near Lemberg,[4] and the rest, to Janów-Lemberg.[5]

Then, a few days later, the final liquidation of the subcamp [on

Petramogila] was called. While the mens' *Appel* was going on, the women and children hid and the men refused to betray the hideouts. The *Blockälteste* was Shmiel Birnboim from Schodnica, Borysław. Schuch, and Wiepert, the arch-criminals, said he was responsible for the women and children hiding, and they demanded that he turn them over. Schmiel Birnboim refused and paid for it with his life. He was beaten so long and hard with an iron bar by a German of the *Reiterzugpolizei,* named Weudz,[6] that he collapsed dead right in front of the column of Jews. The slaughter went on for two months. Then the second ghetto was completely liquidated. Those who had survived were driven into the slave-labor camp at Limanowa, outside of town.

These 1,200 people were held inside the camp until August 1944. Random executions and roundups went on regularly. The camp was run by SS men Tamaneck, Schwartz, Kempke, Lindenfeld, Semmer, Menzanger, Schembach. It's impossible to describe their cruelty. They were joined in their sadistic acts by the Jewish head of the *Ordnungsdienst,* Wolek Eiznsztajn, and his second, Max Heinberg, who profited from what the Nazis left over.

On March 28, 1944, when the Soviet army had stopped outside of Stanisławów, the Germans began liquidating the camp. The Jews had managed to dig a few bunkers in the forests and they broke out and headed there. The Germans were in total panic with no means of transport or escape. For some reason, the front stopped at Stanisławów. This gave the Germans a chance to go on with the extermination. Wolek Eiznsztajn began "agitating" for us to come out of the woods and return to camp, because no one was in any danger now. Life in the bunkers had been very hard and the people let themselves be talked into coming back. Soon, the Germans had deceived about 600 Jews this way and carted them off to the camp in Płaszów, Cracow. Wolek Eiznsztajn started "doing his job" again, and tried getting out the Jews the Germans had missed. They captured fifty to sixty people every day and by June 22, 1944, they again had a transport of 600 Jews ready for Płaszów. For the month starting on June 22 and ending on July 22, 1944, the Germans and Eiznsztajn had forced out another 700 Jews and sent them to Auschwitz.

During that month, the Germans also captured these three Jews: Hofman, Lanek; Hoberman, Fishl; and another man whose name escapes me now. The Germans learned that these three Jews had been the ones to organize the breakout to the bunkers they had prepared in the forest. The German murderers gouged their eyes out and butchered them. These three lost their lives in such a gruesome way for wanting to save their own brothers.

On August 7, 1944, 375 Jews were liberated from the Limanowa camp in Borysław. This is the final total of the Borysław Jews. Naked and barefoot, the miserable remnants of a community the Germans slaughtered with the constant aid of the local Ukrainians and Poles.

Schwebisch Hall, December 29, 1947

Eyewitness Testimony 4. Escape to *Eretz Yisrael*[1]

E.G. Born in Radom, Poland in 1932; escaped to Palestine in November 1942. Recorded in Tel Aviv in December 1942 by the Historical Commission of the Polish-Jewish Refugee Writers and Journalists Union. The then ten-year-old child tells of his life in the Radom Ghetto, the work he did in the factory, which was confiscated from his father, then goes on.

Suddenly, *Froh* Golde Graucher burst into our home. She was crying and said she had gotten a pass to *Eretz Yisrael* but what good was it, since two of her children—a daughter and a son—had been grabbed away from her and deported. This *Froh* Graucher was my mother's friend and she stayed with us till the time she had to leave for Vienna. During the night, as I lay in bed, I could hear my mother crying as they talked together. "Our days are numbered," she said. "That monster, Berend,[2] is threatening to take away our permits. I know we won't survive. But save my youngest child! Register him as the child they took from you. Let me at least have a son, a *Kaddish* in *Erits Yisrul!* Your child is gone, you must!" They fell into each other's arms, sobbing.

The next day, my father contacted a Jewish policeman to try and bribe the Gestapo, and he came round in the evening with a document for Natan Graucher, which was now my name. My father paid 10,000 *zloty* to bribe the Gestapo, but the policeman said I'd have to manage getting out of the ghetto on my own and no one could take me to the train, either, because the Gestapo itself was full of informers. My mother gave the policeman another 10,000 *zloty* along with *Froh* Graucher's passport and a photo of me. *Froh* Graucher was scared to give up her passport because the Gestapo would probably keep it, but the Jewish policeman swore he would take responsibility and bring the passport back. We waited till the next evening, and he came back with the documents like he promised. He said everything was ready—I was going to *Eretz Yisrael!*

It was terrible to be the only one going, but my mother tried to make me believe she would soon follow. As the time passed, we cried more and more. We waited eleven days for the Gestapo to select eleven Jewish women from all over Radom County. The women

were all brought to our home, but not one of them knew I was coming along. On the day I was going to leave, my father and mother
were able to get hold of special passes from the factory. But my
sister and brother weren't allowed off work. We didn't even get a
chance to say goodbye. As the transport was being prepared, a Gestapo agent came over to *Froh* Graucher and asked for her papers.
He said he didn't know if they were in order or not, so my mother
immediately gave him another large sum of money. Suddenly, my
sister came rushing in, begging them to find her a place on the train,
too. During this sad scene, my mother whispered to me to run out
into the street and hide under the baggage in the coach. But the
driver saw me and struck me with his whip—he thought I was trying
to steal a valise. Luckily, *Froh* Graucher came between us and she
was able to push me down deeper under the bags. I stayed hidden
at the bottom all the way to the train station. My parents weren't
allowed to come to the train with us. They couldn't even wave goodbye to me because then I'd be found out. When we got to the train
station, *Froh* Graucher started kissing me so no one would suspect
anything. The other women were still so shocked by this whole
journey they didn't realize a thing. We were still trembling when we
got on the train. The bribed Gestapo agent who was in our house
the night before came into the compartment to check everyone's
papers. I was sure, since he'd gotten his money, he was going to turn
me in now. But he didn't say a word and the train finally started
moving. We stayed on all the way to Vienna. The whole time, I had
to keep forcing myself to call *Froh* Graucher "*mameh*," and every
time I did it, I fought back the tears as before my eyes I saw my
dear mother and poor father, my brother and my sister—who knows
if I'll ever see them again?

Eyewitness Testimony 5. Survival Among Ukrainians

Y.G. Born in Bursztyn, Stanisławów District, Galicia, in 1902; lived
there. Recorded by Icek Shmulewitz in New York, 1956.

In June of 1941, after the German-Soviet War broke out and the
Hitlerites were advancing on our region, the Soviets still held their
position in our town for a week. When they withdrew, it was in an
orderly way, with many Jews, who'd worked for them during this
time, leaving Bursztyn side by side with the retreating Red Army.
Once the Russians were gone, the town became independent for just
three days—no Soviets, no Nazis—the Germans hadn't overrun us
yet. This lasted from a Monday until Thursday. The Ukrainians in

town, many of whom had collaborated with the Soviets, went on a rampage through the Jewish quarter, destroying all our homes, and threatening that as soon as the Hitlerites were here, they'd help them slaughter all the Jews.

On Thursday morning, July 3, 1941, I was out in the fields in back of town, grazing my animals. Suddenly, I saw a column of smoke in the distance, then an army advancing, but whose, I couldn't determine. When they got closer, I saw that it was the Germans. They couldn't tell I was a Jew and asked me the way to Inaszków. I pointed it out. As soon as they'd passed, I gathered the animals from the pasture and headed home. Along the way, a Ukrainian that I knew, a rich peasant, caught up with me and started beating me up. I made it home alive, but had to stay in bed for two weeks because of the injuries. Since the peasant had been the one to attack me, I got myself a Ukrainian lawyer, Skulski—he was a good friend of mine before the war. The Germans still hadn't occupied the town and I wanted this well-known lawyer to take up my case against the peasant who beat me. When I said to this lawyer friend, Skulski, "Help me avenge my life," he answered: "Get out of here or I'll kill you myself!" This was the reply my best friend gave me.

When I recovered after spending the two weeks in bed, I left my house to go out into the street. I ran into the baker in Bursztyn, Yankl Pilpel, who yelled to me: "Look! They're leading away the rabbi, Reb Herzl Landau!"

I turned to see the rabbi being pushed through the streets by the two Ukrainian brothers, Ivantchuk, who were from the village of Martynow. Since I knew these peasants well, I ran up to them and asked: "What's our rabbi done? Why are you taking him away?"

They quickly grabbed hold of me and pushed me off together with the rabbi. But a young Jew from town, Yisrul Shvarts, came up opposite them, and as they lunged at him, he broke free, with the *goyim* chasing after him. They yelled at me and the rabbi to lay flat on our stomachs and not to dare get up before they were back. As those two criminals were chasing Yisrul Shvarts, I jumped up from the ground and ran off. The rabbi, Reb Herzl Landau, also got up and ran behind me. I dove into a vegetable patch in the Ukrainian, Ilki "Goy"'s yard. The rabbi was right in back of me, but in a second, he was cut off by two other young Fascists who beat him to the ground, then dragged him off.

While I was crouching like that in the garden, I heard cries of "*Shma yisruel!*" very close to me, then a volley of shots. It was coming from the *shiel*. The executions went on from three in the afternoon till eleven at night. The Ukrainians herded the Jews into the synagogue, ripped their beards out, then beat, tortured, and finally shot them. By around eleven P.M., Mini Tobiash, the head of the *Yidnrat,* had met all the demands of the local Gestapo chief, who also headed up the Ukrainian militia. He brought him tea, gold watches, and things like that to stop torturing and executing the Jews. After some more beatings as a "finishing touch," they were finally released. The next day, the Jews couldn't recognize each other because most of their beards were gone or were badly burned. The same day, the funeral of Moyshe "the Red," whom the Ukrainians had shot to death, was held and one Jew couldn't recognize the other, though they'd known each other since childhood.

While I lay in the peasant's garden at midnight, shivering from fright and from the cold, my teeth rattling uncontrollably, I had to thrash around on the ground to try to keep warm. The Ukrainian, Ilki "Goy," slept in the shed in the yard and heard someone moving around. He came out slowly, but when he saw me, he grabbed me, threw me into the barn, and pushed me down into some hay. Just at that moment, Ukrainians burst through the door and wanted to know where the Jews were hiding! Had he seen any Jews in the area, then? The peasant said no, and let me stay there all night. He was a neighbor of mine. His vegetable patch bordered my yard. In the morning, I went back to my family. My wife told me she and the children had hidden out that night in the same barn and we hadn't even known the other was there.

Two weeks later, after the Germans had taken over Bursztyn completely, they ordered the Jews to pay a huge ransom. They demanded over half a million *zloty* in silver. In two days, the entire sum had been collected, with all the Jews contributing in this emergency. Mini Tobiash, the *Yidnrat* "Elder," tried to convince us that once we'd given up this sum, the Germans would never bother us again.

I had no money then to contribute the share the *Yidnrat* had determined for me, so I went to the market to sell two of my animals and then to give over the money toward the ransom. But the peasants agreed among themselves not to buy my animals, because they'd eventually get them for nothing anyway.

Before morning, at around three, Pintche Shnayvahs of the *Yidnrat* came to me and asked for my share of the tribute. I led away my four animals and went around trying to sell them, but no one would buy them. Then I went to Kopchinski the peasant's wife, and offered to sell her all four animals for 1,500 *zloty*. This Christian woman said to me: "Here, take these 1,500 *zloty* in silver, buy your freedom and keep the four animals."

The ghetto of Bursztyn was set up as soon as the Germans took over the *shtetl*. The Jews were immediately rounded up from all over, forced into the Jewish quarter, and no contact was allowed with the Gentile side from then on. In the beginning, there were about 2,600 people inside the Bursztyn Ghetto. We were led out of the ghetto every day for hard labor at the quarries in Tarnopol District. The work was brutal and many of us died in our tracks. We were never fed, and all of us swelled up from hunger. The Germans shot us off like flies.

Mini Tobiash gave up his position as Elder of the *Yidnrat* and was replaced by his cousin, Filip Tobiash, who was a lawyer. As his cousin protected the Jews, so this Filip Tobiash was anxious to please the Germans. If they asked for 100 men to work, he got them 125. Mini Tobiash, the first Elder of the *Yidnrat*, became ill and refused all treatment. He said, "I have no use for health while Jews are being tortured and killed! It's better to die!" He perished in the Rohatyn Ghetto on *Erev Paysekh*, 1943. But Filip Tobiash survived the war. He lives in Breslau today—a converted Jew still practicing law.

On October 10, 1942, the Germans hung out the order dissolving the Bursztyn Ghetto and, before the deadline was up, they expelled all of us to Bukaczowce.[1] When we got there, they led us into an overcrowded area where all the Jews of Bukaczowce were forced to stay. There was no room for us on these "Jewish streets." The mayor of Bukaczowce had to call a meeting of the *goyim* on the next street to ask them to move in with their families for a while and let us take over their flats so we wouldn't have to camp out on the sidewalks. The Gentiles wanted no part of it. The mayor then telephoned the German *Landesrat* in Rohatyn[2] to ask for instructions.

The Gestapo chief with the Rohatyn *Landesrat* came to Bukaczowce promptly, and called all the Gentiles out into the street. He assured them the Jews were condemned to die in eleven days and must be quartered in this area till that date. We were staying in the marketplace near where the meeting was held at the time, and we heard every word the chief of Gestapo said. He spoke in German and an interpreter translated into Ukrainian. The *goyim* were out of their flats in a second, and the Jews of Bursztyn came in off the street.

Eleven days later, just like the Gestapo chief warned, the massacre of the Jews from the market square began. The Germans charged through the flats, dragging the Jews out. Those who tried to escape were gunned down on the spot. Half the Jews from the square were shot dead within the hour. The same day, a massacre also broke out in the Rohatyn Ghetto. The Jews were herded into a sealed-off area and machine-gunned to death.

While the Germans were storming the houses and executing the Jews of Bukaczowce, I and my wife and children were given refuge by a Jewish friend, Yisrulke Dahvid. He lived in Bukaczowce and had a restaurant—I knew him for many years before the war. He smuggled me and my wife and our three children into the home of a neighbor, a Jew named Vulf, who was from the village of Szczarow.

We were kept in the bunker Vulf had built into his flat a long time ago, hidden from the outside behind a false wall, with the entrance coming from the attic. I paid him for letting my wife and two daughters, and also a neighbor's wife—Minke Shumer—stay in the narrow hole, but my small son and I wouldn't have fitted in once everyone was inside, so we escaped to the woods. We hid for a while in the Szczarow and Witan forests.

While I was in Witan, I came across a Ukrainian peasant, Ivan Shkurlak, and paid him fifteen *toller*, a pair of golden earrings, and my wife's *kidushin* ring, to hide me and my son. It was on the twenty-second of October, 1942. The peasant took all these things from me and brought me and my son into an empty room in his cottage that had a separate entrance. An hour later, he brought in another thirteen Jews who had also given up all their possessions in exchange for this hideout. They had to give him every last thing they owned in the hope they could trust him. He let us stay there exactly one night. I had also paid the peasant's wife something extra to go to the hideout in Bukaczowce and find out about my wife and children—were they still in the bunker? I gave her the location of the house and she soon came back bearing a sign from my wife.

Once the peasant had the money and gold we gave him, he decided we had more, and he wanted all of it. He got in touch with his brother, Mikhailov Shkurlak, who came by the next night. Later, he walked into our room and told us he'd been sent by the Gestapo to haul us back to the transport of Jews being deported from Bukaczowce. If we gave him money or gold, though, he'd leave us alone. The people were desperate and begged him to let them go, but I knew he was only bluffing. While he was standing there and threatening them, I was by the window. I shot out my leg and kicked in the glass, and not knowing if anyone would follow me, I dived through the window with my son. The cottage was on a hill and we rolled and tumbled all the way to the bottom where the fields were, and then got up and ran where our legs carried us.

We followed the way back to Bursztyn, my hometown, in the dead of night. When we finally got there, I climbed up into Kopchinski the peasant's loft—I mentioned him earlier—and he never found out we were there. Kopchinski was a rich pork butcher. He kept a Ukrainian servant girl at home, Grisha, who had a Jewish lover from town at that time named Yossl Bigel. The Ukrainian girl was madly in love with him, she hid him and fed him and Yossl was safe in Bursztyn. Then the girl found out my son and I were hiding in her employer's loft, but I asked her to let Yossl know where we were and to find out from him what the situation was and what we could do.

She came back and told me Bigel would wait for me near Shpok's Forest—named after the woodsman-caretaker there—and we'd make a plan when we met. I climbed down from Kopchinski's loft with my son and headed toward the meeting place. But Bigel never came —I waited and waited and he never showed up. I went into the forest and met a Jew from Bursztyn there, Shmiel Ober, who was coming from Bukaczowce, and I asked him about my wife and two daughters. He'd heard nothing. But he told me that many Jews had been slaughtered in Bukaczowce and they were a lot better off than the living. This is what Shmiel Ober said to me.

I left the forest with my son and made my way back to Bukaczowce. When I arrived, I headed straight for my friend Dahvid's café. As soon as I walked in, I saw my wife and our two girls running toward me! We couldn't stay in Bukaczowce because an order had been issued for all remaining Jews to be removed to the ghetto in Rohatyn, with each individual allowed to bring along a maximum of up to ten pounds of personal belongings. My wife and children and me were also transported to Rohatyn then—it was October 22, 1942.[3]

When we came into the Rohatyn Ghetto, we joined the last surviving Jews of Rohatyn, Bursztyn, Bukaczowce, Bolszowce, Knihynicze and Żurow,[4] who were forced from their homes, driven out of all their hiding places, and herded together into this cramped area. We had to stay out under the open sky because, by then, a large part of the Rohatyn Ghetto had been reduced to ruins. My older brother, Moyshe, was a good friend of the Rohatyn *Yidnrat* elder, Amarant. My brother gave Amarant 500 *zloty* and the *Yidnrat* then placed me, my wife, and three children in a room which already held fifteen people—not counting the five of us. When we walked into the room, a man named Skolnik, who lived in the next house and had a printing press in Rohatyn, came over to me and said: "Dig yourself a hole—they're coming to get us any minute."

We walked along all the walls, but found nowhere to dig. During the night, we started hacking away at the base of the wall which faced out on the Gniła Lipa River. We dumped all the dirt we were bringing up from our tunnel into the water, so no sign would remain of our work. For three weeks, working only through the night, we dug up a passageway which came out on the path along the river, so if we were ever in danger, we had this way of escape. The work was done during the time the Nazis were reorganizing their plans against us and they weren't deporting us for now.[5] During the day, we could even leave the room and stay outside to work on what we were doing.

But then the Germans started demanding a hundred Jews a week from the *Yidnrat,* and they took them down into the cellar of the building and shot them. Until *Khanike,* 1942, the laborers from the ghetto were left alone. The Germans had executed the ones not able to work, the sick and the old. From then till May 1943, there was a series of *aktsyes* and they also took out laborers from the ghetto. They took six people from our room—men and women. Two women who hid with us in the tunnel died during this time. One was Ite Blekher—she left behind three children—and the other was Minke Shumer—the one who had first hid with my wife and daughters. Another man, Yisrul Shtander of Stratyn, broke out of the tunnel and ran up to the attic to hide. We could hear him groaning up there: "Just a little water, just a little water, I'm dying." Soon there was silence—he died in the attic, there was nothing we could do.

On the night of *Shabbes*, June 6, 1943, the last *Aussiedlung* in the Rohatyn Ghetto was begun. German and Ukrainian soldiers and police massed around the ghetto and fired point-blank into the buildings the Jews were staying in. There had been 3,000 Jews still alive in the ghetto—over half were massacred during the night and the others were shipped out to be exterminated. The 1,500 slaughtered Jews were buried within the ghetto walls. I can still see the husbands and fathers of the butchered women and children digging the graves and burying their whole families.

It was like a furnace in the passageway—people choked to death. There was a young man from Bursztyn, Moyshe Bigel, in the hideout. He suddenly went mad and started snarling and biting everyone. He howled with a ferocity and pain which was no longer human —we were sure they would discover us. Moyshe Bigel had to get out of the hole together with his two sisters and they walked up into the ghetto. We heard the shots as the Germans gunned them down near our house.

This final *aktsye* by those murderers left the Rohatyn Ghetto empty and covered with blood. I took my wife and three children now and we crawled through the tunnel to the Gniła Lipa. When the Germans saw us out in the open, they came after us, shooting while they ran, but we jumped into the river and swam across safely to the other side. The other Jews also came up from the hole but, instead of diving for the water, they ran along its banks and were all shot down.

My family and I crawled out on the opposite bank but we didn't know which way to turn. We lay hidden in the fields near the water for a whole week, gnawing on the cobs of corn which had dropped from the stalks. In the end, we had no choice but to try and find our way back to our hometown, Bursztyn. We stumbled into the *shtetl* in the middle of the night and crawled back up into Kopchinski the peasant's barn loft—you know who I mean. He didn't hear us up there. We stayed in the hayloft for a night and a day—it was during a terrible heat wave and we had nothing to eat.

While we were walking to Bursztyn, we lost our little eleven-year-old girl, Dreyzhe, and my older brother, Moyshe, picked her up along the way. While we were lying in the loft, we heard our little girl screaming in the distance. She was together with my brother, Moyshe, his four children, and my wife's sister and her husband. They were all captured by the Nazis, beaten and tortured, and dragged off to be executed. We heard the screams of our dearest ones but could do nothing to save them.

We were slowly starving, lying like this in the loft—me, my wife and our children, a boy and a girl. We couldn't keep it up any longer. I climbed down from the loft and went to Kopchinski the peasant, asking him for a bite a food. He turned white when he saw me, wanting to know where I'd come out from. When I told him I was up in the loft with my family, he started cursing me and screaming, that because of me, him and his whole family would be executed. When Kopchinski's youngest daughter, Danka, saw her father like this, she said these words to him: "*Tata*, we must help a good man like Y____ is—we might even save his life! Pretend we don't know he's up in the loft with his family!"

Kopchinski finally agreed to let me and my wife and two children stay in the loft for a couple of days—no more. But we hid out there for over three months. Every so often, he—and also the other members of his family—would bring us up a bite of food. At night, I climbed down from the loft and roamed through the countryside, looking for cucumbers, radishes, and apples to keep us alive.

The three months passed and the hysteria about escaped Jews quieted down—mainly because almost all of them had been captured by now and either sent off to extermination camps or shot dead on the spot. I came down from the loft and walked into town. I went to some peasants I knew to get a little food. Soon the whole town knew that the last surviving Jew was still wandering about. The Germans got out their trained dogs and started looking for me. I ran back to the loft, to my wife and children. The Germans came after Kopchinski, wanting to know where the Jew was! The peasant told them there was no one else here, though we were up in the loft. But the Germans surrounded the house and looked for us everywhere, while Kopchinski's wife walked up and down, wringing her hands and begging God that the Germans won't find us. When it was all over, we had to leave the hideout for good.

It was late at night, my wife and two children and I crawled into a vegetable garden belonging to an old Ukrainian priest. We climbed up to his cottage attic and he didn't hear us up there. My wife and two children and me hid out in the attic for two months and the old priest didn't know about it. During the nights, I let myself down from the window and dug in the fields looking for food. This time, I also went to nearby villages where I wasn't known. I waded through swamps, swam across rivers, hunting for food through the countryside and bringing back what I could to my family.

One time, when I came back to the priest's attic after looking for food, I saw that my wife and daughter were gone. My son came with me to help find food. While we were away, the priest's son had climbed up to the attic to fix the roof and he suddenly came upon my wife and daughter. He says to them: "I don't see anything, I don't know anything," but he told them to leave the attic. On that same day—once it was dark—my wife and child came down from the attic, crawled into the vegetable garden, and hid there.

I found them late at night, but it was impossible to hide there. We had to return to Kopchinski the peasant's yard. We let ourselves down into his ice cellar and hoped he wouldn't see us. We shivered in the cold for a week. There were a few potatoes scattered around and we had to light a fire to bake them. I also stole out at night and brought back a little food. By the end of the week, Kopchinski came down into the cellar and found us. He tells us to get out, with the excuse "I see no end to the war. I let you hide once, but I won't sacrifice myself and my family."

Shabbes at night, my son and I head for the woods but I managed to talk Kopchinski into letting my wife and daughter stay in the ice cellar another week, till I can find a place for us to hide in the woods.

I walked through the whole forest with my son. Along the way, we came to Shkurlak the peasant's cottage, where the thirteen and me had hidden in the beginning for money and gold. As I walked into his hut, I was jumped by two Russian partisans with guns. They were both drunk and started beating me up—and my son, too. They knew I was a Jew but accused me of being an enemy agent because only Gentile partisans operated in these woods, and what was I doing there, then? Suddenly, Shmiel Grotnas, a Jew from Bukaczowce, who was with the partisan unit the Russians belonged to, walked into the hut. He knew me and told the Russians to stop beating me. They shouted at Grotnas that if he said another word, they'd take his gun away and shoot him together with me.

A few minutes later, another Jewish partisan—Kalmen Shtreyger, a baker from Bursztyn—came into the hut. He also tried to get the Russians to stop beating me, and he finally convinced them and tore me away from them. Kalmen Shtreyger took me and my son deeper into the woods where we came upon a large encampment of Jews who had formed a partisan unit. The group was only active in the forests and was made up of Jews from Bursztyn and Bukaczowce—each and every one of them was armed. Altogether, there were around 130 people. The leaders of the group were three soldiers who'd served in the Russian army and escaped a German prison camp. Two of them were the Russians who had attacked me in the peasant's hut. Two of the leaders' names were Sashka and Bashka, but I can't remember the third. Bashka was a Russian Jew, but he never admitted it openly. There were also women in this partisan unit in the woods—and whole families, parents and children.

A few days after I met the Jewish partisans in the woods, I headed back to Bursztyn and Kopchinski the peasant's cottage, so I could bring my wife and daughter back into the woods with me. I went with an armed escort of several partisans. We walked through the yard, brought out my wife and daughter from the cellar, and Kopchinski wasn't aware of a thing. My wife was so weak walking through the woods that her legs buckled and we had to carry her across our shoulders.

After a while, I was handed a rifle and made a member of the partisan group. We would go into the fields at night and steal pigs and cattle and all kinds of food from the peasants and bring all of it back into the woods, so that everyone had enough to eat. At the start of their operations, before I joined them in the forest, these Jewish partisans had walked into Bursztyn one night, stormed the police precinct, and "liberated" a stockpile of rifles. Only two old gendarmes were on guard at the precinct, and they put up no resistance. They left the gendarmes alone. Then the partisans operated along the roads to Bukaczowce, attacking German convoys, killing many soldiers, and taking their guns and boots. In a short time, the partisans had full supplies of arms, clothes, as well as food.

Me and my family stayed in the woods with the partisans for three weeks, until we were ambushed by a German patrol along a forest path. They shot nine Jewish partisans during the attack, and took twenty-one partisans prisoner. During this German assault, me and my family along with a neighbor of ours from Bursztyn, *Froh* Ita Mandelberg, got away. When we saw the Germans overtaking us, we just threw ourselves down into the snow and shut our eyes— we refused to witness our own execution. The Germans ran up to where we were, and suddenly, *Froh* Mandelberg jumps up and demands to know the reasons the Germans have for shooting us! As soon as the words left her lips, the Germans blasted her from all sides. Two Germans pointed at us and one said to the other, *"Lasse die!"*

After the Germans were gone, we staggered to our feet and limped back into the dense forest.

My son, who was now seventeen, left the forest on January 8, 1943, with a few other boys—this was before the German ambush—to look for food. The full moon lit up the whole region and they were captured by Ukrainians. They broke away and the Ukrainians chased them, firing without stop. The other boys were all shot dead by the Ukrainians, but my boy was captured alive. My son was brought to Rohatyn, interrogated, and tortured to make him tell them where the partisans in the forest were staying. But my son wouldn't tell them, and they shot him.

My wife and daughter and I stayed in the woods with the Jewish partisans till the twenty-third of August, 1944, when the Red Army began its offensive to drive out the Hitlerites.

After Liberation, my wife and daughter and I came back to Bursztyn, our former hometown. There was nothing there but ruins. Thirteen other Jews were all that survived from our large community. The Soviets took over the town, put the Jews to work at all kinds of building projects, and inducted anyone they wanted into the Red Army. Though I was nothing more than skin and bones after all my ordeals, the Soviets still ordered me inducted into the Red Army. I wouldn't take it and got out of Bursztyn with my wife and daughter. The other Jewish survivors also fled the town.

We settled for a while in Lower Silesia, Poland, but we ended up coming to America.

Eyewitness Testimony 6. The Cycle: Soviet Terror; German Genocide

M.B. Born in Grodno in 1912; lived there. Recorded by Yankiv Fishman in New York in 1954. The witness describes at length the ordeals Jews went through under Soviet occupation in Grodno, then talks about the arrest of his parents for being Zionist activists. Then he goes on.

[Soviet] Jewish officers would come by my house all the time. They talked endlessly—but only on one subject: Jews and Jewish life in Poland before the war. They spoke with such nostalgia—but at the same time, with such a sorrow. It was terrible. I remember this one colonel especially: as soon as he walked through the door, he headed straight for the Jewish books on my shelves. With great emotion, and tears running down his face, he read Bialik in Yiddish. But as soon as I mentioned the hatred against the Jews, the Soviet-style Nazism in the Red Army, they fell silent.

My parents were released in June 1940. My father told me he was never officially charged with any crime or told which decree it was that had freed him. His passport was in perfect order. In May 1941, my parents were arrested a second time. In June I found out they were being deported deep into Russia. This was when the Germans started their offensive against Russia. Their bombers attacked the transport my parents were on, and they were killed from German shrapnel. They, and a long convoy of arrestees. I only learned about them later. We were totally unprepared for the German attack on Russia. For us, the Jews, it meant final disaster. We couldn't run any more—they overtook us with such lightning speed. The roads were blocked by swarms of retreating Red Army soldiers. And the Germans tore them apart. So you see, the civilians were trapped.

Grodne was gripped by terror.

The Germans immediately set up a ghetto for the Jews. It was their first priority. They fanned out through the city, making large-scale arrests of Jews and non-Jews. They started by arresting those suspected of collaborating with the Soviets. The Germans put almost all of them to death in the prison dungeons.

My wife and I left the ghetto from time to time. We hid out several weeks with some Gentiles, but then returned to the ghetto. As long as the war lasted, we could never trust them and always feared for our lives when we were among them. There were constant *aktsyes* in the ghetto. Jews were led away and transported to their deaths regularly. During every *aktsye,* masses of Jews were shot in the ghetto itself. We survived every *aktsye.* How? We didn't plan it. It must have been by miracle. But by the middle of January 1943, when the general deportations now included all of what was left of the Jews of Grodne,[1] we—my wife and I—and again, this had to be by miracle, we escaped from the ghetto. We wandered all alone through the fields in the outlying areas of Grodne and found no safe place. It was strange, but we weren't even stopped once by the German patrols—probably because we had blond hair and looked to them like "Aryans." We roamed through the forests for two weeks, never meeting anyone. There was an eerie silence in the forest. We only ventured from the woods to beg for some food from the *goyim,* and then we went right back in. We spent a few nights inside some barns. We did it without thinking. The peasants simply didn't take us for Jews. But this couldn't last. In the end, the Poles would find out who we were and turn us "dirty Jews" over to the Germans. If we would have had money, we probably could have bought ourselves somewhere to stay. We didn't have a penny. We lived in total desperation, expecting misfortune at every turn. We still had no children then. So it was a little less painful for us.

It was only at the beginning of 1944—after four to five months of dragging ourselves around in total solitude, and in constant danger—that we came to an understanding with a Pole, *Pan* Kowalski. Again, a miracle happened. Kowalski agreed to let us hide in a corner of his cellar where no human eye ever set sight. We went down into that dank hole in a rapture. Kowalski and his wife brought us food and water. They knew we could only pay them if the war ended. That's right. The name of the village was Łososna, not far from Grodne. We were able to stay alive in that cellar, and there was also a trapdoor leading up into the Kowalskis' kitchen. They piled heavy objects over this hatch in the kitchen. The Kowalskis weren't concerned about the money, and didn't much like Jews. Far from it. All they could think of was their hatred of the "dirty *Szwab*." They were getting back at the "invincible" Germans by saving at least a couple of Jews from the Nazi executioner. He took in some more Jews. You can imagine how terrified we all were down there. All of a sudden, voices of Poles demanding Kowalski give over the Jews— they heard say—were hiding here somewhere. We heard Kowalski yelling back at them furiously: "Oh, yeah!? Where the hell are they, then?! You know my house! You find them if you can! Come on!! You tell 'em to keep their stinkin' rumors to themselves!!!"

Another time, we hear a drunken German bellowing: "Hey you, where you hiding your *Juden?!*" From the cellar, we made out this terrible fight between a German and the Kowalskis. We heard them beating this stubborn man. The Kowalskis' screams were unbearable. We were sure these were our final moments. The Germans would certainly find where we were now. Our peasants would break down and confess their "crime." But it didn't turn out like this. They held fast. They were too proud. They were what people call "true patriots." And the same thing happened over and over again. The Kowalskis were, of course, constantly denounced directly to the Gestapo. We began to feel our resistance weakening. We felt that these crises were straining us beyond our endurance. As a way of keeping ourselves coherent, we tore at each others' skin and scraped each others' faces. Germans came and went. Each and every day. Poles came and went. Mad wolves prowling over our heads for their prey. And suddenly, misfortune strikes: Kowalski's wife has a heart attack. We hear the doctor come. There's a lot of movement upstairs. *Pani* Kowalski's carried out. We pray for her life. Kowalski came down and spoke to us that day, telling us everything. She was in the hospital four weeks.

The Germans stopped coming. The house was locked up and shuttered. Abandoned. Then she comes back and we hear her say to the doctor: "*Panie Doktorze,* it's been my fate to have bad people denounce me for hiding Jews in my house. They got the Germans to come, and they, too, came every day, screaming and beating my husband and me. Can you believe it, can you believe it, *Panie Doktorze?!*"

We spent a year and a half in that dungeon of Kowalski's. *Pani* Kowalski recovered after her heart attack and we came out of the cellar alive. One and a half years! It was now May 1945.

The Red Army finally advanced on Grodne. The first Jews surfaced, came out of their hiding places, came out of the woods. A few days later, the first Jews started arriving from Germany. Emaciated people with numbers tattooed on their arms. And the first Jews were now let out of Russia. These were Jews from Grodne, but they also came from other places. They roamed through the city looking for relatives, looking up addresses where relatives might be found. The city itself was left relatively undamaged, but it was a rare event if someone found a family member alive.

A committee was set up in the city to dispense relief to the refugees. But the Soviets put an end to the committee almost immediately. No relief! While the Reds are here, there'll be no relief! . . .

Eyewitness Testimony 7. The Last Jews of Ozorków

B.L. Born in Ozorków, Łódź District, in 1925; lived there. Recorded by B. Frenkel in a DP camp in 1946.

I, B—— B——-L——, born in Ozorków April 2, 1925, daughter of A—— B—— and S——, maiden name L——, was a pupil at the local public school until the outbreak of the Second World War in 1939. At the age of fourteen, I started to endure the sufferings of the *Khorbn* of our people.

Already during the first days in September, the town fell to the Germans, and they began the extermination of the Jews. They dragged people from their homes and shot them in the squares and courtyards for no reason. Soon, the *shiel* on Pilsudski 16 was in flames. All the *sifre toyres* and the *talaysim* and the *sfurim* turned to ash. After the fire, the charred ruin was turned into a cavalry stable for horses. They start rounding up Jews in the streets, load them into trucks, and the people are never heard from again. In the first days of winter, 1941, the men are transported to labor camps in Poznań. My brother was among them. He never came back. On April 10, 1942, ten young Jewish men are selected and led off to the square in the "new town," right in the middle of the marketplace. Before them stands a gallows. These ten wretched men are then hanged by their own brothers' hands. The SS forced all the Jews from the ghetto to assemble in the marketplace and witness the killing. After the noose was pulled tight around his neck, one of the condemned men yelled out: "I'll find no rest in the grave till you who survive avenge me and all of us the Germans have murdered, when the war is over!" I was overcome by this and fainted. A forty-year-old Jew named Friedman was shot by the Nazis because he was blind. My older sister—her name was Karola, she was thirty years old—lived in Łódź from before the war. Another sister of mine, Bela—she was twenty-five—went to see her often. Bela would smuggle medicines and food from Ozorkow into Łódź. When the Łódź Ghetto was sealed off, the smuggling came to a standstill. She couldn't come home to Ozorków anymore, and

was trapped inside the ghetto. I worked in a furrier workshop outside the [Ozorków] Ghetto. We were brought there early every morning, and marched back into the ghetto at night. In 1941, all free
movement was forbidden. The Jews were put under house arrest.
Then, in the afternoon, the SS stormed in, sounded an alarm, and
made everyone come down to the street and line up in the courtyards.
Then we were marched off to Kosciuszko Street and locked up inside
the elementary school building. After that, inside the *gymnazye*. We
were told we'd be examined by doctors but it turned out that they
only paraded us naked before regular SS men, who stamped us
either A or B. When the *selektsye* was over, they segregated everyone stamped B. We learned later that they were taken to Chełmno,
near Koło, and gassed. I lost my mother during this *aktsye*—she was
stamped B. I also lost a married sister and her three children. We
three remaining sisters, along with our father, were put back to work
and we suffered terrible hardships until the summer of '42. In July,
a new *aktsye* takes place. A group of able bodied workers are selected
as laborers and sent into the Łódź Ghetto. My sisters and father and
me were among this group. The rest of the Jews were sent to their
deaths. We arrived on the *Balut*[1] square in the Łódź Ghetto carrying
our small bundles. We had to leave all our belongings behind, scattered in the street in front of our homes. They separated a small group
from us and led them back out to clear away the remains of the
Ozorków Ghetto. After all the goods were arranged for shipment to
Germany, the group was taken back inside the Łódź Ghetto. Suddenly,
the Gestapo surrounded them, condemned them for sabotage, and
machine-gunned most of them against a wall. The *Älteste der Juden,*
Chaim Rumkowski, had the rest of us led away and confined in a
school building. After a few days, we three sisters and our father
went to stay with our elder sister who lived on Lutomierska 14. My
father became a watchman. I got work at the husk factory.[2] We
were given the same rations as the other Jews in the ghetto. A month
later, the horror of the *Sperre*[3] is imposed.... On Monday, September 7, 1942, the *selektsye* begins in our part of the ghetto. We run
like poisoned mice when we see what's going on: huge numbers
of people fail the *selektsye* and are pushed into wagons, then unloaded at the *Umschlagplatz* on Drewnowska 75, the building which
used to be St. Józef's Hospital. There's nowhere to hide and we have
to surrender to the SS. By a miracle, we escape death. My sister
Karola and her two-and-a-half-year-old child already stood in the
wagon. In the final moment before departure, they were suddenly
separated and she found her way back to us. After the *Sperre* was
ended, I was assigned to work at the garment factory on Lagewnicka
Street, turning out military uniforms. I work here without interruption from now on. It's true, we were slowly starving to death, but

we thought we would avoid being deported by working here. I had to work a hard, long day on twenty-five *deka* of dark bread with some soup and, very rarely, I begged some potato peels from a kitchen. I made "*Laufigs*" [?] cutlets from them. This is what they were called in the ghetto because they're made from turnips and roasted ersatz coffee. Because we were always at work, we were never caught during the *aktsyes* of 1943. But the summer of 1944 put an end to all our hopes, even though we were on the verge of Liberation. We expected to be freed any minute. News was secretly spread through the ghetto that battles were raging in and around Warsaw. We also resisted for a long time and prevented them from rounding us up for deportation. Hans Biebow[4] the murderer tried to appease us. He asked us to assemble on the square opposite our house on Lutomierska 11 to 13, where the Jewish fire brigade were also stationed. Then Rumkowski apepaled to us to come out, but we would have fought it. The garment workers were prepared to resist to the end. The entire ghetto was looking to these tailors. The Nazis knew the battle would be bloody and too costly, and they were forced to liquidate the ghetto. A curfew was called where we were staying, but we crossed over to another part of the ghetto. The rationing stations were closed down. No bread was distributed for eight days. The garment workers called public demonstrations but starvation overcame the masses and they submitted to the will of the ghetto chiefs. They ordered the ghetto evacuated and even agreed to the tailors' demand that their leader, a Jew named Grossman, be allowed to leave with them on the first transport. These deceitful Nazi criminals even piled on cut materials, the looms and other machines, and loaded them onto freightcars with us. Along the way, the wagonloads of machines and merchandise were detached from the train and we continued the trip in sealed, stifling cars to Birkenau, Auschwitz.

Eyewitness Testimony 8. An Escaped Slave Laborer

R.K. Lived in Siemiatycze, Białystok District. Recorded by Duvid Shtokfish in a DP camp in April 1945.

I was born in Lublin in 1905 of very religious parents. I'm a builder by trade, but during the occupation I did other kinds of work—like loading logs onto trains, collecting garbage, and mixing cement.

I married in 1928. My wife and three children were killed in Treblinka on November 19, 1942. I also lost my father and mother, my brother and my sister-in-law and their child.

From 1925 on, I lived in Semiatitch,[1] Bielsk Region. There were around 5,000 Jews in my *shtetl*—about 66 percent of all the people. The overwhelming majority of them worked in the chemo-ceramic industry, at the shoe-manufacturing plant, and in the shoemaker and tailor shops. There were also many artisans and weavers who worked at home and some shopkeepers and petty merchants.

On the first day of the "siege"—this was on November 2, 1942— the Nazis drove 500 Jews into Semiatitch from the surrounding areas. Though Semiatitch was a border town right on the Bug River, the Nazis tried to prevent us from escaping to the Soviets by annexing the town right from the start, on June 23, 1941.

Every day at least ten people perished inside the ghetto, which was just recently imposed. There were no births. We knew of some isolated instances of mental breakdowns.

A few days after the start of the German encirclement, the Gestapo marched the entire Jewish population—including women, children, and the old people—out of the ghetto, and made us tear out the weeds between the rocks around the *shtetl*. Three people resisted and were shot that day, and the overseers beat us terribly because none of us did the work like we were told. Soon, they ordered us to put on the yellow patches.

Special squads of Germans from the "Todt Organization"[2] started arriving and they got the local townspeople to order the statue of Lenin standing in the Semiatitch marketplace demolished. They showed their hatred by dragging all the Jews out and forcing us to the market square, beating us the whole time without pity. They hurled one Jew live into the river and he drowned. They draped a *talis* over the director of the Jewish *Folkshul*, Yihude Kogut, put a *toyre* crown on his head and made him deliver a eulogy for Lenin in front of all the people. He had to yell, "Down with the USSR!" The Jews were then ordered to smash off Lenin's head but we wouldn't do it. The Germans and the Polish police fell on us with bloodlust. These killers obliterated the statue themselves and ordered the pieces taken down into the Jewish cemetery.

For the moment, they only arrested those Jews found eating meat because this was forbidden us, even though they threw us bones and scraps we had to gnaw at to "entertain" them.

At the start of August 1941, the Nazis exacted a tribute from the Jews amounting to 140,000 rubles. We were inducted into slave-labor battalions for clearing away the rubble of the houses flattened by German artillery, and also for hauling all kinds of cement blocks and boulders to build fortifications. Since the Germans wanted to spare their beloved horses, they had us lay down tracks and ordered us to pull the cargo by hand.

All our property was confiscated and we were taxed regularly, having to bring them valuables like furniture, clothing, linen, china, and sets of service, gold, and more. Besides these major confiscations, the Germans kept breaking into our homes under all kinds of excuses and robbing us of everything we had left.

Jews were allowed on the streets for only three hours a day—from two till five in the afternoon. No one was permitted to set foot out of their house at any other time, even to see to their physical needs. It was forbidden to open a window or to look out into the street.

The ghetto in Semiatitch had been set up on the second of August, 1942. While we were being transferred into the ghetto, the Germans inspected every bundle and lifted out all valuable contents. Every ghetto inmate was alloted 1⅒ square meters living space, and the height of a room never rose above 2½ meters.

The Germans were especially cruel to the *Judenrat* and the Jewish police they created. Once, they ordered the eleven Jewish council-men—excluding the *Präses*—to clean out the town cesspool and to cart off the excrement to the outskirts of town. There wasn't one instance of this Jewish committee giving a Jew over into the hands of the Germans.

We were marched from the town every day to the labor sites. The Germans rationed out twelve *deka* of bread a day for a laborer from the ghetto, and six *deka* for a nonlaborer. We used to smuggle a few potatoes back from the labor sites in our pockets.

There were no workshops or factories in the ghetto. The Germans imposed a head tax and the *Judenrat* had to collect money from the Jews constantly for ransoms and to postpone the lesser evil decrees.

A public kitchen, which was started in the ghetto, used to distribute over 1,500 free meals a day.

We knew people who became *baley-tshive* after having been athe-ists all their lives.

The ghetto in Semiatitch was in existence about three months. Our suffering can't be described. Then we heard that the final liquidation of the Warsaw Ghetto had begun.

Once Semiatitch was incorporated into the Third Reich, we felt that the liquidation of the Semiatitch Ghetto was far off, even more so because the Germans kept giving us assurances about it.

On Monday, November 2, 1942, at half-past four in the morning, we woke to find the ghetto being surrounded by Gestapo and SS. People instinctively rushed to the wires, cut them, and broke out. The Germans fired without stop and killed several hundred people. A small number managed to reach the woods. They formed them-selves into a partisan unit of about one hundred combatants and fought the Germans from the forests. In the fall of 1943, the unit was defeated and scattered by the Germans.

The operation of expelling the Jews from the ghetto and trans-porting them to Treblinka was carried out only by Germans. Disre-garding the warnings that were hung up around the ghetto after the

Jews were shipped to Treblinka, that anyone approaching the ghetto would be shot, the local people took the fact that no guards were posted as a signal to break into the Jewish homes and plunder everything in sight. They were ecstatic over the Jewish catastrophe, but at the same time they were terrified. They knew the extermination of the Jews meant their end, too.

I was given this account of the annihilation of the Jews of Semiatitch by Binyomin Rokh, an inhabitant of Semiatitch who escaped from Treblinka. These are his words:

> . . . The last Jews of the Ghetto were packed off into freight cars and sent through Czeremcha-Białystok-Małkinia to Treblinka. They were detoured from the shorter route of Semiatitch to Treblinka by way of Sokołów Podlaski—a two-hour journey. The people were needlessly tortured by this longer way to break them down and deceive them. We got to Treblinka in the evening, but were kept locked up inside the train all night long. At dawn, everyone was dragged out of the trains, pushed into the gas chambers and exterminated. Because I was a carpenter, I was put to work in the carpentry stalls of Treblinka and I managed to hide out during this slaughter. . . .

> About half a kilometer from Małkinia, I broke through the roof grating of the speeding train. Since the opening was so small, I had to strip my top clothes off, keeping on only my underwear, and jump out into a twelve-degree frost. Several dozen other desperate Jews tried the same thing all along the train, but the guards shot them all since they showed up as such clear targets against the white fields of snow. I was the only one to escape death, because I didn't run for the fields but threw myself down alongside the tracks. I dragged a German guard by the sleeve down after me—he bounced and crashed all over the gravel and lost his automatic. I grabbed the gun and shot him through and also got away with his revolver. I managed all of this because I was in one of the last cars and as I jumped, I landed at the very end of the transport which only had one German guard.

> In the first month of my escape, I hid out in different Polish villages.

> On December 4, 1942, I was in hiding in the Semiatitch region—I ran into five more Jews from Semiatitch. We dug a bunker under a peasant's barn—the Pole knew about it—and waited for the Red Army's advance here.

Eyewitness Testimony 9. "Going Through" the Camps and Prisons

W.L. Born in Warta, Kalisz District, Poland, in 1924; lived there. Recorded by Icek Shmulewitz in New York, December 1954. The witness describes the outbreak of the war and the persecution of the Jews in his hometown. He talks of the conditions in the Warta Ghetto in 1940, and continues.

The Ghetto also had a Jewish security force. Their *Älteste* was Yosif Obrentsh. The *Älteste* of the whole ghetto was London. The Germans hanged him afterwards. Obrentsh, the police elder, was later deported to the Łódź Ghetto, and from there they took him to Auschwitz where he was probably killed.

They used to take the Jews from the ghetto and put them to work for the town doing things like clearing the snow from the streets, building roads, cleaning the German houses, and more. Even in early February, before the ghetto was in existence, the Germans hounded me out in the middle of the night to clear the streets of snow. I was lightly dressed and became very ill. To this day, I'm still sick with rheumatism.

In September 1940, the *Volksdeutsche* caught me in the streets of the ghetto together with other Jews, pushed us to the Sieradz train station where the *Arbeitsamt* was, and we were registered for work in the outlying labor sites. They put us on a hay wagon pulled by a horse and led us away. Midway along the road, I jumped off and dove into a potato field where I hid for some time. Afterwards, I walked back to the ghetto. A month later, I was again caught in the streets of the ghetto with some other people. We were stuck into open boxcars and headed deep into Germany. As the train was speeding up not far from Kalisz, I jumped out. The German guards shot at me but their bullets just whistled by. I made it back to the ghetto again.

In November 1940, the "Jewish Committee"[1] of the ghetto put together a transport of 100 Jews to be sent away as laborers. I was working in the ghetto for the Germans then at repairing watches. I was deceived and included in the transport even though I'd been given work and the only ones being sent away were those for whom there was no function in the ghetto. A ghetto policeman, A—— Z—— —today he's in Israel—came over to me and told me to report to the "Jewish Committee" to fix the large wall clock there. I walked into the committee room where the other Jews of the transport were already detained and there was no way of getting free. German prison personnel took us "off the hands" of the "Jewish Committee" and tied us all up—100 young Jews bound one to the other by rope to prevent escape. Then we were shipped to Dorenfeld,[2] near Leszno in Poznań. We were put to work tending the fields of German nobility. We were locked up in an infested camp and never fed. Only Jews worked here—about 120 men.

After being kept in Dorenfeld for a few months, I was taken out with a group of men and brought to the city of Poznań. We were put into the camp barracks of the Remu et Co.—this was an enormous labor enterprise through which the inmates were transferred to different labor sites. We were mainly put to work digging up a canal for a man-made river. We slaved at the project for twelve hours a day, and walked the distance to the site and back to camp on foot every day—two hours each way. We were given almost no food. Remu was an old and huge mustard factory before the war. The plant had been divided up into barracks—the bunks for sleeping were put in later. Germans kept watch over us at work all day long. They couldn't stop beating us. I was working in the division of the *Sager und Werner, Ostdeutsche Bau-Gesellschaft*. The overseer in our *Kommando* was a *Volksdeutsche* named Stelmaszczyk, a wild murderer—he wandered around with a club and bludgeoned the inmates to death.

During one period, a typhus epidemic spread through the camp and many Jews died. The sick were never treated or given any medicine. They were just dumped into a separate corner of our barrack. I also came down with typhus then, but I got into the camp infirmary for four weeks.

After I recovered and left the infirmary, I was sent with a group of convalescents to the quarantine camp at Eichenwaldau.[3] There was no food for us there and every second inmate died. The only doctors were a few Jews and some people practicing folk medicine. But they couldn't do anything for us because they weren't allowed to keep any medicaments.[4] I was inside the quarantine camp for four months, then sent back to Remu and put to work digging the canal again. Up to that time, I had gotten some packages from my home, and I was able to survive this ordeal.

In the spring of 1942, I was taken with a transport of 500 Jews to Malta, a manor near Poznań. We did the same kind of labor—digging man-made rivers. They rarely gave us our rations, and flogged us the whole day long on the project site. After enduring Malta for several months, I was sent into the Łódź Ghetto with a transport of 1,000 other Jews from the manor.

I arrived in the Łódź Ghetto toward the start of 1943. After they inspected and registered our transport, we were taken to the ghetto prison on Czarnecki Street. They kept us locked up in the cells for three weeks. It was so overcrowded inside, the only way to sleep was standing upright. We weren't permitted to bathe or given a change of linen for the whole three weeks. The prison guards were Jewish policemen who walked around with clubs. The prison warden was called Kol and addressed as *"Pan Komisarz Kol."* Later, he and the others were sent off to Auschwitz. He treated the Jews in the prison cruelly.

On a certain day, Hans Biebow and his aides came to the prison and started inspecting and interrogating the Jews of our transport. From their behavior and the way we were guarded afterwards, we knew for sure they were sending us to Auschwitz. I decided on an escape plan to try to save myself.

The prison on Czarnecki Street was surrounded by a tall wooden barricade topped with barbed wire. I climbed up on the wooden wall which faced Franciskanska Street. This was on the seventh or eighth of April, 1943. It was evening and getting dark. As I was climbing the barricade, a Jewish policeman—a certain T—— from Łask—who guarded the prison from the street, spotted me. He sent out an immediate alarm to the other policemen. In that second, I dropped straight down from the wall and landed on the policeman's head with my wooden clogs. T—— collapsed on the concrete, blood pouring from his face. The night was now pitch-black and I got away. I ducked into some ruins on Franciskanska Street which had been gutted for their wood beams. While I was lying there during the night, I heard them lead away the 1,000 Jews who'd been brought from Poznań with me, from the prison. They were loaded onto trucks and driven off. When I got to Auschwitz afterwards—I'll speak of this soon—I met a handful of survivors from this transport who told me the whole convoy had been taken straight from the prison into the furnaces.

I have to tell you something which happened in the Łódź Ghetto prison. When our transport was brought inside, the Jewish policemen from the Łódź Ghetto found out from us which of the Jewish "auxiliaries" who'd been brought from Poznań with us had mistreated us during work. After the men were identified, we were avenged. The "auxiliaries" were picked out of line and thrown into solitary-punishment cells.

The following morning, I left my hideout in the ruins on Franciskanska and smuggled myself into the ghetto. I immediately headed to where my relatives were staying—they were deported from Warta into the Łódź Ghetto earlier and their status was legal.[5] I was in the ghetto illegally. I wasn't registered and had no official ration cards. My relatives let me stay with them and the rest I got by stealing. During the nights, I stole into the cultivated plots in the ghetto which were scattered between different buildings—they were called dzhalkes.[6] I ripped cabbages, beets, and other vegetables from the ground and this is what I lived on. Finally, I was given legal status in the ghetto and treated like everyone else.

After becoming legal, I was given a job at the watchmakers' workshop, fixing watches. I worked there about five months. Suddenly, the Jewish police started arresting those who were imprisoned when they were brought into the Łódź Ghetto and had escaped. They found a hundred of us in the ghetto who'd broken out of the prison and I was among them. They put all of us back into confinement on Czarnecki Street. This time, we were locked up in the high-risk wing where hardened criminals were kept before the war.

We were held at the Gestapo's disposition with our fate unknown, locked up till the Gestapo decided what to do with us. There were twenty other Jews put into the cell with me. We had room to move this time. Each one of us 100 men was given a special place to sleep. We were given soup and 300 grams of bread a day. They called us "*Setka*," from the Polish, because there were 100 of us. After seven months in the prison, many of us were let out into the ghetto. I was also let go. By now, it was the beginning of 1944. I was later put to work at construction in Marysin, outside of Łódź. We built barracks which housed factories producing heaters for the *Wehrmacht* at the Russian front. These were small apparatuses the German soldiers carried around to try to keep warm in the deep frosts of the Russian winter. I worked on at Marysin until August 1944, when the Łódź Ghetto was liquidated.

I was then sent to Auschwitz with the remaining Jews from the Łódź Ghetto. I was put in Barrack No. 21 and for three weeks we did nothing. The camp we were in at Auschwitz was called "the Gypsy Camp" because the Gypsies had passed through it before us. We were told the Germans never exploited the Gypsies for any kind of labor, but burned them immediately.[7] The barrack I was in held 600 of the last surviving Jews from the Łódź Ghetto.

After three weeks in Barrack 21, I was taken by transport with other inmates—most of us were Jews—to the camp at Stenzelberg, near Waldenburg.[8] We were put in quarantine there and did no work. On a certain day, the Germans rounded up all the Jewish youths in camp aged thirteen to fourteen who had passed for adults till then and transported them back to Auschwitz. Many of these kids were shot trying to escape out of the railroad cars.

From here, they later took us to Wuestegiersdorf.[9] There was a labor camp near town, but our transport was held over in the transit zone. We used the time there to form our own theater troupe which performed every Sunday for all the inmates in camp. The show we did consisted of songs, monologues, and skits in Yiddish, Polish, and German. The repetoire was completely prewar. The moving forces of the group were Shameh Roznblum[10] and his partner who used to appear in Łódź. From Wuestegiersdorf, we were brought to the huge labor camp at Wolesberg which held over 3,000 inmates. We bored huge tunnels through the mountains in which the Germans built the missiles—V-1 and V-2—they used to bomb England. The Germans also produced synthetic benzine in these tunnels. We slaved almost round the clock and were fed miserably. In the time I was in the camp, 10 percent of the inmates died. I was kept in Wolesberg until February 10, 1945.

When the Allied fronts closed in on Germany, the camp was evacuated. Our transport of less than 3,000 inmates was led deeper into the countryside on a forced march. Many people fell behind from fatigue and total exhaustion and the German guards shot them dead. The death march lasted three full days. We spent the nights in the forests. The Germans handed out bread they had with them once a day—we had to eat while walking. On the third day, we walked into Friedland, near Schwiednitz on the Czech border. They herded us into two big barns and gave us nothing to eat. People sat down and died in their place. The dead were dragged out and buried in two large common graves. I can remember the half-dead ones lying among the bodies. They were still wheezing, completely exhausted and spent, and the Germans ordered us to bury them along with the dead. [As the witness describes this scene, he interrupts himself several times to ask if the world knows anything of these two common graves, if any memorial stone has been erected in Friedland?—I.S.]

The Soviet front kept advancing. We were held in these two barns for ten straight days—over 1,000 people died during that time. I survived only because I told the Germans I was an expert watchmaker. There were many German soldiers stationed there working on vehicle repair. They wore defective and broken watches and when they heard I was a watchmaker, they gave me all their watches to fix. I was let inside the captain's office, and that's where I sat repairing the watches. The captain kept bringing me extra watches to fix and I was given enough food—I was even given some of the food that was brought in for the captain, or his leftovers.

After keeping our dying transport locked up inside the barns for ten days, the Germans loaded us into open boxcars that used to carry coal and we were sent deeper into Austria—to Mauthausen. Our transport was only kept in Mauthausen four days—they didn't want us inside the camp, there was no room, it was bursting with inmates.

From Mauthausen, they dragged us off to Ebensee, near Gmunden. There was a major labor camp here, but also a crematorium in which the inmates were burned. Again, we were set to work boring huge tunnels through the mountains. Residences were installed inside with all the conveniences, just like a regular city. We were kept in the camp barracks, but led back and forth from the mountain labor sites where we dug the tunnels. The barracks were livable, but the food was like poison. We were carted off to Ebensee from Mauthausen in open cattle cars, in the freezing cold, and many hundreds of inmates died along the way.

I was liberated in Ebensee by the American army on May 6, 1945.

Three days earlier, before the Americans came, the Germans hanged
four inmates in our camp. The four were hanged because they tried
to buy bread from the overseers. In the last three days before Liberation, there was nothing to eat in camp. We felt that Liberation was
so near—everyone wanted to cling to life, not to collapse from hunger
and exhaustion in the final minutes before the miracle happened.
These four inmates had torn the gold teeth from out of their own
mouths to get some bread from the overseers for it. For this, they
were hanged.

On May 4, 1945, when we got back into camp from the labor site,
we saw the German camp guards piling into trucks and speeding
away from the camp. We didn't know if they'd be back, but for now,
the Hitlerites ran from the camp and left us to ourselves. On May
fifth, the watch was taken over by Austrian men, civilians, who walked
around with their guns drawn. We weren't marched off to work that
day. On May fifth, during the night, the Austrians fled, too. And by
the morning of the sixth of May, when we walked outside, we didn't
see one guard—we were completely free. The camp was encircled
by extremely high-tension wires and no one wanted to risk breaking
out. On the same day, May sixth, in the afternoon, the first American
soldier wandered into camp.

Eyewitness Testimony 10. The Autumn of Prague

M.G. Born in Plzeň, now Czechoslovakia, in 1914. Recorded by Mikhl
Zylberberg in London in January 1957. The witness tells of her life
prior to and after the annexation of Czechoslovakia and describes
the situation in Prague after March 1939. She talks of the preparations being made to deport the Jews of Prague and goes on.

On the whole, the people were subdued. In Prague itself, we strained
under the aggravating restrictions—having to wear the yellow *mogen
david*, being forced to comply with all the anti-Jewish laws while
the Gentiles were free to do as they pleased. But we imagined we'd
only be sent off somewhere as laborers and would stay there till the
war ended. Besides, we were sure they'd only send us among Jews.
In either case, people were resigned to make the best of it.

The prospects for the older people looked worse. They couldn't
imagine starting life over in a completely new world, with the conditions around them deteriorating so badly already.

Two days later, we were taken to the train station under SS guard,
with the Gestapo standing on all sides. Our route passed through
the streets of Prague and thousands of Czechs lined both sides as an

expression of their sympathy for the Jews. Many of the men removed their hats and some of the women wept openly when they saw how cruelly the Nazis treated us, old and young, and the small children, too.

Even now, no one dreamed they were sending us to Poland. We thought: Holland, Belgium, Germany—but never Poland. That they were sending us to Jewish ghettos in other places was very far from our minds.

We were deported in October 1941. They loaded us on a regular train, ten to a compartment. The trip was hard. There was no water or any kind of first aid, but it was hardest on the children, the babies needing special care.

The SS patrolled the cars for the whole journey, constantly taking head counts to make sure no one had escaped.

On the following day, the train suddenly came to a halt and the SS started screaming "*Raus!*" We saw young men closing in on the train with clubs, rubber truncheons, and wearing colored hats topped with a *mogen david.* At first, it all seemed like some masquerade. We had no idea where we were or who these people in disguise were. After an hour or two, we were given to understand that this was Marysin, on the outskirts of Łódź, and that the masqueraders with truncheons and clubs were the Jewish police and fire brigade.

It took us over an hour's march till we got to the Łódź Ghetto. We were all put into one building—a transport of over 1,000 people, thirty people to a room. This is when our hell really began. There was no water in the building, just a pump in the courtyard, and for these 1,000 people—only four lavatories. In the meantime, it got colder from day to day, snow began falling and everything froze solid. Our condition was desperate from the start. Of course, there was no food anywhere, though the first two days we still had the little we brought with us from Prague. But after that—we were overcome by starvation.

After a few days, a new transport was brought from Prague and these people were also crowded into our house.[1] The situation got so bad that we gave in to despair and lost all hope, becoming totally apathetic to our surroundings. In every room, people sat around in a stupor, picking typhus worms and lice from their clothes—though it was pointless to try to stop all the filth from spreading. There was no end to it.

After a week, our transport was removed from the building and detained at Franciskanska 15. The conditions now beggar the imagination.

I can never forget something that happened then. All of us were suddenly ordered to line up immediately on *Hamburgplatz.*[2] Thousands of Jews were huddled together, guarded from all sides by

German military and Jewish policemen. No one knew what was about to take place.

Then a gallows was quickly raised and, right before our eyes, they hanged a young man.[3] The Germans blared through their loudspeakers: "This is the way everyone caught trying to escape the ghetto will end up!" We now had no more illusions about the kind of world they'd brought us to. I don't want to tell you things about the Łódź Ghetto you might have heard. It wasn't possible to survive these conditions. Of my entire family and friends, most died of hunger. My mother died January 13, 1943; my husband, February 6, 1943. My cousin, Dr. Erich Herman of Prague, was hospitalized with diseased lungs. The Gestapo charged in, dragged the patients out of their beds, and shot them to a man. He was one of them.

The horrors of the *seleckcja* we underwent! I really feel that those who were immediately sent to the gas chambers suffered less than the Jews inside the ghetto who had to endure torture and starvation and ravishing disease for years until they could stand no more. I mean, you understand, those who wouldn't believe what was waiting for them until it was too late.

I worked at a factory that made shoes out of straw; then as a clerk in the same building. It was considered better work—the kind you got "for life." When they liquidated the factory, I was moved into another plant that turned out greatcoats for the military.

After the sixth of February, when my husband died of hunger, I was left all alone and struggled on in this hell till the end of July 1944. I was then deported to Auschwitz.

Three months before the Auschwitz *aktion,* I broke my leg and was put in the hospital. I was kept there two months. It was considered suicidal to be caught inside the hospital. The Germans would come in and execute everyone in bed—the way I mentioned before. Somehow, I managed to keep alive. I have to admit, that I also felt lucky to be in the hospital, sometimes. One of the reasons was I didn't have to stand out in the cold, rain, and frost for hours, waiting for a bite of bread or that watery soup. Inside the hospital, they gave me a small ration of bread and soup without my going through that torture.

The day they transported us to Auschwitz, I was still hobbling on two crutches. As the *selekcja* started inside the camp, I instinctively threw the sticks to the side. This happened just as Mengele himself, that infamous SS officer of Auschwitz, began doing the choosing. Even while we were undergoing the *selekcja,* we didn't imagine that they were going to send us straight into the gas chambers, that our fates were being decided by that flick of his wrist.

The day they deported us from Łódź, everyone was given a piece of bread, some cigarettes, and the people were all really quite calm.

They wanted to believe they were only being transferred to another ghetto, and the worst that could happen would be more work. We couldn't conceive of something worse than the Łódź Ghetto.

When we came into Auschwitz the next day, we were struck with the impression of having entered an insane asylum. The look of the camp, the appearance of the inmates as they stood around the platform, the way they moved—it all seemed like some colony for the demented.

The *selekcja* was started instantly—old people, children, the sick to one side; youths and the ablebodied to the other. During the whole time, I kept close to a woman acquaintance of mine from Prague, *Frau* Stein and her child. When their turn came, the mother and child were pushed off with the old and the sick, and I was sent to the second group.

I wanted to take my friend's child with me, but a *Kapo* came between us and said, "Save your own life, let the child alone."

As we walked into the zone, we still carried our small bundles and the bread rations. From both sides, long-time inmates stood and yelled: "Eat your bread!" We started to eat it. When we came to a certain area, everything we had was grabbed from us. We were lined up completely naked and then they started processing us into the camp. There were thousands of other people[4] who'd also come in that day and there wasn't enough time to put everyone through the same ordeal. Because of this, many of us got out without having our heads shaved or numbers tattooed onto our arms.

Once inside our area, I ran into a *"Makherin"*—a young, pretty girl whom I'd gone to school with in Prague. She helped me in the beginning, and because of her, I was able to stay alive. She got me work for a time, cleaning up in the barracks.

I spent about six weeks in Auschwitz altogether—the whole time in "D" *Lager—Durchgangslager*—from where the women were sent either to the gas chambers or to different labor camps.

We were forced to stand at *Appel* for long hours every day. It was now August 1944, and the sun burned like fire. The nights were bitter cold, with the wind howling through the barracks, and we had nothing to cover ourselves with.

The saddest part of all this, and something I can never forget, is the way the *Blockälteste* and her helpers treated us. Though they were Jewish women, they acted more like wild beasts from the forests, beating us and kicking us all the time, and showing us no pity at all. They, themselves, lacked nothing, though. They were mostly veteran inmates who'd been in camp over three years and had gone through the same hell in the beginning we were going through now.

I met a cousin of mine inside Auschwitz—he was still a boy—named Karol Hibak, and he helped me a lot, too. He was a laborer in the camp and brought me soup or a piece of bread many times. He'd been in camp a long time and knew all its ways. He kept repeating to me that if they sent me into the gas chamber, I should position myself right under the gas exhaust, because like this, I'd be gassed instantly. If I stood away from the pipe, it could take from five to ten minutes. I never had to experience it. But tragically, he was the one to perish, and I remained alive.

At the end of August, I was sent to Bernsdorf, near Trautenau in Sudetenland, with a group of twenty women. This happened under very unusual circumstances. While I was still inside the "D" *Lager,* some female camp supervisors came in and started picking out the young and healthy women. They took eight girls from our barrack. We thought it might turn out well for us. There were no Germans with them, and to us this was a sign that it wasn't a *selekcja* for the gas chambers. Some women were also selected from other blocks—about thirty of us all together.

The Jewish *Blockälteste* took us before a German medical examiner in a completely different section of the camp. The "doctor" really molested us, poking his hand into every part of our body as we stood naked before him, and he finally qualified twenty of us for some kind of labor. We still had no idea what all this was about. They gave us linen, clothes, and shoes, and brought us to the camp gate. Five soldiers were waiting for us, and they marched us away right through the center of town, to the regular train station in Auschwitz. For the first time, we stood among ordinary people, most of them German civilians. Everyone else was waiting for the train. When the train pulled in, we were put into special, comfortable compartments and then the cars started moving. We were never told where they were taking us. The next night, we were in Bernsdorf.[5] The soldiers led us to a weaving mill—a large, modern factory where we were kept till eight in the morning. When the director arrived and saw us, he got very upset. Yes, he'd ordered twenty women as workers, but for November—not now! It was our great fortune that this director disliked the Nazis and decided he wouldn't send us back.

Around 200 Jewish women had been working at the factory for a long time—most of them were from Poland. The situation here was tolerable. Some of the overseers were fanatic Nazis and violent anti-Semites, of course. But compared to the Łódź Ghetto and the camps, it was paradise. This is how we felt about this factory after having been in Łódź and Auschwitz.

For the first two months, the twenty of us had no work assigned to us. Afterwards, we were given work with gas masks and this is what we did till May 1945.

While walking through the village during those last days, we saw Hitler's picture in a shop window lined with a black band. This is when we found out something was happening. The director also tried encouraging us at work sometimes with these words: *"Durchhalten, es dauert nicht mehr lange."*[6] He said this under his breath. He himself was terrified of all the Nazis in the factory.

The director was an intelligent man. He started treating us better when he realized Nazi Germany was crumbling. Not like the idiot Nazis who believed right up to the last minute that their *Führer* would save them. They mistreated us terribly all the while—even worse at the end.

Up to the last day, we didn't know if Liberation was near.

On the day when there wasn't a single German soldier left in the village, the director appeared before us during the midday break and said these words: *"Meine Damen, wir sind frei."*[7] He said the war was over.

When we walked out into the street, the villagers started greeting us from the windows. We felt that we were free now.

A day later, the Russians were in the village. I returned to Prague and lived there for three years.

In 1946, I married a second time—to my present husband. We left Prague during the Communist upheaval of 1948 and settled in London.

Not all of it can be described. There are things we lived through, we witnessed, that we can't begin to talk about. Such things that have no equivalent in words. It remains inside us as our deepest part—we, who saw with our own eyes what the Germans are capable of.

Eyewitness Testimony 11. Defiance

V.K. Born in Wilno in 1913; lived in Kaunas. Recorded by B. Frenkel in a DP camp in 1946. The witness talks briefly about the first war year in Kaunas, his fleeing to Wilno, then back to Kaunas, of the forced labor in the camp at Praveniskis,[1] the selections and executions which decimated the camp's inmates, and the final death march, about which he continues.

Me, and a friend called Eliezer, were part of the last group—about twenty people. We knew this was the end, so as they led us over a bridge in the evening, we jumped into the water and clung to the underside all night long. At daybreak, we headed toward Kovne.[2] We were attacked by two Lithuanian assassins along the way who wanted to finish us off. They ordered Leyzer and me to dig our own graves. We dug the shovels into the ground, suddenly flung the dirt in their eyes, killed them, and buried them in these same graves. We got to Kovne, but it wasn't till evening that a woman neighbor pointed out where I might find my wife and children. I remain in the Kovne Ghetto for about a year and do slave labor at the airstrip. This was in 1942. My wife was forced to work at the airstrip, too, but she was caught in the *aktsye* by the ghetto gate and hauled off to the Riga Ghetto.[3] The children remained with me. In 1943, the children and me also get sent to Riga. I work here as a bricklayer and furnace stoker. Eight days after I arrive, twelve Jewish policemen are executed—accused of smuggling arms into the ghetto.[4] While I was working in Pren,[5] I stole weapons from the stockpiles and smuggled them into the Kovne Ghetto, where I handed them over to the partisans who operated from the surrounding woods."

Eyewitness Testimony 12. Caught Between Enemies

M. G. Born in Luka-Wielka, Galicia, 1915; lived in Mikulińce, Tarnopol County. Recorded by Icek Shmulewitz in New York, December 1954. The witness recounts his experiences during the outbreak of the war and under Soviet occupation in Mikulińce, then continues.

All that time, the Ukrainians made pogroms on the Jews in the area. They murdered a large Jewish family. The *goyim* butchered the head of the family, Velvl Okun, because he'd served in the Soviet militia. They murdered Okun's wife, his mother-in-law, then they rounded up the whole family and slaughtered them.

As soon as the Hitlerites took over our *shtetl*, the same Ukrainians who had just collaborated with the Soviets now collaborated openly with the Nazis. That first day, the only Germans to enter the *shtetl* was a Hitlerite squad of about ten soldiers. They armed the Ukrainians immediately and, together, they shot up the retreating Soviet soldiers who were still on the outskirts of town. About 300 Red Army soldiers were wiped out that day.

The Hitlerites started dragging the Jews outside the town for all kinds of deadly work on the roads, also making us clean streets and things like that. We were then forced to dig large pits for the 300 dead Soviet soldiers. I was among the group that buried the Red Army soldiers that day. We dug the pits out of the field where they'd been gunned down. We just bulldozed the bodies into the open graves.

Then the Hitlerites lined up half of the Jews in the *shtetl* and told them they were going to be taken to work at the beer brewery which was just outside of town. This was the excuse, but they were really being led off to be shot. When the column got near the brewery, a tall Hitlerite officer cut them off on the road and ordered them turned back. They were brought back to the *shtetl,* but a group of about twenty-five to thirty were kept in place before the brewery. A Ukrainian named Kobulanski lived at the brewery. This peasant and the other Ukrainians there threw themselves on these last Jews with a fury. They ran them through with spades and pitchforks, and the screams of the dying could be heard all the way to town. A German squad stationed at the brewery wanted to put an end to the death agonies and screams, so they shot them dead. Most of the Jews were young people, boys and girls. . . .

The Germans kept rounding us up and sending us away to hard labor. All money, gold, and furs were confiscated. There was no ghetto created for the Jews but we had a *Yidnrat.* Its head was Dr. Yegendorf. The *Yidnrat* got a lot of help from Simkhe Zaltsman, the rich merchant. They treated us badly but it wasn't their fault because the Germans kept demanding the collection of ransoms, that they provide Jews for the labor battalions, that they make up transports of people to be taken to the camps or shot. There was also a Jewish *Militz* which used to escort us to and from the labor sites, and also to our execution. Some Jewish militiamen were worse than the Germans. Not one of them survived.

When I realized that all this was only going to get worse, I left for the village of Miszkowice with a group of friends. There was a large manor here that had been worked before the war and which the Nazis had converted into the seat of the *Kreishauptmann.* The Hitlerites had made a Pole we knew from before the war—a good Christian—caretaker of the manor. Five or six of us went to him in the beginning to try to convince him that he needed farmhands, and to take us on. The Pole gave in, then we got food and a place to sleep so that we didn't have to be afraid all the time the Germans would find us. The Hitlerites knew there were Jews on the manor. Out in the fields, the Ukrainian farmhands constantly fought with us. When the Jews in the *shtetl* found out about us, more came to the manor and after a while, we set up a kind of voluntary work camp in Miszkowice. There were about fifty of us working here, mostly young people—men and women. We were there about a year. My older brother, Yankiv, worked on the manor with me. Later, my sister also joined us at work.

After we worked the fields for a year, the Hitlerites put out a decree for all Jews to be rounded up and sent to the Tarnopol Ghetto. My brother and sister and me decided to resist and not let ourselves be taken like the other Jews of the manor. We looked for some way out. We came to an understanding with the caretaker, Koliwicki the Pole, that we'd hide in the courtyard while he looked the other way. He did like he said.

We stole into one of the barns on the manor, dug a pit under a stack of hay, and stayed down there for six months. One night a week, we came up and went to the caretaker's cottage. His wife left out a large bowl of food—barley or potatoes—with some bread, so we had enough to eat. We never met the caretaker's wife and she didn't look out at us when we came in the night. We were terrified walking to and from the caretaker's home for food. Peasants came all the time to bale hay from the stack we were hiding under. Once, they got so close, they were just one motion away from uncovering us. We dove into another pile of hay and hid there. We still came to the Pole's door during the nights, and his wife left the food out for us like always.

One *Shabbes* morning, while we were lying under the hay in the new hiding place, young peasant couples came in to do some threshing. They started taking apart the stacks of wheat we were hiding behind. Just as they were about to find us, I, myself, called to a Ukrainian peasant, Shudlovski, I knew before the war. I told him we were hiding here and not to give us away. The peasant quietly called over the old foreman, the Ukrainian Sechko, and we asked him to help us. He threw some hay over us and moved the peasant couples off to another spot, away from where we were hiding.

The Ukrainians on the manor and the field help started grumbling about Jews hiding out in the barn. They started coming one by one, without stop, and tried to make us confess how many Jews were hiding here, altogether. This happened in the winter of 1943. The Ukrainian field hands and the peasants brought us a pot of soup once. Another time, when all the peasants had gone off to work the fields, this other Ukrainian foreman, Mishko Kormilo, stayed behind. He came for us and took us to a different hiding place for the day. He told us we'd be better off staying up in the stable loft where no one would ever think of looking for us and we'd be safe there. If we were ever in serious danger, he told us, we should come to him— he'd help us. We climbed up into the hayloft of the stable nearby and lay there for eight straight days without food.

On a certain morning, German military and Ukrainian police swooped down on the manor to grab field hands for labor in Germany. The Ukrainian peasants tried to get out of being sent to Germany by scattering for cover in different barns and stables. Some of them scrambled up into the loft where my brother and sister and me were hiding. When we saw the Ukrainians crawling around on the rafters looking for somewhere to hide, we jumped down from the loft and ran for the fields.

We ran away from the manor and crossed a small bridge into the forest. Night fell and it got completely dark. A Ukrainian police guard was stationed by the bridge and he'd seen us running over. He turned his searchlight on us, aimed his rifle, and shot at us again and again. We tried to get out of the line of fire by skirting the edge of the forest and ran toward the village nearby. We dove into some bales of hay stacked in front of a peasant's hut. The Ukrainian police guard swept the area with his light but couldn't find us. He stood right over the bale of hay we were hiding in, shining his light through it up and down, but he must have been blind because he didn't see a thing.

Later, we crossed over to another village, climbed up into a stable loft, and no one noticed us. The stable belonged to an Ukrainian peasant I knew. After spending the night there, we came to the peasant and asked him to hide us. He wouldn't do it. We stayed there all day but had to leave in the evening. It was a winter night and freezing cold. We asked peasant after peasant to put us up, but they refused. And these were all peasants I knew well, you should know.

Finally, we had to go to the Ukrainian foreman I mentioned before, Mishko Kormilo, who told us he'd help if we were ever in trouble. I hadn't known this peasant before the war. We got to know him working on the manor of the *Kreishauptmann.* Kormilo's brother was a gendarme.

We offered to sell Mishko Kormilo a watch and some clothes because we just couldn't hold out any more and we wanted to give ourselves up voluntarily inside the Tarnopol Ghetto. This peasant tried talking us out of going into the ghetto, and told us he would hide us. Mishko Kormilo the peasant was so poor we gave him the watch and clothes for nothing. He took us up to the loft of his shed and spread the only ten bales of straw he owned around us. He also got us some food. By the way, this peasant, Kormilo, was a practicing thief.

We lay in hiding in the loft for eight days when we suddenly heard there'd been a burglary at the manor where Kormilo worked as foreman. He was suspected, and police came to search his hut. They climbed up into the loft looking for the stolen goods near where we were hiding. The police overturned the whole attic but didn't touch the ten bales of straw where me and my brother and sister were hiding.

After this scare, Kormilo wouldn't let us stay any longer. His wife and mother hated the Jews and badgered him for letting us hide here. Kormilo smuggled us into the manor of the *Kreishauptmann* where we worked earlier. He took us down and hid us in the ice cellar. We lay there for three days and nights stretched out on the ice. All we had to eat was the frozen ice. On the third day, a peasant woman came down to the cellar and spotted us. She was an old Ukrainian maid. When she saw us lying like that on the ice, she started crying and took pity on us. She brought us some food right away.

We climbed up from the cellar after the woman left—we were

afraid they'd find us now—and went back to Mishko Kormilo again. He finally took us into his hut and let us stay in a "bunker"—a large covered pit under the floor where he kept potatoes during the winter. We stayed in this hole till Liberation. Kormilo's wife and mother knew we were hiding there, but they started treating us differently. They brought us food now. To cover for his "sin" of hiding Jews, Mishko Kormilo would go to the meetings of the *Banderovtsi* and ranted wildly about: all hidden Jews must be flushed out! Kormilo, himself, would then reenact for me these appearances before the *Banderovtsi*.

When the Soviets came into Miszkowice in March of 1944, my brother and sister and me came out of hiding. We walked back to our hometown of Mikulińce but met very few surviving Jews. We found out that my father and mother were deported to the Tarnopol Ghetto and perished there. We left Mikulińce for Poland, then headed for Germany. We had also wandered in Lower Silesia and later joined the *Brikhah* through Czechoslovakia, Austria, and Germany to get to *Eretz Yisrael*.

Eyewitness Testimony 13. A Child in the Camps

J.A. Born in Cracow in 1931; lived there. Recorded by Icek Shmulewitz in New York in February 1955. The witness describes the war's outbreak in Cracow, the Cracow Ghetto during the first and second deportation actions of 1942, then she continues.

But since my parents had work, I wasn't taken out of the ghetto when they deported the other children. My parents worked at this time in the *Nachrichten Geräte Lager*,[1] where cables, telephones, wires, and things like that were made and sent to the German front lines.

The second *aktsye* in the Cracow Ghetto was started in the summer of 1942.[2] Even the masses of Jews who were working and carried official work permits were led away, supposedly because all economic productivity was being suspended. Some permits were extended with attached blue slips, *Ausweisen*, meaning these people could stay on in the ghetto. Half of all the people in the ghetto were deported during this *aktsye*, along with almost all the children. My parents got these blue-slip extensions so they could keep working, but my problem was critical—they were deporting all the children of the parents still allowed to work in the ghetto. I remember that the people were then led off to Majdanek.

I was able to hide out while this *aktsye* was going on. This is how it happened:

The wives of both the *Yidnrat* members and the Jewish police lived in one building in the center of the ghetto, which also served as the headquarters for these groups. During the second *aktsye*, the heads of the *Yidnrat* and the Jewish police took their wives, children, and close relations back inside the building—they were exempted from this deportation. While the children of the ghetto were being lined up in rows, I hid out in a garbage can which stood in the courtyard of the *Yidnrat* building. I crouched inside it in the most horrifying moments—when they went from house to house searching for Jewish children. When it was all over, I ran into the *Yidnrat* building where the wives and children of the men and Jewish police were, and I rushed in among a group of children. Outside, in the ghetto, they were leading away the children and the adults with them. My father also stood on line with those being taken away even though he had a blue-slip permit, an *Ausweis*. But he paid out 500 *zloty* and the *Yidnratler* got him taken out of the line.

As night fell, the people—most of the children, the old, and the sick—were gone, and I ran back home. I came in to find my family and the other family staying with us still there. My mother was sure they had taken me with the other children. When she saw me walk into the room, she burst out in tears of joy—as if I'd come back from beyond the grave.

My mother paid the *Yidnrat* a specified sum of money and they wrote me out a false birth certificate making me older than I really was. The document said I was sixteen, but I was really only eleven years old. Now, the Germans would no longer consider me a child and there was less danger of being deported with the other children. Soon after, my parents gave the factory overseer some jewelry to take me on as a worker. I was eleven, looked like I was going on five, and was passing for a sixteen-year-old. . . .

The Cracow Ghetto was liquidated at the start of 1943.[3] Most of the people still left inside the ghetto were taken to the death camps. Those who could still work were interned in the Płaszów Concentration Camp. The entire Cracow *Yidnrat* was lined up against a wall and executed inside the ghetto. The 100 Jews who worked at the factory—including my parents and me—were taken to Płaszów. There, my mother and I were put in the women's camp and my father was separated from us along with the men. The 100 of us were taken to work at the factory from Płaszów just like we'd been taken from the Cracow Ghetto. After two months in Płaszów, I was no longer allowed to work at the factory because the Germans said my strength was failing and I could no longer do the work right. They had me work at the brush factory in Płaszów for the time. I could no longer see my parents, either, because the 100 Jews who worked at the factory were locked up inside and never let out—they were no longer part of Płaszów as they had been till now. I heard that this happened because the Poles and Germans of Płaszów⁴ protested against the Jews appearing through "their" streets.

Selektsyes took place all the time now, and the people were sent either to other labor camps or to Auschwitz. The most tragic *selektsye* was the one in August 1943. Children, sick people, and the aged were hunted down, herded together, and packed off to Auschwitz.

There was a children's home in Płaszów where the workers left their children for the day. The children of the *Jüdischer Ordnungsdienst* were also kept here. I was put inside this home with many other children while the big *selektsye* I just mentioned was going on.

The head of the Jewish police in Płaszów had been a suspected informer, but said he'd only been a milkman, in Cracow. His name was Chilewicz.⁵ He knew I was going by a false birth certificate, that I was still a child. His wife was the head inmate of the women's camp. Soon, during an *Appel*, Chilewicz's wife took me out of line and sent me to the children's home where all the other children were being gathered for deportation. She said I was also a child and belonged with them.

There were about 500 to 600 of us inside the children's home. The building was sealed behind barbed wire and guarded by Gestapo agents and not the sentries of the *Ordnungsdienst*. I spent only one night inside this children's home. The following morning, they started loading the children into trucks headed for Auschwitz. I felt sure they were leading us away to die and I decided to escape. As they were pushing me toward a truck with the other children, a German guard stopped a moment to light his cigarette. He stood spread-eagled. In a second, me and three other children—a boy and two girls—dropped out of line and, running low on the ground, we shot through the German's spread long legs. We broke for the latrine. The German whirled around and fired but he didn't hit anyone because we dropped to the ground as soon as we heard the first of his many shots. He couldn't come after us because he was afraid if he left the other children, they'd break away, too.

The camp latrine in which the three children and I hid was exposed. As we stood there, we could be seen from all sides and we were afraid they'd spot us. So I quickly ripped out one of the boards covering the pit and jumped right into the hole, into all the excrement. The children jumped down after me. The last child dragged down the board I had ripped out with him, and this saved us. The latrine ditch was very deep because they dug the waste out every few days. We edged the board in between two walls of the pit and sat over the feces on it for six long hours, not knowing what to do or how to get out.

When the *aktsye* had finished, after the children and the old people were gone, the Jewish women started coming into the latrine to

relieve themselves in the ditch we were in. The excrement was dropping all over us. We screamed and yelled to them for help, but no
one could hear us because we were down so deep. So we dug our
feet into the pit wall, and holding each other up, we used the board
to bang on the floor above our heads. The Jewish women finally heard
our screams and knocking, they yanked the boards out of the floor
and pulled us up. Two children were half-faint from the stench
they'd breathed in during the long hours at the bottom of the pit, and
collapsed. There were now no other children left in the camp—we
were the last four Jewish children of Płaszów.

The women brought us inside their barracks and hid us in the top
bunks. We were separated—each one of us to a different barrack.
The women got one of the Jewish doctors in the camp to come see
us and he gave us shots against cholera—this was all done secretly,
of course. We were hidden inside the four separate barracks for a
week. The women took very good care of us and brought us food.
Finally, the head of the women's camp—Chilewicz's wife—found
out about us and informed the camp commandant, Goeth.[6] This
German said to her that if we four children had the guts to jump into
the waste to save ourselves, then we should be spared and not deported like the other children. This is how we were able to remain in
camp legally. We were the only children there and were really well
taken care of—this was because the thousands of Jewish women who
lost their children to the death camps treated us like their own.

My mother no longer believed I was alive—she again thought I'd
been taken away with the other children when they cleared out the
children's home. Someone who took food to the factory where my
mother was locked up let her know I was alive and that I was still
inside the camp. When my mother heard I'd survived, she went
straight to the factory supervisor and begged him to let me come
to her, to let me work by her side. The supervisor was a German,
Captain Fischer—a decent man. This German gave in to my mother's
pleas and went to the Płaszów Gestapo chief himself to take out a
permit that would let me work in the factory with my mother. Captain Fischer then sent his adjutant, Hilbig—also a German—to bring
me to my mother by auto. My mother had no idea this would happen—she didn't even believe they had really listened to her at all.
But Captain Fischer and his aide were kind—it's because of them
I'm alive. [As the witness recounts this episode, she's noticeably
moved when speaking of the two Hitlerite officers.—I.S.] From then
on, I stayed at the plant with my mother and the others—we worked
together past the summer of 1943.

In the beginning of 1944, all the men were taken out of the plant
and marched back to Płaszów. My father was among those taken
away and I saw him that day for the last time. When my father came

back to Płaszów, he met a friend from Cracow there who was assigned to making out the work schedule in camp. Many Jewish youths
from Hungary, aged fifteen to sixteen, were being brought into the
camp then. My father's friend made him . . . supervisor for the over
200 Hungarian Jewish youths who were used for slave labor and
this was how he got out of doing the work which would have killed
him shortly. [The witness's exact words were: "My father's friend
made him *Kapo*—" but she quickly corrected herself, changing it to
"supervisor."—I.S.]

My father was a quiet and kind person. Having a child himself,
he never goaded these Hungarian Jewish youths to work. The youths
became undisciplined and rebellious. Once, the camp commandant,
Goeth, rode his white horse up to where my father's *Kommando* was
working. He ordered the youths to line up for an *Appel*—he wanted
to take a head count. After he finished counting, it turned out that
two youths were missing. During the *Appel* that same night, my
father got twenty-five lashes across the face with a riding crop.
Goeth, the camp commandant himself, was the one to administer
the whipping. The strokes completely lacerated my father's face and
Goeth forbade anyone at the hospital to treat my father. But being
a pharmacist, my father had many acquaintances who worked at the
hospital—they pilfered the medicaments from there and treated my
father secretly. A few months later—it was in July or August of 1944
—my father was sent to Mauthausen in a transport of many Jews
and he was killed there.

In September of 1944, they liquidated the Media Equipment Plant,
and everyone was taken back to Płaszów. My mother and I were also
returned to the women's camp. The group of 100 women from the
plant was held in Płaszów for six more weeks, then we were transported to Auschwitz. They crammed us into two lorries and the
traveling took all day.

When our group of 100 women were led into Auschwitz, there
was an orchestra playing at the camp entrance. We were taken into
zone C, where the transit camp was. As we passed through the zone,
they shaved the hair off our heads and bodies. Jewish women cut
our hair—*Kapos*—but SS men stood guard. After they shaved us,
we were lined up naked outside. We had to pass in front of a team
of SS, and they were the ones who decided which of us was healthy,
able to work. Most of us were still strong enough, because in the
camp where we worked before, there were food rations given out.
Then, each of the women in the group was given a dress, a pair of
shoes, but no undergarments. We were passed into a barrack where
we just milled around—there was no work here. This was zone C,
the quarantine camp. We were there for six weeks.

We found out that they were planning to send us away to Germany for labor, but this didn't happen, because a typhus epidemic broke out at that time in the Auschwitz camp. This was in summer, 1944. It was November 1944 before they could take us out and bring us to the camp at Gundelsdorf, in Germany. We were shipped in freight cars used for cattle. This voyage lasted a full three weeks. When we finally came into Gundelsdorf, we were immediately dragged off to do the same kind of labor we did at the *Nachrichten Geräte Lager*. Later, about a hundred Jewish men were also transferred to us from the camp at Flossenburg to do the labor. Three women came along with this group, German SS, who were put in charge of guarding our women's *Kommando*. We worked in the camp six days a week, ten hours a day. The same German guards who were in control of us in the last camp by Płaszów, were now also stationed in the factory to watch over us. Besides them, there were now these three female SS supervisors from Flossenburg, and together, they oversaw everything. They didn't beat us—they saved all the torture and beatings for the men. We were also given larger cuts from their rations.

We were in the camp at Gundelsdorf till January or February 1945. One night, they cornered a group of 100 women and led away seventy, leaving the thirty others behind. The men had all been taken out of the camp before. My mother and me were among the thirty women who were left behind in camp. After this, we were made to work for another four weeks, about. When the Americans started bombarding the village, our group of thirty women were rushed off to a truck and taken away to Helmbrechts. There was a big concentration camp there for about 3,000 women. Most of the women were from Poland—there were also Jewish women there from Hungary and Greece. No one did work here.

The American army kept advancing, and the Germans gathered up the whole camp and took us all out on foot—without any of us knowing what our destination would be. The SS men who were pushing us on didn't know either—they were just running with us away from the American artillery barrages. They could only take us along the roads during the daytime—the nights we spent in village stables that we passed on the way. Food was thrown to us once a day. The German guards used to collect burnt potatoes in the villages, and this is what was left for us. This forced march lasted two long months.

On May 2, 1945, we came into a forest near Husinec, which is in Czechoslovakia by the German border. Of the over 3,000 women who had started this march, only 120 women were still left standing on their feet. Most of the women had died along the way from hunger and exhaustion. Many were just shot by the SS men because they couldn't drag their feet another step.

As we walked into the forest near Husinec on the second of May, the SS men ordered all of us to lie face-down on the ground. We were sure they would just shoot us all now. We lay like this with our faces in the ground for long hours into the night. In the darkness, a few women started lifting their heads a little and saw none of the SS who'd been guarding us around. They had run away somewhere while we were all lying facing the ground. It was the middle of the night and we huddled together in the forest.

In the morning, May 3, 1945, we walked out of the forest toward the village of Husinec. The women of our group split up and started going from house to house where the Czechs lived. The Germans had all abandoned the village. The Czechs told us the Americans were coming near. The Czechs brought together all of our women who were wandering around in different places and we were all taken inside a large theater hall. The Czechs started bringing in some food and we all stretched out on the floor to sleep. Doctors started coming in to treat the sick and emaciated women. Of the 120 women who had survived the forced march of 3,000, another forty women died right there that day in Husinec. . . .

[The witness was brought by the Labor Zionist Alliance to America, where she became active in Jewish affairs for the first time. Her social life was spent almost exclusively with other Jewish youth who had survived the war. She was completing a degree in physics when this interview was conducted.]

Eyewitness Testimony 14. Infanticide

M.L. Born in Chełm, Poland, in 1914; lived in Łódź. Recorded by Icek Shmulewitz in New York in November 1954. The witness talks about the situation in Łódź at the outbreak of the war. She describes her escape to Kielce with her husband, then getting trapped inside the Kielce Ghetto. After recounting incidents of persecution by the Polish populace, she continues.

The small Polish boys chased the terrified Jewish women, then jumping around them and pointing straight into their faces, yelled: "Żydówka! Żydówka!" Whenever the Poles came across a Jew outside the ghetto, or discovered a Jewish hiding place on the "Aryan" side, they demanded huge sums of money to keep quiet about it. The Poles were paid consistently over a very long time, but in the end, they always betrayed the Jews who paid them, too.

My husband and child and me were all of us together in the Kielce Ghetto until its liquidation. The first major *aktsye* in the Kielce Ghetto was on August 20, 1942. The second *aktsye* happened a few days later, and the third *aktsye* followed on August 29, 1942.

They completed all three *aktsyes* in just one week and deported all the Jews out of Kielce. A little over 1,000 people—the last group of the transport—were separated from the rest and left behind in the labor camp. The first thing they were made to do was to clear out the ghetto of all the valuables the expelled Jews had to leave behind. When the people were led out of the Kielce Ghetto, they were told they were being sent as laborers and there was no reason to take along bags or trunks which were too heavy, since they'd be given new bags at their destination. But they were told to be sure to take their jewelry because, they were made to understand, there was no point leaving such precious things behind.

Most of the Jews in the Kielce Ghetto knew beforehand that the Germans were deporting them to their deaths. They found out for sure right after the first transport was taken out. Two young men—Moyshe Mydlo and Yosele Vaser—were among those on the first transport. Two days later, they escaped back to the ghetto and told us they'd been inside Treblinka—and what they saw there. As soon as they were inside the camp, the inmates let them know it was an extermination camp. They immediately found somewhere to hide, then jumped into a boxcar full of clothes being taken back out of Treblinka and this was how they got away. There was nowhere for them to hide later, so they had to come back to the Kielce Ghetto. Once inside the ghetto, they started spreading the news of the killing that went on at Treblinka—they described how the Jews of Europe were being annihilated. There were some who took advantage of the fact that no one believed Mydlo and Vaser. A certain Spiegel, a German Jew who was the *Älteste* of the Jewish police in the Kielce Ghetto, expelled these two young escapees from Treblinka out of the ghetto, saying they were spreading panic among the Jews of Kielce.

As I said before, the Kielce Ghetto was liquidated on the twenty-ninth of August, 1942. My sister—she also came to me from Łódź—was deported to her death that day, too. Me, my husband and child—we were in the group of 1,200 people left behind from the ghetto to start a labor camp with.

Once the labor camp was operating and there was no more ghetto, the Germans deceived the *Yidnrat Älteste*, Herman Lewi, and murdered him by great treachery. He and his whole family, together with all the other councilmen—a group of over twenty people—were taken out to the *besoylim,* to the cemetery. They were ordered to dig a large open pit and the Hitlerites shot every last one of them separately. Each one had to witness the shooting of the one before. Herman Lewi was the last one shot. He was sure the Hitlerites would spare him after shooting all the others. He begged and begged them to let him live, but it did no good.

When the camp of the remnant of the Jews on Jasna Street started functioning, the Hitlerites came in to announce that anyone wanting to go to Palestine could. They took down exact information from everyone on how much family they had in Palestine and it looked like we would soon leave. Most of the people registered then—they had some relatives in *Erits Yisrul*—and we felt certain we would all get out. My husband and child and me also signed up to go because we have family in Israel. But the Germans just laughed at us afterwards and humiliated us.

We did every kind of labor at the camp, but we worked mostly at the lumber mills located on Zagnańska, Odrzeja, Jasna Streets and other places. Purim, 1944, an *aktsye* was carried out in the camp against the Jewish doctors and nurses and their families. A truck pulled up and they were all loaded on. They were told to bring along their medical instruments as well as bedding and clothes because they were just being transferred somewhere else. This group of Jewish doctors and nurses, together with their families, numbered sixty-six people. The truck brought them to a field in Pakosz, not far from the Jewish cemetery, where they were blown apart with hand grenades. Before these sixty-six people were herded into one spot to be executed, they were stripped naked—the Germans thought it a shame to waste the clothes the Jews were wearing, they didn't want the clothes getting all bloody and torn from the shrapnel.

Poles living in the area described to us later how the group of Jewish doctors and nurses was obliterated. The Poles said the Germans had an extremely hard time trying to kill the doctors' and nurses' children. The children wouldn't stay in one place—they ran all over the cemetery—and as they ran, the Germans pelted the "moving targets" with hand grenades and massacred them all. The Germans left one Jewish doctor alive in the labor camp—Dr. Reiter— and also a nurse—Proszowska. These two ultimately suffered the same fate the rest of the Kielce Jews did. Dr. Reiter died right after the war. The nurse Proszowska died at the hands of the Poles in the Kielce pogrom a year after the war, in July of 1946.

Still earlier, in May of 1943, the Hitlerites murdered all the other children of the labor camp. This happened on May 29, 1943—the day my child, too, was killed. That day, the Hitlerites and their Ukrainian henchmen stormed into the camp and grabbed every child to the age of fourteen—babies, too. The heartbreaking scenes of tearing infants from their mothers and not letting children say good- bye to their parents will remain with me forever. At the same time, the Germans were grabbing a group of old and chronically ill people who were in the camp with us. They led out about forty children and the parents weren't told what they planned doing to them. The Germans said the children were being taken to Germany where they'd be put under proper supervision. My little boy, who was then three years and three months old, was among the children they took away.

In the morning, when we got to the Henryków lumber mill for work, the Poles who were working there told us what happened to the forty Jewish children who were led away. They described the scene of the children being taken inside the cemetery and blown up by hand grenades. They said it was the most gruesome butchery imaginable. When the Germans got the children between the walls of the cemetery, the Poles said, the children knew right away what the Hitlerites were going to do. The children started scattering in different directions and the Nazis couldn't get them into one spot. In the end, the Germans cornered them. They chased and hounded them from one place to the other for a very long time, till the Jewish children were now all pinned into a corner of the *besoylim,* trapped between two walls with nowhere left to run. They were inched back tighter and tighter into the corner by the German soldiers and their Ukranian underlings who blocked them off on all sides. Then the Germans bombarded the children with hand grenades and tore them apart.

We were locked up inside the Henryków labor camp with 500 other Jews. We stayed in wooden barracks and worked in the lumberyard. We worked alongside the Poles who were there as regular laborers—they got paid and returned home at night. We Jews were given a piece of bread and a little soup for the work we did.

The warehouse was right next to the barracks we were in. There was also a small shed there for disinfecting the clothes, cleaning and polishing the work tools, motors, and similar things. Once, in the middle of the night—this was the winter of 1943—the warehouse with the finished wood products was set on fire. The flames raged out of control. Soon, they spread to the factory. The fire had been started in the disinfecting shed. We were sure, that night, that we would all be led out and shot. This disinfecting room was run by a young Kielce Jew, Yankl Zylberberg. He had set the disinfecting-machine meter at too high a temperature and it exploded, causing the fire. In the morning, the Germans removed Zylberberg, put him in detention, and kept him there several weeks, torturing him unspeakably all that time. They beat and whipped him, trying to make him name the person who had got him to burn the factory down. This young man, Zylberberg, denied without letup that anyone had put him up to it, and protesting his innocence, admitted he'd probably been careless and set the machine's temperature wrong.

Then, we were called out to an *Appel.* When we got outside, we saw a gallows in front of us. Immediately, a car with Yankl Zylberberg inside pulled up. He was ashen-faced and numb with terror. Some Germans held a quick mock trial out in front of the gallows so that all the assembled Jews would hear the charges. The sentence was then read aloud, condemning him to death for sabotage. Suddenly, Zylberberg yelled out: "I'm innocent!" While he was screaming, a German kicked him in the groin till he doubled over. Zylberberg then called out these words to all the people: "Jews! Avenge my young blood!"

A close friend of Zylberberg's was forced to tie the noose around his neck—that was the German order. As the friend got up on the stool to try and work the rope, he broke down in tears and Zylberberg said to him: "Don't cry. You're not to blame."

On August 1, 1944, the few hundred Jews left in our camp were lined up, then transported to Auschwitz. The same transport collected the Jews from the other subcamps in Kielce, and also a large group of Jews from Skarżysko[1] who were loaded onto our transport when the train passed through that *shtetl*. We came into Auschwitz the next morning.

After they pulled us from the wagons, the transport was divided up, with men to one side and women to the other. I was torn away from my husband that day and never saw him again. As soon as we were inside Auschwitz, we saw the huge chimney shooting black smoke into the air. The people, suffering from total exhaustion, stumbled around, covered with tattered, filthy rags—they seemed completely crazed to us. Our transport was mobbed on its arrival in Auschwitz by the Jews from Kielce who'd been deported before us. The people came to the platform because they were wild with worry about what had happened to their loved ones all this time. But we tried to make them tell us what was being done to our people here in this camp they'd brought us to—Auschwitz. Khayim Poslushni, the well-known *Poyleh Tsiyin* Left activist from Kielce—he's in Israel now—was also among the Kielce Jews who surrounded our transport. When we asked him what they were planning on doing to us in this camp, Poslushni answered: "You'll need luck—the chimneys are smoking."

Khayim Poslushni then told us to drop the packs we'd brought with us, to leave them behind in the wagons and not drag them around after us because soon they'd be taken away from us anyway.

I was then put into Block 18, right next to the camp of the Czech Jews. I did all kinds of totally useless labor the Hitlerites thought up to torture and exhaust us. I hauled bricks and rocks from one spot to another together with the other women. The horrors of the camp *Appele*—you can't imagine them. We're driven from the bunks in the middle of the night or before daybreak and have to stand naked out in the rain and snow. While the *Appel* goes on, they beat us and hound us without letup. I can still see the many Jewish women breaking away and running at the high-tension wires, then throwing themselves against them—this was how they committed suicide.

How we envied those women then—they had the courage to do it! [At this point, the witness murmurs to herself almost uncontrollably about the horrors of those days.—I.S.]

In the beginning of 1944, they transported me along with a group of Jewish women—almost all of us were from Kielce and Radom—to Ravensbrück. There were 1,200 of us on this transport. We were carried in cattle cars.

When we got to Ravensbrück, they put us into the *Transportenblock* where people were held till transfers were arranged out of the camp. We didn't work here, but they never stopped torturing us anyway. One time, a German civilian came to us, stripped us naked and examined us—poking and tapping us all over our bodies—then he selected out those who could still work. A transport was immediately drawn up—I was also included—and we were sent to Malchow-Mecklenburg,[2] in Germany. There were 800 Jewish women in this transport.

At Malchow, the transport was unloaded inside a camp for Russian and German women prisoners—there were also many Jewish woman deportees from Hungary working here. We slaved in local munitions works housed in bunkers deep in the forest. Each day, we were marched to the bunker labor sites from the camp over long distances, suffering the whole time from starvation and frost. German guards held dogs to us on every march.

Even though the torture was intensified in the camp at Malchow-Mecklenburg, we endured and knew, somehow, that the war was coming to an end. I don't remember how, but we also heard President Roosevelt was dead. Along all the ways we marched from the camp into the woods and to the bunkers, swarms of German refugees, evacuees, stricken with fear, ran in the opposite direction. The German women, too—the overseers of our camp—now seemed desperate and lost, they couldn't terrorize us now like before. We knew the war was ending, but we didn't believe we'd live to see it. I also remember how one of the German officers, a high-ranking chief in the camp, had Jewish women sew him a civilian suit overnight, and he ran away from the camp dressed in these civilian clothes.

On April 20, 1945, the camp for French prisoners, which wasn't far from our camp, was inspected by a commission of the Swedish Red Cross. The French told this Swedish Commission that our women's camp was nearby. On a certain morning, as we were getting up for the *Appel* before the march to the woods, we saw through the wires that white cars with the Swedish Red Cross Commission—most of them were men—were driving up to the camp entrance. As soon as they drove in, they exchanged some words with the *Lagerführer*, then asked for a list to be made up of certain women in the camp—only the Polish women, and those Jewish women, who came from

Poland. We felt then that something good was happening right before our eyes, a change, but we didn't know what. We didn't sleep that night but watched through the wires from the barracks, looking out to where the white cars of the Swedish Commission stood.

In the morning, we were chased out to the *Appel*, but with more brutality than usual. The Germans confiscated all the bread we were holding and we were sure then they were going to lead us off for execution. The Jewish women from Hungary hadn't been included on the list with the Polish women and the Jewish women from Poland, and for this reason, they felt very sorry for us. We, too, felt like they did—we were the ones who were going to die. The *Appel* dragged on while the German women, the overseers, beat us without pity. We felt they were trying to get back at us for something—they yelled as they beat us that we'd soon be better off than they were. [The witness now explains, as an aside, that the Jewish women were so hardened by then, so resigned to expecting the worst, that they gave up all hope of staying alive.—I.S.]

We were marched through the gates, loaded onto waiting trucks, and driven toward an unknown destination. The drivers on the trucks were Canadian soldiers, if I'm not mistaken. After a long time, we found out from the members of the commission and these drivers that they were taking us to Sweden.

We were let off in Copenhagen, which was under Nazi occupation, but we were received well. A special commission of the Danish Red Cross greeted us on our arrival. They gave us adequate food, new clothing—we almost lost our minds from all this sudden attention. We were in Copenhagen for just one day. They loaded us into a ship and took us to Malmö, Sweden. We were very warmly greeted here, too. Our transport was processed by a special commission which handed every woman new clothes and good food as we passed through. The ailing women of the transport were taken into the hospitals and the healthy women were brought to Doverstop. It was like a fairy-tale village in breathtaking mountain scenery—we were wined and dined here on the very best.

In July of 1945, I began working as a nurse at the hospital in Malmö. I was assigned to the respiratory section. While working there, I met a patient, also a homeless Jew, who was brought to Sweden after Liberation. His name was A—— L——, *A Lodzher,* and we became good friends. When he was released from the hospital, we married. We were married in February 1947.

The whole time I was in Malmö, I also worked as a nurse in a children's hospital and my husband worked as a salesclerk in a store selling military uniforms. On March 15, 1951, a girl was born to us in Malmö. In December of 1951, we emigrated from Sweden to America as DP's. We came with the ship *Gripsholm* and arrived in

New York harbor on January 10, 1952. My husband's been working this whole time in a sports jacket factory, and we manage all right. We have a nice three-room apartment with all the conveniences. We read the *Post*, and from time to time, go to a show.

Eyewitness Testimony 15. Religion and the Instincts

M.G. Born in Strzemieszyce, Galicia, in 1915; lived in Brody, Tarnopol District. Recorded by Icek Shmulewitz in New York in 1954. The witness recounts her experiences at the beginning of the war in Brody, and then under Soviet occupation. She describes her escape to the "Aryan" side of Lemberg (Lwów), and continues.

My husband was dragged from the house and later killed with the other Jews. He was taken to a death camp.

My sister and I were left alone in the house, because in the beginning, the Nazis only took the men. They were all lined up, and, for a short while, held inside the same Polish school where the Jewish children had been kept before. Later, a Jewish woman told me that if I had pointed out my husband to her earlier, she could have saved him. She used to take food into the school—she would have dressed my husband like a woman cook, she said, and got him out of there.

In a few days, an *aktsye* was started against the Jewish women.[1] I was working under an assumed identity as a housekeeper, and the Germans left us alone, not checking our papers yet. Jews who were starving would come to my house and I helped them and gave them food. At that time, every Jew had to wear a white armband with a *mugen duvid,* but I didn't wear this band because I was passing for a Christian. My looks helped me in this. I just walked into the stores and did the shopping. I managed to get hold of an *Arbeitsschein* for my sister, which cost a lot of money, and she wasn't taken yet either. Housekeepers and women with permits who did "useful" work were spared at this stage of the war.[2]

After a while, I started dealing in forged ration cards. I risked my life, went into the stores to get produce with the cards, then sold it later. I bought these forged German ration cards from Poles. I knew about a Polish resistance organization in Cracow which was issuing these forged ration cards during that time. They were sold in many cities all over Poland and brought in lots of money the Poles used in their underground work. Poles also traveled from Cracow to Lemberg [Lwów], bringing the cards along to sell. At first, I bought them second- and thirdhand. Later, I got them firsthand from a Pole who came from Cracow and only sold these cards to the most trusted people. My contact was a former judge from Cracow, a Pole.

There were three other Jews dealing in these forged ration cards in Lemberg, also under assumed names and posing as Poles. I only found out after the war that they were Jewish. One of them was from Vienna, a former newspaper editor. . . . Though I kept risking my life. I later made lots of money from these transactions and kept on giving the hungry Jews free food.

Then, at the end of 1941, they started an *aktsye* against the Jewish women housekeepers, too. The *aktsye* was begun on this side of the bridge—where my sister and I lived—but on the other side, the *aktsye* was already over. My sister was in hiding then and I begged God, I prayed for Him to help me.

Suddenly, I felt this impulse. It happened while the Gestapo were poking their snouts into everyone's face, checking to see who was Jewish and who not. There was one of them standing at every step of the way. I took a deep breath and strutted across the road, walking on to the trolley stop at the corner of Zamarstynowska. With my heart pounding wildly, I waited for the streetcar to come and pleaded all the while that the *Aybershter* save me. The Gestapo came up to me, stared into my face, but *Hashem-yisburekh* dropped a veil over their eyes. The streetcar came along, I climbed in and rode over the bridge to the other side where the *aktsye* was through. Since my sister had papers proving she could work, she was in less danger.

After we were across the bridge, I took a second streetcar into the crowded Gentile section where hardly any Jews could be found. I got off at Zamojski Street but had nowhere to turn. I stood there stopping Poles on the street to find out if anyone knew of a room for rent. The Poles took me for one of them and gave me the address of an eighty-six-year-old Polish woman who had a room at Zamojski 18. I went there and met the old woman, who was named Kaminska. She rented me a room in her flat, thinking, of course, I was Polish.

A Jewish committee was set up in Lemberg around then, but I don't remember if it was called the *Yidnrat*. A man named Rokeach,[3] a Lemberger, was on this committee and he put me in contact with a Pole, who was supervisor over the building I lived in, and also other houses. This Pole knew I was Jewish. He had me registered and got me a pass under the name "Marja Lipska, Pole." I was also able to have my sister brought to where I was staying, and the same Polish supervisor also made her out a forged document which gave her name as "Różanska." Later, after I paid him some money, he also made me out some papers with the same name. He got me a *Kenn-karte*, bringing it from Warsaw. Afterwards, I started dealing forged ration cards to this supervisor. He got my sister a *Kennkarte*, too. All this time, I had a feeling that the supervisor, with his connections on the Jewish committee and the way he had us registered and got us documents, was a Jew disguising himself as a Pole.

But later, I had strong suspicions that he was the one who had betrayed us to the blackmailers who extorted all our money and threatened to denounce us to the Germans. I'll speak about them soon. . . .

At the beginning of 1942, a Pole came to my room and said he was sent by the Gestapo and I should follow him. That's when I felt that this Pole had been sent by the supervisor who had once helped us.

No one besides the supervisor knew I was a Jew. I took out a large bundle of notes and gave them to the Pole, who started counting them up. My sister who lived with me—my other sister and brother who stayed behind in Brody were killed—was in the other room. When the Pole finished counting, he said it wasn't enough, to give him more. I got him to agree to pick up the rest of the money at another spot. It was then I knew for sure he wasn't a Gestapo agent but a plain extortionist. A second woman—she was Polish, too— would block my way at the entrance to the building and demand money. The Pole kept coming after me and demanding money. I saw that it was hopeless, that all this would come to a bad end, so I abandoned the flat together with my sister.

I put a notice in the papers saying I was looking for a place to stay, without mentioning my name—I was afraid the same Pole would come around to blackmail me. During this period, a lot of Poles were taking in Jews under assumed names. First they took all their money, then they denounced them to the Gestapo and stole everything that was left behind. Because of this, there was nothing but empty rooms wherever I looked. The papers were barraged with offers from "willing" landlords. I picked out a boarding house on Ossolinskich 13 and went there. I rented a room from a family—a husband and wife with a small child—named Mikosinski. The husband was a printer. There were two entrances to my room through two separate doors. One opened up onto the hall and led out to the courtyard, and the other adjoined the Gentile family's flat. Naturally, the family thought I was a Pole. This was midsummer, 1942.

I wanted my sister to come stay in my room but I was afraid for her—she was a classic Jewish beauty. She had big, round, dark eyes, long black hair, and a strong nose. I dyed my sister's hair blond so she'd be able to walk through the streets. Then I got her into my room secretly through the hallway entrance and the Gentile family didn't know she was staying with me. I told my sister straight away: "I've brought you to this hiding place but I don't know if this can save you." I hid my sister in my room for two years and she never left it once all that time. During the day she hid out in a closet and at night she slept in the bed with me. I brought her everything she needed. Every time I left the room, I locked the door facing the Polish family's flat, locked the door leading out into the hall, and left the other key inside so the family wouldn't be able to get in. They let me have the room for two years.

I've been religious from my early childhood. I kept it up even during the war when I faced death every moment. I ate no meat, didn't ride on *Shabbes,* and things like that.

I had to support the Polish family I was staying with by giving them food and other things. I had to, because I couldn't register. I'd left my old room and didn't want anybody following me. The Gentile family knew this but they figured—they told me this time and time again—that since I was a Pole, the Hitlerites had probably tried to get me into a labor battalion headed for Germany, and because I lived with them, I was able to get out of it. So I pretended it was true and had to pay them back with food. I kept on earning money through the forged ration cards, getting provisions from the German storehouses and giving the family a cut.

Once, I was in the marketplace near the coal stalls buying cheese and eggs and things like that. A Polish woman came up to me and told me to follow her to her flat where she'd sell me produce cheaper than at the market. I went to this woman a couple of times—she did her smuggling on Sloneczna Street—and bought food from her.

One time, as I walked into her room, I was confronted by a Ukrainian militiaman who sat at the table with a dog by his side. She said right away she had nothing to sell me. I didn't lose my head because of the militiaman but acted as I always did when I came to see her. I knew then that she'd betrayed me. The dog pounced on me and snorted at my handbag. The militiaman said it was a bad sign, the dog sniffing at my bag like that. He wants to see what I've got inside. I opened my bag but the militiaman found nothing there. Then he asked me for my papers. I had my forged document on me, the *Kennkarte,* but I told him I hadn't brought it with me. I suggested he follow me home and I'd show him the papers. I figured that once I got him away from the *goyeh,* I would bribe him. There was another reason I couldn't show him my papers: the Hitlerites were stamping all official documents at that time with small swastikas. You could only make the stamp out with a magnifying glass and the Hitlerites were masters at detecting fake swastikas. There was no proper stamp on my forged papers and this would have given me away immediately.

The militiaman said my idea was out of the question and I had to come with him. I started begging him to let me go. I motioned to the Polish woman to leave the room. Once she was gone, I gave the Ukrainian money and a large-stoned ring my husband had given me when I became a *kahle.* I always kept the ring with me so that in case of danger I could buy my release. He grabbed the money and the ring, then ordered me to come with him. He told me to walk ahead, he'd be two steps behind, and if I tried to run, he'd shoot me.

While we were walking like this, I again tried pleading with the militiaman to let me go, to give me a chance to escape. I offered him huge sums of money I didn't even have. The militiaman said he'd never do a favor for a Jew—he couldn't stand 'em!

I prayed all the while I was walking ahead of the militiaman. I said the words of the *payrik* in *Tilim,* "*Ashre yoshvi vayseykhu,*"[4] which I knew by heart, and pleaded silently: "Father mine in heaven, he thinks I've fallen into his hands, but only Your strength holds me. Help me. Whatever I do, whatever I say, make it turn out for the best." [The witness cries as she repeats these words.—I.S.]

The Ukrainian took me to the precinct on Lyczakowski Street. As soon as we were inside, he took out the money and ring I'd given him, laid them on the table, and reported that I'd tried to bribe him. An officer came in and asked who I was. To this I replied I was a Jew. I did this to save my sister who was back in my room, hiding. I knew they already found out I was Jewish, so if I denied it they'd start interrogating me, take me back and search my room, and then they'd also find my sister.

When I told the officer I was a Jew, he said in Ukrainian: "Look at the courage of this Jewess! The city's *judenrein,* and she walks around without an armband!"

That was when I got the impulse to make up a story and I don't know where it came from. I heard myself saying that my mother was a Gentile, and my father was a Jew. My mother worked as a maid for my father—I really did say this—they lived together, and I'm the result of their union. "Why should I be blamed for my mother's sin?'" I demanded of the officer.

Then he asked me right away if my mother had married my father legally. To this I answered no. I was put in a solitary cell in the detention center. During the night, the same militiaman to whom I'd given up so much money came to the cell and let me out without a penny fine. He also gave me back the ring and the money I gave him.

After Liberation, I ran into the Jewish editor from Vienna who had passed for an "Aryan" and helped me spread the forged ration cards. . . . He explained to me then for the first time why it was they released me, even though I admitted I was part Jewish. I'll get to this soon.

It turned out he had been issued forged documents by the Viennese Jewish *Kehileh* saying he was German. He was sent to Germany and employed by the Gestapo, and this way was able to save many Jews. When he felt his cover was in danger of being exposed, that the "earth was burning under his feet," he ran away to Lemberg, where he lived on the "Aryan" side as a Pole.

He told me he heard that the Germans had a law: if one of the parents was Gentile, their child was considered a *Halb-Jude,* and if such mixed parents hadn't legally married, then their issue was a

Viertel-Jude and three-quarters Gentile. [After what I told them], they considered me three-quarters Gentile and let me off.

But I'm convinced that *Der Aybershter* put it into my head to say what I did, because I had no idea then there was any such law. It pained me to offend the radiant memory of my mother, who was a strictly observant Jewish woman all her life. But I behaved at that moment by the dictates of my instincts.

I lived with the Polish family under my assumed name a while longer. My sister hid in the closet the whole time we stayed in that room.

In May or June of 1944, the Soviet army started its bombardment of Lemberg. We lived across the way from the municipal military headquarters, and there was an antiaircraft gun on a nearby hill. Our neighborhood was flattened. Three bombs exploded right by our building. My sister and I lived on the third floor and there were 104 tenants altogether in the building. When the bombings started, the tenants ran down to the cellar, but I couldn't go down there with my sister because I was afraid the Poles would be able to tell she was Jewish, and then I'd be exposed, too. Besides, our building was packed with Gestapo, who also ran for the cellar when the bombings started.

I finally had no choice—the bombings were devastating—and my sister and I also went down to the cellar, just like the others. By the way, this was just before the war ended. When the *goyeh* in whose flat I was staying spotted me with my sister, she knew right away my sister was a Jew and the woman finally realized I was Jewish. This Polish woman then said to me that a Jewish family had offered her a fortune to hide their child but she refused because she, too, had a child and didn't want to risk its death. "And since it was God's will" the Polish woman said to me, "I hid the both of you for nothing."

This was how—by running down there and hiding in the cellar with the others—my sister and I survived the war, how I was able to stay alive with the help of *zayn libn numin*. Me and my sister— who's observant, too—fasted every Monday and Thursday for as long as the war lasted.

After the war ended, we stayed on in Lemberg till May 1945. . . .

As a testament to my surviving the war because of God's help, I now help out handicapped religious boys in Brooklyn. . . .

Eyewitness Testimony 16. The Polish Nobility and Clergy

S.F. Born in Warsaw in 1912; lived there until September 1944; was inside the ghetto until April 1943. Recorded by Yankiv Fishman in New York in 1954. The witness describes her life on a labor gang of

Poles and Jews working in the fields of a requisitioned manor near Warsaw. She was separated from the group just prior to the outbreak of the ghetto uprising when the Jewish farm laborers were deported by the Gestapo. She talks now of this scene.

The Gestapo squad called to the lord of the manor to come out. Fijalkowski appeared and they pounced on him like wolves, slapping him and screaming: *"Juden seinen bei dir!"*[1] It was no use when he protested that the German authorities had given permission. They beat him up so bad all his teeth came flying out of his mouth. Next, they ordered all the Jews to come out with their hands up. They were all marched off to a waiting truck and beaten and humiliated without mercy. I ran straight into Lady Fijalkowska's chamber, crying to her that I was finished. She led me down into the cellar and told me to wait there until they'd gone. But a Polish policeman broke into the house yelling: *"Gdzie jest Żydówka?!"*[2] I was told there's a Jewess in here!" The lady couldn't talk him out of it. He ran down to the cellar and found me right away. He dragged me up to the ground floor. I kept crying and kissing his hands: "Tell them no one's here! Give me a second and I'll be far away!" He did. He must have been an angel of some kind. He let go of me and in an instant, I flew through the back door and out of the house. When the truck was gone, I went back into the lady's chamber. She wouldn't let me stay. She herself was still trembling from what had just happened. I knew I had to go now. I left the estate and walked through an open ditch by the side of the road. I stayed down there till morning.

As the sun was coming up, I fell into a panic. I knew no way of escaping my horrid fate. I went back to Lady Fijalkowska again. I clung to her, crying and pleading for her to save me. Her answer was telling me there was no reason to panic—I didn't look "too much" like a Jew. She talked me into going to the nearby monastery and asking for sanctuary from the father, Edward Wojtczak. He was supposed to be a kind man and a friend to the Jews. I went. What else could I do? A sister answered my ring and asked what it was I wanted. I told her I had to see the father. She didn't say anything— just looked me up and down as if trying to figure out who I was. She told me to wait. A long time passed. The father himself came out to see me. A tall man, gray-haired—he looked about sixty—with a kind face. I started crying and said I was a Jewish daughter. I took out my purse with the little money I had left and some jewelry I always carried with me for whenever I had to buy my way out of getting killed. I told him I would give it all away to the sick people in his infirmary. The priest looked at me with understanding and said: "I don't need it. You might have to use it someday. Where will you go now? It's night already." He took me inside the monastery. I felt lost in this darkness. There were only small candles flickering over the heads of the marble and bronze icons. It was all horrifying. I sank quickly into a sleep.

At five in the morning, the priest came to me. He took me to his cell, gave me some food. I was beginning to feel that my fate was changing. He told me that in two hours, his real sister was coming here to talk things over with me. It was true—she really came. A nearsighted woman, she stared straight into my eyes as we stood nose to nose. She was simply radiant with kindness. She kissed me and calmed me down. I offered her my little bag with all my possessions.

"I'll only hide it for you. Hitler won't be around forever," she said.

She combed out my hair so I'd look like a Gentile girl. She changed my clothes. She took me with her. We got on a trolley and she took me to Pulawska Street, to her unmarried sister. This sister was caring for a Jewish child—a girl of about two. Such a beautiful and wonderful child you've never seen. The child treated her like a mother and she simply cherished the little girl.

"And you say," she says to me, "that I'm a cousin of yours."

The priest's sister had a buttons-and-notions shop downstairs. I stayed in her flat and sometimes I came down to help out. My Polish was perfect.

Soon, Germans came and took over the store, letting only *Volksdeutsche* run it. I happened to be there that day. You can imagine how scared to death I was. After that, I never left the room. That's right. I made it too obvious when I ran back to the room like that—but I was so scared.

The priest came. He comforted me. "Don't worry," he said. He told me to go back inside the monastery and to stay there till he got me papers and a job. I was now back inside the cloister. I learned all their prayers and the group recitativs the nuns sang.

The priest went to see Fijalkowski—the lord of the manor where I worked on the labor gang. It turned out they were very well acquainted and he brought me back the *Kennkarte* of a real Gentile girl—Zofia Rychlinska of Białystok who had just died in the Warsaw Hospital. The father accompanied me—I was supposed to be a simple farm girl now—to the Gestapo, to have me registered. The Gestapo were completely cynical. They stared at me maliciously— they knew perfectly well who I really was—but since a Catholic priest had come along, they didn't feel like starting the investigation.

So now I had the identity card of an "Aryan" Christian girl and my name isn't S—— V—— anymore, it's Zofia Rychlinska. I keep attending the services in the convent and sing along with the nuns.

The priest did me more favors. He got me a job with Dr. Newiadomski on Marszałkowska 87—a completely Gentile street—and I worked for a Gentile family. The priest had mentioned me to the

doctor a few times. The father didn't want to take on another person
in times like these! The doctor finally agreed.

I got along in Dr. Newiadomski's house. Sleep, food, and a couple
of *zloty* a week. I helped take care of his house, and also his office.

The father also arranged a marriage for me. I told him I would
only take a mate after the war. Not now. I was feeling secure. I
recognized Jews on Marszalkowska Street. I begged God they would
survive all this. The doctor had two sons—young men—students at
the University. The doctor's whole family was involved in the Polish
Underground. I could tell this easily from their conversations. They
didn't keep their guard up with me. After all, I was Father Wojtczak's
protégé. But despite all this, they were all—especially the two
younger sons—rabid anti-Semites. They always toasted each other
at Hitler's "accomplishment" of ridding Poland of its Jews. Poland
was now *judenrein*. I wanted to scream out but couldn't—it was
really, really hard suppressing my hatred of them.

Comes a day, the doctor gives me some money to get something
at the store on the ground level. The regular servant girl was busy,
or she was sick. I went down. While I was inside the store, I noticed
a civilian standing outside and staring hard at me. He didn't move
the whole time. This could only mean he was waiting for me—he
must know I'm a Jew. I panicked. There was no back door to the
shop. I got up all my courage, and in a second, while the suspicious
man was turning away, I rushed right past him—but not back inside
the building. I ran around the corner to Wilcza Street, which had an
alleyway with an entrance to the doctor's building. I was overcome.
I felt for sure the man had seen me turn into Wilcza Street. It was
all too much for me and I was expecting the worst. The window of
the room where I slept faced out on Wilcza Street. During the night,
I lay in bed staring at the building across the way and listening like
a madwoman for any footsteps in the hall. Suddenly—a great tragedy.
I saw the building across the way light up from top to bottom. There
were megaphone announcements and alarms and sirens going off,
and sounds of beatings and tortures. I hear loud screams and crying.
Every window is lit up. It seemed to go on forever. And then everything went dark and quiet. In the morning, the neighbors told me that
during the night the Gestapo had looked for a Jewish girl in the
building across the way but couldn't find her. "How do you like
that?!" they said to me. This was in February of 1944.

Three weeks later, I was in the priest's cell and Fijalkowski walked
in. He was as pale as the wall. He didn't say anything. I got scared—
something must be wrong. He was the one who got me the identity
card. I tried to keep up appearances and say something pleasant. But
he was lifeless. The next day, I had to go back to the priest to find
out what was going on and again, I met Fijalkowski. I tried sound-

ing cheerful: "How can such a rich lord find the time to spend two whole days at a priest's side?" I teased him. Then, it suddenly dawned on me that he was hiding out here, and it was because of me. His caretaker had denounced him to the Gestapo for giving the identity card of his servant girl, Zofia Rychlinska, to a Jew. The Gestapo rushed over to Fijalkowski's estate, found the place abandoned because he'd escaped through a back door, so they beat up his father and mother and arrested his wife and children. It was like this for many sad days until the priest was able—for a huge sum of money and through personal contacts—to free Fijalkowski's family and have the whole matter disposed of.

Another time, the doctor gets a telephone call: "Tonight, your neighborhood'll be a meeting ground for 'doctors.' "[3] He had to leave the house. We were terrified. And what if they came and picked me out to check up on? I told the doctor's wife I was going to the priest and would be right back. I didn't go to the priest. I went to a Gentile woman friend who used to bring the milk around to the doctor's every day. I told her I had nowhere to sleep that night. She said right away I could sleep there—and gladly. We both slept in the same bed. We talked on into the middle of the night. The woman left the bed to turn down the gas, but she must have left it on a little. I couldn't fall asleep. I kept thinking of what might be happening at the doctor's house. My head was hurting. Then my friend started groaning "O Jezus, O Jezus," and suddenly, she dropped from the bed like a stone, with a loud thud. I revived her. I turned on the gas. The whole room filled up with gas fumes. In the morning, when I came back to the doctor's, he looked at me angrily and wanted to know where I had spent the night. "You look simply awful, Zofia, simply awful." I made up a story that I was feeling ill so I slept over at a friend's house. The doctor gave me some pills.

By now, it was November 1944.[4] The Germans picked up young Poles on the street and arrested them. The doctor's wife sent me down to buy some things, but the street was unsafe. The stores were locking up. The streetcars stopped running, stopping still midway on their routes. I ran home, scared out of my mind. I described to the doctor what was happening in the streets. He tried convincing me it was nothing. That wasn't shooting—it was only thunder. But I felt that what was going on in the streets was like a revolution. The Poles in our neighborhood started leaving their buildings with guns. Armed Polish lookout men were positioned by every building. There was an uproar —the uprising had begun! Poles lead captured Germans away. Our side of Marszałkowska, the odd side, belongs to the Poles—the other side, to the Germans. I'm drawn into the fighting. I stand guard over German prisoners. Germans are slaughtered by Poles. But the Germans eventually win. The rebels had to surrender on Poznańska

Street. They had to cover their heads with white handkerchiefs. I surrendered then, too. They loaded us onto trucks and took us to Pruszków.[5] I spent over two days in Pruszków, lying in a field. There was nothing to eat. From there, I was taken to Lehrte, in Germany. This was only a transit camp. Our heads were shaved here. We were given slips of paper with the kind of *Kommandos* we were assigned to. A Ukrainian asked me if I preferred working with chocolates or with iron. I answered chocolates. We were led off to Grossleben[6] and lowered into salt mines. It was a cruel trick when I saw we also had to make bombs here. It pained me terribly to do this kind of work. I had also never imagined that women would be given such hard labor. I slaved to total exhaustion and was starving to death. Wherever I worked, there were only women, thousands of women—also Ukrainian and Russian women. They were our oldest enemies and the most vicious anti-Semites. Enemies to the Poles, too. They beat us and cursed us and humiliated us. They were ideal partners for the Germans.

It happened that once, at night, a woman in the bunk on top of me dropped some straw on me. I lost my temper at her but she let fly such curses that I got hot and cold all over: "Stuff it, stinkin' Jewess." Two days before, a German had threatened that if there were any Jews among us and we didn't turn them over immediately, we'd all be exterminated. I felt I was beginning to swoon. I broke out in a cold sweat. I didn't sleep at all that night, barely survived till morning. I was the first one into the latrines so I could meet the woman and beg her not to cause my death. But as soon as she saw me, she waved me away with her hand: "Just don't you worry yourself." But she knew I was a Jew, and all the other women had heard about it, too. The women I shared the bunks with now made life unbearable for me, but they didn't denounce me. I couldn't endure my fear anymore. This nightmare of suffering went on for a year, but I still held on.

Everyone started saying this was going to end with our being shot. We had heard, more or less, that the Germans were capitulating, that these were the final days of the war. By now, many Russians and Ukrainians had run away. A German then gave the order that anyone found escaping would be shot. The breakouts came often, and they were large-scale. People were really escaping! We heard the Americans were positioned right near the camp. My fear was so strong— what if I didn't survive these final minutes before Liberation? I didn't know what to do. The camp commandant, a German, is running around screaming at us not to dare escape. In the morning, they brought us into the Targemund Forest. I saw with my own eyes how the Germans were burning our mutilated brothers—they were half-dead but some were still very much alive. My blood ran cold. The camp commandant—the old camp commandant—orders us to hang out a white kerchief, to surrender only to the Americans. None of the Polish women would do this—let him do it himself! And he did. He hung out the white flag. Then he disappeared from sight. There were no more camp commandants. The Americans rolled their tanks into the camp. All of a sudden, an American yells to me: "You're Jewish?! You look like a *yidishe*, come here!" He talked half English, half Yiddish. I was completely disoriented. I didn't know who or where I was. It took a long time before I could walk over to him, and with tears in my eyes, I told him I was Jewish. I drove ahead with them into the village of Lehrte and spend two weeks in a hospital here. From here, I left for Warsaw. I met my husband, D—— F——, there, and we married.

Eyewitness Testimony 17. From Deception to Rescue

Kh. K. Born in Zarżyn,[1] Galicia in 1913; lived there. Recorded by B. Frenkel in a DP Camp in 1946.

During the registration, the *selektsye*, I was taken out of the line of workers and told to go left—meaning they had condemned me to die and I would never leave this place alive. Anyone who dared to speak up, to say they could still work, was shot on the spot. The *Judenrat* tried to get us released to our homes and to shorten the time of detention. To get this done, the *Judenrat*, headed by its *Präses*, Vekhner, had to hand the local Gestapo several kilos of gold as a ransom. It was collected from all the Jews. We knew this didn't mean complete release, only a postponement of death for a couple of days. I returned home, but I tried to occupy myself somehow, so I went to a gardener who used to buy tools from our store before the war. A commercial agent from Poznań was staying with him, and it was only later that we learned he was really a Jew in hiding. This neighbor pulled all the strings to get me and many others employed by the German *Arbeitsamt*. He went so far as to bribe the officials to do him this favor. I start working in Zarżyn and fourteen of us lived as a group in a house belonging to Jews. These hardships dragged on till September 1942, when they started the extermination of the Jews from all the surrounding towns and villages: Rymanów, Krosno, Korczyn, Jasło, Dukła, Żmigród, and Sanok.[2] The *Aussiedlungen* were done in the following way: A day earlier, a German official drove into our *shtetl* and picked out around 200 young people up to the age of thirty from among all the Jews he had ordered for a lineup. A ghetto was made ready for them. These were only skilled craftsmen. They turned out military equipment in a workshop. A second group was pushed off to the highway as a labor gang. Then they had to demolish all the Jewish homes and clear out all the belongings of the murdered Jews. Later, the Germans promised them they would all be transferred to another labor camp. Everyone was given bread, some marmalade, and a piece of soap. To discourage them from resisting, the Germans acted like no extra guards were needed—but the next day, all the Jews were shot. At the same time—this was in autumn 1942—they issued an order for all the Jews in Sanok and in the surrounding woods who were in hiding, to come out peaceably and surrender, no one would harm them because they were needed as laborers. These sadists went through a formal registration procedure where every person was questioned and assigned somewhere and then they waited an extra two weeks on purpose. The Jews believed all these lies and hesitantly crawled back into Sanok at night. Then the Gestapo picked a day to assemble all these former escapees and, still lying to them, led 520 Jews off to Zasław,[3] where they were massacred. All the other women and men aged sixteen to forty-six were packed into open cattle cars. Their cries pierced the heavens. Many of the men were wrapped in *talaysim,* and clutching *tilimlekh* in their hands, they prayed for God to perform a miracle and save them. They were all taken away to the death camp at Majdanek.

On the fourth of September, 1942—it was the most beautiful day you can imagine—an order was given for all the [remaining] Jews to assemble in Zasław by Monday, the seventh, through Tuesday, the eighth. This was eleven kilometers from Sanok, where six large graves had already been dug. A warning came with the order threatening anyone found in the town on Wednesday with execution. About 6,000 Jews came together at the designated spot. Death met these poor people in the most horrible way. The condemned were ordered to strip naked in front of the open grave. They had to place their clothes in a neat pile to avoid splattering them with blood so the murderers would still be able to "enjoy" them and pick out the hidden valuables inside. The people had to cross a plank. The Germans opened fire with their machine guns but many Jews who were still alive collapsed and dropped into the pit because their legs couldn't support them on the board anymore. So many of them were like this—half-alive. The earth dumped over the victims still heaved many days after the slaughter. The Ukrainian beasts brutally grabbed the small children by the legs and smashed their heads into the walls till they were pulp. These scum said it was a shame to waste a bullet on them. Bigger children were torn from their mothers and herded into sealed freight cars—as many as could fit in. The cars were packed to the limit, just like regular freight. The children began suffocating after a short while. Mothers who wouldn't separate from their children were shot on the spot. Or the children were shot first and then their mothers. A mother begged to be shot first but these monsters said that first she had to witness the death of her child, and only then would they shoot her.

During this bloody slaughter in Zasław, my mother, two sisters—one was married and had two children—and my other relatives were all killed. They were shot there on the ninth of September, 1942. The screams of the victims filled the countryside for miles around.

On the fourth of September, 1942, a Gentile woman named Kuzaniak—she was a neighbor of ours from before the war—told me not to let them take me to Bukasko because they were bringing us there to die. She found this out from her son who was a gendarme and she told me I must escape. She also said that because of my blond hair I could pass for a Gentile. I did what she told me—I jumped off the wagon that was leading us to extermination. Night was falling. I ran into the fields with my girl friend, Rukhl Sheyves. We walked through them till we came to the fields called Lasy Podkarpackie.[4] A Christian woman, Stanisława Laskowska, took pity on me. She lived in the village of Długie. Before the war, she used to come to our store to buy material. At first, this Gentile woman hid me in her barn for ten days, and then I went into the stable for a long time. She brought me food. When there were raids or searches in the village, she sent me into the woods, but she left me food, hiding it where I could get it at night. When the weather held, I hid under the forest trees, but in the winter, I hid out in a cave. When the Christian woman was told there would be no trouble for a while, she took me into her home. I washed myself there, I even slept in the same bed with her. She made many sacrifices for me. In uncertain times, when I lay hidden in the stable with only a piece of bread wrapped in a kerchief, the mice crawled all over me and finished the bread before me. Once, while I was hiding in the forest with a group of ten people, we were ambushed. It was during a raging blizzard—it was freezing cold and the snows were very deep. I only managed to get one shoe on before I ran away from there. Because of this, half of two toes on my right foot froze off. I had no bandages but I kept my foot in a rag and kept it on from January till April. It was only then I tried taking the rag off. As I did, pieces of my toe came off. The Gentile woman Laskowska now took care of me. Because of her goodness, I survived the *Khorbn*. Afterwards, I had to wander over many areas before I was liberated.

On the twenty-sixth of December, 1949, I arrived in Bremen, from where I left for the United States where I've been since January 26, 1950. The Christian woman, Laskowska, came to join her husband in the United States after the war, and she visits me from time to time. I also go to see her and we spend a nice time together. I just gave her son, Mieczyslaw, who stayed behind in Zarżyn, Poland, some property which I had there. It's made up of lots over which four houses can be built. These holdings were left for me by my parents as a part of their legacy.

Eyewitness Testimony 18. A Jewish Woman During the Occupation

R.H. Born in Vaskovici, Rumania, in 1908; lived in Cracow. Recorded by Mikhl Zylberberg in London in May 1955.

In 1939, I was married in Cracow. My husand, who was from Vienna, was active in the Socialist Party, and when the Nazis occupied Vienna, he escaped to Cracow. My husband was a locksmith by trade. Both of us worked in the metal foundries.

When the war broke out, my husband and I fled from Cracow, heading for Sandomierz. We were afraid to stay on in Cracow because of our political past.

We plodded on for two weeks until, finally, we reached Grzybów.[1] The situation all along the roads was critical from here and we had to return to Cracow.

When we got back to the city, I was told they were letting everyone from the other side of the San River cross back over. Since I was born in Rumania, I tried getting an exit visa to return there. I succeeded. The German authorities issued transit permits for me and my husband. We reached Przemyśl and spent the night in the stockyards. In the morning, we crossed the River San and we were now on Soviet territory. We were able to get across because the entire region was in turmoil and no one stopped us to see if we were Jews.

From Przemyśl, we left for Lemberg. The conditions here were miserable: nowhere to sleep, no food, and we had to get out of the city, finally arriving in Stanisławów. Here, both of us worked and eked out a living.

On January 6, 1940, the Russians deported us to the Stalingrad region. My huband worked here in his locksmith trade and I worked in a preserves plant. We were under a loose control, but there were severe economic shortages in the area.

After six months, I started going through the procedure of getting a transfer to Czernowitz, where I had many relatives. After exerting a lot of pressure, I was finally given permission. The route took us through the following cities: Stalingrad, Lemberg, Stanisławów, Śniatyn, Czernowitz. We were detained by the NKVD in Stanisławów, even though we had authorized domestic travel permits. We were both transported to the town of Rohaczyn,[2] where there was a major detention camp for Jews from every region. The suffering that went on here was indescribable. There was nothing anyone could do here. Starving people milled around and dropped in their tracks from hunger, exhaustion, and deprivation. My husband and I decided to break out and to steal across the border into Czernowitz. We swam across the River Prut at Cheremosh, and headed deeper into Bukovina. We only moved at night. We dragged on all week long under the most dangerous conditions until we finally reached Czernowitz.

All my relatives were alive. I was so relieved. But the city was in total chaos.

Czernowitz became the last place of a refuge for Jews from all over Europe. There were German Jews, Czech, Polish, Austrian Jews, and from other countries. Some of them managed to stay alive and find something to eat, but the majority lived in extreme want.

But cultural life thrived. Many concerts were held, a daily Yiddish paper was published, and the Yiddish theater gave constant performances. The biggest producers in the theater were the Kiev Jews, but some were also from Czernowitz, like Misha Bernshtayn—now in Rio de Janeiro—Salo Shafer, and others. I saw the production of Goldfaden's *Di Kishefmakherin*. The Communists were the ones who controlled the cultural activities in Czernowitz.

I got a job here working in a mill. My husband also worked there—as a stoker.

The mill was owned by a Jew named Trichter. But the Russians had deported him to Siberia, and his wife committed suicide. The new manager of the mill was a Russian named Koritsky. He took advantage of his position and pilfered countless sacks of grain from the storehouses. We were afraid there would be purges against us, the workers, so we explained the dwindling supplies to the higher authorities. When an inspection commission arrived, Koritsky got them all drunk and was left to do as he pleased. News of these activities spread through town and a second investigative squad was sent. The manager was removed, but he had to have his last revenge on the handful of Jews at the mill. He singled me out and denounced me to the NKVD, charging that I had entered Czernowitz illegally and was a "wrecker" of the system.

This ended in a trial where both me and my husband were sentenced to eighteen months in prison, and then exile into a remote region of Russia. All our passes and other documents were immediately confiscated.

I wrote out a long appeal and brought it personally before Luca, the political commissar of Czernowitz and, later, finance minister of Rumania. His secretary, a Jewish woman named Kagan, took me in to see him. He looked the paper over, then had a letter sent off to the highest authorities in the city.

Some time later, a second trial was held, and we were both released. We got new jobs and stayed on in Czernowitz until June 21, 1941, when the war with Germany broke out.

As soon as the country was attacked, we fled deeper into Russia. The train carried us past Zaleszczyki and Czortków.[3] The bombardment was continuous and the train came to a complete stop in the

Czortków woods. There were about 6,000 other Jews on board. We had no other way out now and everyone started running off in different directions. My husband and I, along with a cousin, reached Probużna.[4] The Ukrainians kept attacking us, robbing everything we had and beating us up to within an inch of our lives. A young Ukrainian slut bludgeoned me till I was caked with blood, but a Polish family took pity on us and let us spend the night.

By morning, the first German squads were pushing through. There were no Jews living here but the Ukrainians kept pointing to us, yelling, "*Jude! Jude!*" The Germans were pressing ahead too fast to have time to do away with us so they left us to the Ukrainians. A peasant walked up to my husband and cousin, drew his knife and tried to kill them. I threw myself at his legs, kissing his feet, and in the meantime, the two fled. The Ukrainian became crazed. He picked me up and flung me over the cliff into the river. I survived by a miracle. I tried finding my husband and cousin, and came upon them late that night.

During this time, the German patrols were forcing the Jews out of the surrounding forests and herding them together in Czortków. They were all lined up on the Czortków public square and executed.

The Czortków Jews huddled in fear inside their own homes. My cousin and I were saved through a miracle. We crouched near the house of a Jew who lived at the edge of the square. My husband was among those shot. Seriously wounded and splattered with blood, he had fallen under the bodies. Around midnight, he crawled slowly to the garden wall. We helped him over and got him inside the house.

For two days and nights, the Czortków Jews dug graves for the people who'd been executed. My husband, who was barely alive, was also forced to join the labor gangs. A Ukrainian then split his whole back open with a spade. He was losing so much blood, his shirt congealed to his skin. I drank the blood which poured from his wounds.

We stayed in this town for three days. The officials reported that all foreigners had been executed. The last few survivors were forced to flee Czortków. The local Jews were afraid to hide us.

We left town, wandering aimlessly. The Ukrainians kept attacking us and beating us up. I knew we'd never survive this, so I asked them to take us to the gendarmes. We had heard that a Ukrainian lawyer was made police commandant. I hoped and prayed that by speaking Ukrainian with him, I would arouse his sympathy. And this actually happened. We were led into the gendarmerie, and the commandant, who had some intelligence, let me have my say. I showed him our documents and begged him to give us a pass through Stanisławów and Śniatyn back to Czernowitz.

As I was speaking to the commandant, German soldiers came in to relay some orders. The commandant knew no German, so I was the interpreter for the conversation—from German into Ukrainian.

The commandant kept us under arrest all night, and at ten in the morning, gave us a pass to Stanisławów. We left town and after two or three hours of wandering, came up against the German army heading for Czortków.

A young Ukrainian was following us and when he sighted the Germans, he ran up to them yelling, "*Jude! Jude! Jude! Juden Czortków!*" making the motion of cutting his throat with his finger. This meant that the three of us were Jews and that we were responsible for anti-Ukranian massacres in Czortków![5]

Our hands were bound and tied to horses and we were led off into the woods. An officer gave the order, and soldiers began digging a grave. Knowing that this was to be our end, I begged to have my final say before dying. I ranted and raved that the German law permitted the condemned a last wish. "*Was willst du, Hund?!*"[6] the officer snarled. I said I wanted to speak to the ranking officer. One of them turned around toward me and I started counting off all the places we'd passed through, and denied we were residents of Czortków. I begged him to untie my hands so I could show him the documents proving we were innocent. This helped confuse them. When he saw the documents, he immediately ordered the digging stopped. We were tied up to the horses again and led back to Czortków.

As we walked into the town, the Ukrainians surrounded us and started beating us again. When the officer saw this, he drew his sabre and yelled: "*Weck, Hünde, zum schlagen sind wir da!*"[7] Though the Ukrainians didn't know any German, they could tell from the way he said this that they were supposed to maintain some kind of order.

After a formal hearing in front of the Ukrainian commandant, we were set free. We again left town, but after a short distance, we heard an uproar from the forest. Suddenly, groups of Jews were driven out and pushed past us on all sides. We got caught up in the column, and they hounded us and pushed us all the way to Stanisławów. We numbered into the thousands. All this happened in the first half of July, 1941.

We were divided up in Stanisławów—the old and the children separate, and the young people separate. The young and healthy were assigned for labor by the SS and *Schutzpolizei*. The old people and the children were goaded from one spot to another. Some of the people from areas outside the region—especially those who had the means—managed to find shelter with local Jewish families. Me, my husband, and my cousin, we labored under the German guards. The work was grueling and we got nothing for it—no food, and no place to sleep.

Thousands of people camped out under the open sky, sprawled over the grounds around the *Judenrat*. Hunger grew from day to day, and epidemics raged out of control. There was such suffering, I can't describe.

The *Judenrat*, headed by Goldshtayn, involved itself with the people. They distributed bread to everyone, along with a couple of lumps of sugar, and tried to relieve the misery.

There was an order posted by the German authorities in town which prohibited Gentiles from selling food to Jews, not even milk for Jewish children. Our children swelled up from hunger and fell like flies.

This is what life was like until the thirteenth of September, 1941.

During this time, my eighteen-year-old cousin from Sadagura, Moyshe Burg, was murdered by the Germans. It happened like this: Jewish youths were marched every day from Stanisławów to Chryplin, to pull out the iron girders of the bridge which had been salvaged from the Dniester River. One time, when my cousin collapsed under an iron girder, not having the strength left even to lift it off him, the Germans beat him and mutilated him till he was completely unrecognizable, then threw him into the river. The same thing happened to hundreds of other Jews who succumbed from hunger and exhaustion.

My husband became ill and couldn't get up from bed anymore. I went out to work every day, cleaning the barracks of the *Schutzpolizei*.

As I was returning from the barracks on September thirteenth, I saw the Germans rounding up Jews—old and young—from out of their homes, at gunpoint. I ran home through the side streets. My husband was lying in bed. My uncle, Yisruel Burg—a religious Jew with beard and *payas*—was staying with us, together with his four daughters and three grandchildren. They had no idea what was happening right in the center of town. I burst in screaming: "Save yourselves!" I grabbed my sick husband and we ran along the banks of the Bystrzyca River, to a street which was now empty of all Jews. We both of us hid out in an alcove. A boy of about eight or ten was hiding in the attic of the same house. A German came in, and the child, thinking it was his mother, who had come back, called out *"Mameh!"* The German pulled him down by the legs and shot him right there. We saw this through a crack in the wall.

When we heard nothing more outside, we walked into the street. When we got near the center of town, we saw many *goyim* standing around and gawking as a horse dragged a Jewish woman over the ground—her black hair was tied to its tail. Her whole face was completely disfigured and there wasn't the slightest sign of life from her body. Most of the crowd was hysterical with laughter, and some wept and wrung their hands.

We wandered around completely disoriented for about an hour, till night fell. In desperation, I decided to try and hide in the barracks I was working in earlier. I found the section with no windows or doors, climbed in through the open side, and we stayed there overnight.

We looked out over the fields and the new *besoylim* at Zagwoźdż.

We saw Jews being pushed into prepared graves and executed at the bottom. Some of the victims were hit by the bullets, some suffocated or drowned in the blood of the many people who were shot on top of them. The slaughter went on till midnight. We heard the steady bark of *"Heil, Hitler!"* mingle with the agonizing shrieks of the victims.

At midnight, the shooting stopped. The few survivors were ordered to run from the *besoylim*.

The next day, Jews were again working inside the barracks. We snuck in among this group as they were leaving work in the evening. After the massacre, a small number of Jews was still alive in the town —those who were away working.

More than 65,000 Jews[8] lost their lives during this massacre. A few victims were still alive inside the mass grave. A cousin of mine, Vulf Kotcher, also came out alive. He was soaked in blood from head to foot, clawed by the people writhing in their death agonies. His expression and state of mind were from another world.

After that night, we had to endure new terrors. We few Jews were registered all over again. The *Judenrat*, still headed by Goldshtayn, continued to function. We were put back to work and the *Judenrat* again had to provide the Germans with everything they demanded.

Everything I'm telling you now is like a grain of sand by the sea— absolutely nothing compared to what happened.

On September 13, 1941, thousands of Jewish families from the neighboring towns were deported into the center of the city. People were herded in from Drohobycz, Stryj, Sambor, Kałusz, Tłumacz, Bohorodczany, Nadwórna, and around 22,000 Jews[9] from Carpatho-Rus. Thousands of Hungarian Jews were also transported into the city. There was no ghetto in Stanisławów. Again there were huge numbers of Jews in the city, packed into every section of town. Thousands of families milled around in the streets and courtyards, until the next *aktsye* cleared them away.

Six weeks later, the Nazis began the final extermination of the Jews. All the people who'd been shipped into the city were now herded together and shot en masse, the same way it happened the first time.[10]

Every two or three weeks, they simply murdered Jews at random. The Germans stormed into homes, heaving grenades and shooting up the people who tried escaping through the windows.

During October and November of 1941, the ghetto in the city was formed officially. A major registration was forced upon us, and every Jew was selected for one of three destinations: (1) Those with authorized identity cards were grouped under A and labored outside the ghetto. (2) Those with no authorization were grouped under B and put to work inside the ghetto. (3) Any Jew categorized as group C was to be deported to a concentration camp. The Jews of group C were assembled and sent off as a transport to Auschwitz.[11]

My husband and I were put into the first category.

There were two concentration camps in the ghetto—one on Młynarska Street in the sausage plant, and the other on Długa, inside the mill. Both camps were bursting beyond capacity.

People dropped like flies inside the camps. The inmates were systematically starved, and every morning, we workers had to pull the wagonloads of dead bodies out of camp.

The ghetto infirmary was housed inside the mission house on Długa Street. The Germans carried out two mass executions here. The doctors were shot together with all the nurses and patients.[12]

We were given one kilo of bread and six *deka* of sugar a week for our labor. Jews were constantly rounded up by the Ukrainian police and forced into labor gangs. Sometimes they tossed them a piece of bread, but most of them gave nothing for the work. We had to steal the food left out for the pigs and dogs. Anyone caught for such a "crime" was immediately turned over to the Gestapo. The condemned were led away to the courthouse square on Bielinska and shot.

On the last crucial night of the liquidation of the ghetto, we both hid in a cellar belonging to our cousin, Frahde Finger. The cellar entrance was through the room above, and was covered with a rug. The cellar was turned into a hideout for our cousin and her three children, her sister Shoshe and her three children, and me and my husband. We were terrified of the police dogs who always sniffed out the Jews in their hiding places. We had a lot of paprika in the house and emptied it all out on the rug by the cellar entrance, so the dogs would back off. This saved us from certain death.

That same night, a neighbor and his two daughters—one was a teacher and the other a clerk—committed suicide. In the morning, when we climbed up out of the cellar, all three of them were hanging from the rafters, with their *mugen duvid* still on their arms. This was in the beginning of 1942.

The archfiends, the butchers of the ghetto, were Krieger, chief of the SS, Streicher of *Schutzpolizei,* and Schat, a Viennese who robbed all the property from the Jews.

Their name for rounding Jews up was *Judenjagd.* The curse they always used was *"lausige Juden!"*

There was a standing order that every German must be saluted. If a person raised their hat, they were beaten savagely, and if they didn't, they were almost killed. The Germans couldn't stand it when people cried during the massacres. Whenever someone cried, they were clubbed to death, and we kept hearing: *"Nicht weinen!"*[13]

I can't mention everything. I can describe what was on the surface, but the things underneath—I just can't tell you this.

In the winter of 1942, the Germans again chased all the women and children out of their homes and herded them inside the *besoylim.*

When the men returned from the labor sites in the evening, they found their families gone. Later that night, the workers were also included in the roundup. The men kept watch all night long and when the Germans were sighted, a signal was given. If someone managed to get away, they were spared temporarily.

This was the way they murdered and tormented us till *Paysekh*, 1942. At the end of *Paysekh*, the Germans ordered all the Jews to demolish the ransacked homes, and most important, to salvage all the iron and other metals. We labored twelve hours a day, without food, without water, and when the day's work was done, they chased us at gunpoint through the city streets. This was a sport to them. For us long as they kept it up, we were forced to sing! The sidewalks on both sides were packed with Ukrainians gawking at the "parade" and having great fun on our account. Every few steps of the way, they pelted us with rocks and bricks.

One time, while my husband was away on the labor gang, I got so hungry I just had to leave the ghetto and find me a piece of bread somewhere. While I was trying to get out, I was captured by a Ukrainian gendarme who brought me to the *Schutzpolizei*. Then they handed me over to the Jewish ghetto police. This meant certain death. The SS, who ran the ghetto police, took all arrestees out to the cemetery and shot them. By a miracle, my name wasn't added to their list and for some reason, I was let go in the evening.

While I was inside the cell at the ghetto commissariat, I watched as all day long they brought in great numbers of people—mostly the old and sick, belonging to group C. That day, even small children had to carry their sick fathers in on their arms. The SS ordered these children to bring in their old and ailing parents.

By October of 1942, there were around 530 laborers left in the Stanisławów Ghetto, including twenty women. Besides us, there were another 200 people sent on a transport for annihilation.

On the morning of the fifteenth of October, we were marched off to work as usual. As soon as we were outside the ghetto, we realized they were taking us off the road to the labor site, and heading us in a different direction. We were guarded by the *Schutzpolizei* and a whole company of Ukrainian gendarmes. Our hearts sank—we were sure this was the end. The police made us stop in the middle of a street. In a short while, those two monsters, Krieger and Streicher, rode up on horses. The police squads snapped to attention and saluted the two murderers. Suddenly, I heard the word "Auschwitz." By now, I knew what Auschwitz meant and I decided to break away from the group, even though my husband was with me. I want to tell you how my husband kept pleading with me to save myself any way I could.

I stood in the first row—the one next to the sidewalk—and quickly tore off my Jewish armband. I threw a kerchief over my head and sprang up on the sidewalk. I acted lame, stooping over like an old woman, and dragged on like this slowly, till I got to the Catholic cathedral. All the time, I was expecting a police bullet any second.

The church had been ransacked and closed for a long time, and the Polish Catholics knelt in prayer outside. A priest stood in front of the group, leading the prayers. I pushed in among these people and dropped to my knees like them. I had a Catholic hymnal with me which I got as a present a while before from a Polish woman, a teacher. I stayed in this position for about two hours.

After everyone had dispersed, I got up and headed for the house of a Gentile woman acquaintance, Anna Romanisyn, at Felesa Street 1. The woman received me kindly, she gave me food, and at night, hid me in the attic of the house. I stayed there for three days and nights. During that time, I had nothing to eat or drink—the woman was afraid of the Ukrainians in the house.

I should tell you now, that three weeks before, while I was working on the "Aryan" side, I went to see the same woman. I noticed a document of hers lying in the garbage, from which I learned that she was a Pole on her mother's side and a Ukrainian on her father's. She was afraid to admit her Polish origins so that's why she threw the document away. I salvaged it then, and kept it—like the most precious treasure.

I now had the document up in the attic with me, as well as a medallion of the Virgin Mary. But I was afraid to leave the attic.

After the three days, I went to an old neighbor of ours named Karol Podbielski. He lived with his mother-in-law and two daughters. He was a railroad man and got home after midnight. When he saw me, he broke down and cried. He gave me food, made tea, but I had to sleep outside in a small stable with his pig. He was very afraid—his house bordered the *Schutzpolizei* post.

I stayed with him for three days. He gave me a change of linen, shoes, clothes, and also money to do my hair. He sent his girl along with me to the hairdresser so no one would suspect me. Three days later, he gave me money and I left for Cracow.

My father was in Cracow together with my two brothers and their wives and children, and also my only sister. I also had good Gentile acquaintances there from before the war, with whom I worked in "TUR,"[14] in the Esperanto Club, and in the socialist youth movement in general. Cyrankiewicz, the present Polish premier,[15] was a good friend of mine.

The trip to Cracow passed without incident. But as the train pulled into the Cracow terminal, a roundup was begun. Anyone without a *Kennkarte* was arrested immediately. I was also put under arrest and taken off to Zielona Street, the police staging ground for people deported to the concentration camps. Everyone was searched and detained till evening, when a Gestapo officer and a Pole arrived to interrogate me. This went on from eight till one in the morning. . . .

[There follows the witness's account of the painstaking examination of her knowledge of the catechism.]

After endless hours of questioning, the Pole said to the German: "Pure Aryan." My eyes lit up but his words were like stabs to my heart.

The morning after, I asked permission to see my "cousin" from the Esperanto Club, Boleslaw Sosul. The Polish interrogator followed me to my friend's. Sosul was standing at the window with his child on his arm. I started calling: "Bolku! Bolku!" and he understood immediately what it was all about. He came out of the house and kissed and embraced me. Then he asked who my "companion" was. When I told him he was from Zielona Street, it was all he needed to know.

The interrogator let me stay with my "cousin" as long as I reported to the police every day.

The Susul family was very poor. I had to go to another colleague from the Esperanto Club, Richard Rawcinski, and he let me stay the few days till I was sent to Germany.

I was miserable here—I wanted to contact my family in the ghetto.

Bolek Sosul walked to the ghetto with me. I asked the Jewish police to send out Ana Sh——, my sister. My sister came up to the barbed wire and I went into the ghetto with her.

My sister then told me that our father, our brothers, and their families were dead. I begged her to leave the ghetto with me. Susul wanted to save her with his wife's documents. My sister's husband was in the Płaszów Concentration Camp and she wouldn't leave the ghetto without him. In the end, I had to leave the ghetto alone. Susul waited for me near the demarcation line.

On the fifth day, all of us had to report to the transfer area where we were taken inside a bathhouse. Here, the SS selected workers from among us while we stood naked before them. Then they shipped us to Wilhelmshaven,[16] near Berlin. . . .

[The witness now describes the harsh prison conditions for the foreign labor gangs, the constant threats against contact with the local populace, and the shuttling back and forth from one labor site to the other, until, after many months, she arrives in Heringsdorf in the beginning of 1944.]

Every day, the police took us by barge across the Spree River to the labor site at the AEG.[17] We got up at four in the morning and finished working at six-thirty in the evening. They gave us nothing to eat at the factory. The work was very hard and they had us under surveillance every step of the way.

In the winter of 1943 to 1944, there was constant bombing. We often picked up leaflets dropped by the Allies. They warned us to break out of the camps before these targets were bombed. But Germans kept us locked up so tight we couldn't even move.

The factory officials singled me out for punishment and just tortured me, giving me the most dangerous work.

I became close with a German woman at the factory and was able to survive because of her. She smuggled in linen, clothes, soap, cigarettes, and food, and gave them to me secretly—it was only this that kept me alive. She risked her life to save me. She also smuggled me out of camp from time to time and took me home. I stay in touch with her, even today. She sends me letters in London. Her name is Elizabeth Enulath of Berlin.

In January 1944, Berlin was bombed regularly and the whole camp was turned to ash. Three hundred and ten prisoners perished. During the bombardment, I took shelter in a small reinforced-concrete bunker. Nobody could get out of the camp—the guards had locked all the gates. Hearing our screams, the men prisoners from the other camp ran over and knocked down the gates which led out to the forest. All of us escaped into the woods.

I reached as far as Köpenick, where there was a camp for Czechs. They took me in together with several other escapees. When the Czech workers were allowed by the German authorities to return home to Prague, they took me along as a stowaway. I was hidden on the train for the whole trip, until we reached Prague. While the German police were inspecting the Czechs' documents, I lay among the bundles under the seats.

After we were in Prague for a while, one of the Czechs took me to the village of Libus, near the city, where I stayed with his sister for the whole fifteen months till Liberation. I worked in the village and was able to support myself.

On May 9, 1945, the Red Army liberated us. I returned to Prague right away. I registered at the Czech and Russian headquarters in the city, to get new documents. They denied me permission. The Russians demanded that I leave for Russia. I refused.

I started working at a metal factory. Later, I worked as an assistant in the social relief center for sick former *Katzetnikn* who were on their way to *Eretz Yisrul*. During this work, I met M—— N—— from Chust, Poland, and married him. We lived together for three years. For all that time, he had a fatal lung disease, and in desperation, he took his own life. This was Prague, 1950.

Later, I met the Polish premier, Cyrankiewicz, when he arrived in Prague as part of a delegation which was the guest of the Czech government.

He asked me to come back to Poland. He told me he would help me start a new life there. I refused. I couldn't return to a country where Jewish blood had flowed like water. I asked him for only one thing—to help me find my relatives, maybe someone had survived. He told me he'd try. Because of Cyrankiewicz, I was able to locate my only sister. She lives in Cracow to this day.

After the tragedy with my husband, I left for Israel. There I married M——H——from London.

My present husband comes from a small village in Poland. He lived in Germany for many years, later he escaped to London. He's a *shames* in a *shiel* here. Again tragedy strikes me. He refuses to understand me—he's cold and distant, and if that's not enough, he'll only speak German. I can't stand it.

I'm really grateful to you for hearing me out. I've unburdened my heart and it feels lighter now. All these years, I had no one to tell my misfortune to. Nobody has any time. Nobody wants to hear about it.

Eyewitness Testimony 19. A Letter to Friends

M. S. Born in 1920.

Rokitno,[1] 2/15/45.

My dear ones!

This is a brief description of my life since the start of the German occupation.

It won't be news to you by the time you read this letter. I tried to avoid writing about it all this time. But now, since you asked me to, I'll try to tell you, in part, what my recent past has been like, my desolation!

This is how it began.

When the country was first shaken by the great calamity, when every heart smothered and stifled its pain, I was standing on the threshold of my cottage in a *shtetl* in Volin, Sarne,[2] watching the swarms of exhausted and terrified refugees drag by. They were hanging out of train windows, the roads were blocked by the endless columns of people. The air was thick with burned gunpowder. We were bombed round the clock by the enemy. And besides this, I was all alone—my husband was on an assignment far away. The house was destroyed by a bomb and this was the time I was in delicate condition. . . .

My heart craved to run with the rest, but how could I leave my devoted friends behind? I was also worried about my health . . . and the health of the child developing underneath my heart.

Dear ones! You often criticized me for being too stingy to give up my property and run like everyone else. It's true. But now you'll be able to understand the reason a little better. I wanted to go to my parents in Rokitno, but by that time, it was impossible. Later, this is what I found out happened to them:

My father got a travel permit to Saratov. But when the time to leave came, my devoted mother refused to leave me behind under any circumstances. She pleaded with my father and brother to go on ahead, but she wanted to come to me. And then the evacuation was over, and all of us were left behind.

I remember it as if it was happening now—those first few days of surrender. On that Sunday, September 17, 1941, from the moment that first German appeared in the streets of the *shtetl*, he showed us what he was planning and what he's known for throughout the world. An incredible barrage of firepower was kept up all day—not a soul dared show their face outside.

Our house overflowed with refugees. They were scattered all over and crowded together on the floor, trembling in fear. Suddenly, we heard the bloodcurdling scream of a Jewish boy we knew. I opened the door in terror and what I saw was a corpse lying on the threshold. This was the first time I really experienced the German's cruelty. I'm not mentioning this only because it's shocking, but because it ingrained itself in my mind as the first barbarous act of a supposedly civilized people. I endured a lot worse, and the more often it happened, the less it shocked me—this was the way it had to be.

My husband went through much hardship before he finally reached home. He was captured and held as a hostage many times. Both of us worked ourselves to the bone. We witnessed the most gruesome incidents. All my belongings were confiscated. White bands with the *mugen duvid* were wrapped around our arms. We were tortured at every turn. Every moment was pierced by the screams of Jews. We were constantly being beaten, tortured, or shot. Every morning, before they marched us off to work, we took leave of each other as if for the last time. Who knew if we'd still be alive by tomorrow?

The Yom Kippur of 1941 in Sarne will stay before my eyes forever. On Friday evening, this order was given: By morning, all Jews, without exception, must line up on the square wearing a new badge—one round, yellow, ten-centimeter-wide patch halfway down our backs, and another one on our right lapel. Anyone disobeying will be shot. That tragic night passed like a torture. We got ready to face the end. In the morning, the streets of our Jewish *shtetl* were swarming with yellow-spotted ghosts. We huddled together and waited—for what? A deep silence fell over the square. Machine guns were positioned on every side. Every now and then, a small child cried or screamed out for its mother. A light plane circled above to prevent our escape. An auto pulled up with the ranking officers and they ordered the *selektsye* of the artisans to begin. I can't describe our suffering to you. The *Schutzpolizei* ran among us like dogs, beating and punishing whomever they got hold of. Several people were shot in the back through their patch as a sport, for *Ziel und Schpiel* (as a target and a game). It was only after many long hours that we were allowed to go home. I went through these punishment drills— *Appele* they called them—five times. To survive in Sarne was now beyond my strength. People said a ghetto was being planned. I was in my last month. The first reports about the mass murder of Jews were reaching us: the first great *Shkhite* at Rovno,[3] and then others, more and more. My parents decided to bring us over to them, no matter the danger, and to have us share a common fate. Travel by train was forbidden us—*Verboten!*—and it meant certain death to go by coach. My father was the only one who would risk his life and come and get us. The conditions hadn't completely deteriorated in Rokitno. We still had our house, a large garden, and an orchard. I recuperated for a time, but not for long. A ghetto was imposed. Several streets were sealed off for Jews only.

My dear ones! I can't describe to you the horrors of the ghetto! People died from hunger, from epidemics. Most of us were swollen from malnutrition. The overcrowding stifled us. And this was the time I bore my child. Doctors weren't allowed to treat Jews. And it was forbidden to bring a Jew into the world.[4] While I lay in bed, sick and terror-stricken, horrendous things were going on all around me. A German drunk accused my father of trying to poison him and he beat him terribly—he tried to kill him then and there. In the morning, my brother was attacked and beaten unconscious for not saluting properly. We were all confined to our beds. But my mother was heroic. She took care of us and comforted us—she saw to all our needs. My mother, who'd been sick herself, somehow now recovered her health. Each day, rumors spread and we suffered every moment. My husband was driven to exhaustion at slave labor. My younger brother, a very talented boy of eighteen, was the only one able to support us and he kept us alive. He worked as an electrician, a metalsmith, he fixed ovens and all kinds of things, he was a watchmaker, a painter, and many times they used him as an interpreter. And besides all this, he also had to work all day long at slave labor. This is how we were able to stay alive until August 26, 1942. My daughter was now a growing pretty, eight-month-old child.

Then, suddenly, an order was passed through the ghetto: everyone must assemble in the morning for an *Appel.* They accused us of having helped many Jews escape to the Russian partisan units. This was the time the first partisan units were forming. They wanted to investigate us and ordered a head count taken. The whole ghetto was overcome with despair. You could see terror on every face. Our sorrow knew no bounds now when we learned that the final *Appel* in the neighboring *shtetl* of Selishtsh[5] that same day ended with the murder of every last man, woman, and child. God! I can't just mention this in passing! My heart still cries out!

I broke into hysterical weeping. The men sat by mum, but my mother kept her head, she started comforting me and calmed me down. There was no way out. We were afraid to go to bed all night. How could we escape in the darkness? To whom? And with a baby! I begged the men not to think of us and to escape. But they didn't— we still wouldn't believe they were going to murder us!

The morning was especially beautiful and clear. My mother started to knead some dough, thinking she'd have time to bake it. My little girl sat up in her crib, looking just like a little angel. She had just woken up from her sweet, childish dreams. My brother left to go out into the street. The Jewish police started carrying out the order of chasing the people from their homes toward the square. My brother ran back into the house, pale as a ghost. I dressed my child quickly and we got ready to leave. My husband broke down in tears —it was a terrible thing to see. After him, we all did. Our home was filled with sobbing. A neighbor came to get us and then we walked out to the square. Big and small, everyone was lined up. Life had become so cheap to us, we were so apathetic, that at first it didn't seem there was anything out of the ordinary. There was only the chief of gendarmes to count how many we were. I can still see my mother when she came over to me with an expression of relief on her face and tried to comfort me: "See, *tekhterl mahns*,[6] there's no one here. Soon, they'll let us go home just like always." The count was taken quietly and quickly. We were only worried that they wouldn't let us go home soon. And suddenly, we heard an order: "Men to one side, women to the other, line up in rows of six!" We clung to each other. Everyone started panicking. We lost control of ourselves. I started trembling like I had a fever. My father, my husband, and my brother were separated from us. My mother held me by the hand, and it was very hard for me to keep a grip. She wanted to lighten my burden and took the child from my arms.

A moment later, a cry that pierced the heart rose from the 15,000 people and filled the skies: "Run, they're killing us!" The Germans and the police converged on the square. Shots rang out from behind the windows. I don't know how I reacted. I only remember this enormous weight suddenly falling on me. I started twisting and squirming and finally crawled free from under the dozens of bodies on top of me. I couldn't see where my mother and child lay. The bullets whistled past me. My dress was drenched with blood. I felt I was hit! No—someone had fallen on me. Whether they were dead or wounded I'll never know. The square was completely covered with bodies—some dead, others were wounded, and many were in shock and paralyzed with fear. Wild screams pierced the air. I couldn't get up anymore, there were people falling all over me. Slowly, I regained my senses. Death was staring me in the face. God!

What do I do?! Where's my *mameh?!* My child?! I thought of getting up and running home. Maybe my mama and child were already there. But it was impossible to move. I started crawling over the bodies. Our house was nearby. But I saw policemen shooting from the staircase. I was afraid to crawl any further because they were right in front of me. I felt my heart stop beating.

And then, in the middle of this mass of crazed, dying people, I spotted my father. With the little strength I had left, I began calling him, hoping he'd hear me somehow. What happened then, I don't remember—I lost consciousness. When I came to, I was lying among sacks of potatoes. We were covered with thick clusters of bean shoots. My father dragged me under constant fire to this place outside town with his last remaining strength. We were in the middle of a field. I was delirious—all I wanted was to return home. I longed so much for my child. I thought of no one else. My father started calming me down. My flesh was torn and gashed. The sun beat down without letup but the earth underneath me was damp. We couldn't move a muscle, or the camouflage would crumble. Then a dog prowled around us like a shadow and kept howling till nighttime. We heard the shooting all day long. A volley of shots, then cries and groaning. We heard people running near us and the police chasing after them with dogs. I was suffering terribly from thirst. My mouth dried up. My breasts ached so. We were only able to stand up late at night. Suddenly, we heard a voice: "*Panie* S——, don't leave us here, let us come with you!" A young fifteen-year-old girl and a seven-year-old boy jumped out from the other side. My blood ran cold from fright. Afterwards, the four of us started out on our lost, roving new life.

The moon shone brightly, as if in spite. I saw my father by its reflection but I couldn't recognize him. He'd turned white as a dove. We entered a forest. I was seized by a primitive fear. Every tree, every bush, the shadows, took on the shape of a German. It was freezing cold. The mosquitoes sapped our feverish blood. I was wearing a light summer dress. I lost my shoes on the way and walked barefoot. The children also. We walked a long distance from the town. We walked all night. We just let ourselves go, and trailed behind, sick and exhausted. My father had been a woodcutter and he knew how to get through the forest. By daybreak, we had reached a narrow river. To quench my thirst, I threw myself down at its edge and gulped down water till I could hold no more. The sun came up. We decided to hide in the forest for the day, and to move at night. The children fell right to sleep, like logs. Blood flowed from my feet. My breasts felt heavy as stones. I writhed in pain on the ground like a snake. What would happen now? Where could we go? We recuperated all day. Again, night fell. Now we had to have some food. The children couldn't stop crying. We spent the whole night walking again. I watched my father's strength failing him. We decide to reach the hut of a forest caretaker my father knew from before. He was known as a kind man. All our hopes were on him. But what will we do with the children? The caretaker was so poor, himself, that four people would be a hard imposition. Again, daylight came. Hunger gnawed at us and we started picking berries. While we foraged through the bushes, we stumbled on a group of Jews. It was twilight by now. A woman lay stretched out over the ground, covering her two small children with her body. There were also two men there. We left the children with them and the two of us went on to the caretaker.

It was a moonless night and we walked in total darkness. No one saw us or heard us as we reached the clearing. And just like thieves—so that even the dog couldn't sense it—we crept into the hay shed, and fell down completely exhausted on some hay in a corner. Still trembling—who knew what would happen tomorrow?—we fell into a sleep which made up for all those days. Some kind of Christian feast was going on at this time. The caretaker surely wouldn't be in a rush to work in the shed on a day like this. We woke up and expected God knows what kind of reception. The sun climbed very high and broke in through the cracks in the door. The world hadn't changed. It was bright and beautiful, only we were in darkness. Darkness. Our fate lay in the hands of the man we were expecting. All of a sudden, I heard the door open—the caretaker saw us. He froze. For the first time in my life, I saw my father cry. I looked the owner straight in the eyes. He walked over to my father and fell on his shoulders. I was delirious. He brought us in food right away and dug out a pit for us behind the corn. His wife bound up my aching breasts. I got better. I could go on and on describing our sufferings. We stayed in that hole for nine weeks. We were overcome with panic many times. Every dog's bark, every sound, filled us with terror. We were worn down by hunger and filth. Waiting breathlessly for the sign of a hand setting down a bowl of baked potatoes and salt, twice a day. He didn't have a penny. We had to escape out the back more times than I can count. The Germans kept coming around with their dogs. Finally, we had to leave the caretaker and run away.

I'll never forget that night. With a piece of bread and a bottle of water, walking sticks in hand, we set out into the world, not knowing where or to whom. The night was black. A freezing rain trickled down without letup. My feet were bound in layers of straw woven together from husks. My father thought of going to some acquaintances, former workers of his. To reach them, we had to cross twenty-five kilometers of woods. And only at night. We walked alongside a train track. It's impossible to describe this march to you. Our limbs had atrophied from going unused so long. My foot bindings came apart. Every ten hours or so, we rested up in the mud. I could see that my father's strength was failing, but there was nothing I could do. And we had to reach our goal by daybreak. We were coming near the village. Here, too, we were met by a decent man—no one ever forgot my father's kindness. We were confined to an attic here for twelve weeks. We suffered unbelievably. We never saw a soul. Later, large partisan units were sighted and they took up positions in the area. This is what saved us. The Germans raided the village less and less. The peasants started to think of us as people again. They also gave us some work to do. We left to live in the forest. My father set up a tannery there. He started making leather goods. I wove, and worked in the fields. We grew used to living in the woods. To a life in a bunker. A group of Jews now formed. The situation was calm. We had enough food now. We put on normal clothes again. We got rid of the worst thing—the *filth*. We started getting ready for our second winter and even built a little cabin in the woods. Over this period, we had many encounters with death. We fell into German hands during an ambush in the forest. We escaped from the bunker where they were pinning us down, but then the murderers captured us again. They couldn't tell we were Jews. Many, many times more, we came close to being killed. It's impossible even to imagine our suffering. Every second we were struck with terror. And like dumb beasts of the forest, not knowing what was going on around us, we were suddenly rescued. The Red Army freed us from a long captivity and an inevitable death. We were let out of prison, but we had nowhere to return to. And no one to rejoice with. A miracle—to be alive. We went back to our hometown. What I saw caused me so much pain, I couldn't even lift my eyes anymore. We went to a neighbor, a *goyeh*.

Here, I found the truth of what happened. My mother and child managed to get back to the house. She put the child to sleep. A German broke in and beat them brutally, pushing them out toward the train with all the others. They were taken to Sarne, to the staging ground. My husband and brother had gotten away. They were caught the next day and forced to drag together all the corpses inside the *shiel*. Then, a day after, they were also brought to Sarne. They joined the others there—my mother and child.

They endured for three days. My husband carried water for my hungry child in his shoe.

A short time passed, a few days. The front was a few kilometers from our *shtetl*. We were bombarded from all sides. I became sick with typhus. Then my father got sick. His weakened heart couldn't stand the inhuman suffering. He died. I lost the most precious part of my life. I was left all alone.

My dears! My past is the past of the whole Jewish people. Be well.

Your M——

Eyewitness Testimony 20. Inside the Gas Chamber

R.K. Born in Łódź in 1919; lived there. Recorded by Icek Shmulewitz in New York, July 1954.

Three days later, I was inside Auschwitz. After they pulled us off the trains, they tore the men and women apart. We cried and grieved as they pulled us—entire families—away from each other. I jumped down off the train with my mother, who was then fifty-three years old. They tried to separate us but I wouldn't let go of her. I pulled at her sleeve to keep us together until a Hitlerite smashed me with his rifle butt. I still carry the sign.

I was taken to the camp police structure where the Gestapo was really in charge. Two paths led out from the back. One was for women and children who were told they were being taken to a separate camp. I learned afterwards that this path led to the gas chambers. As we walked through the open zone, an orchestra was playing and we were ordered to dance. Then we were taken inside a bathhouse. Had to leave all our things there. We came out of the changing room completely naked. They lined us up in a row. And with young Gestapo and Hitlerite officers, men and women, in front of us, they cut off all our body hair. While they were doing it, these German women tore whole clumps of hair from our genital parts. As long as I live, I'll never forget the moral degradation they forced me and all the other women through.

Afterwards, we were ordered inside special barracks. I was put in Barrack No. 19 where there were 1,100 other women. Ten women or more had to find places on bunks which had room for only two people.

At 2 A.M., when sleep is deepest and a person could forget their misery for a short while, we were roused violently and forced to run out and get coffee. Then they woke us again at 4 A.M., screaming and beating us to get out of the bunks for the so-called *Zeilappel*. We stood on the drill grounds naked and barefoot, our breasts and other parts of the body exposed, in snow and rain, from four at night till nine in the morning. We weren't permitted to move even a muscle. And if anyone had to relieve themselves, it was done underneath, while the overseers were beating us with clubs.

Then, we were pushed back into the barracks, given a thin slice of bread with margarine, and coffee. At eleven in the morning, we were led out to the latrines, and whoever stayed there longer than five minutes was beaten over the body with clubs. We were then driven back into the barracks, and at 1 P.M. they brought us the midday meal in large pots. A bowl of soup for every five girls. At two o'clock, we were again taken out for the *Zeilappel,* and couldn't move till five, no matter if it rained or snowed or if a cold wind blew. Many women collapsed dead in their places. Later, they chased us back into the barracks.

Two days after I was brought to Auschwitz—on September third—a *selektsye* was started for who would die and who would live. We were lined up again completely naked in front of the Gestapo men, who turned us around over and over till they decided who would work and who wouldn't. The Hitlerites sent me over with the group who weren't picked for work. They gave me and the other 300 women and girls some clothes, and told us we were headed for a different kind of work. They ordered us to strip again and some of the women were let inside a bath. There were small cells inside, big enough for about fifty people, but they pushed 300 women in. Each woman was pressed tight against the other. We didn't know what this place was for. Inside, I saw my former teacher from Łódź, *Froh* Shafir—her maiden name was Kropivnik—and she pointed to the pipes sticking out from the corners of the ceiling, she said they were gas pipes. Standing inside this chamber, you could smell the gas from before. We stood like this for two hours, terrified of what was about to happen.

When the two hours were over, a "supervisor" came in, a Polish woman, who told us not to cry and get hysterical because they were taking us to a special camp for convalescents, so that later, we'd be able to work again.

Soon, we were really led out of the chamber, given clothes, and taken into a field where they held us all day. In the evening, they drove us back inside the barracks.

I remember a certain woman in the chamber—Pajewska, the wife of a doctor from Łódź. She was sent to Auschwitz with her two children, who were immediately seized from her. As soon as the woman walked into the chamber with us, she knew where she was, that soon we'd be burned. She started screaming: "It's not enough that you've taken our husbands and children from us, now you want to kill us, too, so that not one witness will live to tell what you did to us Jews!!"

The woman was short and thin. She took advantage of a second when the chamber door was opened and she broke through. Hitlerites caught her, brought her back inside the chamber, and right before our eyes, they beat her till she was unrecognizable—they busted five clubs over her small, frail body. This woman is alive today. I don't know where she lives.

I spent five more weeks inside the barracks. I remember the *Blokowa* of Barrack No. 19 where I stayed, especially—she was a Jewish woman from Czechoslovakia. *Erev* Yom Kippur, 1944, this woman put a white tablecloth over the barrack oven, lit some candles, and told all the Jewish women to walk up and pray in front of the candles. All of us went up and the barrack was filled with an unbearable wailing. The women again saw their annihilated homes. *Froh* Rotshtat, the famous violinist from Łódź,[1] was also kept in our barracks. The *Blokowa* brought in a fiddle and asked *Froh* Rotshtat to play *Kol Nidre*. She refused, saying she couldn't play because her heart was bursting. The *Blokowa* threatened to beat her, to put her on punishment details, if she didn't play. When *Froh* Rotshtat began playing, the Jewish Blokowa suddenly lost control and started pushing us away and clubbing the Jewish women, yelling: "Enough! You've had enough pleasure!"

In October of 1944, I was brought to Bergen-Belsen along with many other transports. From Bergen-Belsen to Elsnig.[2] We were shipped in sealed freight cars. When the Russian front advanced, I was led out of Elsnig with other women. They made us march for two weeks straight—walking night and day—without a bite of food. We stumbled and collapsed along the way, many women died in their tracks—they were beyond exhaustion—or were shot. Afterwards, they loaded us into sealed railroad cars again, and took us further. On a certain night, we were attacked—strafed and bombed—and the train came to a complete stop in the middle of nowhere. The railroad cars started catching fire, but the Hitlerites wouldn't open them. Over 120 women and girls of our transport were charred to death that night. Because the floorboards of the train kept collapsing, many jumped free, and I was among them.

The women scattered in every direction, into towns and villages deserted by the Germans, who had left everything behind. I reached the outskirts of Berlin on foot, and went from there, again by foot, to Poznań, and from there, I took a train to Łódź.

I stayed in Łódź until December 1948. I came to Paris through legal means. The "Joint" helped support me there for several months and I learned tailoring at HEPUD.[3]

In January 1950, I married H—— K—— from Łódź, who had arrived in Paris in February 1947.

Eyewitness Testimony 21. A Child's Passage Through Hell

Kh. K. Born in Piotrków, Poland, in 1928; lived there. Recorded by B. Frenkel in New York in 1947. The witness talks about the persecutions and massacres of the Piotrków Jews during the first year of occupation, then he continues.

In the summer of 1940, although I was a youth, I volunteered to work under the Germans in a glassworks so I could get out of being rounded up in the streets. All of these raids ended with the captives being murdered. The jobs at the glassworks were punishing. I had to stand over a fire for days on end—during the night shift, too. When my painful work was done, I had to go straight out to the coal cars which had come in during the night, and without rest, unload the coal or other cargo. If I didn't, they would have killed me.

In the fall of 1942, while I was working the night shift, they started the *aktsye*[1] which took the lives of my parents, two younger brothers, and one of four older brothers. When the liquidation of the Jews was complete, a camp was set up for the 2,000 people who survived— among them, a small group of women and children—and all of us were packed into one compound. Of all the children in the city, only about 100 were left alive. Some people, who had managed to hide out during the *aktsye*, were eventually discovered by the Nazi killers through the help of Polish informers. These Poles, who at first had hidden the Jews, now robbed them of everything they had, and finally turned the people over into the hands of the German murderers. The Piotrków Rabbi, Reb Moyshe Khayim Loui—*Hashem yinkoim domoy*[2]—was part of our group, but in the very first days, the Germans dragged him out and shot him right in front of our eyes.

The Jews who'd been hiding that were captured, were held inside the *shiel,* and from there, they were taken to the Rakow Forest where they were shot. The children who hid with them were killed immediately in the most sadistic way. They smashed the children against the walls and ripped them apart by the legs. The Nazis ordered the Jewish police to regularly submit specific numbers of Jews for extermination. They complied because they were promised they and their families would be spared. The Jewish police carried out these cruel orders fully. Their turn came later, when a large number of them were themselves slaughtered by the Nazis.

Food in the camp was minimal—I was given watery soup and a twenty-*deka* piece of dark bread a day. Many people had money, so they bought extra food from the Poles who worked at the glassworks and in other places. I had no money, though—my parents were gone—and this forced me, after slaving away all night, to sign up for day labor at clearing out the homes of the murdered Jews. During the work, I hid a few pieces of linen, or some clothes—even though I could have been killed for this. I sold these things to the *goyim* for a piece of bread. While I was working at clearing out the houses, I came upon the most horrifying scenes. In many homes, the Jews who'd been shot dead were still lying in pools of blood on the floor, and in their beds. Full plates of food still stood on the tables. I was a youth of barely fourteen, and this depressed me beyond words. These catastrophic experiences shattered my nerves and today, I still suffer from it.

When the Germans started losing battle after battle, they wanted to exterminate us quickly, so they dragged together a transport of 950 Jews—I was among them—and sent us to Ostrowiec.[3] Several smaller transports were made up for other slave-labor camps.

In Ostrowiec, they carried out regular executions, which had to be witnessed by everyone. Once, a Jew tried to escape and three Jews were shot in retaliation. Many of us couldn't look as the death squads fired at them, but the Nazi killers turned their guns on us, and many of us were fatally wounded. Another time, again, several people were shot because one of them tried to hide a couple of dollars. Among those executed were two brothers named Zakhchinski. After them, another victim named Gutholts was killed. For turning some rubber hose they found into soles for shoes, several men were shot in front of our eyes. To survive Ostrowiec under such conditions was almost impossible.

In the summer of 1944, when the Soviet army entered the region, the Nazis quickly sealed us into freight cars and shipped us away to Birkenau, Auschwitz. Our transport from Ostrowiec numbered 1,800 people. Here, the women were separated from the men, and then all of us were put through a *selektsye*. Many were taken off immediately to perish in the gas chambers and crematoria, and the rest were pushed into the bathhouse. The *selektsye* which was done in Ostrowiec ended with the immediate shooting of all the sick people.

I was put into the "Gypsy" camp. I spent two weeks in this hell—half-alive and half-dead—and then they sent me out for slave labor. Once I was outside the camp, I was given the striped prison garb. They put me on a transport to Świętochłowice.[4] In German, they called it Eintrachthütte. Here I worked in a scrap-metal warehouse and at putting down roads, under *Kapos* who always carried whips. They hanged several Jews in the camp, again, for trying to escape. These unfortunate souls refused to endure the terrible ordeal. Among the victims was a Hungarian Jew named Roth.

We were kept here from September till mid-November, 1944, when they took us off to Buna.[5] I worked at the turbine plant inside this camp. Every *Shabbes*, executions were carried out, mostly by hanging. Our "crime" was that we couldn't withstand the murderous labor. The "guilty" ones were locked up in an underground bunker, and the victim had to stay down there till *Shabbes*. Then the sentences were carried out. Many were given twenty-five lashes and everyone was forced to watch. I, myself, was given five lashes. My "crime" was not being able to keep step in line. Others were strung up between the posts of the high-tension wire. They had to stay like this for twenty-four hours without moving, in snow and frost. They were electrocuted if they moved a muscle. I was held at first inside *Block* 3 of this concentration camp, then in *Block* 32. The *Blokowy* was a demented criminal, a *Mischling*—his name, *Yimakh shemoy*, was Alfred Wedel.

I worked in *Kommando* 62. We stayed inside this camp until January 1945. At night, they forced us out on foot to Gliwice.[6] Five thousand of us left the camp, but only about 3,000 of us got there. Anyone who couldn't keep up the fast pace, or who fainted or collapsed, was shot on the spot. The cold and frost was torture. Barely 2,000 half-dead "relics" were piled into open cattle cars and brought to Buchenwald. We stayed alive by eating snow, and once, the Germans threw three loaves of bread into each car. They did this on purpose so we'd claw each other scrambling for the bread. This hell lasted eight days. Many died of asphyxiation. We trampled the corpses underfoot. I was injured in this way and arrived in Buchenwald in February of 1945, an invalid. I was operated on and spent four weeks in the hospital. The conditions here were impossible. Coming out of the hospital, I only had one shoe because I lost the other one on the way to the hospital. I had to walk around like this, then stand at the *Appel* in the cold and frost with one foot shoeless, just wrapped in some rags. Later, I was sent to the block for invalids and youths. For several days before our liberation, the Nazis kept leading out transports of Jewish *Katzetler* to their deaths. Through a miracle, our group, which was marked for extermination, was saved, and we were liberated by the American army.

I spent six more weeks in Buchenwald, because I was included in a convoy organized by a chaplain in the American army. His name is Rabbi Schechter. Since we were youths, they sent us to France and we spent the whole time there in a hostel under the auspicies of the OSE Institute. I was taught to write and to read there, and I also did some work, getting enough food, until the year 1947, when I emigrated to the U.S.A.

Eyewitness Testimony 22. Spontaneous Resistance

Z.H. Born in 1908 in Zawichost, Radom District, Poland; worked there as a driver. Recorded by Duvid Graysdorf in a DP Camp in December 1947.

. . . The Jews of Zawichost were deported during October 1942. Everyone was forced to march the ten kilometers to the Wikozy train station by foot. The people were made to wait twenty-four hours under the open sky. A terrible thunderstorm broke out just as the people got to the field, and it rained on them for hours. They were then jammed into freight cars and shipped to Treblinka. Jews were herded in from the surrounding areas and piled into the already overcrowded transport, which numbered some 5,000 to 6,000 people.

There wasn't a Jew left in Zawichost, but two kilometers from the *shtetl* there was a labor camp where about 1,700 Jews continued slaving away at the most deadly kinds of labor. We had to work wading through swamps and ponds for days on end. The Jews of many neighboring towns—Radow, Shidlovtse,[1] and others—worked here. Every day, many victims fell dead; some because of the constant beatings and others from exhaustion and hunger.

When the Jews saw what had been done to the community of Zawichost, they decided to assassinate the camp commandant, the SS man, and to liberate the camp. They first killed the guards keeping watch by the commandant's quarters. Then they stabbed the commandant with a stiletto. Everyone broke out and all the Jews scattered into hiding in the woods.

Eyewitness Testimony 23. Life in the Lublin Forest

A.G. Born in Lublin in 1912; lived there. Recorded by Icek Shmulewitz in New York in January 1955. The witness describes the events in Lublin after the outbreak of the war; his experiences in the Piaski Ghetto, near Lublin, until the liquidation of the ghetto. He was able to escape through a bunker and continues at this point.

I came out of the bunker all alone—it was the dead of night. I jumped over a wall, but a Polish policeman saw me. He yelled for me to stop but I kept on running. He fired a couple of times but missed. Running wildly, I rushed down the next street and found myself back inside the ghetto. It wasn't completely by accident—I was desperate for a drink of water and couldn't have kept running without it. As soon as I started drinking from the ghetto well, a group of Polish policemen rushed at me. I ran out of the ghetto again, with the policemen after me, but they couldn't catch up.

I stumbled and ran through the fields all night long, not knowing where I was headed. Suddenly, I saw that I had reached the *besoylim*. As I rushed through it, a dog jumped out at me from behind a grave, still tugging at pieces of flesh from the Jews who'd been shot and dumped here. The corpses in the shallow open pits were barely covered over. As the dog scurried by me I nearly collapsed in fright. I finally got out of there and raced through the fields away from the

cemetery. I passed many peasant huts along the way. I drank from
cattle troughs to quench my thirst. When I drank my fill, I got up
to run, but soon I was overcome with exhaustion. I crept into a
peasant's shed and lay down on the hay to rest. But then a dog ran
up and started howling, so I had to keep running. I walked and ran
all night long, till at daybreak, I reached the Skrzynice Forest near
Lublin. This was in the fall of 1942.

When I was finally inside the forest, night fell. Right at the edge
of the forest, I saw a woman jump up from the fields and dash in
between the trees. I caught up to her. All I said to her was, "*Amkho?*"
The woman answered, yes, she's a Jewish daughter. She told me that
deeper in the forest, her two small children lay hidden together with
other Jewish women—some of them old—and their children. Altogether, this group of women and children numbered twelve people.

The woman was from Lublin and she told me that during the
deportation from the Lublin Ghetto, she and her two children and
the other women with their children escaped into the forest from
the ghetto. Polish peasants confronted them in the woods, but they
took pity on the women and children and let them live. She said she
was on her way from the village where she'd gotten hold of two
bottles of water—she had a small kettle in the woods and wanted
to boil the water for the children. As we were finishing talking, we
came upon the spot in the woods where the Jewish women and children were hiding. Before me was a horrible sight:

The women and children lay stretched out on the ground, bundled
up in rags. The small children cried terribly and a fire had started in
the underbrush and was spreading all around them. . . . [After the
fire was put out] and I asked them how they had managed to keep
alive, they told me that every evening, they were visited by a good-
hearted Jewish youth from Łódź, Yulek Rozenshtayn, who was taken
out of the *Lodzer* Ghetto with other Jews in 1940,[1] but had escaped
from his transport. He stayed in the woods somewhere and the
peasants thought he was Christian. For two years, this young man
worked as a caretaker for the forest warden. In the end, the warden
found out he was a Jew and got rid of him. The women told me he
visits them every evening and brings them beets, potatoes, and other
things to eat. I waited for him, and that same evening, I met Yulek
Rozenshtayn.

We became friends right away. He told me he sometimes still went
to see the warden for whom he'd worked, and the warden gives him
bread. Yulek Rozenshtayn told me he couldn't stay in the area long,
because the peasants make raids in the woods to capture Jews in
hiding, and strip them of everything they own. The peasants also
beat the Jews up—sometimes, to death. This young man told me a
peasant woman lived near the forest with her children—her husband
was taken away for forced labor to Germany. At night, Yulek Rozen-

shtayn comes in through her yard and sleeps in the cellar, and the peasant woman doesn't know a thing about it. During the day, of course, he roams through the woods.

Yulek brought me down to the woman's cellar. We stayed there and talked our situation over. In the morning, I took up potatoes from the cellar and brought them to the women and children in the woods. While we were standing around the campsite fire, baking potatoes, a Pole and a Russian, both armed with rifles, attacked us. They stripped off my boots and suit and then left. This Pole had been exiled from Poznań and the Russian was a Soviet soldier who escaped from a German camp. Both of them hunted the woods for Jews, and when they found them, they robbed them of everything they had.

Yulek and I returned to the peasant woman and she gave me some wooden clogs to wear. Then we took two shovels and an axe from the woman and went off to dig a bunker in the forest for the women and children, who had to lie on the sodden ground. It took us several days to finish the bunker. We padded it with straw and burlap, the children and their mothers went down inside and baked and ate potatoes there. Now they had some means of security.

A reward of a quarter-kilo of sugar was offered by the Germans to any Pole who revealed the hideout of a Jew. During the night, while I lay in the woman's cellar with my friend Yulek, a mob of peasants stormed into the woods, dragged the Jewish women and children from the bunker, and took them off to the Germans. The women were forced to go on foot, and the children were dumped into a wagon. The women and children were taken to the Gestapo in Głusk. At dawn, when my friend and I left the cellar to take the potatoes to the women and children in the woods, we saw the peasants hauling them away in the distance. We decided then not to return to the peasant woman's cellar, but to stay in the woods.

The next morning, we watched a priest and a peasant roll a wagon into the forest to get firewood for the church. We went up to the priest and asked for some bread. The priest said he had no bread with him, but in the afternoon, when he came to the forest for more wood, he'd bring us some. Later, he did bring us bread and two bottles of milk. The bread and the bottles were hidden under the straw in the peasant's wagon, and he didn't know it. While the peasant was busy gathering wood, the priest told us to go to the wagon, where to look for the bread and milk, we found it and left.

After my friend and I had enough to eat, we decided to get guns to protect ourselves, since we were always in danger of falling into the hands of the Poles. We decided to ask the peasant woman in whose cellar we used to sleep, about guns—maybe she knew something about them, or maybe her husband had a gun, or maybe the Polish army hid guns in her house after they were demobilized?

When we got to the woman's hut, it was already very dark. She got scared when she saw us but we calmed her down. The woman was furious because we took the potatoes from the cellar and left her and the children with nothing to eat. We promised her, that if the world was ever made right again, we would repay everything. When we mentioned guns, we sensed from her words that she knew something about them but wasn't willing to help us. Finally, the woman told us to climb down through a trapdoor—there was a pit down there covered by a boulder where her husband had buried something when the Polish soldiers were demobilized.

My friend and I got down in the pit the woman spoke of, we started digging, and found a rifle there, manufactured at the Radom munitions works. We also found a revolver with bullets down there. The rifle and revolver were very rusted. The woman gave us paraffin and rags, we went off to the woods, and for a whole day, we polished the rusted guns. We loaded the rifle and revolver with the bullets and crossed into another part of the woods.

My friend and I headed in a completely new direction. During the night, we stole into a peasant's yard. When the peasants saw we were armed, they gave us bread and other kinds of food and we went back to the woods. This was in the Chmiel Forest. While we were there, we heard volleys of shots from the Skrzynice woods. At night, we returned to the peasant woman who lived near the Skrzynice Forest to find out what the shooting was about. She told us the warden informed the Germans there were partisans in the woods—meaning us—that we had attacked him and taken his rifle. Later, Germans and Poles came into the woods with their dogs. The dogs started sniffing out the Jews hiding in the forest and the Germans shot them. There were many Jews who were safely hidden in the depths of the forest, but they panicked because of the dogs and the soldiers and abandoned their shelters. They ran for the fields where the Germans shot them all. But many Jews didn't leave the forest. They stayed inside their hideouts. After the Germans had finished in the forest, they went after the Jews hiding in the villages.

My friend and I went to the Skrzynice Forest to find the Jews in hiding the peasant woman had told us about. Walking through the forest, we saw smoke in the distance—some small fire was burning— and we crept up quietly. When we got to the clearing, we saw Jewish families I had known in Lublin, Głusk, and *shtetlekh* near Lublin, gathered in a circle. They were baking potatoes over the fire, and as we came near, they told us there had been a raid in the woods yesterday—the shooting we'd heard—but they hadn't given up their hiding place, lying flat all day, and because of this, had saved themselves from the Germans and the Polish peasants.

When we asked these people in the Skrzynice Forest how they kept alive, they said that one of their group, Yisruel Fingerkurz of Głusk, heads into the countryside to peasants he knows, and they always give him potatoes. The peasants warned him the last time out, though, not to come round anymore, because a search was on for Jews in hiding and they were afraid, themselves, of getting caught for what they did. The group of people also told us there was a young Jew wandering around the forest, who kept to himself. He was called Heniek[2]—he was from Lublin—and had belonged to the Polish partisans, but the Poles robbed him of everything, so he left them and came to these woods.

As my friend and I were standing and talking like this to the group in the forest, the young man appeared out of nowhere. He recognized me from Lublin and told me it was true—he'd been with a Polish partisan unit. He wore a cross around his neck—he said he had a good Polish accent, the Poles couldn't tell he was a Jew. Heniek soon realized, though, that whenever Jews joined the partisan unit to which he belonged, they were taken on only to be shot the same night. He was scared they would find out he was a Jew and shoot him, too. So he left the Polish partisan unit and came to the small town of Osmolice.[3] In Osmolice, he went up to a peasant for bread, but the peasant recognized him from the partisans and knew he'd run away from them. The peasant found out he was a Jew and dragged him off to the Germans. At night, he escaped through a window and came back to the forest. The young man told me he was afraid to stay with the other Jews in the forest because they talk loudly and yell among themselves, so he keeps his distance from them.

Then I told him my friend and I were armed and we also had a gun for him if he decided to join us. I suggested the three of us take our guns and search around for food to bring back to the Jews hiding in the forest, and later, we would decide what to do next. The young man took the rifle and left for the village that night with me and my friend. The peasant watchmen who stood guard in the village during the night took aim to shoot at us, but when we said we were partisans, they held their fire. The peasants gave us bread, potatoes, and butter, and we took these back to the forest where our people were hiding. Later, we told the peasant watchmen to inform the village chieftain there were partisans in the woods, and not to arm any more peasants in the village at night against Jews looking for food, and to stop handing us over to the Germans. We went back to our group in the forest, and now had a supply of food for a few days.

They told us there were other Jews hiding in the forest, but they were scattered all over, and one didn't know where the other was. Snow started falling, and this was bad, because we left tracks in the fields and villages when we went to get hay for our bunker. That same day, the forest warden came to us and asked that we leave the area because the Germans were tracking us by our footprints.

Our whole group crossed to another forest near Pieczków.[4] We brought along shovels and dug a large bunker in this new spot where we hid for a long time. This bunker held fourteen people—men, women, and two children. The food we had was the bread and potatoes we brought along from the forest we'd just left.

While we were there—near Pieczków—we again heard shooting from the Skrzynice Forest. During the night, my two friends and me—we were armed—headed for the peasant woman who lived near the Skrzynice Forest. The woman told us the Germans were in the woods because informers led them to the bunker where the Jews had hidden. We walked through the Skrzynice Forest till we saw the Germans tossing grenades into the bunker we'd hidden in before. After the grenades went off, the Germans realized there were no Jews here—we'd escaped in time, before the informers had gotten to them.

We knew we had to get arms at any cost if we were going to form a partisan unit which could resist the Germans. At night, the three of us went to the peasant Skulski looking for guns we heard he'd hidden. We threatened him and told him we knew about the hidden guns he denied having. We told him if he didn't give us the guns, we'd take his wife and children from the hut, shoot him, and burn everything down. The peasant still refused to give us the guns.

Then the three of us took bundles of straw into the hut and set them on fire. His wife cried and begged Skulski to give us the guns, but he kept denying he knew anything about them. Then Yulek and me stayed with them while Heniek went to get the village chieftain, to order Skuski to surrender the guns. When the chieftain came, he said to Skulski: "Can't you see this is an organized, integrated partisan group? Give them the guns!"

But Skulski the peasant denied he knew anything about any guns. Then the chieftain took us aside and told us Skulski had robbed and murdered countless Jews who were in hiding—that is, when he didn't have the Germans do it. When I heard this, I lost control completely. I told my two friends to take the peasant's wife and children away, and for the chieftain to get them somewhere to stay. The house burned, and my friend raised his gun and shot Skulski dead.

After we shot him and the house was all in flames, the peasant's wife told us to climb down to the foundation where we'd find the guns. We rushed right into the hut and put out the fire. We lowered ourselves down and started digging where the peasant's widow told us to. We then found two rifles and a full crate of ammunition. We carried this back to the forest where our people were. We told the chieftain to inform the peasants in the village that if partisans came, they should surrender their guns, and if anyone informed or retaliated against the Jews in hiding, we'd put the whole countryside to the torch.

We took the guns into the woods and cleaned them for a whole day. We armed two more men with these guns. One of them was Fishl Spivak from Głusk, and the other was called Avrum, also from Głusk. By now, we were five Jews—all armed—and we decided to make a campsite in the woods and stay there till the snow melted. We held out in this hideout for two months. At night, we'd go into the villages, to rich peasants, and take bread and potatoes from them. They were afraid of us, gave us all kinds of food to eat, and this is what we lived on for the whole two months.

In the spring of 1943, the five of us armed ourselves and went to the Skrzynice Forest again, to see if there were any Jews still alive. We roamed through the woods all day until we finally reached a spot where a group of Jews—young men and women—were sitting around a small fire. When they saw us coming up with our guns, they rushed toward us, crying from great excitement and emotion. They said there was an integrated partisan group in the woods—meaning us— who'd killed a peasant and terrorized all the other peasants in the region to stop marauding the Jews in hiding. We five armed Jews again went into the village and brought back bread and potatoes for the young Jews hiding in the woods.

One of the Jewish girls, who went into the village to sew for a peasant woman, told us that while passing a peasant's hut, she saw the Pole and the Russian—I mentioned them earlier—who kept up their attacks against Jews. The five of us left right away and sur- rounded this peasant's hut. We watched through the windows with- out being seen, and saw the Russian sitting and eating. We waited till the peasant's wife left the hut to go out into the barn—she left the door open—and we stormed into the hut. First, we grabbed the Russian's revolver and told him we wouldn't shoot him because he's Russian. We demanded to know where his Polish "partner" was. The Russian took us to a peasant's hut and called out the Pole we were looking for. As soon as the Pole walked through the doorway, we shot him dead. He was a "*Slęzak*" murderer. We let the Russian go, and told him if he proved himself, we'd consider taking him into our partisan unit after a while.

We gave the Russian's revolver to a Jew in our group in the woods, Sender Zusman from Lublin. The five of us returned to the woods near Pieczkow and the other people stayed on in the Skrzynice Forest. We met Jews who were hiding in the Pieczkow woods, but we brought them to the Skrzynice Forest so all the Jews would be together. All in all, there were twenty-six of us in the forest: men, women, and the two small children, a brother and sister, Srul and Faygaleh B——. These two are grown now, and live with their parents in the Bronx. In the beginning, everyone hid in one small pit in the ground which was covered over. Later, we dug a large bunker farther back in the woods, where we could all stay together comfortably.

One morning—it was a Sunday—some peasants came to collect firewood near where we were. They spotted us, and the next day, Germans were here. We had all left the bunker by chance and were roaming around different parts of the woods. Only Itche Klayman of Głusk stayed behind in the bunker. There was something wrong with his foot and he couldn't walk. The Germans broke into the bunker and shot Klayman. The rest of us took up new positions deeper in the woods. We started shooting back and the Germans retreated from the forest. We all came together again afterwards, and moved to another part of the forest. Soon, the Germans had us surrounded and fired at us from all sides. During the exchange, they shot Fishl Spivak's wife, Yosl Aynshtayn, and a young woman named Masheh. The rest of us escaped still deeper into the woods.

We got together at night, and decided to regroup in the woods near Mentow.[5] The Germans ordered the Poles to cover up the Jews who were shot with earth and leaves, right where they'd fallen. A few days later, we returned to this spot, dug up the mounds where the dead Jews lay, and buried them in four separate graves, one next to the other. At the head of each grave, we placed boards, and inscribed the name of the person who'd fallen, their place of origin, and that they'd fallen in battle against the Nazis.

Eyewitness Testimony 24. Expulsion from the Town of Auschwitz

B.Y.H. Born in Auschwitz in 1926; lived there. Recorded by Dr. Y. Bornshtayn, no date or place mentioned. The witness tells of the effects of the start of occupation on the old *shtetl*. He reveals the procedures used to construct the concentration camp at Auschwitz with local Jewish slave labor. He now discusses the first expulsion at the end of 1940 to the Government General.

They ordered that the *shtetl* of Auschwitz must become *judenrein,* so gradually, everyone was forced to leave. The selection of the first 1,000 deportees took two weeks. Whole families were led away with all their things. Whoever had large sums of money tried to buy their reprieve. The people were taken near the city of Lublin and confined in the small villages of the area.[1] This transport took away my grandparents—my father's parents. It was the first really terrible ordeal the people suffered. Every family mourned, each home was filled with weeping. The rabbinate called a day of fasting, loud prayers rose from every *Shtibl, Tilim* was heard from every window. Everyone felt this was the beginning of the destruction of Jewish life. We all kept repeating the phrase: "Who knows if we'll ever meet again?"

To assemble in the *shiel* was outlawed—the Germans saw to this right away. Then, they set the *shiel* on fire and tried to burn it down. At the start of 1940, we suddenly heard this explosion rip through the *shiel*, but we were able to put out the fire. The community leaders carried out the *klei koydesh*, as well as the *sifre toyres* from the *shiel* and distributed them to different Jewish families for safekeeping. All gatherings of Jews were forbidden, and we couldn't *davn* publicly in the *kloizn*, but had to gather privately in each others' homes to make up the *minyen*. We kept watch at the door in case a German stole by. The neighbors close by used our house for the *minyen*. The *sifre toyre* was hidden in a small cupboard in the wall. When the order was given for the 1,000 Jews to leave town, everyone fasted. Women and children, too. The *rasn kvurim* of the old women was heard from the *besoylim*. The family was in a total state of shock. I could never have imagined a sorrow like that which descended on us after they took my father's family away.

In the week of *Puysekh*, 1941,[2] the *Judenrat* made an announcement for all the Jews to be ready to leave the town within three days, taking along whatever they could carry. The people were divided up in three groups headed for different destinations: Bendien, Sosnovits, and Chrzanow.[3] The *Judenrat* arranged for the local Jews in these towns to accommodate us. The Germans hitched together a few dozen carts and horses for the old and sick people, because it was over two kilometers to the train. People couldn't stop crying on the march out of the *shtetl* because they were being forced from a home their ancestors had settled and lived in for centuries. The way was littered with abandoned belongings the people couldn't carry anymore. Many fainted and collapsed in the streets. The Jewish doctors tried reviving those who'd had attacks. The *sfurim* and *gemures* were all buried earlier, for the most part. Many *sfurim* were buried in the *shiel* courtyard to prevent their being desecrated by enemy hands. The *sifre toyre* and *mezuzes* the people took themselves. The expulsion from Auschwitz was carried out by the German border patrols. They were correct toward us and some even tried to help. In contrast, the *Volksdeutsche*—most of them were former local Polish subjects who lived alongside the Jews—trailed after us with anti-Semitic slogans and curses, rejoicing over their "revenge." They were only looking for people to drop their belongings so they could swoop them up and steal them. Mostly, we were stunned by the correct behavior of the German field gendarmes toward us—that was why so few tried escaping. It was only inside the train that the transport was taken over by German SS, dressed in black, skull and bones.

Of all the Jews who had been in the *shtetl* before this deportation, only the *Judenrat* was left behind now with another fifty people to clear out the deserted Jewish homes. What they did with the Jewish belongings they gathered together, I don't know. Two weeks later, the *Judenrat* and the fifty people were removed to Bendien and Sosnovits. After exerting a lot of pressure, some of the *Judenratler* were co-opted into the *Judenräte* of Bendien and Sosnovits.

After the SS took control of the train, no one was allowed off the transport—not even for a drink of water at the station—until they brought us into Bendien. After the endless despair we suffered in those stifling cars, the kindness the Bendien Jews showed us was a great comfort and encouragement. The Jewish youth of the city received us at the train station with warm nourishment—milk was prepared for the children, food was distributed to everyone—and their generous and sincere Jewish hearts revived us. People were assigned by the Bendien *Judenrat* to help us carry our things and we were housed comfortably. Our family was given a separate room by an old couple named Fayershtayn. They empathized with us because of our suffering. They did everything to support us and help out. The reaction of these people gave our whole group new spirit and hope.

I have to tell you that at first we were afraid there would be antagonism between us—we were considered Galician Jews and the local Jews were part of Congress Poland.[4] But now, all I can do is praise those Jews of Bendien [who are no more], but who made us feel there was no difference between us. The Bendien Jews sympathized with all our troubles. A few weeks later, our relatives, who were deported with the group to Chrzanów, arrived. They escaped from Chrzanów unseen, and since they were in Bendien illegally and so couldn't get a room, they stayed with us. The Fayershtayn family was very considerate, even though there were five new people. Later, a room was found for them to stay in.

The Bendien *Judenrat* advised all young people to volunteer for the labor battalions headed to the German camps, because if they didn't, they were assured, their families would certainly be "resettled." I wanted to spare our family, so against the wishes of my mother, *Oleyhu hashulem,* who wanted me to hide, I joined the labor battalion voluntarily. I left home, and didn't even say goodbye. We were divided up into special groups and assigned to different camps. I was transported to Birkenhain[5] together with a group of 100 people. This camp was made up of five or six long barracks surrounded by barbed wire and guarded by SS. We worked from morning till night laying railroad tracks. My job was filling in the spaces between the crossties with gravel. I was young and had never done any manual labor. I got terrible blisters and my hands swelled up. The sanitary conditions in camp were unendurable. There was no water inside the camp—it had to be brought in by barrel. We became dirty and lice-infested very quickly. The worms drove us crazy. There wasn't enough food. We tried getting more at the work sites. We'd plead with the civilians for some bread. After twelve hours of labor, I had to polish the boots of the guards. They gave me a few pieces of bread for this. I could speak German, so I was given the "privilege" of polishing their boots. Many envied me for this.

During this first period of life in camp, I not only suffered from the hard labor, but from loneliness and the fact that I hadn't bid my mother farewell. My nights were a torture, racked by nightmares. My only thought was getting out to see my mother one last time and saying goodbye to her like I should. The idea obssessed me day and night and I started planning an escape. It took seven months before I was given the chance of working at the wire fence surrounding the camp. No one saw me cut a hole in the fence through which I could crawl. One afternoon, when, unexpectedly, the work ended early, I rubbed off the *mugen duvid* which was smeared on my garb in oil paint, and tore my way through the hole. The camp was twenty-five kilometers from Bendien and where my mother was. I ran for about fifteen kilometers, then got on a trolley which drove into Bendien. At night, I came to my mother's room. I had stolen through alleyways since it was past curfew—it was only allowed to be outside in Bendien till eight P.M. Those caught out later, were arrested. They were also shot. I darted from doorway to doorway till I got to the house where my mother lived. I knocked, and my terrified sister opened the door. Everyone froze with fear, as if I'd come back from the dead. Now was the first time that I heard my mother had been sick for three months and I thought this must have been the feeling which gave me no rest through those nights. After we rejoiced for a few hours at my coming back, I decided to return to the camp because I was scared something might happen to our family when it was found out I had broken out—they were sure to retaliate and strike at my family. I was given a picture of the family to take back with me and a separate one of my father, and some money from the little they had. I took my leave of them and started my trek back to the camp. I went with a feeling of calmness—now fate could take its course. I had said goodbye to my mother. It was still dark when I got back.

The next day was *Sylvester*, 1944. During the day, we worked at clearing the fields around the camp. At midnight, we were roused by the SS guards who chased us, screaming and hitting us the whole time, from our bunks to the *Appelplatz*. They charged into the barracks screaming "*Raus!*" and beat us without looking. We were driven out with no clothes on and beaten all over our bodies. They paraded us up and down the *Appelplatz*, and made us run till we dropped. We were brutalized on the *Appelplatz* like this for three hours. Many had to be dragged back inside because they collapsed from the cold—they just froze up. This was the surprise the SS gave us on *Sylvester* of the new year.

After two weeks of this, they sent us from the Brand[6] camp to another camp at Gross-Masselwitz,[7] also in Germany. We lived in a cement-block shed which was used as a stable for horses before us. Most of us worked in the cement plant. We hauled in wagonloads of sand and rocks. I was emptying out a wagon when a wheelbarrow fell over on my hand and crushed my thumb. Many hours passed before I was taken back to camp and I was then driven into Breslau under guard to have the finger treated at the hospital. The guard told me the hospital had been a Jewish one. I was treated decently and the finger was operated on. For a time afterwards, I did no heavy labor in camp—just swept the grounds with my one good hand.

During this time, the SS *Sturmbannführer*, Lindner, inspected the camp regularly. He never failed to select a transport of sick workers for the Auschwitz crematoria. He also came when I couldn't work. This Lindner was going to send me off to Auschwitz with the other sick inmates, but a camp doctor—a Jew from Zator[8] named Modner— and the medic, Dolek Haas, tried to stop him. They risked their lives doing this for me, telling Lindner I'd be able to work in two days. It cost you your life if he felt you were bluffing. He sent you to Auschwitz just for opening your mouth. But I was saved, by their pleading, from a transport to Auschwitz which would have surely led to my death. Two weeks later, I was put back to work at the labor site.

I had a *landsman* in camp who came from a family of rich *Khsidim*, named Zajdband. He knew my parents, too. He was a *Kapo* in camp. When I met him, I asked him to help me. He looked me up and down with a sadistic smirk on his face, then told me to remove my hat. He suddenly struck me over the head with his rubber club and beat me again and again till I was delirious from the pain. This Khayim Zajdband was one who reached the height of sadism in the camps. He was condemned in Poland in 1947 to twenty years hard labor.

In May 1944, we were taken out of Gross-Masselwitz and sent to the Dyhernfurt *Konzentrazionslager*. We worked here at loading and unloading freight trains. We laid tracks here, too.

It was 1945 and we felt the war was coming to an end. The Germans couldn't "do their work" on us any more, either, because of the constant bombings. At the end of February, we were shipped out of camp. They packed us into trains—100 men to a coal car—and we were sent toward Bergen-Belsen. On the way to Bergen-Belsen, we passed through the town of Zelle, where we stopped at the train station. Other trains stood near ours, packed full of soldiers and ammunition. It was evening. Suddenly, an air squadron of British bombers swept over the town and leveled it. The railway was completely destroyed. They forced us to stay inside the railroad cars. The SS Guards were crouching beneath us, under the cars. When the bombing began, people on our transport were hit, and when some of us tried to take cover in a nearby forest, the SS opened fire on us. The bombing kept up all through the night, hitting our cars, too, and now most of us risked running clear of the trains. The SS guards lost control over us because they were also getting blown up. We all scattered to the forest and ran further into the countryside of this region. Many of us were killed by the SS. Others were hit by bomb shrapnel and were wounded. Some of us got hold of civilian clothes and changed into them, but as soon as we took off our caps, they could tell we were *Katzetler* because there was a strip shaved down our scalps three centimeters wide, from the forehead to the nape of the neck. This way, when an escaped *Katzetler* was found, he was shot on the spot. It was only on the following day that they started looking for us and captured us. While they were hunting for the escapees, many of us were shot. There were about 150 victims, a third of them were killed by the bombs. After we were caught, we were taken on foot into the *Konzentrationslager* at Bergen-Belsen.

On the day of Liberation, I was infected with typhus and lost consciousness the day after. I found out about the cyanide-poisoned bread[9] when I recovered from the illness. In mid-April, we were freed by the English.

Eyewitness Testimony 25. Down the "Aryan" Side by Steamer

R.M. Born in Warsaw in 1908; lived there. Recorded by Hersh Vasser in Warsaw, November 1947.

... Polish acquaintances of my husband, Y—— M—— (he was a metal goods supplier for the military) kept warning me not to stay in the ghetto. They felt it was certain death. Even if they hadn't insisted so strongly, my eyes showed me every day I wouldn't last long in the ghetto. Finally, I decided to get out.

In the beginning, I stayed at Opocinska 45 with my husband's Polish acquaintance, Bielski. I tried to give the impression I was a Pole, too. I was given the name Jankowska. This is the name I was known by till recently. An officer of the first cavalry battalion out of Praga, Lieutenant Stefan Jankowski, with whom my husband had dealings, gave me his late wife's birth certificate. This is how I was able to register and get a *Kennkarte*. I made out a forged passbook for my daughter Sheyve with the help of our Polish acquaintances. I made it out under the name Sabina Jankowska, born in Wlodzimierz-Wołynski. Besides Lieutenant Stefan Jankowski, the people who helped me were: Major Biguszewski of the cavalry battalion—he died during the occupation; Chorąży, Baruch, and the Kwiatowski family—Henryk and Helena Kwiatowski.

Stefan Jankowski had me and my daughter registered as residing in his home at Praga 3. I had no money. I often had to accept invitations from Polish acquaintances to have dinner at their homes. First, I traveled to Grodzisk, near Warsaw, and later to the Lublin region. I smuggled food into the ghetto, and this also helped keep me alive. The police often confiscated all the food I was carrying. Because of my destitute condition, the Bielskis at Opocinska quarreled constantly. After talking things over with my family in the ghetto, I decided to go back. This first phase on the Polish side lasted about half a year. After I moved into Sienna Street 27 with my husband's family, I started providing people with homemade meals. I would leave the ghetto, risking my life every day, so my child would have something to eat—there was no other way. I was active like this for a few months. But the "business" finally lost all its "customers." Feeling myself slowly dying of starvation, I decided to leave the ghetto once again. I want you to know that as long as I struggled against the Germans, I was full of energy, never felt helpless—no setback discouraged me. I wanted to survive the war. I pawned the last few valuables I had for about 150 *gildn,* tied together all I owned in a small bundle, and with my little Sheyve, left the ghetto by way of Chłodna Street.[1]

We spent the first night at the Kwiatowskis'. *Pani* Helena Kwiatkowska introduced me to *Pani* Jadwiga Górska—she knew I was Jewish, too—whose husband, Władysław Górski, ran a buffet on the steamboat *Goniec* of the Wistula Line traveling the Warsaw-Sandomierz route. I helped out in the buffet. The steamship served a main water artery and, naturally, a huge amount of smuggling was done on the Wistula steamships. The smugglers were degenerate types. In the beginning, I didn't think I would hold out, but knowing what was waiting for me back there, I resigned myself. Every five days, I would spend some time in Warsaw with my young daughter. I left her at Zajęcza 13 in Powiśle,[2] with the widow Ninet. I paid her twenty *gildn* a month. I was given food on the ship, but no pay. I worked on the steamship all summer long in 1942. After a while, I started smuggling again, too. Władysław Górski—he still didn't know I was Jewish—lent me the first 300 *gildn.* I sold smuggled goods in Warsaw and, from time to time, also inside the ghetto. During this time, it was impossible to even come near the ghetto—the big deportation to Treblinka had started. I helped Polish smugglers through the river checkpoints—the main police checkpoint was at Dęblin.

One time on the river, I made the acquaintance of *Pani* Jadwiga Szot from the village of Jakubowice near Sandomierz. I asked her to take care of my child, whom I had to leave behind in Warsaw. She agreed to it. We didn't discuss money. She was an honest peasant woman in her forties, simple and reliable. There was a Jewish woman on the same steamship from Jozefów-nad-Wisłą who also smuggled. Górski found out who she was but didn't betray her. I knew, too, but she didn't recognize who I really was. One time, a lice-infested group of Jews near death—men, women, children—was let on board, and they came part of the way with us to Sandomierz.

Another incident from this period: On a certain day, while we were at anchor in Dęblin, a gendarme detained a well-dressed man. When he found out he was a Jew, he dragged him onto the shore and started beating him without pity. The crowd also called me over to have a look. The onlookers yelled: "Shame! Shame! In front of everyone!" Then I walked on to the shore, and without saying a word, took hold of the gendarme and brought him back to the buffet with me. The ship captain and some other men lifted the beaten Jew into a cabin and I revived him. Then the crowd wanted to make sure he was a Jew. I wouldn't let them. I said: "It's all the same whether he's a Pole, a Jew, or a Russian! What matters is, he's a human being!" This had an effect for the moment. The next morning, this man got off at a port of transfer and headed for Sandomierz. When he took leave of me, he assured me he'd never forget what I'd done for him. The passengers—common Polish people—had one opinion on the Jews and this was their "answer": The trouble with the Jews was they had never "gotten theirs," and though the Germans were maybe too brutal, it was either them—the Jews—or "us."

I got by without running into any Germans the whole time I was on the steamship *Goniec*. Wasn't beaten once. I held my head high. Not out of desperation, but because inside me I felt a great reserve of strength which drove me to act compulsively.

This is what happened once: Some stolen goods which the gendarmes confiscated from one steamship and the Germans loaded onto ours, thinking it'd be secure here, were stolen by the smugglers on our ship. Górski was also mixed up with the smugglers. The gendarmes tried to force me to give them the name of the guilty one. I told them nothing. Out of gratitude, Górski allowed me to bring my little Sheyvele on board and she was fed just like me.

During one of my short stays in Warsaw at this time, I met Zofia Szarecka at Wolska Street 42. This happened after I left the steamship and managed somehow to settle down in the village of Jakubowice, about two kilometers outside Annapol Lubelski.[3] I had taken advantage of my acquaintance with Górski, and gotten to Warsaw by steamer. Zofia Szarecka had built a hideout into her flat and let four Jews stay there. For a whole month, I cooked for them, bought them food, and was their only contact with the outside world. But I couldn't endure it any longer because my longing for my child and my anxiety over her safety drove me back to Jakubowice. I kept in contact with the group, though. The four were assisted by the

"Underground Committee for Jews in Hiding,"[4] and they arranged for 1,000 *gildn* to be sent to me and my daughter every month. Another unusual occurrence in the Hitler era was when a Gentile woman and I, together, took on two Jewish children, who were lowered down in bound sheets from a third-story window at the time of the general deportation.[5]

After going through all these ordeals, I became sick with the Bazedov disease. My life in Jakubowice was one long chain of misery. I hired myself out to peasants, pawned, bartered, smuggled, just to get hold of the bare necessities. My Sheyvele stayed with the peasant Szot. Through his attempts, she was signed up at the elementary school. But to pay her way, she had to tend his cattle and goats in the morning hours. As long as the war lasted, the child ignored that she was Jewish. Many times, I didn't think I'd survive the war, maybe because rumors were spread that I was Jewish, maybe because of my impoverishment and desperation. And again a lucky coincidence saved me in those tragic days. I was walking in the forest once—it was toward the end of 1943, and I knew all the woods and country-side like my own pocket—when I ran into a Soviet partisan, an engineer. I told him of my hardships, of having lived in Warsaw. He reacted to all this by promising me that the Russian and Polish parti-sans wouldn't harm me. The villagers heard about it and took a whole new attitude toward me, even though I hadn't told it to anyone. I kept in touch with the partisan assault units till the very end, and just before the Red Army got here, I even directed two escaped Russian prisoners-of-war to the partisans in the forest. But I was de-nounced for this and had to run away into the woods with my child and hide there till Liberation.

Eyewitness Testimony 26. On Both Sides of the Ghetto Wall

A.G. (maiden name R.). Born in Warsaw in 1923; lived there till the war. Recorded by Mikhl Zylberberg in London in the early 1950s. The transcription was a Yiddish translation from the Polish original.

As soon as the Germans occupied Warsaw, our business was con-fiscated, and by the next day—looted clean. The valuables and notes my parents had in the bank were all blocked. This was the start of great suffering for us. My younger sister and I stopped going to school and we lived from hand to mouth.

In the summer of 1942, a massive *Aussiedlung* was begun. At the start, we weren't threatened directly because we had gotten work through some social agencies. But after a time, this didn't matter anymore, and my uncle Henryk had to pay a huge bribe to get us inside Hoffmann's Linen Mill[1] on Nowolipki Street. The *aktsyes* never stopped at the mill, either, but luckily, none of our family was deported. The greatest tragedy of my life happened in the *selektsye* on September 6, when my only sister was separated from us and deported, leaving only my parents, a cousin, and me alive in our home which once held so many. The Jewish *Gmineh*[2] helped provide for my grandfather, my uncle Henryk, and a cousin during these hardships.

As soon as the *selektsye* ended, my parents started thinking of how to get me over to the "Aryan" side. My uncle had many contacts in the Polish Underground, and he started making a plan that would get me, my grandfather, and two cousins, settled safely on the "Aryan" side. I stayed in the ghetto till March of 1943. One day, my parents took me from work and told me, suddenly, that during the night, my grandfather and I would cross over to the "Aryan" side.

We were guided through underground labyrinths at three in the morning by my uncle's friends, Dr. Ringelblum and P. Miller. They helped lift us over the ghetto wall, and two contacts met us on the other side. A Polish policeman in blue uniform—he'd been bribed—acted out an arrest and led us away to his contact on Chłodna Street. There, we were brought to *Pani* Elżbieta, my father's and cousin's former secretary, who had stolen across to the "Aryan" side before me.

She hid us in her flat for a month. One time, the door was broken in by uniformed Poles from Silesia who were set on capturing us, and we got away with our lives only because we still had a little money left. Afterwards, we were put up in a flat belonging to a Polish sailor, Roman, in Praga. Roman lived there with his wife and mother and worked for the Polish underground.

I only stayed there a short while. Roman was always bothering me and we were afraid his jealous wife would denounce us to the police.

My grandfather and my little cousin stayed behind at the sailor's and I ran off to another contact on Bednarska Street. The flat was being used by an old prostitute who put me up for money. I had my own room here and was left pretty much alone. One night, Germans came in. At the last minute, I jumped out of bed and hid for over an hour behind her dresser which was blocked off by the open door. The Germans were looking for valuables and I escaped death by a miracle.

The lady of the flat grew fond of me and decided to help rescue me. She talked things over with her sister in Miłosna,[3] who agreed to take me in for money. Her name was Szatkowska. Her daughters came to get me and took me back to Miłosna. I was here, supposedly, as the mistress' visiting niece. When I crossed the threshold of this new home, I saw two women inside, but I didn't know which was my "aunt." I called out loudly, "*Ciocia! Ciocia!*" and one of them then threw her arms around my shoulders and said, "My dearest Kazia." This is how I learned who my "aunt" was supposed to be.

In the morning—this was on a Sunday—*Pani* Szatkowska's daughters took me with them to church. I had no idea what I was supposed to do inside. I decided to watch my cousins and do what they did. I was breaking out in a cold sweat the whole time. The "cousins" didn't follow the service at all, they just gossiped about their girl friends in church. When we walked out of the church, we were surrounded by their boyfriends who decided the new "cousin" was the "spitting image" of Szatkowska. After the midday meal, I had reached such a point of fatigue, I just dropped into the deepest sleep of my life. Suddenly, I felt someone staring at me. I started from my sleep in terror. There was a young man lurking near the bed offering his "profoundest apologies," for he'd "only come to see his neighbor's new cousin." He left the room immediately.

In the evening, a whole bevy of my "cousins" arrived, along with strangers from the neighboring hamlets, all carrying on in the most vulgar and disgusting way—things I had never even imagined. Later, nothing they did would have surprised me.

I stayed with them while the uprising in the ghetto was in full force. One day, the head of the household showed up and said that another Jewess from Warsaw was coming. She was in hiding with her grandfather but the old man was unable to survive. From the way *Pan* Szatkowski talked about it, I knew right away he meant my grandfather and my cousin, and later, she told me the details of my grandfather's tragic and heroic death.

The day of April 19, 1943, we heard explosions and heavy gunfire, and saw flames shoot up from Warsaw in the distance. The fighting kept up all the time. By nightfall, the neighbors had all packed into the house to ridicule the Jewish uprising, swearing and overjoyed that finally, "the Jews were frying up, real nice meat patties." I kept thinking of my parents, uncle, and all our loved ones who were inside the ghetto. The young neighbor, Baranowski, kept me company often. I felt he sympathized with me though he didn't know who I was for sure.

One night, a week after I first came here, the mother woke me to tell me there was some kind of man here to see me. It was my cousin, who, half-dead, had jumped from a train taking him to Treblinka. He fought alongside my parents inside the ghetto and was taken prisoner by the Germans during a battle. The three of us were now together for three months. I was the only one—because of my "Aryan" light features—who could leave the house. My cousins—the boy and girl— hid all the time in a storage closet over the first landing, near my room. After my cousins, another Jewish family was brought in.

The daughters became jealous that Baranowski came to see me so often, and they told him the secret—that I was a Jew. I knew, myself, that the situation was critical, and decided to tell Baranowski that for the good of both of us, we had to cut our ties. When Baranowski came in and I started suggesting delicately that we end our relations, he broke in to say he knew everything, but it didn't matter. He promised to help me take care of my affairs as much as he could. I told Baranowski I wasn't alone, and he agreed to help my relatives, too.

Now our hosts, together with their daughters, decided to rob us clean, then turn us over to the police. Baranowski found out about their conspiracy and let me know. When the hosts realized Baranowski knew what they were planning, they decided to throw us right out on the street. While I was away in Warsaw trying to find us a new refuge, the Szatkowskis evicted my cousins from the house. They were immediately arrested and shot at dawn. I survived because of Baranowski. He found me a place in Pasieki, a village far from Warsaw. I spent the whole summer of 1943 there, till the fall. I was supposedly there on vacation. By autumn, I had to leave. Baranowski found a new place for me to stay in Grodzisk,[4] and I got on a train that was going there. At the Tluszcz station, the Germans surrounded the cars and dragged people off, to be sent to Germany as laborers. They took everyone off to Praga, to Skaryszewska Street. That's where they were registered and packed into trains headed for Germany. I was trembling with fear. Anyone could tell I was different from the others by my face, the clothes I was wearing, and the way I moved. They lined us up on Skaryszewska Street, took down our personal data, and collected our *Kennkarten*. While the official was writing down the information off my forged documents, an aide came up to tell him something. In a flash, I risked everything and swooped the *Kennkarte* off the table. The official lost count and continued on to the next person in line. This was how I kept my false identity safe.

The next day, they sent over a medical team to inspect us. All the women had to parade past the examiners completely naked. [As it happened, the witness had by chance just finished a bottle of buttermilk which got her tongue white and made it possible for her to convince the German doctor she was sick.—M.Z.] The following day, all those who were put down as sick were taken to the clinic at the hospital. We were guarded by armed Germans and Polish police. The Germans were lax, but the Poles didn't take their eyes off us even for a moment. One of the patients' sons told Baranowski what was going on here, and the next day he came with fresh linen and clothes, and got me past the guards.

Afterwards, we stayed on in Grodzisk. Here, the time passed without incident. We were here till Liberation.

Eyewitness Testimony 27. A Youth in Buchenwald

H.E. Born in Dęblin, Poland, in 1928; lived there. Recorded by Mikhl
Zylberberg in London in December 1958.

When the war broke out, I was eleven.

I worked the whole time in Dęblin—I wanted to save my father.

The Germans beat me up, tortured me, and were going to hang me.
But they had a *selektsye* from among five of us friends and they
picked another one of us and hanged him. They charged us with the
"crime" of looking for food.

Afterwards, they took us to the Chenstokhov[1] Concentration Camp
where the Germans shot all the children.

This happened in 1944.

We worked at the munitions plant in Chenstokhov. They gave us a
liter of soup a day—it was really just water. There was a potato floating around in the soup somewhere, but it crumbled apart as you
touched it.

When the Russians stopped less than ten kilometers from Chenstokhov, we were immediately sent off to Buchenwald. No one
worked in Buchenwald. You just waited to die.

From Buchenwald, a whole transport of us was sent over for labor
in another camp, in Nordhausen.[2] They forced us to haul boulders
and cement blocks without stop. We were building an entertainment
hall.

Later, when there were no more rocks, they shipped us to Wipke.
We spent about two months in Wipke, building a factory.

By this time, my finger had swollen up completely from all this.
The medic at the camp, a Negro, was going to hack my finger off.
He was a psychopathic killer. He couldn't stop whipping me. Once,
he asked me how old I was. When I answered I was only fourteen, he
punched and kicked me till I was covered with blood, and he
screamed the whole time: "Only fourteen?! Only fourteen?! How've
you survived this long?!"

I've still got welts all over my body from those blows.

In Wipke, we could see the war was coming to an end.

The Americans and English bombed the area day and night. Mor-
tar shells landed right in front of us.

The Germans packed thousands upon thousands of inmates into
small freight cars, and no one knew where they were taking us.

The Americans and English bombed and strafed the train and
killed hundreds of inmates. We could have run off. No one had the
strength to move. We ate nothing for many days and were dying of
dehydration.

Later, the SS guards marched us off further. At night, five of us dropped from sight and ran for the woods. We now had absolutely no strength left, and just crawled along on all fours. The SS bombarded the transport with grenades, and fired into the group from all sides. Every last man—around 3,000 men—was slaughtered.

The five of us lay in the woods for five or six days. I can't remember exactly how many even if I tried—how could you count those days?

Suddenly, we saw Americans, and we got up and stumbled into the village.

I was able to get to London with a transport of Jewish children selected by UNRRA.

Eyewitness Testimony 28. "Medical Experiments" in Auschwitz

M.F. Born in Sosnowiec, Russian Poland, in 1910; lived there. Recorded by Yankiv Fishman in New York in 1954. The witness describes the conditions in Sosnowiec under German occupation. He gives some new details about the role of Moyshe Merin.[1] The witness escaped to the Soviet Occupation Zone but had to return home. He now goes into the *Aussiedlung* of October 1942.

There were piles of dead Jews in the street. The gutters were full of bodies every day. Fear gripped the Jewish community. At the end of October and beginning of November, 1942—only three months after the Germans set up the ghetto—the first deadly *Aussiedlung* of the Jews took place. All the Jews of Sosnovits were brought to a large square, supposedly to have their papers stamped. They actually stamped a few documents, but about 8,000 passbooks weren't touched. These people were told to wait off to the side. This is how they were condemned to death. They were hauled off quickly to the train and sent to Oświęcim.[2] With very few exceptions, they were all exterminated in Oświęcim. As the people were being pushed from the trains, the Germans shot many of them without provocation. Among the victims sent to Oświęcim, and who perished there, was my aunt, who had raised me. She was forty-eight.

The year 1943 began with the smell of death for us Jews of Sosnovits. We knew already what they did to our brothers and sisters in Oświęcim. Even on days when we felt this wouldn't happen to us, we really knew the tragedy would cut us down sooner or later.

We started building bunkers. Bunkers were constructed in every courtyard and inside the buildings. The bunkers were well built and so well camouflaged, the Germans could never find them by themselves. Twenty people stayed in the bunker together with me and my family. It was down deep in the ground. The walls were reinforced with huge rocks. The door was completely hidden, but my child's crying gave our hideout away to the German. This was our saddest moment. We were all taken out of the ghetto. This happened August 1, 1943. The pavements were blown up to get us out of the bunkers. The Germans were now in the last stage of liquidating the Sosnovits Jews. The SS brought down a holocaust on the ghetto. No amount of pleading or bribery could stop these killers. The order was for every Jew to be taken to their death, *now!*

During the first *Aussiedlung*—in November 1942—the head of the *Kultusgemeinde*, Yankiv Merin [sic], believed that as *Präses*, he still had authority, and the Germans would take his opinion into consideration. He had managed to postpone the deaths of many people, and of course, his own family. He even used to condemn the Germans to their faces, protesting they were engaged in crimes against the Jewish people.[3] Now, this same Yankiv Merin was silent. He knew he would die now, too, and that all the German promises had run out in a pool of blood. Yankiv Merin and his whole family were deported to Oświęcim with all the other people. The Germans took special care to make sure not one member of the Merin family survived. All of them perished.

The road from the square to the train was lined with crowds of Poles and I saw many of them celebrating and glad.

We only had luck in one thing—the journey to Oświęcim didn't take long. It's not far to Oświęcim from Sosnovits—it only took a day.

My wife held our child in her arms. The child was four years old. All I could do was think of ways to save my dear ones from death. I took the child and held it in my arms. This was my last hope—that this way, I was saving my wife from death. We knew the German "work ethic"—let a young woman without a child live—and I could only hope they would let me and the child through, too. I was only thirty-three years old. I looked a lot younger and hoped I could save the child by my usefulness to them. I really believed this.

We were dragged off the trains at Oświęcim and clubbed and screamed at the whole time—my wife was pushed into the group of women with no children but they passed me over. As soon as those devils saw I had a child in my arms, they pushed me into the group headed for the crematorium. We knew for certain now what all this was about, what would now happen to us. The Germans and Ukrainians and the Jewish workers made no secret of it, either. And here something completely unexpected and unbelievable happened, which I'll never understand, and which haunts me to this day. A German brought my wife over to me. He grabbed the child from me and gave him to her. Then, with great brutality, the German pushed my wife into the group to the crematorium, and he dragged me back to the group selected for labor. All this happened so quickly, with such sureness—it was as if planned—that we were paralyzed. We couldn't say a word. They were taken away and I never saw them again.

I was brought with the group into Birkenau—the labor camp of Oświęcim. This is how we were processed: I was pushed in front of a table. I had to stretch my arm out and have a camp number tattooed on it. A *Kapo,* a French Jew, stood on the table and made sure everyone kept order. When the needle was stuck in, I jumped from pain, and the *Kapo* kicked me right in the mouth so hard, a tooth flew out and blood ran all over my chin. And the *Kapo* screamed with laughter like an animal at the way I doubled over.

Birkenau was like hell. Everything rotted and stank, if you can imagine it. We weren't permitted to cover our feet, but had to walk barefoot. We were given only drops of water. They did this by plan. Food—practically none. Every *Älteste* beat us. We were whipped for the smallest "sin." They beat me day and night. Our lives became cheap—which was what the killers wanted.

Erev Yom Kippur, 1943, this is what happened: They called a *selektsye*—they did it all the time. People were dragged off to be killed. Of my own will, I ran over to the group condemned to die. I was clubbed over the head. This German shrieked at me: *"Nicht wenn du willst, nur wenn ich wolle!"*[4] When I saw I couldn't even die when I, myself, wanted, this is when I decided to take hold of myself. I suddenly had great strength and courage. I realized we couldn't just drag ourselves around as if we were lost. I announced to the Germans that I was a tailor—and a good tailor. I was taken back inside Oświęcim, to the workshops. I was given work. It was much safer here than in Birkenau—cleaner, and there was enough water to survive. We were given shoes. Once a week, we got a change of linen. Everyone slept in their own bunk.

But there were different horrors: they did many "medical experiments" on my body. They bled me almost every day. Many times, they cut out strips of my flesh. Not only couldn't I make a sound, I wasn't even permitted to wince. One time, they summoned me. I saw a commission of "doctors" standing in front of me. The Germans examined every part of my body. One of them screamed into my ear: *"Herausreissen!"* This meant I was to back out running. I couldn't understand the whole procedure—why they checked my body, what they wanted from me, and why they told me to run out backwards. I also saw another young Jew in front of the commission. A few days later, when I saw him again, he was deathly pale. I spoke to him. He was so depressed he was almost without life. He told me—they castrated him. He broke down and cried at the way fate had treated him. This young man knew the German "doctors" had just released me from such torture. Why? This I don't know.

I was kept here for a year and a half. On January 18, 1945, I was transferred to Dachau. It was almost like a sanatorium here. The food was better and there were also medical examinations.

Eyewitness Testimony 29. Friendship

F.F. Born in Tomaszów Mazowiecki, Poland, in 1924; lived there. Recorded by Yankiv Fishman in New York in 1954.

. . . In May 1943, the last few remaining Jews of Tomaszów—I was among them—were taken to Bliżyn.[1] We were transported by train for three days, which was torture, since before the war the same way took three hours. They gave us no food on the train. Whatever someone brought with them was all they had. Those who didn't bring any food were given some by the others.

The Bliżyn camp had just been built. When we were brought in, we met some Jews from Radom here. By this time, Jewish transports were arriving in Bliżyn almost every day, and soon 2,000 Jews had been deported here. They put us to work as tailors, shoemakers, carpenters. It was all for the Russian front. We would have survived the work if the Germans hadn't forced us to meet impossible slave quotas, and put wild *Kapos* over us. The *Kapos* were Jewish. They beat us—but even worse, they reported bad workers to the Germans and that was the beginning of real hell. Some of the *Kapos* were from Tomaszów and were quiet, ordinary people before the war. No one would have believed they were capable of becoming collaborationists and traitors.

There was total starvation at Bliżyn. Those who were "in commerce" at the wires, selling the *goyim* their possessions for something to eat, still had to risk their lives. The Germans shot you for such a "crime." Neither my father nor I did it. We starved to the end. A year to the day after we came to Bliżyn, my father died. Died of hunger. He was fifty-four years old.

They kept me in Bliżyn till the camp was liquidated. I was there fourteen months. On July 30, 1944, I was taken out of Bliżyn and sent to Oświęcim. I was the only one of my family left alive now. I was barefoot, ragged, and sick. In Oświęcim, they tattooed a number on my arm. My number is A-15794.

When they brought me to Oświęcim, the Germans selected me for the group they let live, and sent us into a bathhouse. This happend in the morning. They took off my clothes. They threw them to the side to be disinfected. I stood naked all day waiting for the clothes. At night, my smock came out of the bath. It was thrown onto a pile, a mishmash of rags. The Germans goaded us so we wouldn't stand still, and it was impossible to find my own things. You grabbed whatever you could. They did this on purpose, so we, Jewish women, would walk around in rags, half-naked or completely naked. I grabbed a small skirt, one that belonged to a little girl.

They sent me for work outside the camp. I had to dig trenches on the banks of the Vistula with a shovel. The work was backbreaking and they stood guard over me with a revolver and a club. I got sick. My body was covered with abscesses.

I watched a group of Gentile arrestees pass by me at work. One of them, a young man of about seventeen or eighteen, fell out of the line and ran over to me. He looked long and hard at me: "Is that you, *Panna* S——?" and he ran back. Then I suddenly realized who it was —Kazik. How people had changed. Is Kazik really in Oświęcim, too?! I knew Kazik from Tomaszów. He was from our neighborhood. He lived with his mother and a sister. They came to Tomaszów from Poznań after the war broke out. Their family name is Wonsowski. They fled Poznań because Germans were persecuting Poles there. The Wonsowskis were decent people. I became friends with them. I visited them and they came to see us. I was glad he recognized me but it pained my heart that the meeting was so short and that I hadn't recognized him. The next day, Zosia, Kazik's sister, walked into our *Block*. I recognized her immediately. We fell into each other's arms. She told me she heard about me from her brother, from Kazik. She gave me her dress as a gift—such a precious possession! She worked in the kitchen, and Kazik worked in the warehouse where they kept the clothes of the Jews who were burned in the crematorium. They were both sent here as political prisoners. The dress Zosia gave me not only helped me stay alive from day to day, it saved me from death during the *selektsyes*. These selections went on all the time. You were condemned to death during the *selektsye* not only if you were sick, or couldn't endure the slave labor anymore, but also if they found a tick on you, a scab, a boil. My body was covered with sores. Especially the legs. Zosia also gave me a pair of leg stockings. I stood at the selection in Zosia's dress and stockings. The top part of my body was naked, but without boils. Luckily, I passed all the *selektsyes*.

Kazik came, bringing me pants and a piece of bread with butter. These were all such precious gifts. They were even more precious as symbols of human friendship. This was very important in staying alive and kept up my hope I would survive this ordeal. When Kazik came to see me this time, he was sick, feverish.

Eyewitness Testimony 30. Descent into Hell

K.G. Born in Końskie, Kielce District, Poland, 1923; lived there. Recorded by Zalmen Kaplan, August 1947, in Israel.

I was fifteen years old when the war broke out. The place I lived was in Kinsk,¹ Kielce District. The Jews around me were terrified— both because of the fighting, and the Hitler Occupation, which was sure to be a catastrophe for us.

Our hell began right in the beginning of September 1939, when the Germans firebombed the *shtetl* from the air. Many houses were destroyed then. The people ran in panic into the surrounding countryside—some into the woods, some to the fields, or into a nearby village. The people fleeing were shot up by German planes strafing them with machine-gun fire. They also dropped bombs in the forests. These were the first war casualties. We spotted two German spies in civilian clothes along the roads, who were signaling their pilots with mirrors. The Jews were enraged—they grabbed them and threw them into the flaming houses the Germans just bombed, and they were burned inside.

On the night of the seventh to the eighth of September, after a heavy artillery barrage, the first German units entered the shtetl, the Jewish townspeople who scattered into the surrounding countryside, now started straggling back. A special military squad detained all of them, and then assembled them in a large field on the outskirts of the *shtetl*, where they were kept without food and beaten savagely.

The people were forced to stand under the open sky for two whole weeks. An assault squad in town rounded up a large group of Jews and hearded them into the municipal park. SS men lined the streets and beat them with clubs as they passed through.

Luckily, no one was in my way and I just ran straight into the park without getting beaten. They kept hitting us inside the park, too, and ordered us to dig a large pit. Many hours later, the order was given for the Jews to start running. The people were shot at with machine guns. The grounds were covered with twenty-three dead people, among them—my close neighbors:

Moyshe Shlenski, Yashke Kronenberg, Mendl-Duvid Aznberg, and the restaurateur, Tsukerman. They were killed on September 12, 1939. The event crushed me, and since I wouldn't give in to this kind of life, I decided to commit suicide. I stole into our flat, left a note on the table, ran out to the first well I saw, and threw myself in. The well was very shallow and the water hardly reached my knees. A neighbor passed by and heard me groaning. She called to the other neighbors. A ladder was dropped and they dragged me out.

I decided to run away and be free of the German. My older brother managed to escape to Russia. That's where I planned to go, too. I was joined by another of my brothers. When we got to Lublin, we saw Jews being dragged out of cattle cars, savagely beaten, and robbed. The *Volksdeutsche* really went wild and left their bloody marks on us.

I got lost from my brother, but to go look for him in the city, I had to move through two rows of Germans who beat and kicked everyone passing between them. Once I got to the city, I met him and a few other kids from my *shtetl*, who were planning what I was. We decided to try and get back home first, and came to a small train station outside Lublin, where we climbed into freight cars and got back to Kinsk without incident.

My brother was beaten terribly at the station and collapsed unconscious. The local Jews nursed him back to health, but he lost no desire and kept running. After three months of endless wandering, he still hadn't reached his goal and came back.

All this time, the suffering of the Jews increased terribly. On the sixteenth of August, 1940, I was shipped into a civilian camp at Hrubieszów. We worked under severe and tragic conditions. We labored on the roads from daybreak till late at night. We slept in a small, cramped barn loft. After a couple of months, I was released and sent home.

We formed another group of young people wanting to escape— this time, including my married sister and brother-in-law. And again, we failed to get across the border. On the way back, I stopped over in Warsaw, where I had to put on an armband with the *mugen duvid* for the first time. After all these failures, I decided to return home and stay with the rest of the family.

Soon, a ghetto was set up and all the Jews were concentrated inside. The penalty for leaving the ghetto was death. Every day, the Germans demanded that the ghetto laborers line up in a column and march off for work needed on the outside that day. No wages were paid.

I saw there was no way out of this, so I decided to try to get onto a nearby German farm on the outskirts of town. This way, I was sure not to be sent to remote areas for hard labor. My younger brother wasn't inducted into any labor battalions, but was sent to Skarżysko-Kamienna, to the HASAG plant, and he vanished there. In the beginning, I did routine farm work, but later, because of my painting ability, I was put in charge of a warehouse and spent the whole time painting countless signs.

This situation lasted till the first *Aussiedlung* in the *shtetl*.

It happened on the twenty-seventh of October, 1942.

During the night, the gendarmes surrounded the town and blocked anyone leaving for the labor sites in the morning. The same evening, the civilian authorities, together with the chief of the *Judenvernicht-ungsbrigade,* called out 150 people—I was among them—and sent us to the farm to build barracks for ourselves. The group was made up only of artisans—carpenters, shoemakers, tailors—and also a group of youths—boys and girls—to work on the farm. I barely managed to say goodbye to my sister who gave me her picture with this inscription: "If you survive, remember, you live to take revenge." I was put to work doing what I did before—painting signs. We heard that all the other people were sent to Treblinka.

The work on the farm lasted till January 4, 1943. On that night, the farm was surrounded by field gendarmes. Everything was taken apart, loaded onto freight cars, and sent to Uyazd.² Our *shtetl* was *judenrein.*

We arrived in Uyazd at night, and before we came, they lined up the Jews of Opoczno and Tomaszów Mazowiecki. At daybreak, the whole column, under an escort of crazed Ukrainians and gendarmes, was led away to the station. This was winter, the sixth of January, 1943. The Ukrainians hounded us mercilessly—anyone unable to keep up was shot. There was a woman and a small child with us, who couldn't run quickly, so a Ukrainian pushed her over into the snow banks by the fields. He shot the child dead, then he murdered the mother. This happened all along the way.

After we marched for many hours, we finally got to the station. We were pushed into boxcars and they spared no beatings while doing this. They packed 180 to 200 people into each car. As soon as someone was squeezed in, they were locked into place between the others and couldn't move at all.

Now, our hell really started. People were asphyxiated from the overcrowding. The screams of the dying, the crying of children, passed any known extreme. From time to time, when we passed through a station, some people hurled snow at the trains, and this dropped in through two small openings. By morning, there were thirty dead people inside the wagons. The stronger ones started heaving the bodies out and someone jumped down with every dead body. This was done to distract the guards from what was really going on. But not everyone managed to jump free, and some were spotted by the Ukrainians and shot. Some didn't jump right and were killed when they hit the ground.

The wagons emptied out and we were left behind. After traveling all day, the train rolled into a small station with the sign, "Treblinka." That's when I finally decided to jump off, especially since the fields were all covered with snow and my thirst was terrible. I stripped off my coat—to fit through the opening easier—and as the train moved toward the platforms in the camp, I jumped through perfectly, without getting injured. A woman from Tomaszów-Mazowiecki also jumped after me. We were the last ones to break out of the wagon.

As soon as I hit the ground, I dropped on my stomach and lay flat till the whole train passed by. After a few moments, I crawled over to the woman who jumped with me. She also fell without getting hurt. We tried to find our way out of here, but didn't know where the paths led, and just picked the first one. We kept pushing snow into our mouths all day, till our hands froze. Two hours later, we came into a small village called Złatków. We walked into the first hut we saw—an old peasant woman and her many children lived here. The woman knew right away who we were and from where we'd come, because it happened many times before. She advised us to get out of the village because Ukrainians came by all the time to get vodka, for which they paid a fortune. She suggested we go to Kosów-Podlaski,[3] which was about thirteen kilometers away. There was a ghetto there where they kept the Jews of the area, who were later sent to Treblinka.

From the way this straightforward woman talked, I realized she knew what was going on in nearby Treblinka, especially when she said a few peasants from the village had "met the same fate."

We had no choice and headed for Kosów. Along the way, we asked a peasant for directions, but he tried talking us out of going there, telling us how we could get to Warsaw. As soon as I heard this, I agreed to it, because I knew there was still a ghetto in Warsaw. The peasant checked to see no one was coming, and took us off the road into his hut. His wife realized who we were and prepared some coffee and bread for us, but we only drank—we couldn't eat, even though we hadn't had a bite of food for three days.

In the evening, his brother-in-law came by with a wagon to take us to the station at Sadovne.[4] We handed over the money he asked for and set out on the road. The cold was unbearable—about thirty degrees below zero, Celsius. Halfway there, the peasant asked for more money. We had no choice and gave him the few coins we had left, and a golden ring. After taking us a few hundred meters further, he suddenly stopped and tried to throw us off, into the dark forest. I had nothing left to lose and threatened that if we were caught by Germans or Ukrainians, I'd tell them he helped us escape. He got scared and took us all the way to the station. The building was small, unlit, and not a soul was there. We sat on a bench all night shivering from the cold and waited for a train. At dawn, peasants who were involved in food smuggling, started arriving. My companion also took her place on line for a ticket, and we started gathering courage for the trip, which at that time was almost suicidal. But we were ready for any consequences. There were no incidents on route. We weren't even stopped at the exit to the Warsaw station. We headed straight for the peasant's cousin at Hoża 26—he'd given us the address in the village. My companion tried making contacts on the "Aryan" side, and was able to stay there safely.

I was very hesitant, and afraid of falling into the hands of the "extortionists"—these were criminal types who saw to it that Jews on the "Aryan" side were captured, blackmailed, then turned over to the German. I decided to head for the ghetto. I found out there were a small number of Jews working outside the ghetto. I waited near the labor site till evening, so I could march back in with them. I said goodbye to my companion and took the number 8 trolley to Żelazna Street. I got off 200 meters before the checkpoint, and waited for the right moment to dash into the ghetto. There was a group of Jews in front of me, and across the way, there was a wagonload of Jews in white armbands with the *mugen duvid.* I went up to the wagon and told them where I had just been. They said for me to climb up. There was bread and soup for the ghetto on the wagon. One of them handed me a white handerchief. Luckily, the Germans let the wagon through without searching it thoroughly.

The next day, I met someone else who'd jumped free of the train. He jumped off at Koluszki. His leg was injured in the jump. He also had stolen into the ghetto. During one of the *aktsyes,* I was caught and sent to the labor camp at Rembertów[5] on one of the transports.

The work conditions were agony. We had to haul fifty-kilo shells under a steady beating. For food, they gave us 1½ kilos of bread a week, and once a day, half a liter of watery soup. We slept in freezing barracks left behind by the former Jewish inmates.

After a few days, I succeeded to get placed in sign-making work, helping a Pole from Rembertów, who worked at the factory. Through him, I could also "organize" a little bit of bread and potatoes, and so we suffered less from hunger. After a while, he got spotted typhus and was immediately quarantined. Though the doctor forbade me to see him, I went to bring him some cooked food. Finally, I caught the disease, too, and stayed with my friend at Mila 36. On April 19, the Resistance Movement started its operation inside the ghetto. I hid out in a bunker and, sometimes, in a cellar. There was shooting and explosive devices going off all around us. Flames were everywhere, and by April 25, the fire reached our building. There was no choice now, we had to surrender.

We were marched through a forest of flames and cinders which reached to the sky. Ukrainians and Lithuanians guarded us all along the way. We were assembled at Zamenhofa 19, where 1,000 Jews already stood waiting. Machine guns were positioned all around and a final search was begun. Everyone was forced to give up whatever they had. You can imagine how many victims were killed just because they happened to be standing in a particular way.

Late that evening, SS *Brigadenführer* Stroop[6] drove up, and gave some instructions I couldn't make out. Everyone was ordered to put their hands up, and this was how we marched to the *Umschlagplatz* by the Danzig terminal. They crowded us into a three-story building there. During the night, Ukrainian Guards and SS men came in looking for gold and jewelry. They bludgeoned people to death. In the morning, they took us out to the courtyard. There were Ukrainians, Lithuanians, and SS men on the steps, who swung at the people as they were coming out with rifle butts and whips. Small children were grabbed from their mothers and smashed head-first into the stone wall. This went on till they finished loading us into the freight cars. Another train stood across the way with "Poniatowa" painted on its sides. We called to the people inside it to tell us what was written on ours. They called out—"Treblinka!"

I knew there was no hope left now. The security on the transport was too strong—a guard on every car top and on every step. It was impossible to jump. Someone tried anyway, but he got hit with every bullet fired and fell away dead.

As we passed through the smaller stations, shots were fired in through the openings, wounding and killing many people. We came into Treblinka in the evening and the transport was immediately taken to a holding area near the platform where we were kept locked up all night long. We were all racked by thirst. We started pleading with the Ukrainians for water, promising them whatever we had or had hidden. A young couple with a child gave up a gold cigarette case set with diamonds for a bottle of water. As soon as he got the water, the husband took a long drink. Then the wife gulped down the rest, not leaving a drop for the child. Once she had finished drinking, she broke into hysterical laughing. She had lost her mind. A father and daughter tried bartering with a Ukrainian to let them out of the wagon. He let them out, then shot them down. At the other end of the car, a group of people swallowed cyanide, dying instantly. This was the most horrifying night of my life.

At seven in the morning, the train started moving into Treblinka II. We were pulled off the trains and pushed into a small enclosure. Women and children were torn away from their husbands and fathers. Right in front of our eyes, the dead bodies were flung out of the trains. The work was done by the local camp Jews, who didn't say a word all that time—they were guarded by the SS. In a few moments, only men were left standing on the grounds. I didn't even see them take the women and children away. We were lined up ten across, then marched single-file past an SS man with a riding crop in his hand. He said nothing, just flicked the whip right, left. He pointed me to the left. Those pointed to the right were pushed through a small opening which closed automatically behind each one, and we couldn't tell what was happening to them. The 320 of us were herded together in one spot and the SS now permitted us to be given as much water as we could drink. Since the water was brought to us by Jewish workers, we managed to get a few words out of them and found out we'd been spared from the ovens. Among these workers, I recognized Nusn Shvartsfieter from Warsaw, who was staying with his family in our town when the war broke out and was taken to Treblinka with the first transport. Of that entire group, only he and one other person were left. And where were the others? He lowered his eyes. I couldn't say anything after that.

A new group of thirty-five was selected out—violinists, artisans, painters, and handcraftsmen—they were kept together. At noon, we were loaded into freight cars—sixty-five men to a wagon. A trough of water was put into every car, along with a bucket for our bodily needs. Everyone was given six breadsticks for the way.

On April 29, we were brought to Lublin, to the square at Lipowa Street 7, where thousands of Jews were being assembled.

The day after, several hundred people were added onto our group, and we now numbered 807 men.

We were being led to Majdanek on foot.

As soon as we started marching, an SS junior officer cut across our path and exchanged words with the SS officers who were controlling us.

Fifteen minutes later, they marched us back to the square. We were guarded by Ukrainians under *Oberschaarführer* Fuchs.

We found out from the local prisoners-of-war and Jewish inmates, that they were sending us to the Heinkel *Werke* in Budzyn, near Kraśnik.[7]

After many hours, they loaded us into trains, and we were in Budzyn by evening. Two barracks had been put up for us. The usual inspections started, but this time, the *Lagerführer*, Fuchs, shot a man and ordered seven elderly people stripped naked. A Ukrainian shot each one separately from behind, and dumped them into a grave. In the morning, after disinfecting us and putting us through a bath, the rest of us were registered, and they also took down our trades.

We were taken for dangerous work to Airplane Factory He. 111, located five kilometers from the camp. Everyone had a red cross label glued to their knees and back. We were marched to the factory under an escort of Ukrainians. The plant stretched on over a huge area and was sealed behind barbed wire. There were special guards on the perimeter, stationed every fifty meters.

The factory was run by a special *Werkschutzkommando* and by Party functionaries. We were assigned many overseers. I was assigned to painting and spent the whole day painting signs. We could endure this work, but as soon as we left the factory grounds, we were taken over by Ukrainians who pushed and hounded us while we walked, and made us sing all the way to the camp.

At night, after the camp *Appel,* each *Kommando* was brought a pot of soup and a loaf of bread for every ten men. It took many hours till they handed out the rations, then they permitted us to lay down in our bunks—only to get up before dawn and head for work again. It didn't always go without incident. There were times—and this happened a lot—the *Appel* dragged on for many hours. You were sure to be shot if you were found with an extra ration of bread, or a change of shirt, or if the red cross on your back had faded a little, and other petty "crimes" like that.

Now, two new transports of men and women arrived—one was from Hrubieszów and the other, from Bełżec. While we were out on the labor site, we heard that one of the new *Katzetn*, Biter from Otwock, was discovered keeping gold in his tin cup—he hid it under a fake bottom. We knew something drastic would happen that evening. After the first *Appel*, at sundown, he was led out stark naked. He followed behind with a rope round his neck yanked by a Ukrainian named Otto, known for his bestial acts. They lined us up in a double column. As he passed between us, everyone was ordered to beat him. The *Lagerführer* Fuchs followed behind with a drawn pistol and a club, making sure everyone carried out his punishment. We wanted to put him out of his pain, and decided to beat him thoroughly. A few moments later, he dropped down, unconscious. He was dragged off to the side. The Ukrainian ran for some water, and the *Lagerführer* tried propping him up. After reviving him, Fuchs took a club and stuck it in his mouth, breaking his teeth and tearing apart his lips. The victim fell, dead.

I slaved at the camp till January 1944. The camp commandants rotated during this time, but our conditions didn't change at all.

They were supposed to transfer us to another camp near the factory. Before they took us out of camp, the former *Kommandant*, Franz, put on a "spectacle" before his departure. The "spectacle" consisted of leaving behind over twenty dead bodies in the camp. After a few days, they gave us striped "prison pajamas" and transferred us to the new camp with a new administration and guards.

Now, major changes began happening. The Heinkel *Werke* was relocated to Rasztok,[8] and in its place, they installed an enormous machine plant to repair damaged vehicles sent back from the front—which was now getting nearer and nearer. In May, they decided to evacuate the plant because the Russian army was so close by. Our camp was also liquidated. The people were transferred to various camps. Five hundred were sent to Radom, a few hundred to Mielec,[9] 150 to Starachowice,[10] and 150 to Ostrowiec-Kielecki. I was sent with this group. The ones left behind, who weren't evacuated, were later sent to Wieliczka,[11] and then added to the Mielec transport afterwards. I didn't do my usual work in Ostrowiec. They used me in building a cement factory. German civilians were the overseers and they treated us with extreme cruelty. After twelve weeks, the work was stopped and we were locked up inside the camp. Some people tried breaking out through the wires, but they were shot down. After many days like this, they loaded us into trains and sent us to an unknown destination. It was the end of July 1944, now.

At daybreak, the train stopped alongside some high-tension wires in a brightly illuminated area. This was the camp of Auschwitz. We came in just as they were forcing everyone out of the barracks for the morning calls.

As the sun came up, they opened the trains and lined the men and women up in groups of five.

We were taken inside a large barrack. On the way there, I looked up and saw those buildings topped by the huge chimneys. The crematoria.

From there they took us to another structure where they shaved our heads. We were pushed into a large chamber with shower fixtures in the ceiling. We looked at each other in horror—what would happen now?! Would there be gas or water?? A couple of minutes later, we breathed easier—water shot out. We got out of our clothes and they were disinfected. Then we had to pick up whatever they threw us. I got a jacket which could have held another person inside, and the pants were like that, too. When everyone had some clothes, they lined us up in fives again. We were marched out of the Quarantine Block and put inside Block 6. Then the "initiations" by the *Block-älteste* and the *Sztubowa* started. They introduced themselves with thick clubs, which came down hard on shoulders, heads, or wherever else they landed. They put us through a drill: *"Mützen ab! Mützen auf!"*[12] After a two-hour session, they led us into Block No. 5, where our vital statistics were marked down, Then, everyone was tattooed on the arm with a number. The number they gave me was B-4231.

When I was talking with an old camp inmate, once, he said: "Your transport was lucky—you didn't rise to the heavens in smoke."

We lived with these daily drills for many weeks. During this time, people were sent off to different factories. I also tried to get sent to work somewhere, just so I wouldn't have to watch the black smoke shooting out of the crematoria.

All the while, new transports kept arriving from the *Lodzer* Ghetto.

I was registered as a locksmith and sent to the Zenith factory about ten kilometers outside of Świętochławice, near Katowice. I came there on August 16, 1944, in my striped rags.

The camp there held about 2,000 people from different nations, and also a huge number of the most degenerate SS personnel and guards. The *Lagerälteste* was the infamous killer from Poznań, Bruno *"Häftling Nummer Eins."*

The conditions were tolerable in this camp. They let us wash. There were shoemaker and tailor workshops, and we also got food. I worked painting signs here, too. They gave me extra bread and cigarettes for it. For a time, I also worked inside the camp itself, and was forced to paint landscapes for the SS administrators. This got me an extra ration of bread and cigarettes, and I used them to help my friends. The Russian army was so near—but they still wouldn't come.

At the start of 1945, they evacuated us to Mauthausen in Austria.

Three days after we were evacuated, the Russians came in to Świętochławice.

We were brought to Mauthausen during the night. They dragged us off the train immediately and marched us to the camp in a terrible frost and blizzard. After marching for many hours, we got to the camp. They held us out in the open all night long, then marched us off to the bath in small groups. This transfer took till the morning. During this night, several people were beaten critically. They died during the day. By morning, we were all inside a sealed-off quarantine camp and put into four blocks: 21, 22, 23, 24. Inside the *Block*, everyone got a different number—a metal tag tied to the left wrist. All of us also had a number glued to the left side of our jackets and the right side of our pants. My number at Mauthausen was 123863.

When the Allied and Russian offensives began, many camps were evacuated and transported here. The camps in Sachsenhausen, Grossrosen, and others, were among these. In a short while, the number of people in the camp reached 1,200.

Besides the tortures and hunger, a new misery arose—overcrowding.

Whole groups of people had to be sent to the nearby labor camps of Melk, Ebensee, Linz, Gusen I, Gusen II, and others. Because of the new transports arriving every day, they murdered countless numbers of people, and pushed the new inmates in in their place. The crematoria fires of Mauthausen and Gusen I never died down, there were so many bodies. They had to dig enormous pits and dump 500, 1,000, even 1,500 corpses into each pit. After seven weeks, I was ordered out on a transport to Gusen II, sixteen kilometers from Mauthausen. This was one of the worst camps I was in. They put me into the sixth *Block*.

Early in the morning, they sent me out for labor that lasted a full day. The work was divided up over a twenty-four-hour period, both day and night shifts. We had to drill through the mountains, then reinforce the tunnels with concrete. They were planning to use it for a Messerschmidt airplane assembly plant. The former laborers had completed one section. The overseers were very cruel and brutal to us. No one was sure they'd live to see the next moment. Both at the labor site and back in the *Block*, they murdered us for no reason. The ones who beat us the worst were the long-time inmates, the male *Kapos*—all from the underworld. They weren't only German, there were many Poles, Czechs, and Spaniards. The death chambers were always full of naked corpses waiting for the furnaces or a mass grave. A *Sonderkommando* for the dead was selected to carry them out and "dispose" of them.

In April, I was called out for night work. When the overseer saw the yellow patch on my jacket—the patches were made especially for the Jews in camp—he started beating me so hard and long with a shovel, without any provocation, till he broke both the shovel and my arm. I knew I had to keep on my feet and continue working at any cost, because if they took me to the infirmary, I'd lose the work and my life. So I told no one and kept working though there was no end to it and no rest was allowed.

I worked and suffered like this all week, but I felt I couldn't endure any more, and had to go to the infirmary.

In the morning, they didn't call me out to work, but wrote my name down in a ledger. They put my arm in a cast only after three days. I was confined to the *Block* and given the duty of floor sweeper. A week later, they order a *Block* curfew and let no one out. The *Block* clerks of every barrack ordered all the disabled and the inmates they despised to assemble, then they drew up a list. A number was burned into their chests with an acid stylus. My turn came. The metal tag wasn't tied to my wrist because of the cast, so they beat me hard and told me to get the number. This saved me.

In the meantime, the *selektsye* carried out by the Inspector-Physician Nickolus, was halted. I used this chance to break out of the *Block*. I ran to *Block* No. 17 where the inspecting physician was a Jew, Marcus, who was with me at Świętochławice. Since he knew our block "elder," I asked him to help me out of this crisis. He agreed. I headed back to my *Block*. This Dr. Nickolus was coming back in a few minutes to finish the *selektsye*.

I knew I didn't have a moment to lose, and I risked going over to the *Blokowa* and mentioning Dr. Marcus. The *Blokowa* understood what I meant and decided to help me. In a couple of minutes, Dr. Nickolus comes. The *Blokowa* takes me over to him and says: "He's healthy, he can work." The doctor lets me pass, but under one condition: the cast has to come off, and I have to report for work tomorrow. I said I would, of course. Those selected for death were pushed off into a corner and then lined up on the *Appelplatz* just as a terrible thunderstorm broke out, soaking them to the bone. They herded them together from all the barracks, then threw them into *Block* 17. They were tortured all night long before they died, beaten without stop as they stood on the flooded grounds.

The *Blokowa* tried talking me out of going to work, even wanting to hide me in the *Block,* but I said no—I didn't want to risk certain death.

The next day, I went to the labor site as usual, but kept the cast on, hiding it from sight under my sleeve. The work was constantly interrupted—we could hear the Allies closing in.

It was mid-April, 1945, now. I was working the night shift during this time. Toward morning, when all the Jews on the night shift were assembled for the march back to camp, they suddenly herded us together in a transport and sent us back to Mauthausen, where we were concentrated near the main camp. Two days later, when a large group of Jews had been assembled—most had been brought here from Hungary in 1944 and were in better condition than the Polish Jews—we were handed over to Austrian gendarmes. They were old men. After a grueling forced march of three days, we were led into the camp at Gunskirchen, near Wels. The camp was deep in the woods. A few thousand Jews were gathered here. We were given less food than ever before. The ration was just a tuft of bread and a quarter-liter watery soup daily. About 200 people died every day.

On a certain evening—this was May 4, 1945—we heard a half-hour-long artillery barrage close by. We paid no attention to it. A little later, the camp head walked up to every one of the guards, individually. Soon, we heard inhuman cries.

The guards all broke rank and ran, throwing away their guns.

I couldn't utter a sound, in amazement. People broke down and cried, others laughed hysterically. We didn't know what to do with ourselves. After a couple of minutes, a group of friends and me started walking to the highway, looking to all sides to see if we weren't about to be shot. It was only then we realized we were free. Other freed inmates started breaking into the food supply houses.

In the morning, American units occupied the nearby village of Wels.

Now I realized how exhausted I was—I couldn't keep on my feet after fifty paces.

On the eighth of May, they brought the others and me to the hospital in Wels where the Americans treated us.

Eyewitness Testimony 31. The Truth of What Happened to Dr. Schipper

Deposition of *Khazn* Y.L. to the Jewish Historical Commission in Poland, 1947.

I was sent to Majdanek near Lublin on May 10, 1943, with the last transport of Jews from the Warsaw Ghetto. Majdanek was divided up into five zones. I was sent to Zone [inaudible], second *Block*, Barrack 20. I was there four weeks, then I was transferred to Zone 3, *Block* 6, where the *Blockälteste* was a Warsaw Jew, a former butcher. When he saw me, he says to me: "*Herr Khazn*, thank God, you're in luck! Fate's been good to you!"

"What do you mean?" I asked.

"Because you've fallen into my hands," he answers. And he goes on—he's musical, likes *Khzunim* and *Khzunes*.

"I was," he says, "a member in the Warsaw Synagogue, heard lots of *Khzunim*, opera singers. In one word, *Herr Khazn*, under me, you'll sing every evening after work, and for this, I'll try to get you some extra food—*Zulage* in camp talk."

The next day, when I walked into the *Block* after work, I was met by a whole group of personnel, who were asked to come hear the Warsaw *Khazn*. These were the camp privileged, the *Blockälteste*, *Blockschreiber*, *Kanzilarieschreiber*,[1] *Kücher*, *Stubdienste*, and the like. They ran the camp. After I sang a few pieces of *Khzunes* and *recitativs*, and some opera arias, I was given an extra liter of food and a bread ration—the most prized treasure in camp.

Not a few of my friends envied me for this "reward" I took back to my bunk to eat. Not a few of those people thought, "What a lucky man the *Khazn* is, getting so much food just for singing a few songs!"

After I finished eating, the *Küchälteste*, a Slovakian Jew, came over to me and asked me where I worked. I answered him by showing him the bruises on my head and back, and I told him if I had to work at the same kind of slave labor for just a few days more, he'd never hear me sing again—the *Kommandoführer*, the *Reichsdeutsche*, would surely finish me off first. He took pity on me—I don't know whether because of my singing, or on me personally. I have to say, the Czech and Slovak Jews in camp aren't much better than the Germans. When it came to the Jews, every one of them was armed with a club and ready to beat up any victim. Right away, he had me assigned to the kitchen as a potato peeler, and told the *Blockälteste* that in the morning, before the *Kommandos* were selected, I should be brought inside the kitchen. At six in the morning, I already stood in the huge potato hangar, packed in with 300 other men, all peeling potatoes. Of these 300 men, about 100 were Poles who were kept separate from the Jews. You met Jews there from every walk of life: doctors, lawyers, merchants, peddlers from Nalewki Street, as well as *Khzunim* and rabbis.

As I walked a little further into the shed, I noticed, sitting off in a corner, the renowned Jewish historian, the former *Sejm* deputy, Dr. Yitzhak Schipper. I was shattered, seeing this great man sitting bent over, all shriveled up, holding a pocketknife between his fingers, and peeling potatoes. While I was watching him, I wondered how Dr. Schipper managed to slip through the *selektsye* of older people sent off to be incinerated, and why hadn't he found a way to escape from Warsaw, to save himself from the clutches of the Germans, gorging themselves with our blood?

After I calmed down a bit, I went up to him and introduced myself, asking him if I could sit down by his side. He answered my question by pointing out the shed overseer, a former Polish lieutenant, who had to approve my request. I walked up to him and asked permission to sit next to Dr. Schipper. He didn't think twice but brought his club straight down on my back with such force, it paralyzed me, while he screamed: "Where do you think you are, dog?!—home??! You forget you're inside a concentration camp!!!"

This was the reception I got, my first day as a potato peeler inside Majdanek. Don't think it was so easy to be a potato peeler. You had to pay dearly for this job—gold teeth, gold coins, precious stones, and so on. Besides all these things, you existed only through the influence of the Czech and Slovak Jews in camp, who ran the whole "system," the *Schreibstuber* [sic], *Blockälteste, Blockschreiber, Shtubdienste,* and the others.

I was obsessed with the desire to sit next to Dr. Schipper, so I asked the "chief" in our kitchen, the Slovakian Jew, to intervene. After I paid him off, I got my place. The following morning, I was already sitting with Dr. Schipper and I started to get to know him. During our talk, he pointed out I had to be extremely careful the former lieutenant didn't notice us talking during work. For such unheard-of nerve, they gave us ten lashes across the bare bottom, no matter who it was. Plus, you had to work quickly and steadily to meet the imposed quota. Each of the potato peelers had to fill six crates with peeled potatoes, and anyone not meeting the quota was removed from their place in a day or so, and sent for punishment labor. Disregarding all these risks, I just had to talk with him, with Dr. Schipper, to make the time pass easier and maybe to learn something through the benefit of his age. I put many questions to him, but he said one thing only:

"My dear friend, I won't survive this—I've already endured so much. I was beaten so hard at work once, they had to carry me back to the camp."

He uncovered his two swollen legs, which were already so infected, pus ran all over them.

"*Frand Dokter,* why don't you go to the dispensary, or into the infirmary?" I asked.

He answered that no one ever left there alive.

In a few days, Dr. Schipper's health had deteriorated so badly, he couldn't stand on his feet any more. One of my duties and obligations was to go with his son-in-law into *Block* 11 before work was called, and carry Dr. Schipper in our arms from there to the potato shed, where we sat him down at his place. We did the same, after the work was over. We carried him back and forth like this for about four weeks, until one day, an order was given for everyone without exception to vacate the shed and come out to the *Appelplatz,* where a medical inspection of the whole camp was going on. When we heard this horrifying news, we knew how it would end.

Every last person was threatened with the crematorium during these sudden *Appele,* because, of course, the crematorium workers had to have something to do. Trembling from anxiety, the doctor's son-in-law and I ran from one *Kapo* to the other, trying to find some way out for Dr. Schipper. Different plans were made, but we decided finally not to take Dr. Schipper out to the *Appelplatz* since the best way to save him was to try and keep him hidden—and this is what happened.

We went out to the *Appelplatz,* and the doctor stayed hidden. The *selektsye* lasted many hours and was carried out by an SS military-medical commission. It took the lives of over 300 men—only Jews, because other nations weren't subjected to *selektsyes.* The people chosen were sent into *Block* 19, where all the sick were assembled, and when their number was sufficient, they sent them off to the gas, and burned them later in the crematorium.

This kind of selection happened every few weeks. As we filed back in, Dr. Schipper was already seated at his work. When he saw us, he started crying from joy. We comforted him and told him the *Appel* was tragic, but of 6,000 Jews, about 300 were selected out. The commission must have had orders for workers, and had to pass most of us.

The doctor couldn't be consoled, though, because he knew what was also waiting for him. Abject, starving, and exhausted, we kept peeling the potatoes and carrying the sick doctor back and forth. Until on a certain day in July 1943, the great Jewish historian breathed his last. He died a "natural" death, unable to bear the work and the beatings any longer. But he didn't die as a *Gamel*[2] or as one who couldn't carry his load, but as a sick, exhausted, exploited inmate, a *Häftling* of the historic death camp, Majdanek-Lublin.

Eyewitness Testimony 32. Collective and Individual Resistance

V.H. Born in Podwołoczyska, Tarnopol District, Galicia, in 1909. Recorded by David Graysdorf in a DP camp in November 1947. The witness is talking of the massacre of the Jews in the Tarnopol Ghetto.

After they liquidated the ghetto,[1] the Germans started tearing down the labor camps around Tarnopol. On July 12, 1943, panic broke out in the Hlobocek camp, where everyone expected it was about to be liquidated. Many Jews broke out and ran into the woods. *Obersturm-*

führer Rokita[2] heard the Jews had run off, and postponed the liquidation of the camp for a few weeks. When General Katzner's[3] aide, that murderer Hildebrand[4] arrived from Lemberg at the end of July 1943, we knew the time had come to act.

After we finished work, the camp was locked up and no one was let out. A great uproar broke out. People took their lives in desperation. At four in the morning, large groups of SS and Gestapo, together with Ukrainian militia, surrounded the camp and started firing at the people inside. We resisted. There was a resistance unit in camp and we'd been organized. Germans were killed, but the resistance was broken in the end. The remaining inmates were led off to the Petrikow Forest and shot.

The executions went on for three days until the second of August, 1943, when an announcement was posted for all Jews left in the camp to report for work registration and they wouldn't be harmed. The people didn't believe the German promises and wouldn't let themselves be taken out. A few days later, Rokita came and promised all kinds of privileges to those who registered for work. Many people were talked into it and did like he said. Before the march to the station, they were given rations of white bread, butter, jam, and marmalade; they were also allowed to take their things along. The Germans sent them to the train unguarded. After boarding them into the wagons, the doors were bolted shut. Suddenly, trucks were driven up, the people were chased from the train into the trucks, they were sped off to the Petrikow Forest and shot to a man.

When they began the executions, a friend and myself decided to make a break for the woods. We were armed with two stilettos. That night, we ambushed a Ukrainian guard, bashed his skull in, and broke out. We hid at a Gentile's house—we knew him from the train station. We stayed in hiding for a long time—till March 24, 1944, when the Red Army came.

Eyewitness Testimony 33. Breakout to the Forest

Y.G. Born in Minsk in 1892; lived in Stołpce, Nowogródek District, Poland. Recorded by Icek Shmulewitz in New York, January 1955. Witness recounts his experiences at the outbreak of war in Stołpce, under Soviet occupation, during the Hitler Occupation, inside the ghetto of Stołpce during the *aktsyes*, conditions at the labor camp in Świerzeń Nowy, near Stołpce, and continues.

The Jews in the labor camp at Shverzhen[1] started talking among themselves of saving their lives by breaking out to the woods. But nobody dared to organize this escape—no one knew how to go about it. We used to get messages from the outside—passed on to us by Gentiles coming into the camp for work—from a Stołpce Jew, Elyohu Inzelbukh, who fought with the Soviet partisan units in the Słuck Forest near the camp. Many Jews fought in the units called "Zhu-kovtsy" and "Chaipayev."[2] The battalion commander was Gilchik, and Pavlov from Moscow was the overall commandant of the brigade. Elyohu Inzelbukh, who sent us the messages, told us to prepare for a certain day when they would liberate the camp.

At the end of January 1943, a young Jew infiltrated the camp. He was Hershl Posesorski[3] from Warsaw, who'd fled to Stołpce as a refugee, and then escaped to the woods, joining the Zhukovtsy and Chapayev brigades I just mentioned. The brigade commander sent Hershl Posesorski to organize the escape. Posesorski arrived with four other Jewish partisan youths. The other four waited outside the camp. They were well armed. Posesorski then stole into our compound, and dressed like the other inmates. He stayed with us for two days, worked with us, ate and slept with us.

During these two days, Hershl Posesorski organized a group of forty people, who prepared for the escape from the camp. But every-one else learned of it right away and tried very hard to keep it secret. The camp was divided at that time into separate zones for the men and women. I didn't want to escape—I was afraid.

It happened on a Friday night, around nine o'clock—we see the Jews running through the camp in the dark. My wife and daughter talked me into escaping with the others. We ran up to the barbed wire perimeter of the camp, near a stream. The guards on the high watchtowers were elder Germans and they'd just climbed down to warm up. We cut through and pulled apart the wire by the stream, and people rushed through into the water. About 180 Jews escaped that night—men and women, both—and Hershl Posesorski led the breakout.

When the 180 reached the opposite bank, they started running alongside it to skirt the camp and head for the woods. We heard the Germans yelling that the Jews had escaped! Soon, they were firing mortars and flares into the night, but no one was hit. The Germans were afraid to chase us because they were sure we had to be armed. Hershl Posesorski with the other four partisans led all the people into a forest called the Werbow Wood.

Soviet partisan representatives from the Zhukovtsy brigade came to us later, and took us back with them to the partisans. It took three days and nights. The men went on foot; the women, the sick, and those too exhausted rode behind in wagons taken from the peasants in the countryside along the way. By Monday morning, all 180 escaped Jews had joined the Soviet partisans.

During the march, my wife, daughter, and I got separated from the group, and we walked deeper into the woods. At the other end of the forest, we saw a small, lit shack in a clearing, a kind of cottage. When we walked in, two Polish orphans came up to us—a little brother and sister, who were left there without their parents. I gave them a five-ruble gold piece, and asked them to let us hide there. The two orphans were so poor and miserable, and were overwhelmed by the golden ruble I gave them. They took us down to the empty potato cellar, and we hid there. Once a week, on Sunday night, I left the hiding place. Some peasants I met, Poles, gave me potatoes and bread, so I went there. I brought this food back to my wife and daughter, and this kept us alive. Later on, I payed the two orphans back in Russian paper rubles for letting us hide in their cellar.

After we were in the cellar for two months, the Polish orphans told us they were scared to let us stay any longer. We headed for the fields right away and hid in a peasant's hayloft. He never found out we were there. We couldn't keep this up much longer and decided that my wife and daughter would stay in the barn and I'd go into the forest to find the partisans. I later found a small group of Jewish partisans in the woods. I wanted them to take us, but they couldn't because their unit commander, a Jew from Słuck named Epshteyn,[4] warned them that any strangers they harbored would be shot. We found out later that this Soviet-Jewish unit commander gave this order because there was fear German spies were infiltrating the partisans.

The group of Jewish partisans led me into the forest near Yavishche,[5] left me at a certain spot, and said they'd come back for me. I lay there all alone for five days and nights, without food and drink, but the Jewish partisans still weren't here. So I left the forest and walked into the village of Yavishche. The village was full of Soviet partisans. I went up to a peasant woman, and asked her for a sack. I picked up bits of bread and potatoes here and there, put them in the sack, and took them back to my wife and daughter, who were in our hiding place seventy kilometers away.

Walking on a forest path at night with the sack of bread and potatoes, I met up with two Jewish partisans who were from Shverzhen. They said they were headed for the same area I was, so we went together. Every few kilometers, they walked into villages in the Shverzhen region, and requisitioned all kinds of produce from the peasants, taking it all back to the other partisans in the woods. These two Jewish partisans were well armed. The peasants were afraid of them and gave them anything they asked.

The two now accompanied me to my wife and daughter's hideout and took the three of us back with them. They brought us into the Polesnya Forest, and we stayed there. They helped us dig a bunker, gave us a tablecloth to cover it with—a kind of tent over a pit—and we lay in hiding for about six weeks. Jewish partisans in that forest knew about our hideout. They came to us and brought us food.

While we were hiding in the woods, I met two Polish peasants. One of them was from Polesnya—he was called Adam Trus. I didn't know them before the war, had never even seen them. The peasants helped us a lot—they brought us food, water, and other things. I promised the peasant, Adam [S]trus, that if I survived the war, I would give him many things I'd hidden in Stołpce.

After a while, we were joined in the bunker by Itchke Khananski and his wife and two little daughters, from Polesnya, I was glad because Khananski knew the woods well and it was easier to get food and to escape, if we had to.

One time—this happened on *Shvues,* 1943, at around four in the morning—a Hitlerite patrol came into the forest with a band of armed Byelorussian peasants, and started shooting whoever they found. We scattered to different parts of the forest, hiding behind trees and bushes, and no one knew where the other was. The Germans ran around with the Byelorussian peasants and kept on shooting. This lasted all day. When night fell, the shooting stopped, and we came out of our hiding places. I found my wife right away, but our daughter was missing. We started looking for our daughter deep in the woods, and in the end, we found her, dead—she was shot with a bullet through the mouth. We buried our daughter, Masheh, who was then twenty years old, in the woods, in the very spot the Germans shot her down.

After this tragedy, my wife and I left the forest. We walked for about fifty kilometers away from the place the Germans had found us, into another forest near the village of Kapula.[6] When we got there, other Jews came out to greet us. There were around thirty of us all together—men, women, and children. There were no bunkers here. We cut bark from the trees and patched together shelters to sit in. The younger people in the group went into the nearby villages to requisition food from the peasants. The peasants were afraid of us. They gave us food, thinking there were many partisans in the woods, in whose name we came. The peasants were afraid we'd burn their village down, like the partisans did to many others when they were refused food.

Our group of thirty people stayed in this one spot in the woods until the summer of 1944, when the Soviets got here. After Liberation, all of us returned to Stołpce and also to Shverzhen, where some of us were from.

My wife and I, along with other Jews, returned to our hometown, Stołpce. The town was burned to the ground, and only a handful of Jews survived. We met only one cousin of mine there—Ezriel Tunik and his daughter—and the three Kaplan sisters. They were three little girls who were hidden in a Polish woman's home for two years.

The few surviving Jews and me only stayed in Stołpce for nine months, then we left for Poland and the German DP camps. The Soviets had immediately inducted the young Jews into the Red Army and these boys have never been heard from again.

During the entire war, my wife and I didn't know what had become of our twelve-year-old daughter, who had gone to stay with a sister of mine in Minsk ten days before the outbreak of the German-Soviet war. When we got to Stołpce after Liberation, we learned our daughter was alive, and was being held in Tchkalov, RFSSR, with my sister who'd been evacuated there. Later, our daughter came back to Stołpce.

Eyewitness Testimony 34. Survival in Italy

K.L. Born in Podwołczyska, Galicia, in 1896; lived in Merano, Italy. Recorded by David Botwinik in Montreal in 1954.

We lived in Merano until August 1939, and had a large wholesale textile outlet there. A short time before the war broke out, the Italian government issued a decree—it was printed in all the papers—for all Jews not born in Merano to leave town and go somewhere else. We asked the Milan rabbi for advice. He told us to travel only to places where there were very few Jews.

We left all our valuables—furniture, china, silver—with an Italian warehouser, since we felt we'd be back soon, and only took the bare essentials with us. There were many Italian Jews in Merano then, and some Jews from abroad like us. Everyone traveled somewhere different. My husband and child and me, we went to Lago di Garda in northern Italy with two other Jewish families. We stayed there a while and had only as much food and drink as we had brought money for—which was very little.

On the sixth of July, 1940, at six in the morning, a *carabinieri*[1] we knew suddenly came to us and took us before the *municipio*,[2] which was just opposite our house. We left, believing we'd be right back, and took nothing with us. I left our room in a housecoat and slippers. When we were inside the *municipio*, a *maresciallo*[3] read us a proclamation indicting us for being Jews, and we were put under arrest. He told us to leave the child behind—he was only taking us to Brescia, to the *questura*,[4] where we'd be set free. But I didn't give in, and took our three-year-old child with me. They hired a private car, we climbed in—escorted by three *carabinieri*, who handcuffed my husband—and after an hour's drive, we arrived in Brescia. But instead of taking us to the *questura,* we were brought inside the prison and down into some dungeon, where they said to us: "*Signore—destra, e la signora—sinistra.*"[5]

I picked up my child and started walking where he said, but the *maresciallo* tells me to leave him behind. So I ask, "And with whom do I leave him?"

"*Ce pensa io,*" he says. "I'll take care of that," he says.

I got so upset I said to him: "Just try taking my child and I'll break your head!" There was a tool lying there. "Why did you trick us and say you were taking us to the *questura?!*"

It seemed this had an effect, because at ten in the morning, they took us there. But they deceived us again, and finally locked us away in a dungeon—my husband was separated from me and my child. They started taking our fingerprints like they do for the biggest criminals, and a whole series of "mug shots."

At seven that same evening, two deputies came for us, put me and my child in an auto, and rushed us off to Trea, Macerata Province. I was locked up and kept inside a camp there. My husband was sent to another place—Isola Gran Sasso. I became very sick in Trea, and the Italian camp authority requested from a higher source to unite me with my husband and allow me freedom of movement. Four weeks later, I joined my husband, and they transferred us to Orsogna, *Provinsa* Chieti. We remained there from August 1, 1940, to September 1943.

There were no guards over us in Orsogna, and we lived under a kind of house arrest. Because of this status, we were also given 13½ lira a day to live on. We were able to get by on this. There were ten other Jewish families in Orsogna in the same situation we were. Besides us, there were about sixty families there from other nations— like Bulgarians, French, Egyptians, and English families. The native Italians knew we were Jews but let us alone. In September 1943, the Germans occupied the town and started digging trenches against the English and Americans. The mayor gave an order for the arrestees to evacuate the town and go somewhere else. That's when the two of us started roaming the *campagna,*[6] staying in the stables the peasants let us sleep in, with the Germans always right behind us.

The front was spread out all around us. German artillery pounded the English, and they returned fire—shrapnels flew from all sides. We had to walk through all this until we couldn't go any further, having to come to a sudden halt about a hundred meters from the front line. To walk in any direction in the Orsogna-Pescara region at that time was dangerous. We couldn't decide which way to turn. Then we sighted a mountain not far from us, and climbed to the top. Luckily, there was a shovel lying there, and my husband started digging a trench, but he only managed to make a hole about half a meter deep. We got in and started to scrape into the sides to widen it, and this is where we stayed. Peasant cottages were scattered all around us. My husband would climb down to the fields and gather up the *polenta*[7] left out for the chickens and also the food the peasants threw away, and brought it back to me. *Gott mahner,*[8] what I went through there!

The month of December came, the rain and snow poured down on us, and my child became sick with swollen glands. My husband broke out in sores all over his chest and stomach from the filth and lice. God in heaven, those days in that grave in the earth! And there were other misfortunes: We were in the pit four weeks when a German came upon us and told us to get out of the "trap." My husband still had his Rumanian passport then, and buried it in the ground. We dug it up when the war ended, and used it. But now, at an hour past midnight, we had to get out of the pit and start walking.

We passed through the lines, but the artillery kept thundering and shrapnel shot passed everywhere. We walked and walked from one village to the next, my husband in his ragged suit with the pack behind him, and me carrying the child, my feet bare and bloodied—I lost my shoes along the way. Stopping finally, we saw some light coming from a house. My husband thought peasants lived there and went and knocked on the door. Curses flew at him from inside and someone called out loud in German: "Get your gun and shoot him!"

The blood went out of my face—I knew my husband was in danger of his life. I ran to the cottage and shouted in German: *Was wollen sie?!*[9] The *whrl* gave a start and began apologizing. He was sure, he said, this was a disguised partisan, or an enemy agent. The *whrl* was a German soldier, and they were quartered in every house in the area. He started acting kind to us, taking me for a displaced German. He gave us food and drink, and in the morning, their Red Cross came, and one of them washed, treated, and bandaged my foot. Afterwards, the German soldier took us into the town of Chieti, and wanted to help us some more—we barely got rid of him.

Many Italian refugees from all over fled to this provincial capital, Chieti. Chieti was a center of activity for the front. We met the mayor of Orsogna, where we'd been kept before, here—he was a fine man. He made out false papers for us as Italian Gentiles. Our real name, L——, he changed to Curi, the Jewish-sounding names to Italian-sounding, and so on. The mayor of Orsogna was himself a refugee in Chieti and knew, of course, we were Jews. It was because of him we were able to survive. After getting the false documents— one set of documents covered a whole family—my husband still had to go to the Germans to get them stamped. How my heart pounded while he was there!

We stayed in Chieti all of January 1944, until an order was given for all refugees—meaning all Italian refugees, and this is what we were now considered—to evacuate Chieti. There were many of us, so we were piled into passenger cars—Italian autos confiscated by the Germans—and sent to Macerata. There were six other Jewish families among these people, passing for Gentiles, like we were. In Macerata, they put us up in an Italian school, and we had to stay there. The local Italians, working for the Germans, brought all of us food. Two weeks later, we were sent further on. We traveled about 150 kilometers, till we arrived in Ancona. The English started bombing the town, and we were taken down into concrete bunkers, which protected us from the air attacks.

The bunker was flooded with water, and it was impossible to stay down there. It was decided that three people would be chosen to intervene for us with the authorities. And those Italians had to pick my husband to be the leader! The two others and he went to the German commandant and said it was impossible to stay down there because of the water, and requested to be sent somewhere else. The German commandant had an auto transport made ready, and our group of several hundred people was driven northward to Pesaro. There was no room for us here, and we had to be taken to Forlì. In Forlì, we were all put into a school building again. Right after that, the school was bombed, and we were rushed into a cloister nearby. The Don Bosco Hospital was also housed in the cloisters, and the Germans brought all the Italian civilian casualties from the bombings in Forlì and the countryside, here. When I got inside, the Fascist woman director told everyone I spoke German, then she informed the German authorities.

As a refugee in the cloister, I was given the job of interpreter, and I was able to help different people—I also saved many from death. One time, two escaped American prisoners-of-war in civilian clothes came to the cloister. One of them spoke broken Italian and the other knew a few words in Yiddish—he said, "Ikh, Yid."[10] I took both of them into my room on the first floor and gave them food and drink. They stayed in the cloister for a short while, then left.

Every day now, the bombings got worse and worse. Since the electricity was often cut, German soldiers came to the cloister all the time for candles. And sometimes they came just to steal all kinds of objects—icons, chalices, and other things. As soon as I said a word in German to them, they all ran off. Other Germans often came to harass the priests—and the cloister was packed with them—saying this one or the other was a spy, and had to be shot straight away. But I saved them when I broke into German. I was thought of as some kind of angel of mercy by everyone in the cloister. The monks, out of gratitude, presented me with a silver rosary attached to a small inlaid case, and every time I went to speak to the Germans, I took it with me so they'd be even more convinced I was a Gentile.

The Italians trembled every time a German came into the cloister, and they whispered, *"Tedesco! Tedesco!"*[11] It was only I, they
thought, who could speak to the Germans freely, unafraid—though
inside, my heart was pounding like a hammer.

The only one who knew this, but couldn't understand why, was
the hospital doctor. He was sure I was German, and said to me:
"You've got it good—why's your heart beating so fast?!"

When the English got nearer, the German military command retreated from Forlì and were replaced by the SS command. They
were stationed in the building next to the cloister. This was around
October 1944, just before Liberation. One time, two young Italians
climbed up into the cloister tower to fix the bell, and suddenly a
massive bombing raid began. Two SS men ran up and accused the
two Italians of being saboteurs. They were hustled off and condemned to be shot at three P.M.

The priest elder went to SS headquarters and asked for their release because they were innocent. The SS then grabbed the priest
and threw him into the dungeon, too, to be shot along with the two
youths. Now all the priests and monks came to me, and begged me
to go to the SS to try and at least get the priest off. I was so afraid—
my husband was in despair—these were the worst Germans. I
couldn't refuse when everyone thought I was a devout Christian, who
also spoke German.

I took the rosary and went to SS headquarters. As soon as I walked
in, I heard them say: "Throw her into the cellar, too—she'll have
company." Suddenly, I yelled in German: "Is this the kind of reception I'm going to get!? Where's my priest?!" and I kept running
the rosary between my fingers and pressing it to my breast.

They acted surprised and said: "Which priest? What priest?" So I
went on: "I swear to you, he's no spy—I've known him twenty-five
years and pray in his cloister."

They let themselves be persuaded, and brought the priest up from
the dungeon. His whole face was smashed in, and I wiped blood off
with a handkerchief. Then I called to the two boys to come up from
the cellar, and I said to them: "Go home, take the priest with you.
There's brave lads." I spoke to them in Italian and translated into
German for the SS. I kept this up with all my strength: "It's not
right for you to treat our priest like this. You fight at our side, and this
is how you treat us!"

They apologized to me. There was an SS doctor there, a commandant, and some other SS men. One of them asked if I wanted a
glass of cognac. I replied I was ill and couldn't drink, but I asked
him to give me a whole bottle as a gift. I wanted it for the hospital
in the cloister, for all the sick and injured. The SS doctor gave me
a bottle of cognac and asked if I wanted a side of beef. So I said,
"Giben sie mir."[12] But instead of a piece of meat, he gave me half a

pig, and two SS men carried it over to the cloister. I gave it straight to the director of the hospital, and said it was for the wounded. He thanked me deeply.

The SS were sure I was German, or of German origin. Some of them came to the cloister just to have a chance to talk with me, and complain that they would have to leave soon because "Tommy"[13] was on his way, he was practically here already. One of them was from Cologne, and invited me to visit him after the war. Another SS man gave me his picture, and wrote on the other side: "*Zu Erin-nerung an das Zusammentreffen zweier Landesleute in Froli.*"[14]

When the bombings reached saturation level and the English started their last push, these SS ran to me and cried, "Run! or the English will get you! If you want, come with us, get in our auto, we'll take you to Brenner Pass!" My answer was: "Someone'll be here for me in a minute. I've got my own transportation."

At one in the morning, my husband and child and I are lying in the cellar under the cloister, afraid the air raids might hit us, and I hear one of the SS knocking on the window: "Come on! Tommy'll be here any minute!"

And I thought to myself: "Go break your filthy neck!" but I said, "*Gehen sie, es wartet auf mich ein Auto.*"[15]

The English were here in the morning.

Eyewitness Testimony 35. In Holland

N.R.G. Born in Przedbórz, Kielce District, Poland; migrated to Holland in 1938; survived the Occupation in Heerlen. Recorded by B. Frenkel in a DP camp in 1947.

In 1942, all Jewish stores and flats were officially confiscated. The stores were locked up, and they only let us stay in our homes till they shipped us to the camp. This was in the summer of '42. The transit camp was called Westerbork, and from there, everyone was sent to Germany.

During the *aktsye*, a good friend to the Jews—his name was Dr. De Jong—saved hundreds and hundreds of Jews from the *Aussied-lung* by taking them into the municipal hospital. He gave the people special medicines and injections that disabled them temporarily. He put many of them under sedation like this, till they lost conscious-ness. Then, when the Nazis came to take the sick away, the doctor said it was impossible, they couldn't be moved. We—that is, me and my husband—spent three months in the hospital like this. Later, a Dutch police agent came to us, and told us they were getting ready to empty the hospital of all the sick Jews. His name was Jongen. He wasn't married, and lived with a family on Molenberg Street.

He came into the hospital at night all alone, led a group of Jews away to his house, and put us up there. Of course, all of these people were able to support themselves.

Some of us hid in the attic of this house for two years until the war for Holland ended in 1944. The Gentiles brought us food. It was barely enough to survive on. If there was a roundup planned, Jongen told us, and we hid behind a false wooden panel which blocked the entrance. There were ten men and women in our group altogether. Children were hidden separately in other places. Jongen came to us all the time, sitting with us, and gave us news about how the war was progressing and what was happening in the city—who the Nazis had caught, or that the Gentiles were throwing the Jews out of their hiding places for not being able to pay up any longer, or the Jewish victims murdered in the city. During a major search operation in 1943, when the landlord of the house was detained, Jongen advised us to leave, and led us out in the middle of the night to another hideout till the raid was over. Afterwards, he brought us back to the house. Whenever anyone was sick, he brought a doctor. He even got my husband to the dentist to have a toothache treated. We were taken to the doctor and dentist at night only. There was a room for us to wash up in the attic. We cooked the food we were brought ourselves. My husband was the only one who *davent* daily. We had brought linen and clothes with us.

In the summer of 1944, the American armies liberated us when they took Holland. Dr. De Jong didn't ask for anything from us after the war—he was proud to have been able to help us during such a tragic time.

We repaid Jongen the agent's kindness generously. The three children we kept in our group at the end also survived, and after the war, they were reunited with their parents. The Dutch government helped us temporarily and lent us furnished flats. Some, as a compensation for their ruined lives and businesses, received money.

Eyewitness Testimony 36. Paradox in Belgium

L.M.P., daughter of N. and M.V. Born in Belgium 1932, only daughter. Father was a metalsmith and activist in *Poale Zion*. Recorded in Israel in the early 1950s.

I remember when the war broke out in 1940, we fled to the south of France by train. The cars were packed with people, and there was a

lot of commotion and hardship. I couldn't really understand what was
going on, but one thing I knew—the Jews were in terrible danger,
and we had to run away from the Germans. We finally arrived in
a small village in southern France, and later, they transferred us to
a large camp in Agde.

After a few months, we came back to Brussels. I even went back
to my former school. I remember the first time we, the Jewish children, stood in front of the building with our yellow patches—but
nothing unexpected happened. The Belgian children left us mostly
alone.

1942 was the last time I had a birthday party in Brussels, and many
Jewish children came—also some non-Jews. Right after that, the
deportations started. My parents immediately took me to La Louviére
to stay with a Belgian family. They treated me well.

I was put into the convent school in La Louviére. No one there
knew I was a Jew except for these two nuns. But they didn't treat
me better or worse than any of the other children.

I can remember this incident now: The two nuns called me into
their cell, closed the door behind them so no one would come in,
then held out this piece of *matzo* to me. They said: "Today is your
Pesach, and if you were home, you'd be eating these *matzos*." They
told me not to go outside with the *matzo*, but to eat it right here,
and I did.

I found out they got the *matzo* from two Jewish girls, who were
also at the school, but they were later deported. I was the only Jewish child left at the convent, but I was instructed in religion and went
to Mass with all the other children.

I didn't feel the pressure so much, I just didn't want to be different
from the other children. I fell under the influence of the teachers
and became very fanatical.

I even begged the priest to let me convert, and to tell my parents
about it. He called my father in to have a consultation with him. My
father explained to the priest that I wasn't twenty-one yet—when I
reached that age, I could decide to whom to be loyal. In the meantime, it was still too early, and there was no reason to rush into these
things. The priest said no more about it, and I also stopped running
after him to convert me.

But at the same time this was going on, I was trying as hard as I
could not to forget Yiddish. Every evening, after prayers, I lay in
bed and repeated quietly over and over all the Yiddish I remembered
from home.

We spoke Yiddish in our house, and I knew both French and Yiddish. Where I got these contradictory impulses from—on the one
hand, wanting to escape being a Jew by converting, and on the other,
my passion to retain Yiddish—I don't know, I really can't understand

it. But this was how I was until Liberation. As soon as my parents took me back with them, the last traces of this foreignness left me forever.

I came back to the school I had been in before, and the Belgian pupils were kind to me. At the same time, I got drawn into the Borochov Youth Movement, and identified myself with Israel from then on. In 1951, I came to Israel with my parents, and joined Kibbutz Mishmar Hanegev. I got married on the kibbutz in 1952 to a member from France, who's been in Israel since 1946.

Eyewitness Testimony 37. Child of a Mixed Marriage

L.R.B., maiden name M.; lives in Tel Aviv. Recorded by Ella Mahler through Yad Vashem in Israel, 1960, in English.

I was born in Berlin in 1928, the only child of a mixed marriage— my father's Jewish, my mother was German. My father, L—— M——, born in 1892, was a professional writer and radio performer. My mother, G—— L——, born in 1896, was a housewife.

I came to Israel in 1949 together with my mother. She died in 1957 in Nahariya. My father stayed behind in Germany, and lives in East Berlin now.

In 1956, I married J—— B——, a commercial agent, born in 1926 in Pilica, Poland. J—— came to Israel in 1947 with Youth Aliyah. His parents, two sisters, and two brothers were killed by the Nazis during the occupation of Poland. J—— himself was interned in several labor and concentration camps. I remember the name of only one camp—Skarżysko.

My father was forced to give up his work as a writer immediately after Hitler came to power. From 1933 until the outbreak of World War II, he worked as a commercial agent. In 1939, he was inducted into a labor gang as a repairman on the *Reichsbahn*,[1] earning thirty-two *Reichspfennigs* per hour, minus a 15 percent "Jew tax." He was arrested during the big *Aktion* of 1943, which was supposed to make Berlin *judenrein*, and was kept under a week's detention in one of the Berlin *Sammelläger*. As a Jew married to a non-Jewish woman, he was released, then put through a *Selektion* with other Jews in order to sort and pack away the archives of the *Berliner Jüdische Gemeinde*.[2] All the institutions of the Berlin Jewish Community were closed during the *Grosse Aktion*,[3] their staff were deported, and the buildings were taken over by the Gestapo—all except for the old office building and its archives, the Jewish Hospital, where sick Jews were nursed till they were strong enough to be deported, and the Weissensee cemetery. What remained of the once-flourishing Jewish community of Berlin was, symbolically enough, the records of the past, the sick, and the dead.

I attended the segregated school for Jewish children, and finished eight grades by 1942, when all the schools for Jewish children were closed down. After the Jewish schools were closed, the Jewish youth past the age of twelve were sent away for forced labor. I—along with a group of almost 200 Jewish boys and girls—was assigned for work at the Weissensee cemetery. I remained there till late autumn, 1942, when I was transferred to other kinds of labor—clearing the streets of Berlin pounded to ash and rubble by the English and American bombers.

Before the *Grosse Aktion* of 1943, the 200 boys and girls assigned to the Weissensee cemetery worked mostly as groundskeepers. Since no Gestapo or SS man ever entered the cemetery premises, either before or after the *Grosse Aktion* of March 1943, Weissensee had become—for the adults as well as for the children working there— a kind of refuge. We felt safe there—if not from the bombings from above, then at least from the dangers of our immediate surroundings.

After the *Grosse Aktion,* of the large group of 200 youths who'd worked at the cemetery, only three were left alive: two boys and me—all of us children of mixed marriages. Of the large staff of adults, only eight were left, including Rabbi Martin Riesenburger—all of them married to non-Jewish women. We three children had to help out in all kinds of work: digging graves, burying the dead, cleaning the grounds and the buildings, and helping the rabbi arrange secret services on Rosh Hashanah and Yom Kippur. These services were attended by many Jews who risked their lives.

My parents and I were liberated in 1945 by the Russian army. This is how it happened:

In April 1945, when the Russians marched into Berlin taking one quarter after another, and the civilians were still seeking protection from the shooting, in the air-raid shelters, a small group of Russian soldiers entered the shelter of our building, where all the tenants, including our whole family, were gathered. The Russian soldiers were looking for German soldiers and Party members. My father stepped forward and announced he was a Jew, and he was pushed brutally toward the exit by a Russian corporal. The Russians had been told there wasn't a Jew left alive in Berlin. So the corporal was sure my father was lying. Only after the Russians questioned the German tenants, and went up to see the yellow *mogen duvid* affixed to our flat, was my father saved from the further fury of the Russian corporal.

I, myself, have written about my life and experiences during the war until the capitulation of Berlin. I chose to write it in English, though German was my first tongue.

I came to Israel in 1949 together with my German mother, who didn't want to live separated from me, her only daughter. I came not because I wanted to be in this country—I knew very little about Israel then—but because I didn't want to stay in Germany. Right after the war, I worked for the Sochnut in Berlin for two years. This was my first contact with people who were close to Israel.

My decision to emigrate was strongly influenced by a chance remark I overheard in a movie theater. They were showing a newsreel of the opening of a Jewish institute in Munich—there were some bearded Jews in it. A German woman sitting behind me said to her acquaintance: "Just look at those, will you! I thought we finished them off long ago!"

Once in Israel, I, and even more surprising, my mother, became very enthusiastic about this country, though we struggled hard. We settled in Akko, lived for five years in the Old City, then moved to the new part of town. From Akko we went to Nahariya, where I got married, and where my mother lived until three years ago. At present, I and my husband live in Tel Aviv.

[R—— seems happy in Israel, and feels completely at home. Since she came to the country, she's traveled to Germany twice. She keeps up a correspondence with the German neighbors who helped the M——s during the war. She's also relented in her bitterness toward her father for divorcing her mother, and intends to visit him some day.—E.M.]

Eyewitness Testimony 38. Ordeals of a Young Woman in Eastern Galicia

B.K. Born in Rozniatów, Stanislawów District, Galicia, in 1923; lived there. Recorded by Icek Shmulewitz in New York, November 1954.

I lived in the small *shtetl* of Rozniatów with my mother, two brothers, and a sister. There were ninety people in our family altogether. My father died just before the war. My *bahbe*—my father's mother—had a mill in the countryside not far from the village of Rowina, and this is what we lived from.

When the war broke out, I had only a short while to go before finishing the high school. After the Soviets occupied our town on September 17, 1939, I started working in an office as a typist, my sister became a seamstress, and my two brothers were still in elementary school. As long as the Soviets were here, we could go about our lives. The war only first started for us on June 22, 1941, when the German-Soviet battles were raging all around us, and the Hitlerites occupied our region. Just one week after the outbreak of the German-Soviet war, the Hitlerites were already inside our town.

As soon as the Hitlerites came in, they started leading Jews away for all kinds of forced labor. Once these people were driven out, the Ukrainians pillaged the Jewish homes. The Ukrainians also set our house on fire and burned it down.

At the end of 1941, the Hitlerites assembled all the Jews of our *shtetl*, Rozniatów—there were around 3,000 of us—and took us to the nearby town of Kałusz. The Germans set aside a ghetto there, and pushed in all the Jews of Kałusz, Rozniatów, and others they herded in from all the surrounding villages. There were Hitlerite guards, Ukrainian militia, and Jewish police in the ghetto. There was also a *Yidnrat*, which assigned different groups in the ghetto for labor—mainly building roads outside the ghetto.

In March 1942, the Hitlerites put together a large transport of Jews from the ghetto—most were from the rural villages— and took them to a camp in Bryczkow, a suburb of Dolina near Kałusz. I was also on this transport.

Before the war, Bryczkow had a German colony. When the fighting broke out, the Germans ran. By the time the Soviets occupied the town, all the houses were abandoned and the fields lay fallow. Right away, the Germans brought in the Jews from Kałusz, put us into the empty houses of the former German colonists, and forced us to work the barren fields.

I went to work the fields of Bryczkow while my mother stayed behind with my elder brother, Yitskhik [sic], but my younger brother, Khayim [sic],[1] who was then thirteen years old, hired himself out as a field hand to a Ukrainian. He looked like a *shaygets*, so he went to a Ukrainian peasant and told him his parents had been caught by the Germans—he was stranded—and the Ukrainian peasant took him on, certain he was a homeless Gentile boy.

The work in the fields was excruciating, and we were given no food. My elder brother, Khayim, who also worked with me later, swelled up from hunger. The only thing he could do was leave Bryczkow, and go back to Rozniatów to try and bring us back a bit of food. When he got to Rozniatów, a Ukrainian peasant called to him and told him to wait at a certain spot, and he'd bring him some food. The peasant left, supposedly to get some produce, but he came back with Ukrainian police. My brother was immediately arrested, put into the Kałusz jail, and tortured over a period of weeks. In the end, he was taken into the prison courtyard and shot . . . [The witness breaks down crying, and is inconsolable.—I.S.]

My mother, who was with me in Bryczkow, also died the same way. Hunger gnawed at us—there was no food at all. Then, one night, my mother walked from Bryczkow into the Kałusz Ghetto, where her sister was, to get some food for us. I accompanied my mother to Kałusz that night. In the morning, after we got there, an *aktsye* was carried out by the Gestapo, Ukrainian militiamen, and Jewish police. About 500 people from the ghetto were dragged out to the *besoylim* outside Kałusz. My mother and I were among these people.

Our column was stopped in front of the cemetery. They ordered some of us inside to dig a large grave. When the digging was over, the people were ordered to run up to the hole and then they were shot. My mother was shot right before my eyes. They didn't shoot the younger ones then—we were taken back inside the Kałusz Ghetto. I was sent back to the camp I'd just left, to Bryczkow. When we were moved from the Kałusz Ghetto to the cemetery, the Jewish police acted without mercy. They did everything to save their own families. And many of their relatives were on the march back from the cemetery.

Later, I lost my younger brother, Yitskhik, who was working for the Ukrainian peasant as a farmhand. Once, while I was out in the fields, my younger brother, Yitskhik came to me. He told me all the Kałusz Jews had been put to death, and a peasant told him the Jews working the fields of Bryczków—including me—were also going to be taken off and slaughtered. My brother wanted to bring me to the peasant for whom he worked. He was going to hide me in a hay barn there.

We decided he'd wait inside the camp for the day, with the other men, and when I came back at night from work in the fields, he'd take me to the peasant and hide me there. During the day, while I was out working the fields, the Germans stormed into camp and started chasing the Jews out, shooting at them, and hitting my brother, Yitskhik, who was then fifteen years old, with a bullet. [The witness can't stop crying, repeating over and over that her younger brother would have lived, he would have survived the war passing for a peasant, but he died because of her, because he wanted to save her.— I.S.]

When those of us in the fields heard the shooting coming from the camp, we panicked and started running off in different directions. I ran straight into the woods together with a Jewish girl friend, Khane Laufer. Now she's called Frisher, and lives in California. This was just at the end of 1942, or at the beginning of 1943. The two of us ran into the woods behind Bryczków and Dolina. We were there for a day and night, and had nothing to eat. I wanted to know what happened to my brother, who stayed in camp that day, and was supposed to lead me out at night. My heart told me something terrible happened to him.

I left the forest, and went to a place near Bryczków, to a Gentile woman I'd done some sewing for while I was in camp. The woman told me then how my younger brother was shot inside the camp. As we stood there, someone knocked at the door. German and Ukrainian police came in looking for the Jews hiding here. I knew they were looking for me. I rushed into the next room, broke through a window, and started to run. But I stopped, jumped back, and crouched under the window. It was late evening, and very dark. The two policemen jumped through the window after me, but they kept running into the fields, looking for me there.

I didn't go back inside to the woman, but ran into the woods. There was a peasant riding on a sleigh ahead of me, and as I passed, he asked me where was I going? He probably knew I was Jewish, and said I could come with him. At that time, peasants were paid a fifty *Deutschemmark* reward for capturing escaped Jews or uncovering their hideouts. I spoke Ukrainian well, and tried to make him think I was Ukrainian, then I slipped into the woods. I couldn't find my girl friend anymore because she had gone to look for food somewhere. I stayed in the forest, and crept into the fields at night to dig up the winter potatoes the peasants had planted, and this is how I lived. I was alone in the forest for over a year. I spent the nights buried under leaves or in the brush, suffering terrible hunger and frost from the constant cold spells. This was in the forest near Dolina.

Once, I had to spend eight straight days without food, and I couldn't stand it anymore. I headed for a small light glinting from a hut outside the forest. I came nearer to the light, but was afraid to go into the hut. I stood by the side, waiting to see who'd come out. Then this old woman came out, and I went up to her and asked for a piece of bread. I told her I'd go back immediately where I came from.

This old woman thought I was a homeless Ukrainian girl. She took me into the stable, and I could see she was impoverished. She brought me a little bit of warm food, a pair of boots and more. Then I told the old woman I was a Jew. She gave me some food and told me to leave because she was afraid. The old woman said whenever I'd come, she'd give me food. I went to her only at night—she left out food, and sometimes let me spend the night there. Every time I went away, she gave me warm food to take along, though she herself had nothing.

Once, the woman gave me an old, torn sweater to take back into the forest. I unraveled the stitches, and knitted a good sweater with needles she gave me. The woman was overwhelmed when she saw the pretty sweater I made her. Later, she collected old sweaters from her neighbors, and gave them to me to knit into good ones in the forest. The neighbors were supposed to think she, the old woman herself, was making these sweaters. They used to give her food for them, from which both she and I lived.

[The witness speaks with admiration for this Ukrainian woman.

The witness told me if she met her right now, she'd give her everything she owned in a minute.—I.S.]

This old woman, whose kindness I'll never forget, was called Maria
Rudik. And this was how the winter passed until the beginning of
1944. I knew then there were other Jews hiding in these same forests.
Every so often, volleys of shots rang out, Germans and Ukrainians
charged through the woods, shooting and capturing Jews.

One time, during the winter of 1944, I was inside the old woman's
hut. She was away at the time, and I was all alone. If aynone knocked
at the door, or if I saw a stranger coming, I'd run out the back to the
barn and hide in the hay. There was a small cat in the hut that
wouldn't leave me alone. Someone knocked on the door, and I rushed
out the side way to hide in the barn, but the cat ran after me. The old
woman's neighbor, a Ukrainian woman, saw me. She was the wife
of a local gendarme.

When the old woman came back, I told her what happened and
said I was afraid the neighbor would inform on me. But the old
woman calmed me down, and said the neighbor wouldn't tell.

In the middle of the night, as I was sleeping with the old woman
in her small bed, someone knocked at the door. Immediately, the
old woman pushed me under the straw bedding we slept on. German
and Ukrainian police burst in and said they heard there was a Jewess
here! They looked in every corner of the room but didn't find me—
I was pushed down under the sack. From that night on, I never slept
inside the old woman's hut again. I kept coming at night, taking some
food, and left right away. I was careful not to fall into the hands of
the Gestapo or the Ukrainian police because the old woman kept
telling me the Soviet front was closing in.

Once, in May of 1944, I came to the old woman at dawn to ask for
some food. It was springtime in the world and all I wanted was to
survive till Liberation. While I was inside, German and Ukrainian
police surrounded the hut and caught me. They pinned the old
woman against the wall and ordered her to tell them if I'd been hiding
there all this time. The old woman said no, I'd never been there
before. I also told them it was the first time I'd been there. Then the
German and Ukrainian police beat up the old woman and me to
within an inch of our lives.

They dragged us to the Gestapo and started beating and torturing
me to tell them who the Jews were who were hidden in the woods
with me. I remember the Jews hiding in the forest then—these were
the woods around Bryczków and Dolina. They went out at night,
captured German soldiers or Ukrainian police, and shot them dead.
These same Jews broke into peasant huts to take food. I knew these
people in the woods were armed. They were probably bands of Jewish partisans, but I never saw them. I did what I could to avoid staying

with large groups of people because this increased the danger of falling into German hands.

I was taken from the Gestapo in Bryczków to the prison in Dolina. They threw me into the same cell as the old Ukrainian woman who helped me, and besides the two of us, there was no one else inside. The old woman didn't blame me for her suffering, she couldn't understand why they were torturing me so. For two weeks we were kept in the prison under constant interrogation and torture so we'd tell them about the Jews in the forest.

The wife of the Ukrainian policeman, the neighbor who informed on me, tried to get the old woman released, and soon they let her go. When they opened the cell to let her out, the old woman pleaded: "Let this girl out, too—she's innocent!"

I was in the prison cell all alone. I heard the bombing all around us and was afraid I'd be killed sitting inside the prison. Soon the prison warden came to me—he was German—and said I wouldn't be let out of prison so fast, but I wouldn't be tortured either, because I had important information to give them about the Jews hiding in the woods. He said he was sending me to the Gestapo in Stryj, and they'd make me talk.

They took me to Stryj with a Ukrainian youth from the Bryczków camp where we had been brought to work in the fields. I knew him from there. On the way to Stryj, this *shaygets* told me he was arrested for hiding a Jewish girl from Dolina, Regina—I can't remember her last name. He was caught, but the Jewish girl escaped to the woods. She was trapped later by *Banderovtsi* who murdered her in the forest.

I was put into the Stryj prison and interrogated without stop. They used dogs who pounced on me during the questioning, tearing my clothes, gnashing my limbs, while they tried to get my confession.

While I was in the Stryj prison cell, I got to know the Jewish women of the Sobel family of Stryj.[2] The Germans captured them and put them into the prison after being led to their hideouts by Ukrainian informers. The father of the Ukrainian family which hid these people was named Shevchik, and the Germans hanged him in the center of the Stryj marketplace.

I was taken from the Stryj prison along with the women of the Sobel family in June 1944. We were brought to Borysław and put into a camp where there were about 800 other Jews—men and women —who worked in the oil fields. I had injuries all over my body from the interrogation sessions at the Stryj prison, and could barely stand. Two weeks after I was brought to Borysław, the Germans liquidated the camp. Everyone was forced into freight cars and transported to Auschwitz. This was in July 1944. The wagons were overcrowded and soiled—we were packed in one on top of the other.

An hour after the train pulled out, we broke open the door of the freight car, which hadn't been bolted, and the people, men and women both, started jumping from the speeding train. We were already quite far from Borysław. I also jumped off the train. The Germans guarding the transport, shot at us as we jumped from the cars. The Jews who fell clear ran off in different directions. I remained lying in the fields with another Jewish girl from Drubitch.[3] A bullet had hit me in the chest, and I was losing a lot of blood. My friend from Drubitch yanked out the bullet which had stuck in my body, she wiped the wound with grass, I struggled to my feet and we ran back to Borysław.

We came into Borysław during the night. We crept up to the camp to see what had happened to all the Jews. We couldn't see anyone inside the camp. My friend couldn't tear herself away from there. She told me that while the people were being led from the camp, her father hid somewhere, and she had to find him. In the middle of the night, we saw them march the remaining people to a nearby hill, and then they were shot. From our hiding place, my friend witnessed her father shot together with the others.

After this tragedy, my friend went to a peasant woman she knew. I headed for the fields and made my way through them for a whole day.

The next morning, I ran from the fields to hide in the forest. Before I could reach there, a Pole blocked my way and told me to come with him—he'd help me. I was afraid of him, but I had no choice—I couldn't have gotten away from him. He took me to the area where the oil wells were, and finally brought me into this hangar. As I walked into this large shed, I saw many Jews hiding there. I stayed with them. We were there another two weeks, until August 8, 1944— the day the Soviets arrived and took over these regions from the Hitlerites.

After Liberation, I started suffering from the bullet wound in my chest. I also had broken my backbone when I jumped from the train. The chest wound hadn't healed. I came back to Stryj and was in the local hospital for a few weeks, recovering slightly. I spent all of 1945 in Stryj.

While I was there, I became acquainted with Y—— K——, who was from Stryj, and we were married. At the end of 1945, we left for Bytom[4] and then came to Munich. I entered the Gauting Sanatorium for a cure, and stayed there from February 1946, until the end of 1949. All that time, I had to lie in a body cast to straighten my backbone. When I left the sanatorium, we came to America.

We arrived in New York in June 1950 on the ship *General Hershey* as DP's. Both of us have worked in the same shop all these years. We live in a small, two-room apartment, furnished modestly, and we're satisfied with what we've got in America. By big misfortune is that I'm a cripple for life.

We go to the English and Yiddish theater from time to time, to movies and concerts. We read the *Times* and *News*. We also read Yiddish papers—but not often, now and then. We read English and Yiddish books—we're reading Sh. Katcherginski's *Partizaner gayen* now. Our social life is with a group of new immigrants—we know a few families like that, and this is all the contact we have in our lives.

[The witness seemed heartbroken, miserable, because she can't have children—her uterine tract knotted together during the years she spent in a body cast. Because of this, she feels worthless and inferior in her husband's eyes, so she overexerts herself and brings in more money than he does, hoping he'll appreciate her this way.— I.S.]

Eyewitness Testimony 39. The Taking of a Nazi Fortification

R. Born in Warsaw, worked there as a bookkeeper. Fled to Dereczyn, Baranowicze District, Poland, where he was overtaken by the German invasion of the USSR in June 1941. This document is a deposition, in Polish, for the Jewish Historical Commission in Poland in 1947. The witness tells of the bitter treachery the Nazis practiced against the Jews of Dereczyn and the sequence of *aktsyes* which culminated in the almost total extermination of the Jews, numbering over 3,000 pople, on July 23, 1942. He continues.

The partisan activities in the woods which rose from the banks of the Szczara River, and also in the Lipiczańská Forest, started in March of 1942. The first partisan units were made up mostly of Soviet soldiers and officers who escaped from German captivity. The first Jews joined around May and June. We'd been in touch with them the whole time and knew which trails they used, more or less, so a group of us—my wife, too—joined up with them in July 1942. Our group was taken into Borys Bezręnki's "Golanska" unit. Our detachment consisted of twenty-seven people—we had eight machine guns. I was a second gunner, and my wife carried out the duties of nurse. We were the first Jews taken into this partisan unit. There's a shortage of men in our force—the whole unit numbered only 400 people, of them, about sixty are Jews. This was the same time Dr. [Yechiel] Atlas was forming his famous Jewish partisan brigade.

In the early days of September 1942, we carried out our first major operation: the taking of the gendarme precinct fortification in Dereczyn, which was manned by fifteen Germans and eighty Byelorussians. The battle started at four in the morning, and lasted three hours. All the roads leading to Dereczyn were blockaded by our people. The assault unit smashed the gendarme compound with hand

grenades, burned down the dairy annex, and set the precinct fortifications on fire. All of us—the Jews of Dereczyn—took part in the assault.
One of our group—the son of the town butcher—broke into the
Sonderführer's quarters unarmed, did away with him, then led in all
the other partisans, until the arsenal was captured. At the end, he
was killed in an exchange of fire. The panic-stricken, fleeing Germans
were picked off through the slot windows of the fortification. The
results of the battle were: the fortification smashed, five Germans
and eight Byelorussian gendarmes killed. We lost nine men, including four Jews.

After we took the Dereczyn precinct, the first major German coun-
terattack was launched, during which our Golanska unit had to dis-
perse. We splintered off into details of from two to four people, and
took up new positions in the nearby woods. My wife and I, together
with another friend from Warsaw, Yosif Veygmayster, headed for the
Lipiczanska Forest where we joined [Hersh] Kaplinski's Jewish force.
This unit had over 150 people and was reinforced by the Jews escaping from Zhetl.[1] They divided themselves up into three units. The first,
into which me and my wife were taken and which saw the most
combat, was headed by Pinyeh Green. These men were absolutely
fearless and inspired us to battle—men like Pinyeh Green, Sholem
Gerling, Khayim Slomka, Natan Funt, and others.

Eyewitness Testimony 40. Opposition to a *Judenrat*

M.G. Born in Łódź in 1903; lived there. Recorded by Yankiv Fishman
in New York in 1954. The witness talks about the first weeks after the
outbreak of the war in Łódź, and shows the different attitudes of the
Volksdeutsche to their Jewish former factory co-workers. He's speaking of these incidents.

Later, Mazo went to the factory owner and told him he'd wait for
him and the German soldier who'd been to my house, at a certain
spot. They both came. The factory owner was given 600 *zloty* for the
both of them, and they agreed to let me go. Another worker came
over to me at that time—he was also a *Volksdeutsche* but I don't remember his name—and told me in secret that the ghetto was soon
going to be completely sealed off. "Get out in time," he said.

On May 1, 1940, the Łódź Ghetto was sealed off. As an active
Bundist, I took part in the resistance movement of the Bund. Rumkowski, the Ghetto *Älteste*, knew about it. He was minutely informed
about each and every action we took. Biebow, the German chief of
the ghetto, came to Rumkowski, ordering him to assemble 10,000

Jewish children to the age of ten.¹ He said they'd be treated with compassion, and their parents would be better off, too—"impoverished as they were."

Rumkowski called over representatives of all the political parties to see him on this matter. He told them what Biebow was asking of him, and Biebow's threat that if that number of children weren't "delivered," he'd deport everyone in the ghetto. My party was represented by Lederman. Rumkowski said Biebow had implied that during the delivery of the children, he, Rumkowski, would have the right to take out a certain number of children, and the group would be chosen from among the children of the party members. The party representatives told Rumkowski they'd have to consult their central committees. Rumkowski gave them till nine the following morning.

Yankl Nirenberg, an important Bund activist, knocked at my door at one in the morning, and said: "You have to come to the meeting. It's at Lederman's, in the *Kooperativ*."² There were twenty-one of us at the meeting. Lederman reported on what had gone on at Rumkowski's. The meeting was very grave. Sixteen of the twenty-one participants were fathers of small children. I was also the father of two small children. We had all of us already heard the Germans were gassing the Jews. The talk went on till five in the morning. Twenty of the twenty-one—I was among them—voted to reject the "exchange." One of the participants—a woman, a mother of small children—voted to support it. She broke down immediately. I was very active in spreading this slogan throughout the ghetto: "Don't give up the children!"

The ghetto was in an uproar over this *aktsye*. At nine in the morning, our representative, Lederman, informed Rumkowski in the name of the Bund, that this proposal was rejected. What the other parties replied, we never found out. Rumkowski managed to withdraw some children. Children of Bundists weren't among them.

The Jewish police were ordered to carry out this *aktsye* of deporting the 10,000 children. But they couldn't do it. Fathers and mothers put up strong resistance. Children were hidden. The Jewish police were bodily attacked. I hid my two children in the *mikve*, where a comrade of mine worked. The Jewish police called their actions off right away. Rumkowski informed Biebow of this. Biebow kept his word—if he didn't get the 10,000 Jewish children, he'd clear out part of the ghetto. This happened in February [sic] 1942. The Germans removed 20,000 people from the ghetto—men, women, and children. Dragged them all off to Chełmno, where they were exterminated through the exhausts of the sealed freight cars.

In April of 1943, we heard about the Ghetto Uprising in Warsaw, and that the uprising was going on under the most tragic conditions. Our party, the Bund, decided to call support demonstrations to mark the Warsaw Ghetto Uprising. At that time, I was working at Kashev's Textile Plant. Only Jews worked there, like in the ghetto. As a party representative, I immediately called the workers together for a *meeting* right inside the factory. I was the speaker. The gathering lasted eight minutes. The manager of the factory, a Jew, informed Rumkowski about it right away. Rumkowski came straight to the factory. He asked: "Who was the speaker?" The workers answered in unison: "All of us!" Rumkowski punished us for this, and the next day, we were deprived of our soup.

The factory building was right next to a hospital—both were inside the ghetto. There were only Jewish patients here. I was on good terms with the hospital administration. We used to exchange news we received on our clandestine radio receivers. This was at the start of 1944. The hospital administrator informed me that the Germans were planning to deport all the patients from the hospital.[3] I asked him: "Should we try to save the sick children?" "How?" he replied. "I'll organize some people," I said, "they'll smuggle the children out through the back doors into our factory. We'll hide them in the looms, under the balls of wool." The administrator got me help—four nurses. We were able to bring over no more than twelve children. And suddenly, there was an uproar from the hospital—"Watch out! The Germans!" Someone had probably informed. The Germans rushed into the factory with their guns drawn: "Where're the children?!" Of course, we told them we knew nothing. They looked everywhere and found no one. Luckily, the children didn't so much as cough. The youngest child was four, and the oldest, seven. After the Germans were gone, we went to the children and they still wouldn't make a sound. Mothers and fathers came running to the hospital. Unfortunately, we couldn't save more than these twelve children. All of the sick patients and the other children were led off somewhere to a death camp.

In August 1944, the Germans liquidated the ghetto. Every day, they led away 3,000 Jews. Biebow held a speech in the ghetto: "You're being taken away for your own protection, so you won't fall into the hands of the Russians, who're due in the city any minute. You'll be sent to a safe place, but take all your valuables with you at all costs."

Then we heard on London Radio that the crematoria in the camps had stopped operating. Some of us believed it and some didn't. There was nowhere to hide. It was impossible to leave the ghetto. There were Germans in front of us and Jewish police at the back. My wife and two children and me took our place on the *Umschlagplatz*. Everyone was given some bread, butter, and sausage. Biebow came and again said to remain calm. Biebow removed only 800 Jews to stay behind in the ghetto. Everyone else was taken out.

We were packed into cattle cars of eighty to ninety people in each car. My child, Emanuelke, called to me in the wagon to listen to him sing a song. He sang: "*Ikh vil ahaym.*"[4] We traveled for three days. They gave us no water. There was an uproar in the train when someone took the urine bottle for themselves.

We're in Oświęcim.[5] The *Sonderkommando* dragged us off the trains with clubs. The Jews of the *Sonderkommando* were especially hard the way they treated us. The screamed out orders: "*Gepecke lassen!*"[6] People asked, "Why? We were told to take them along!" "You're all going to heaven," they answered cruelly. Then the nightmare of *selektsye* started. Right and left. Old men and old women, and also young women if they had children, to one side, and a small group of young men and young women without children to the other.

A terrible uproar broke out. Screams and shouting. Children were crying, "*Tateliu! Tateliu!*"[7] People ran back and forth under a hail of blows. Later in the evening, we saw huge flames shoot up from the crematorium chimney. I felt the flames were consuming my wife and children. They were, as we knew later.

I was sent into the labor zone. In Oświęcim, the daily selections were made by attacking Jews wildly and at random, then hauling them away. I was there for six days, then they sent me to Dachau where I was kept till the second of May, 1945. They assigned me to the burial *Kommando* here. Meager rations of food were doled out to us. I worked like an animal. Every day, piles of bodies were brought to me to be buried. The death rate climbed wildly, and if anyone seemed exhausted or sick, they were thrown straight into the crematorium, too. This was the system at Dachau: bury the dead and burn the sick. My younger brother, Yishayeh, also perished here. He was twenty-eight years old. The guard, the German who oversaw the burial of the corpses, looked the other way when I buried my brother in a separate grave. I know today where his grave is.

Observant Jews prayed every day though it was strictly forbidden. A Hungarian Jew from my *Block* put on his *tfilin* daily, and on the *yurtsat* of my father, on *Lag boymer*, I said *Kaddish* together with a *minyen*.

On May 18, 1945,[8] we were taken out of Dachau. There were 16,000 of us. Out of these, 3,000 were Russian prisoners-of-war. They kept to themselves. We had nothing to do with them. They were vicious anti-Semites. Everyone was given a piece of bread, margarine, sausage, and a few lumps of sugar for the march. At the *Appel*, the *Ober* announced we were being taken to the Swiss border. "From there, the Red Cross will dispatch each and every one of you to your homes." We didn't believe it for a moment. How could anyone trust a German? Some of us had different ideas: We were being taken to the Tyrol mountains where they'd make us put on soldier uniforms, and line us up against the Red Army. Others simply expected to be led to some spot and slaughtered.

We set out on the march once night began to fall. We had to walk the whole way. The column was lined on both sides by SS guards, and each guard had a big German Shepherd on a leash. A few people began a song, and soon everyone was singing, all 16,000 of us. We sang in many languages, and all kinds of songs—even revolutionary ones. This was how we marched. It was in the dead of night we sang. The Germans didn't put a stop to it. It looked macabre and sounded macabre. We passed through a village, and women tossed us bread. I was lucky. I caught a piece. This isn't what bothered the guards. They got angry and cursed at the women, yelling at them to stop throwing bread—couldn't they see these were "traitors to the *Vaterland?!*"

During the ten days' march, we weren't given a thing to eat. Anyone falling out to scoop up a potato from the field was shot. The Germans finally had to ignore this, too. We started falling out and snatching up raw potatoes which we simply devoured. I finally collapsed from sheer exhaustion, but I had to get back up or be hit by a bullet. Then the march came to a halt. We were outside the town of Betels.[9] It was on the edge of a forest. The Germans ordered us to run down a ravine. We stood frozen with fear, unable to move a muscle. We were all overcome by the realization that they were going to massacre us in this hole. The Germans held their guns to us and shrieked: "Either you climb down or you get shot this second!" With cries of *"Shma Yisruel!"* and *"Oshamnu, bogadnu!"* we stumbled down into the abyss. We filled it to the full and had to spread out around the sides, where we suddenly came upon a huge number of Jews who were also waiting for the terrible end. They'd already been down here a day or two. Night fell and we lay down in the snow and mud. As soon as it was daylight, the Germans started screaming: *"Heraus!"*[10]—to climb back up to the road. We lined up again over the ravine and stood here for three hours. Then we realized the Germans had run off—but there weren't any Russians anywhere near us. It was around noon now. Two old Germans in uniform suddenly appeared—they had the Red Cross emblem on their sleeves. They had guns, too. They addressed us: *"Kameraden,*[11] in just a short while you'll be free. Come to the village with us." The village houses were all draped with white flags. We were put up in all the barns. Germans came in with bowlfuls of warm soup. Liberation. In the morning, we watched the first American tank rumble in. The villagers were out in the street. Every German man and woman tried to give us the impression they hadn't had the faintest idea of what was being done to us. The Americans broke down and cried when they saw us.

After a couple of days, I walked to the town of Betels with some other *Katzetler.* For two weeks, I wandered around in my camp rags, the striped prison pajamas. Finally, someone gave us some regular clothes. I stayed in Betels for three weeks. Then I went to Munich. I started recovering and began thinking of the future. I went back to find out the whole transport I'd been brought to Oświęcim with had been sent straight into the crematorium. It was again made painfully evident to me that I'd been left with absolutely no one.

Then I learned that my brother, who was exiled to Siberia with his wife and child, had been heard from. When the war broke out, they fled to the Russian side and were deported deep into the interior. I waited for them here, in Munich. After contacting so many people and sources, I finally learned what had become of them. My younger brother had vanished during the exile. Whether he died or was killed, I have no way of knowing to this very day. Much later, his wife and child—a girl aged eight—came to me. I married my sister-in-law. My brother's child is now a young woman of seventeen. She lives with us. I treat her like my own daughter. We emigrated to America. Our apartment is in the Bronx.

Eyewitness Testimony 41. Hershl Posesorski, the Partisan

A.I. Born in Warsaw in 1912; worked there as a salesman. Recorded by Duvid Graysdorf in 1948. The witness describes the liquidation of the Jewish community in Świerzeń Nowy on October 5, 1941, and then the conditions in the labor camp of the *Luftgaukommando Moskau-Krakau-Breslau*. He then goes on.

To escape, to save ourselves, to run off to the woods—this was something we thought about day and night. Different groups took opposing sides. The first faction, consisting of the local *shtetl* Jews—mainly the rich—said this: "We've learned from experience that *Lagerdirektor* Domino is a man of his word. If he says he won't shoot us as long as we don't try to escape, we can believe him. And since there's nowhere to run to anyway—the partisans murder the Jews, just like the rest—we should stay in camp and wait for a miracle."

The second faction, which had the support of the majority of the inmates, believed that escape was primary, but had to be timed right, so as many Jews as possible would get out: for the time being, contact must be made with those partisans who can lead us to safety. The third faction, made up a couple of dozen youths, said: "Go *now!* There's no one and nothing to depend on, there's no reason to wait! Don't think of collective retaliation—just go!!"

A German sergeant who was on guard—I forget his name—stood by while the Jews argued, and understood what was being said. He called over a few people and told them: "I know how you feel. I'm a Viennese worker. The day I find out there's danger, I'll let you know." There were a few Germans who gave us their soup rations, and got us some potatoes off the peasant wagons.

There was a young Jew in the Stołpce Ghetto named Hershl Posesorski, a young man of about twenty-two from Warsaw-Praga.[1] He worked at a German labor site. He had to travel around with the Germans a lot and gained their trust. At the end of the summer of 1942, seeing what was becoming of the Jews, Posesorski took advantage of the right moment and made off with two German machine guns. It was said he left them a note on a table with these words: "What I'm doing might come as a shock to you, but I swear to you, when the war's over we'll meet again, and then you'll find out who owes what to whom!"[2] The tragedy is that Posesorski didn't survive the war, and couldn't settle this account with the Germans.

Posesorski's escape made a strong impression on the Germans. They looked high and low for him on the roads and railways, but couldn't find a trace.

Posesorski had a sister in our camp. She escaped from the Stoypts[3] Ghetto during its liquidation and was an "illegal" among us. One of Posesorski's brothers-in-law, Zlotovitch, a carpenter from Warsaw, was also in camp. He was interned in the summer of 1942, after he, too, escaped from the Stoypts Ghetto.

While Posesorski was with the partisans, he could find no rest till he liberated the camp and freed his sister and brother-in-law. He was in "Zhukov's" Brigade. The commander of his platoon was Lyova Gilchik, a Jew from Kopyl, near Minsk, who distinguished himself by capturing enormous quantities of arms, including hundreds of rifles, for the partisans. He couldn't speak Yiddish, but helped Jews at every opportunity and always advanced our cause.

Posesorski reported to the battalion command and told them of a "proletarian force" in the Świerzeń Nowy labor camp, very suited for the partisan units. He explained how he planned to liberate the camp. After the strategy session, the command permitted Posesorski to bring out only those who were armed or able to bear arms. But Gilchik told Posesorski privately, "Don't listen to them. Bring out everyone you can."

In January 1943, the Russians reached Vyelike Łuki, RSFSR. The German defeat at Stalingrad was imminent. We knew the Germans were demoralized—we had to do something.

It was during this time Posesorski got approval to liberate the camp. He was assigned four partisans—three Jews, one Byelorussian. The winter was extremely harsh. Huge snowdrifts. Approach to the camp was almost impossible. There was also a heavily fortified German garrison guarding the town.

Posesorski was given an additional assignment by the Command:

transmit certain instructions to the Byelorussian police to Stoypts who were in touch with the partisans. This was also extremely dangerous. It was about three kilometers from Sverzhne[4] to Stoypts, but you had to cross a bridge over the Neman. There was a strict control at the bridge. We found out later that Posesorski also carried out this mission and had no trouble delivering the instructions.

The group didn't move as one formation, but each one separately. Posesorski was the only one with a revolver, the others had rifles. He left them in Yavishtche, about thirty kilometers from Sverzhne. On January 29, 1943, he walked into town alone. It was impossible to get into the camp—all the Jews were away at the labor sites. Germans and Ukrainians checked all traffic in and out at the wood factory. Despite all this security, Posesorski broke into the wood factory, rushed up to his brother-in-law, Zlotovitch, and the others, and called out: "*Hayom hares oylem!*[5] Today we free the camp!"

Posesorski sewed on the yellow patch and after work, returned to the camp with the whole column of laborers. He immediately contacted the activist cell. They were afraid of informers and decided not to give the plan away yet, but to prepare the mass breakout.

It was on a Friday. The Jews themselves would keep watch so that none of them escaped—the threat of collective retaliation terrified them. The watch was strictest *Shabbes* night into Sunday morning, when the Germans and Ukrainians were too drunk to guard the camp. But on Friday, the "self-watch" was relaxed. A bitter frost and a raging blizzard—no one would leave. Even the same, the "escape artists" looked too excited while getting their bread rations.

Posesorski couldn't be held back—he wanted to free everybody. He summoned the Jewish camp leader, Kazik Raykhman—*a lodzher* —and announced: "In the name of Zhukov's Partisan Brigade, I've come to free the camp. I'm informing you we're surrounded by partisans. I know there are some here who can sabotage our mission. As commandant, I warn you, if anyone tries to stop us—a bullet to the head!"

Raykhman was shocked and said: "This day will be decisive and historic. Not only will no one interfere—I'll go myself!"

Because of the weather, there were few guards watching the camp. Posesorski himself went forward, knocked out several boards in the wall, flung a plank down across the stream, and—the camp was open! He announced that the escape would take place exactly at five. Everyone was to proceed one at a time, without causing a commotion. Posesorski got away with about forty people. They had several rifles, quite a bit of ammunition, and were gone!

As soon as the inmates found out what happened, there was an upheaval. The entire young militant wing had broken out! To be free of the camp—is it possible?! Some tried to calm the inmates, but most of us got ready to escape. We packed together small bundles in a hurry, and with these on our backs, headed for the hole Posesorski left us. Because of the frost, the guards were staying locked in their tower, and saw nothing. We put together a group of about fifty, women and old people, too, and got out.

The plank over the stream cracked. Our feet got wet and froze. We all had frostbite. Not knowing which way to turn in this unknown area, we finally realized we had circled through the snow and drifts, only to come back to the lye heaps in front of the paint factory. You can't imagine our desperation.

After some time had passed, the Germans finally realized the extent of the breakout. A volley of shots rang out. The blackness of the night was split by flashes of mortars and flares. We dropped our bundles and ran wildly. We were led by a young man from Świerzeń who perished later—Velvl Klatchuk. We ran toward the village of Polyesna—we heard there were partisans there. The frost stung us but we were still drenched in sweat. By around eleven at night, we were still two kilometers from Pogoreloye,[6] five kilometers from Polyesna. To pass through Pogoreloye was dangerous—there were many German and Byelorussian police stationed there. To avoid Pogoreloye, you had to add another eight kilometers through unknown land. We decided not to make any detours, but to risk going through the village, thinking there was less danger at night.

We were so disoriented, many of us still had the yellow patches on our clothes. We had no guns, just a hatchet. The group didn't break up, like we should have done. We were all holding each other as we walked, thinking that if we perish—then all together!

In the middle of the night, when we got close to Pogoreloye, we could see fires still burning in the peasants' huts. This could only mean danger! But we walked on. Suddenly, a man runs out of the first hut, yelling: "*Stoi!*" It turns out this is one of Posesorski's men. He was armed. His name was Itsik Portsovitch, the son of a Świerzeń baker, but he was killed later. Our spirits returned. I was now reunited with my brother-in-law. In the midst of these men, our hope knew no limits. Portsovitch sent me to the leader of their unit, Dr. Oferman, from Warsaw—he survived—to report our newly arrived group.

As we walked through the village I could see a lot of activity. Many sleds were being loaded for a long journey. People walked around in white parkas. Oferman told me to report to the Soviet commandant for instructions. He taught me to say these few words in Russian: "*Tovarishtch Komandir, razreshitye dolozhit, shestsdesyat chelovyek,*"[7] and so on. Before I even got the words out of my mouth, the commandant threw his arms around me and roared: "Where have you been all this time!?" Everyone was thunderstruck. It turns out

Posesorski is a good friend of mine from Warsaw and knew me right away.

He gave orders immediately to have extra sleds drawn up for us. We were fed, and at one in the morning, we started our trek in the direction of Polyesna. We rested there for a while, took on other Jewish escapees from the camp, and moved on. At two in the morning, we were about ten kilometers from the old Polish-Soviet frontier. We traveled through a forest all night long, riding and walking, so we wouldn't freeze completely. Hershl Posesorski led the entire expedition.

Of the over 300 Jews who'd been inside the camp, almost all of them had gotten out. But some, seeing the harsh, unknown journey ahead, turned back. Some were shot during the Police pursuit. On *Shabbes* morning, the Germans counted under eighty Jews in the camp. One man, a driver from Łódź, told them the route we took. They jumped into their armored cars and chased us till Pogoreloye— they were scared to go any further. The eighty Jews were tortured sadistically, then taken outside of town on Sunday morning and shot. About 200 Jews from the camp reached the partisans. Over eighty have survived.

At daybreak, we reached a village on the former Soviet side. Peasants came out of their huts, and seeing over 100 Jews, they started crossing themselves. The peasants who came with us were given back their sleds here and sent back. We went ahead by foot. We walked to the village of Yavishche, known as "Little Moscow." The four partisans who came with Posesorski to free our camp were waiting there. To our great surprise, we saw the other partisans strutting around with their automatics, flirting with the girls. Our shock was beyond words. We were still humiliated and intimidated and thought to ourselves, "The Germans were able to take Sevastopol but not this place?!"

Lineup was called—the old *Appel* was now transformed into "*Postroyenye.*" The officers reported to the commandant, "*Zadanye vipolnyeno.*"[8] We fell out of line and were then quartered in huts, two or three men to a hut. Our first order of the day was, where do we find something to eat? The old partisans reassured us and joked: the peasants already know the partisan menu—a partisan doesn't eat bread with milk, only *salo*, whiskey, butter, and plenty of it. The peasants understood this very well. We had breakfast, dried our clothes, and rested a while.

At exactly twelve noon, we marched out of Yavishche. We walked through the historic Lavay Forest. By nightfall, we had entered the village of Lavay. We rested there till late at night. Around 11 P.M., Posesorski came and informed us: "There's been a change of plan, get ready to move. We have information that the Germans are pursuing us, but it won't make any difference. No sleep tonight—we're off this minute!"

An hour later, we had gone by foot to the village of Latvina. We met many partisans there—they were mobilizing the village: all youth, all ablebodied men, must join the partisans. From Latvina, we took sleds and headed for the Polesye Woods. The danger passed, we felt safe.

On Sunday morning, January 31, 1943, we arrived in the village of Zhavolki. The people received us well. We ate, washed our clothes. Some weeks later, after we'd been long gone, a German retaliation squad, reinforced by Radianov's people,[9] came into Zhavolki. They found out how hospitable Zhavolki had been to the escaped Jews. As a revenge, they massed together the whole village, young and old, babies and gray old men, ordered them all to drop to their knees, and shot every one of them.

Like always, Posesorski couldn't keep still on that Sunday we were in Zhavolki. He even saw to the first aid and called doctors from his old partisan units to come and care for the sick. He was unusually brave—always riding ahead on his horse to scout the ways—he trusted no one else with this kind of mission.

On Monday, we left Zhavolki for another village, and came upon something totally unexpected. Yeremenko's battalion was stationed here. It was a big village. Soviet military leaders in dress uniform, large cannons positioned in front of the homes. We were very impressed, but our relief was short-lived—many partisans were staring at us with hate.

We continued on. Our most dangerous moment came when we had to cross the Warsaw–Moscow highway, a major road with heavy military traffic and under constant surveillance. Posesorski scouted out a crossing and brought all 140 Jews over to the other side under the nose of the Germans in their checkpoints.

We arrived at the spot assigned to us in the Polesye Forest. The peasants in the area were extremely poor, famished. We weren't greeted very enthusiastically. We met even higher Soviet commissars here. The commander was called Shustapalov. This is how he addressed us: "We've taken you into the partisan family. You'll be fed from partisan storehouses. Hand over all personal possessions, if not—death!" Anyone who still held on to something parted with it quickly. Inside the village, we were read tracts about the great German defeat at the Battle of Stalingrad.

We could tell the partisans here were hostile to us. We were quartered in the village for the time being—there was a shortage of bunkers in the forest. Sixty people from our group were led into the forest to build bunkers, the rest stayed in the village.

By February 5, 1943, our whole group was staying in the forest.

It looked like a small city. Just passing into this zone made an impression on us. We were escorted in by an integrated unit—there were many Jews here—of the Marshal Zhukov Brigade. A Third Unit was formed out of our 140 people. The Soviet Jew Epshteyn, from Słuck, was commandant of this unit. He gave the Jews a lot of trouble—the complete opposite of Commandant Lyova Gilchik. This Gilchik found out I could sing a little. He always called me over and said: *"Spoi shto nibud, shto a khosid, shtobi vzyalo!"*[10] He often forced me to sing when the other commandants were present, non-Jews. I didn't like this, it embarrassed me. So this Gilchik then treated me to some genuine Russian "blessings" and I was forced to sing. I noticed for the most part that Soviet Jews had a particular longing for Khasidic, liturgical melodies. Whenever Lyova Gilchik had a free minute, he'd yell to me: *"Spoi khasidimlekh!"*[11]

It was rare when we had any time to ourselves. On the sixth of February, 1943, the lookouts reported that the Germans were putting villages to fire off in the distance. We were all put on alert. In the morning—*Podyom!* We took no special precautions. But at nine, an alarm—*"Voruzhye!"* We fell into line, the weak were put on sleds—there were many among us with frostbitten limbs—and march!

The march took two months, with interruptions. Sometimes we rested two to three days, and sometimes two to three hours—whatever the situation demanded. The third platoon, the Jewish one, had a few guns. Food was supplied by those who were armed and involved great danger. This caused a lot of resentment among the partisans. They complained: *"Zachem eto tretya rota?!"*[12] Girls, young wives—they should form a civilian zone and stay in the forest. Why do they drag along after us?!" The Jewish unit often starved. Besides, we were in Polesya, where the peasant has suffered poverty and deprivation from time immemorial. The commandants also protested against the Third Unit, but they always sent us to do the heaviest, dirtiest labor, though we were all half-starved.

Posesorski heard the objections to our Third Unit. He couldn't stand it and knew it would end badly if we didn't arm ourselves fully. He asked the command for ten partisans to go and capture arms. They were released—including a woman, Fela Vaynberg, from Łódź, who perished in Gretsk[13] at the end of May 1943, while on a mission for the partisans. They all left to get guns in the Kopyl area. The mood of our unit improved, we were all sure Posesorski wouldn't return empty-handed.

Our unit had many different encounters in the Maritchanka Forest. The local peasants were very hostile to partisans. Many times, they got partisans who came into their huts drunk on purpose, then called the Germans. Before Maritchanka, we walked from fifty to sixty kilometers without stopping, through swamps and marshland, hungry and cold. When we reached Maritchanka, we thought we'd be able to rest for a couple of days. Famine was widespread. We got hold of some potatoes somewhere. We were so hungry, we couldn't wait to cook them, and swallowed them raw. We tried sending out some partisans from our Third Unit to find something to eat, but ambushes were set everywhere—the Germans or Byelorussians were just waiting for us. They couldn't enter any village and returned with empty hands and stomachs. Our hearts sank. The other units still had some food supplies, our unit—nothing. They used to give us one or two potatoes a day and we ate them raw.

One morning about ten, at the end of March 1943, while we stood in the forest, we heard a short burst of machine-gun fire. We paid it no special attention. It turned out the local peasants found traces of the partisans and informed the Germans. The peasants, with the Germans right behind them, got past the lookout posts unseen and closed in on the partisan base.

Suddenly we heard shooting right next to us. We dropped everything and ran for five or six kilometers through swamps and bogs. Luckily, no one was hit, but all we had left was what was on our backs.

After the ambush, the command decided that the issue of the Third Unit must be settled once and for all—this can't go on! The Germans came after us and even the armed units didn't fight, they just ran away. Yet all troubles were blamed on the Third Unit. It was said openly: "Send the Third Unit away, and let them arm themselves. If you find guns, come back. If not—go wherever the hell you want to!" Other units used to get guns in mixed groups, armed and unarmed, but the Third Unit was always sent out completely unarmed, to a certain death. We tried protesting but it was useless. The commandant of our unit, Epshteyn, treated us cold-bloodedly in this matter.

We set out in small groups, ten to fifteen men to a group. There were German and Byelorussian and Ukrainian police ambushes in every village. The Ukrainians had organized special squads at that time to fight the partisans. We had no clothes, we were barefoot and starving. They gave us eight potatoes for every man as our provisions for the road. We wandered in the direction of the Kopyl region. It was said there were most likely guns there. Long military convoys passed through the area all the time, and it was possible to pick up arms that had been scattered or buried. This was where Posesorski had headed, and we wanted to join up with his group.

We left the Maritchanka Forest on April 7, 1943. We received a pass—stamped and authorized—that no partisans should try and stop us. Though they didn't like it and protested and argued, they had no choice—it was an order from high up and it was good for a month. At the same time, the First Unit also left to get guns. They were told that even if they couldn't get any, they should come back—us, no.

The first group of thirty men left—we were unarmed, with no

battle experience, complete strangers to the area, and didn't know any of the roads. Danger lurked on all sides, and we still had to cross the Warsaw–Moscow highway. We hadn't had a bite of bread for two months. We gulped the few potatoes down raw, unsalted.

As soon as we were out of the forest, we split up into two groups, fifteen men to a group. The bravest one of us, Baba Vahnberg, a Łódź weaver, became our commander. The second group—as we found out later—were active in the Pinsk Forest. Some of them survived the war.

We reached a village. Vahnberg and another man named Berman —a teacher from Mołodeczno, Wilno District—went ahead to scout and we remained in the woods. They were gone for too long and we started to worry. We were relieved when the two came back. They hadn't seen any gendarmes in the village. We ran into the village and broke into the peasants' huts like madmen. We forced them to give us food—even bread to take back with us.

Vahnberg told us to keep moving at all costs. One of us, Rubinlikht, a loom operator from Warsaw, went into a hut to ask for some food. We waited a long time and he still hadn't come out. Vahnberg passed on these orders to us: "Rubinlikht has broken discipline. Don't wait—leave immediately!" After we walked a few hundred meters, we heard cries of "*Ratuystsye!*." We never saw Rubinlikht again.

We came to a small river. We crossed over to the other side on rafts as thin as moth wings, then entered the forest and found bunkers right away—some partisans had probably been here before us. We could tell by different signs that they'd just left. We found a bit of food, a grill, and decided to spend the night here. We made a communal meal and the night passed without incident. We stayed in the bunkers during the day. Suddenly, we see several armed men moving in on us. It turns out they're partisans! We talked things over, they showed us a nearby path—the truth is, though, the more dangerous one.

We started down the path in the evening. We had to wade through swamps in over our knees. The way took five days and nights, from the seventh to the twelfth of April, 1943. We managed to get food in every village, one way or another. Things had gotten better for us in this sense. We encountered all kinds of miracles. Once, Vahnberg went into a hut to find out if the area was safe. He burst back out, pale as a ghost—there are police right in the village! We ran where our feet carried us. Ten minutes later, we watched German and Byelorussian cavalry galloping through the woods.

We crossed into the Lavay Forest in the Kopyl region on the twelfth of April, 1943. This was a partisan zone by now. We were met by Jews. They broke the tragic news to us that Hershl Posesorski had been shot several days earlier by a Russian commandant. This is how it happened:

The unit commandant—Ananchenko[14] was his name, a Ukrainian
—noticed that Posesorki was using the machine gun he took from
the Germans when he escaped. The group Ananchenko led was made
up of Ukrainians. Many of them had served the Germans. In 1943,
many Ukrainian police came over to the partisans. We recognized
several guards from the labor-camp wood factory in this unit. Posesorski was extremely active in the Kopyl region. His heroic exploits
were legend all over the countryside—to the peasants, he was known
as "Hari."

Ananchenko kept demanding that Posesorski hand over the machine gun. *"Eto komsostavskoye oruzhiye,"*[15] he argued, "and you
have no right to carry it—give it to me!" Posesorski didn't give it up.
Ananchenko threatened him: "Give up the machine gun or you'll re-
gret it!" Posesorski just laughed. People who were close to Posesorski toward the end said that Fela Vahnberg was partly responsible.
Posesorski had grown very fond of her recently. She coaxed him into
refusing to give it up—"He can't do a thing to you," she'd say to him.

One night—this was during the eighth to ninth of April—Ananchenko ordered Posesorski to come to a bunker in the Lavay Forest,
and then categorically demanded the return of the machine gun.
Posesorski refused. There was an exchange. Ananchenko suddenly
drew his revolver and shot Posesorski down on the spot. He confiscated the machine gun for himself.

The nine Jewish partisans who had come here to the Pinsk Woods
with Posesorski to look for arms dispersed now, fearing further shootings. We took up positions in Posesorski's bunker. A group of friends
brought him to his rest in the Grove of Fallen Partisans. After a while,
his brother-in-law Zlotovitch arrived. He cut down a birch tree and
sculpted a grave marker with this inscription: "Hershl Posesorski,
felled by a murderer's bullet."

The Soviet commandants tried to cover up the matter. A group of
friends went to see Commandant Shustapalov and demanded the
murderer's punishment—that killer was still leading men! The commandant said now was not the time—there'd be enough time for
punishment after Liberation. The only justice done was that we took
the machine gun away from him.

You can imagine how we felt after all this. We lost the desire to
accomplish what we came for—to get guns. It was hard. The peasants
had stockpiles of guns, but demanded horses and watches in exchange. Without guns, it was impossible to get a thing. We had no
problem with food here. The whole region was full of partisans.
Stealing food from those cruel peasants without frightening them
by gun was humiliating, but we had no choice.

Soon, fifteen more Jews from the Third Unit arrived. As the number of Jews grew, our mood improved. After a while, we saw there
was no point in returning to the Pinsk Woods. The other partisans

didn't help us, they only left us to ourselves. The group of Ukrainians, the former guards at the wood factory, treated us much better than the others did—they were trying to make up for their past crimes, it seems.

The local peasants started calling us the *"Yevreytchiki byez oruzhiye,"*[16] and gave up less and less to us. We even looked for guns at the bottom of lakes and rivers. We usually found only parts of guns—once, even parts of a machine gun. Paysekh Skalke, a carpenter from Warsaw, carved out the wooden parts of a gun. We got a strap from somewhere. I know—the gun had no lock, but we intimidated the peasants with it and it did its job. We even got ourselves new clothes, because we were walking around in rags.

The command then agreed to let us come along with the unit, but at the price of carrying out a dangerous mission—to set the wood factory at the Świerzeń Nowy labor camp on fire. In July of 1943, two of our group—Elie Mandelman, a weaver from Łódź who later perished at the front in the Red Army, and a man named Natek, I can't remember his family name anymore—carried out this operation. They broke into the wood factory and burned parts of it down. But after some time, the fire was put out.

Later, the whole Third Unit, headed by Epshteyn, left the Lavay Forest and came over to us.

Our group was made up only of Jews. It started out with fifty men, later seventy. The news spread that a large group of Jews was camped out in the forest and had plenty of food, and this rumor reached the command. We wanted to rejoin the partisans, but they wouldn't take us.

All of a sudden, there was upheaval—a German attack! The armed partisans scattered. There was no plan of defense, but we stayed behind. We hid out in the marshes. At dawn, we heard the rumbling of vehicles and a short volley of shots. We sent out a scouting party: it turned out there were only a few autos. The armed partisans had run away for no reason—they could have wiped them all out! The Germans took some animals away from the peasants and left.

We headed for the base camp of the partisans who had scattered and found what was for us a treasure: sacks of flour, barley, salt, bacon, furs. We lived off this for a long time.

In August of 1943, Lyova Gilchik came to us and said: "Comrades, we must organize, if not—we perish! The Command is against you. I'll take over the leadership."

The brigade commissar came to us and made a speech: "The Soviet people are being bled—help us fight! In the course of two months, you're to find arms. If not—we'll consider it sabotage. Get pitchforks, prongs, clubs. Kill the enemy! Steal his weapons!"

Mishke Oytser, a youth from Rovne, shouted: "What do we need

guns for?! Someone we know had a gun"—he meant Posesorski—
"and you shot him!!"

We started to organize, forming the so-called "Gilchika" group.
We were part of the brigade named after Chapayev. The brigade
consisted of several units: Zhukov Unit, Donayevo Unit, Shtorsa
Unit, Ponamorenko Unit.[17] These divisions were broken down into
battalions, and the battalions into companies. The Gilchika Group
consisted of two companies. The commandant of the first company
was Mishke Oytser—he perished later in battle against the Germans.
The commandant of the second company was Shmukler from Kletsk
—he's alive. The overall command of the group was given to Gilchik.

Many Jews from Zhukov's division were forced to turn in their
guns and were sent to our group. Our number grew to over 100
people. We tried getting guns, using any means we had to—we considered it our most important objective. In a brief period of time,
most of the people in our company got guns. By now, we had over
fifty rifles, two machine guns, three automatics. The brigade sent
over some rifles dropped for the partisans from Soviet planes.

We carried out many diversionary operations, sawing down tele-
graph and telephone poles and cutting communications lines. We
also blew up railroad tracks.

On the sixth of November, 1943, our group carried out a major
operation. We burned down several bridges used by the German
garrison in the Gretsk area. The following day, we celebrated the
anniversary of the October Revolution with the Shtorsa Division,
who were positioned not far from us. On the morning after the fes-
tivities, a sudden reorganization was started. The brigade general
staff—Commandant Shustapalov and the commandant of the Shtorsa
Division—came for an inspection, and our whole group was ordered
to fall into line while they addressed us: "Your group has our admiration—you've carried your missions out well, you've acquired arms.
As of now, the group stands disbanded! Those with guns report
immediately to the Shtorsa Unit. The others will be formed into a
company of civilians under brigade supervision." The civilian company was formed and supported by the brigade—for a while.

We left the forest on November 15 to be quartered in the village
huts. Partisan base camps ringed the area.

Our morale rose. Day after day, we went out on missions, operating along the Minsk–Słuck highway. We carried out our last big
offensive on June 19, 1944. We blew up a section of the Baranowicze–
Slutsk railway for a distance of eight kilometers. The next day, we
pinned the Germans down with a fierce attack. We killed many of
them. Seven of our own partisans fell on that day.

On June 26, 1944, the Kopyl region was occupied by the Red Army.
We were brought to Minsk and decorated. Many partisans were

thrown straight into the Red Army and fell in droves in battles against the enemy. I want to mention several names now I still remember:

Yankiv Fishman—twenty-three years old, a Warsaw stocking-maker, alive.

Maza—from Stoypts, fell while with the partisans.[18]

Myetek Valonski—a Baranowicze mechanic, alive.

Yankiv Yakubovitch—a weaver from Łódź, alive.

I was inducted into the Red Army. On August 4, 1944, I was wounded near Raseynyay, Lithuania. In November of 1944, I was inducted into the Polish army. At the end of 1945, they demobilized me in Lublin.

Eyewitness Testimony 42. Jewish Partisans in the Bransk Woods

B.H. Born in Siedlce, Poland, in 1917; lived there. Recorded by Yankiv Fishman in New York, 1954. The witness talks briefly about the outbreak of the war and the Soviet evacuation of the city during which he, along with some thirty youths from the "*Ezras yisoymim*" (Orphan's Relief), was removed to Minsk. He was soon inducted into the Soviet army and later captured by the Germans. He continues.

On the thirtieth of April, 1942, we broke out—me and two other Jews and these five Poles. Wlodzio was our leader. Wlodzio was a young Jew from Warsaw. He was a student chemist. He was shot during the escape by a Ukrainian. We ran into the Bransk Woods and joined the Russian partisans. We heard that tens of thousands of Russian partisans were active in the Bransk Woods. The leader of all the groups here in the forest was General Srebrekov. We were armed. I often heard soldiers say, "We should have attacked Gitler[1] first and torn him to pieces!"

The Germans were completely tied down because of us. They were afraid to move. We dominated the whole Diatkov region from Diatkov to Orlov. We kept up constant pressure on the Germans. I belonged to the sapper commandos. I crawled under bridges and planted mines. We were followed by an inspection unit checking to see if we'd carried out our assignments. German trains crashed down off the banks or were smashed on the tracks. We captured tons of supplies headed for the front. I manned a machine gun and stopped the Germans from harvesting the wheat. They did the same when we tried to gather in the crops. Many fierce shooting exchanges broke out over these fields. We finally overran the village and secured the surrounding fields. I belonged to the assault group. There were seventy-five of us. We blew up the three German artillery pieces. A

Interrogation of a Jewish girl partisan.

The sign reads: "We partisans shot at German soldiers."

A group of Jewish partisans in the woods near Parczew, Lublin District, in 1943.

A Jewish partisan group in the woods of Byelorussia.

Jewish partisans from the Vilna Ghetto: Zelda Treger, Rayzl Korczak, and Itka Kempner.

Jewish partisans of Bielski's brigade in the Naliboki woods, Byelorussia, in May 1944.

German was killed and three were captured. The Germans tried to regroup around the village. The fight was to the death. I'm lying in a swamp, without food, and keep up constant fire against the Germans. I don't miss a shot. I can see I'm wiping them out. I lay in this position for five days without sleep. Many of us fell, but we killed much more on the German side. The peasants were with us. It was during this time a peasant accidentally led us astray while leading a group of ours, and was shot under suspicion of being a spy.

The battle to prevent a German encirclement of the Bransk Woods lasted till the major Russian offensive. The attack was launched with massive firepower. I receive a decoration from General Srebrekov, the partisan leader. As a Polish citizen, I participate in the push on Poland. The offensive began in March 1944. By the sixteenth of September. I'm in Warsaw.[2] My assignment is to force Germans out of hiding. I capture them under the bridges. Germans are taken prisoner; Ukrainians and those who collaborated with the Germans are shot on the spot. This was an order.

At Jastrow-Landsberg in Bavaria, several Jewish and Russian soldiers and I liberated a transport of 400 Jewish girls, who were barefoot and almost naked. I was so shaken by their appearance, I was seized with tremors. The Germans, the ones who guarded them, had fled. The girls were in a pitiful state. Some muttered as if they were insane. We were enraged. We summoned the mayors of all the surrounding villages. We ordered them to see to the welfare of the girls. As we looked on, the transport was carried off by truck, and the girls were put up in abandoned German houses. I became close to one of the girls on the transport—she was from Wilno—and we were soon married. The wedding took place in 1946, in Landsberg.

Eyewitness Testimony 43. Jews and Poles Unite in Volhynia

M.V. Born in Tomaszów-Mazowiecki, Poland, in 1912; was a high school teacher there. This testimony, translated from the Polish original, was recorded in Landsberg, Bavaria, on April 10, 1946, as part of the depositions gathered by the Jewish Historical Commission of Poland.

This happened in 1943, when the Germans were staggering from their first big defeats. That was also the year Ukrainian nationalists became very active. They were convinced the time had come for a German withdrawal which would leave in its wake an independent Ukrainian national state upon the Ukrainian earth.

During this year, I was still in the Polish village of Kurdyban-

Warkowiecki, fifteen kilometers from the county capital of Dubno. The village was built on adjoining hills, and straddled the highway connecting Dubno with Rovno. The huts stretch on for a distance of two kilometers, with huge gaps from one to the other. Seventy percent of the inhabitants were Poles, the rest Czechs and Ukrainians. Until June 1941, when the German-Soviet war broke out, I was the principal of the local school, so the villagers weren't exceptionally hostile to me. This was how, in the terrible year of 1943 when the Jews in the Ukraine had long been exterminated, I was able to save myself through forged "Aryan" papers. I was also put up by different peasants, who, to tell the truth, did it with great reluctance. Besides me, twenty-two other Jews found refuge in the village, staying with two Czech farmers. Two Jews also stayed with Poles. Altogether, twenty-five Jews found hiding places in this village, and all of them survived till Liberation.

Every night of that whole year of 1943, the village faced great danger. As soon as night fell, a barrage of shots ripped through the village, and wherever the eye turned—fires. These were the Polish villages set ablaze by the *Banderovtsy* Ukrainian gangs. The Poles were shot and butchered.

Our village maintained a constant death watch, especially the Jews who were hiding here, because the end could come any second—if not at the hands of the Ukrainian gangs, then surely through betrayal by the Poles. For the Poles, there were the cities to flee to, but Jews—where could we run? Gradually, the village armed itself. The peasants had sixty rifles, twelve automatics, six heavy automatics, and up to 400 grenades in their possession. The Jews who stayed with Poles were also armed—including myself and two others—and sometimes, the Jews who stayed with the Czech farmers also got guns.

The attacks came at us in steady waves, but the tightly organized defense didn't break to let the brigands through. I took an active part in the defense. I also used to write proclamations for the peasants on organizing defense and I tried raising the combat morale of the defenders. I'll give you a copy of one of these proclamations. I've also preserved the originals.

The other armed Jews also kept watch at night and took part in the defense of the village. The attitude of Poles to Jews in this village was tolerant as long as they felt their own skins in danger.

For a whole year, practically, we never slept during the night. We were on constant alert. There were pitched battles many times and during one exchange, two people fell—the Pole Antek Wiezinski, and the Czech, Jorko Studenny. Similar bravery was shown by the fighting Jews alongside the Poles in the defense of the Polish village of Bortnica, eleven kilometers from Dubno. The bloodiest fighting in this village broke out on Christmas eve, December 25 [sic], 1943, which was only six weeks before the Red Army came. Fifteen Poles and eight Jews, all from Dubno, took part in this battle. This small unit held out in two houses against an invading force of 400 men. The battle lasted all night and ended tragically for the defenders after they used up all their ammunition. The eight Poles and two Jews were overrun and killed. The others got away and avoided falling into the hands of those savages. The strongest Jewish resistance was put up in defense of the Polish village of Panska Dolina, near the town of Młynów, Dubno County.

This village recruited 160 Polish combatants and had an autonomous Jewish strongpoint 1½ kilometers outside the village, by the wooded area. Kuna Gutenberg, born in Dubno in 1911, a painter by profession, told me the following facts about the defense of Panska Dolina:

> The Jewish stronghold, which was part of a larger Polish one, was manned by fifty Jews, most of them heavily armed. The guns were gotten from the Poles by our liaison men. They requisitioned their own food. During attacks, the two groups united and defense was carefully coordinated. For the most part, the Jews were the first to fight off the marauders, since they also operated from the forests. The Poles built concrete trenches and had modern, low-caliber weapons and even machine guns. On a certain day in July, almost 3,000 rebels attacked, but the small number of Jews fought back with such fury that the Ukrainians fled in panic, leaving hordes of dead behind them on the battlefield—five wagonloads of corpses were filled, not counting those who had jumped into wells, and the wounded. But despite the vigorous organized defense, almost the whole village went up in smoke. The combatants didn't pull out, but lived to see the Red Army arrive.

A joint defense by Poles and Jews was also organized in the village of Zemówka, which was situated between the renegade Ukrainian villages of [names inaudible]. On the fourteenth of July, 1943, when everyone was out working at gathering the harvest, the village was suddenly put to the torch. I could go on about other battles where there was joint defense of Polish villages. . . .

Eyewitness Testimony 44. Tunnel Escape from a Camp

Sh.S. Born April 19,1929, in Iwanicze, Nowogródek District, Poland. Recorded by the Jewish Historical Commission in the Hindenburg DP camp, Germany, in 1945. The witness gives a painstakingly detailed account of the unspeakable tortures and massacre of the Jews

in Iwanicze and its environs by the SS units and the Byelorussian
police, resulting in a *selektsye* where only the young and ablebodied
remnants were sent into the Nowogródek Ghetto. The witness also
brings to light an attack by partisans in the region, many of whom
were Jews, upon a German battalion withdrawing after executing
the old and the children in the Iwanicze Ghetto,[1] in which they
wiped out every last German to a man. He tells then of the liquidation of the Nowogródek Ghetto twenty-two days into Ab, 1942,[2]
during which over 5,000 Jews died, and of his successful attempt to
escape the labor camp where the surviving remnants of the Jews
were concentrated. He continues.

After the liquidation of the ghetto, a census was taken of the Jews
in the labor camp. The counting was done in the morning before
work and at night after work. They threatened that all Jews would
be exterminated if even one Jew was missing from camp. This slowed
down the steady flow of Jews who escaped to the forest.

Early in the morning of May 7, 1943, the census was closed by
the *Judenreferent*, SS man Rauter, who announced that the Jews
whose name he'd call, must report to the kitchen for bread, and the
remainder remains as is. We knew right away this was going to end
badly. Panic broke out among the remaining Jews.

In the crush, some managed to break into the kitchen through the
side ways. After a delay of several minutes, the gate of the camp was
flung open and large units of Byelorussians accompanied by SS detachments marched in. The people left out in the open were immediately surrounded and forced to run through the gates while they
were beaten viciously. They were herded into a field a short distance
from the fence, ordered to lie face down, then five at a time were
dragged off to a pit dug for them and shot. Almost everyone tried
to break free, but auxiliary police were positioned all around the
field and picked the escapees off in a machine-gun crossfire. A woman
named Samsonovitch was kicked by a policeman who ordered her to
move, but she got up, straightened herself out, and gave him two
such ringing slaps, that his snout was torn open and he was splattered
from head to foot with blood. They shot her right away. Three hundred and fifty Jews were shot in that field.

The 250 of us in camp who survived—a scattered remnant—saw
our last illusion of saving ourselves through labor collapse, and we
decided to plan an escape to the partisans in the forest. We organized
an assault unit. The Byelorussian police sold us some rifles and revolvers, and our plan was to shoot the guards once night fell, blow
out the camp gate, and escape. The plan was criticized because the
camp was situated in town and the shooting would be heard by
everyone and this would give us away immediately. We made up a

second plan: When the guard changes and crisscrosses at a certain point, only a handful of sentries keep watch at the gate. They could be overpowered easily and we'd get the right passkey to open the gate through which everyone would escape. We got hold of a key and made a copy. We even smashed the gate open once, but some of our people were unprepared and we had to postpone the escape till later.

As we got up one morning a few days later, we saw that the camp had been reinforced by many SS units and extra police guards. The reason was that the partisans came during the night, attacked the Byelorussian police sentries, and dragged them off to the woods. Again we had to put off our plan of breaking through the gate and escaping.

Then they raised this towering pole topped by a huge searchlight which lit up the whole perimeter of the camp. They did this when it was learned that the partisans were ready to attack the camp and free us. But the young man from Nowogródek, Beril Yoselovitch, gave us the idea of digging an escape tunnel under the camp. Only a few dozen people knew the plan—only those we trusted completely and who were ready to make any sacrifice. We picked the farthest barrack to start digging in because it was right on the fence, and also because the most loyal people, the ones who knew the plan, were kept there.

The people were split up into units—some did the carpentry work, others the digging and getting rid of the earth. The people chosen to do this were those the Byelorussian workshop foremen watched over less because their absence wouldn't be immediately noticed. The same evening we drew up the plan, we started work. We dug a pit into the corner of the wall which bordered the fence and poured the earth into containers we carried up to the rafters. We dug two meters down, then we started digging in the direction of the fence, and here was where we had problems. Because of all the earth, the rafters started sagging and we were afraid the roof was going to cave in. Our plan would fail and the consequences would be unimaginable. We decided to make a routine request of the carpentry workshop foreman: since winter was coming and the barrack walls were weak, and there was such a big surplus of boards anyway, would he let us— after the day's work—reinforce the walls of the barrack? The foreman gave his permission. We got a double benefit out of it: first of all, we used the boards to support the roof of the tunnel, and we also decided to build fake walls into the barracks and pour the earth between them and the old walls. We needed a lot of manpower and skill to do this work. It was then decided that the people who worked on the digging steadily would get ten grams of bread from our daily ration and those who were in the workshops during the day would help digging for four hours at night. The work was done at a furious tempo. After we dug through about ten meters in length, there were new difficulties. The first was that it became impossible to carry the earth out in containers over such long distances. Then, we also had to have light and we had to use the searchlight illumination because the camp had no electricity.

Since Beril Yoselovitch was an electrician, he thought of a way to get us some light. When the guard changed, he busted the searchlight, then was called to do the repairs. He connected a wire to the searchlight pole and ran it the length of the fence and into the tunnel.

It was becoming dangerous and we had to get rid of the earth faster. The carpenters were asked to lay out wooden tracks the length of the tunnel and fix up a large loading cart. We nailed on some wheels, tied rope to the sides, and it rolled backward and forward smoothly, carrying out several cratefuls of earth at a time. Soon, most of the people found out about the tunnel and we dumped the earth out in other lofts. When the lofts started giving way from the weight, we took quilts, tore them up, and spread the feathers up there to hide the clumps of earth. The digging took over three months. The tunnel was more than 250 meters long. The exit was in the woods near the camp.

When the work was done, we passed the word around. There was a lot of opposition to the breakout. We called a gathering and forced a vote. A bare majority voted for escaping. We immediately picked a day and time for leaving the camp. It was also decided those with seniority would split up into two groups, one leaving before the other.

The days were rainy and windy. To cover our departure from all eyes and ears, we decided to wreck the searchlight again and to loosen the metal hoods over the perimeter fenceposts so their clanging from the wind would drown out our steps.

We succeeded 100 percent in everything. While we were leaving the camp, a small number of people decided to remain behind, claiming they didn't want to risk dying this way.[3]

The next morning, when we were already in the woods, we heard that at daybreak, armed SS units came into the camp, ordered to execute us. Fortunately, we were nowhere to be found.

Eyewitness Testimony 45. A Bunker on Franciszkanska Street

M.L. Born in Warsaw in 1910; lived there. Recorded by P. Mints in Warsaw in 1945.

... This was how the Germans always behaved. When the *aktsye* was over, they tried talking the people into believing it had been the last one.

I was consigned to the small warehouse at Franciszkanska Street 32. There was practically no one left to dole out relief to because hardly any Jews were left alive. Besides the work, I was also given a room to stay in. It was January 1943 by now, and people had already started preparing hideouts for themselves, so that when the Germans broke into the flats, they'd find no one inside. Anyone who could, built themselves and their family a concealed hideout. Likhtnshtayn of the *Judenrat* legalized my status and made me eligible for a work permit.[1]

In January—on the eighteenth, 1943—the Germans again started the general roundup of the Jews to ship them out of the ghetto once more.

You might have heard that the Germans also caught a lot of Poles for forced labor then, and the Poles broke into the ghetto to try to hide. I saw many of them myself.

At around nine o'clock in the morning, the Germans stormed into the ghetto and started emptying out the flats. This roundup lasted three full days. They also charged through our building on Franciszkanska 32. The Germans were even deporting those who had *Judenrat* work permits. They were told it was for administrative purposes, but they never came back. The Germans searched all the floors, but they didn't break in on the first floor.

I watched as the Germans led all the people down from the floors out into the street. There was this blonde girl standing among the people. She showed her contempt for the "hunters." After the Germans brought her down, she suddenly vanished. Because she was blonde, they noticed right away she was missing. The Germans were obsessed with finding her and went up to the third floor again to look for her, but she was gone. While they were inside the building, they passed our flat on the first floor again. We trembled, expecting them to burst into our flat any moment, but they didn't.

Those who had built a hideout into their flat in time, avoided falling into the Germans' clutches.

There was a cellar under the warehouse. I advised my friends to come with me and we'd overturn sacks of potatoes to block the entrance, because the Germans would probably return soon. There was a two-year-old child with us. Later on, some had to leave the cellar because of the agonies they endured and went back to their flats. They hid and blocked the entrances with dressers. The Germans came back inside the warehouse again and we heard their steps down in the cellar. They broke into the rooms and forced everyone out.

By January 1943, everyone knew the Germans were deceiving us and all of us began building bunkers into our homes. There was one large bunker in our building, not counting the individual hideouts. The bunker was set up with provisions for eating and sleeping.

It turned out, though, that the bunkers were of no real use—first of all, because from January 1943 until the uprising in April 1943, there were no big *aktsyes,* and second of all, because the Germans blew up the buildings and burned them down to the foundations during the ghetto uprising and, in the end, the people had to evacuate all the bunkers and hideouts after a short while.

I myself hid out in a brick building on a high landing after this building had already been blown apart by the Germans. From my room—to which there was no access because the stairway had given way—I could observe every day how the Germans, over the weeks and months of the Warsaw Ghetto Uprising, gradually set on fire and blew up all the adjoining buildings on Franciszkanska 32 and flushed the Jews out of the bunkers there. From my room in the ruined building, I could hear the Germans counting off the captured Jews. An especially large number of people were concealed in the large bunker of the adjoining building on Franciszkanska Street 30. The well-known community activist and Warsaw merchant Abraham Gepner[2] also hid out there.

The Germans tried to get to our building at 32. They crawled through the ruins looking for the bunkers. And while they were climbing around like this, they sighted the people in the room of the ruined brick building and we were certain now they'd get us. I observed from high up how they were laying the lines to blow up our part of the building and our room in it. They hurled a grenade and one of us was hit.

Suddenly, an alarm was heard. The Germans were called away to another place where a bunker of Jews had been unearthed. Night fell, they left and forgot us temporarily. There was no point in staying here anymore and we lowered ourselves down to the ground from the room on sheets. We couldn't get into the bunker through the adjoining court of the next building at 30—we weren't let in this way. The area gave off such incredible heat, it was impossible to breathe there. People saved themselves with the water from the pumps which had been installed there. This was an enormous bunker under the shops in the building and it extended out under the street. The heat came from the flames over it, which blazed through the whole building. The Germans eventually uncovered this bunker, too, and shipped everyone off to Majdanek.

We moved over into the bunker of our building, but we were forced out and led off to Muranow Square. There, we were all stripped naked and searched thoroughly. They put crates near us and all the money we had on us had to be dropped into the boxes.

There was also this old couple among us. If I'm not mistaken, their family name is Dykman. Their son was a translator from Yiddish into Hebrew. On the way to Muranow Square, she and her husband swallowed some pills. They poisoned themselves. The woman collapsed on the way and the Germans shot her. But the old man's condition was obviously better because the pills didn't work on him—he just kept on with us.

From there, they led us to Majdanek. While they were lining us up in an open zone there, I noticed old Dykman. And he says to me, "Look at this, look at this! One can still live here—and my wife had to poison herself!" The old man didn't realize where he was.

A little later, after hosing us down, the selection took place and all old men were sent off to be burned and, of course, old man Dykman was one of them.

I would like to give you some of my personal observations from the Warsaw Ghetto Uprising.

I was in the bunker from the nineteenth of April till the tenth of May. Even before the uprising, we had an observation post on top of the house at Franciszkanska 34. Up in the attic we had a spot where, with binoculars, we could make out whether the Germans were advancing. The watch was changed every two hours. We got little real use out of it because on the eve of the ghetto uprising, we learned that the Germans were mobilizing the Polish police, so we could imagine what was about to take place. We stopped relying on the information supplied by our watch on the roof and descended into the bunkers.

Our conditions in the bunkers were so hard, you wanted to get out of them as soon as possible. No light or air, and we saw this was the devil's game. We became apathetic and some even started deluding themselves that the Germans were only rounding us up for work. What would it take to convince them the enemy was causing our total destruction?!

By my count, several hundred people participated in the ghetto uprising. There was particularly fierce resistance put up in Wołowa and Swiętojerska streets.[3] The buildings at Franciszkanska 30 and 32 weren't actively defended during the uprising. There were active combatants among us but we played no combat role here for two reasons. First, we had no arms, and second, we knew the battle wouldn't produce certain strategic results. In our despair, we had to turn to new forms of resistance. . . .

Eyewitness Testimony 46. "Wild" Battle Group in the Warsaw Ghetto Uprising

A.H. Born in Warsaw in 1899; lived there. Recorded by Yankiv Fishman in Israel [?] in 1954.

Toward the end of 1942, the German industrialist Toebbens distributed printed leaflets throughout the ghetto, calling on all ablebodied
people and possessors of sewing machines to report to him for work
in his factory. There was relief that day in the ghetto. People seized
at it as a way of assuring your right to life and increasing the chances
of surviving till the war's end. Toebbens had a few factories: on
Leszno 78 and Leszno 40 and at several other sites. I managed to
convince him of the need to set up an annex of his factory, but only
on the condition that I'd be given at least 100 people to do the work,
along with 100 sewing machines. I was able to reprieve this many
people and I also was given the sewing machines. Toebbens got us
a locale at Gęsia 6. My wife and two children worked here and my
father and mother also, my brothers and their families and my sister
and her family, too. We turned out cotton trousers and tunics for the
Wehrmacht. Wages were a pot of soup sent over every day by Toebbens, with a piece of bread for everyone. We slept in the factory
because we felt we were much safer here than spending the night at
home.

This happened in January 1943. Our son pleaded with us to take
him home to sleep. Spending the night in Toebbens' factory was made
an illegal act and this put us in a dangerous position. Our son got
his way. We went home. We now had a flat on Muranowska 17. In
the middle of the night, the SS broke in and took us all away. Led us
down to the courtyard, pushed us into a huge crowd of Jews headed
for the *Umschlagplatz.* Toebbens was told his workers were being
lined up at the *Umschlagplatz.* He came down for us. But he was
too late. My wife and son were already on the train. Toebbens told
me he had no permission to intervene for those who'd already been
loaded into the freight cars. He got me and my daughter released.
He took 399 Jews back with him. We were led to Toebbens' factory
at Leszno 78. I pleaded with Toebbens to let us sleep in the factory
and to let me bring some bedrolls from home. He gave me permission. A few weeks later, an order was handed down for all of Toebbens' workers to come out to Miła Street. Thousands upon thousands
of Jews stood assembled there. A large squad of SS was present. This
was late March, 1943. The SS questioned us about our age and health
to arouse the false hope among us that we were being sent away for
labor. Toebbens again learned of what had happened to his workers.
He came down to Miła Street. He let his 600 Jews go, myself and my
daughter included. Toebbens now called us together at work, advis-
ing us to get ourselves flats in the area around his factories. The
"Toebbens Quarter" ran from Leszno-Żelazna Street to the Karmelicka and Nowolipie intersections on Leszno Street—the side with
the even numbers and the part of Karmelicka which ran into the odd
numbers. I moved into a flat at Karmelicka 5. The whole Toebbens

area was divided off from the ghetto by a wall. My daughter and I were in one room and three young men lived in the other.

After staying there for two weeks, my daughter coaxed me into returning to the ghetto with her. In the middle of the night, we pulled the bricks out of the wall at Karmelicka and Nowolipie, and stole through into the no-man's strip where none were permitted to stay— Jew, German, or Pole. This is the part of Karmelicka-Nowolipie and Nowolipki and Dzielna till Gęsia and Zamenhofa. We hid in a courtyard there till evening when the workers passed by on their way back from the labor sites. We moved in among a group and passed into the ghetto with them. We entered Zamenhofa 21 and found a deserted flat. Since there were mostly empty flats now—almost everyone had been sent to Treblinka, because before the war this courtyard was occupied only by Jews—I brought my wife's brother and his family here. My sister-in-law's sister came, too. For 3,000 *zloty*, I got hold of two work permit cards for me and my daughter.

One time, my brother and I had a violent scene. He yelled at me, "What are you staying here for?! Don't you know you'll have to keep dragging yourself around from one place to the other?! What kind of life will that be?! I'm going to register myself and my family for work at Poniatev.[1] They need us for labor there. Is that worse?! So we'll work like slaves! Listen to me—you should do it, too!" My heart sank. I started screaming at him hysterically, "Have you lost your mind??!! What you're doing is killing yourself—for sure!" And he just screamed right back at me, even louder, "You're a liar!!" and he stormed out. I ran after him. I just wanted to beat some sense into him. I could hardly keep myself from tearing him apart. He did what he said. He registered himself and his family. They were taken to Poniatev. Not long after he arrived, he and his family, together with 15,000 other inmates, were slaughtered.[2]

There were fifty-six Jewish families now staying out in the courtyard at Zamenhofa 21. We were a close-knit group. We assembled an illegal radio receiver and knew what was happening at the front— that the Germans were getting the hell kicked out of them! The loudspeakers in the ghetto only blared out news of German victories. We built bunkers into the attics and in the cellars. Our lookouts lay low on the roof keeping watch for the enemy. As soon as the Germans were sighted, we were signaled and headed straight into the bunkers. The Germans broke into empty flats. We had a few weapons. We gave the Jewish police a clear warning that they had to let us know beforehand—and with time to spare—when the Germans were planning something. They helped us many times with secret information. They themselves hardly believed any more that they were being left alive on purpose. The Germans had already executed large numbers of them.[3] Most of them were demoralized and apathetic. They did terrible things, believing that Jewish women and children were a lost cause anyway, and only the men could still be saved by working for the Germans, so they supported rescuing men—without bribes. Those of us at the courtyard of Zamenhofa 21 threatened to execute them if they didn't act like proud Jews, like whole human beings.

Erev Paysekh 1943. Jews in the ghetto baked what *matzos* they could. Final preparations were made for *Paysekh*. A pound of *matzos* cost seventy-five *zloty*. A bottle of wine cost fifty *zloty*. No other meat beside horse was available. This is what happened at four in the morning, on the first night of *Paysekh*:

We saw the ghetto being surrounded by Ukrainians, Germans, and Jewish police. Airplanes flew overhead. That same day, the first day of *Paysekh*, two Jewish policemen were shot in our courtyard from a concealed position because they hadn't provided us with this information earlier. The Germans called to us through their loudspeakers to come out and surrender, to evacuate the bunkers. Our watch on the roof retaliated by shooting. Bullets rained down on the Germans from every building in the area. Ukrainians then charged into the courtyards. They're cut down by Jewish bullets. The Ukrainians hurled flaming rags they'd soaked in benzine at our building. Our house at Zamenhofa 21 goes up in flames. On the first day of *Khol hamoyed*, we had to come out of the bunkers. We surrendered. Held our hands up over our heads. We stood like this in the street for hours. The SS ran around among us demanding money and gold. I didn't give them a thing. And like this, with our hands over our heads the whole time, we're taken to the *Umschlagplatz*. Groups of Jews were brought here through all the side streets. As soon as we reached the assembly point, we were packed into barracks and the Ukrainians threw themselves on us, beating us over the head with iron bars. We fell over each other. We were kicked and dragged toward the trains. Pushed into the wagons, squeezed in—they were surely trying to suffocate us all. The chlorine which was scattered all around the insides constricted our throats and burned our eyes. There was no water. People hurtled themselves through punctured walls and the smashed window openings. Many were shot as soon as they hit the ground. And then—Treblinka. The transport carried 5,000 Jews here. As soon as we were off the trains, a selection was started, with the men separated to one side and the women and children taken away to the other. Even those who hadn't believed till now that Treblinka was a house of death, realized exactly what it was now—to their ultimate horror. My daughter said quietly into my ear, "*Przepadło, idziemy do matki.*"[4] [The witness cries.—Y.F.] I gave her a large sum of money. Maybe. Maybe she could save herself. We kissed and parted.

We, the men, were now interrogated about our age. I answered, "Fifty." Added ten years. I begged God those evil vermin would send me to the gas chamber. He whipped me a couple of times with his lash because I'd deceived him. All this only took a few minutes. Three hundred and nineteen of us men remained alive. Next, an SS man addressed us in a saccharine voice, saying they'd let us live and we'd soon get food and drink—we'd leave this place yet, not to worry. Money and gold were now handed over. Jewish assistants distributed bread. I whispered to an assistant that I'd give him a fortune if he saved my daughter. And he gave me a look as if to say I was someone who had no idea what kind of a place this was: "They don't exist any more."

Soon we were loaded into freight cars. Now there was too much room. Only forty people in a wagon. There was a water trough and sacks of breadcrumbs inside. We arrived in Lublin. We were told to sit on the ground near the train. There were Jews here from countless places all over Poland. We were all mixed together now. Jews from every corner of the land. Thousands upon thousands. A group of 800 people, including myself, was sent to Budzyn, near Kraśnik. They put us to work at Heinkel's Airplane Factory. On the day we came there, they shot Dr. Pupko of Warsaw.[5] We were led into a bath-house. Since we had to change into new camp rags, I was afraid for the little money I had. A Jewish tailor who worked here saved the money for me. He took a cut. It was hell here. Not a day passed without Jews being murdered. I can't get rid of the horrifying image of the German, Feikes—the camp *Kommandant*—setting that Jewish manufacturer on fire, the one who made the *Tretorn* rubbers.

I was in Budzyn for over a year. Then I was sent to Radom and worked in HASAG. From Radom I was sent to Essenthal,[6] to Germany, near Stuttgart. This was in December 1944. There was a concentration camp here. There were 600 of us, only Jews. I stayed here four weeks. Next, I was sent to Alach.[7] From Alach, we're dragged for eight days along the way to Staltach where the train came to a halt. We couldn't understand why. The train's immobile in the middle of a field! Some day they heard shooting before. Our fear grew. Suddenly, the doors are thrown open—Americans.

Eyewitness Testimony 47. The Uprising in Treblinka

Y.M. Born in Włodzimierz-Wołynski, Poland in 1918; was transported to Treblinka from the Siedlce Ghetto on August 22, 1942. Recorded by S. Olitska in Eschwege, Germany (American Zone), for the Jewish Historical Commission in Poland in 1945.

... The small village of Treblinka lies near the little train depot on the Shedlets-Malkin[1] line, six kilometers from Malkin. It's buried deep in the dense Polish forests. In the winter of 1942, it still functioned as a penal camp for "saboteurs"—like peasants who hadn't turned in their wheat quotas on time, or workers who'd reported to labor sites late. In the summer of 1942, this camp was made into a giant death factory. Millions of Jews were exterminated here—among them almost the whole of Warsaw Jewry, the Jews of Chenstokhov,[2] Radom, Białystok, and Shedlets. Jews from Germany, Czechoslovakia, Belgium, Holland, Greece, and other countries were also brought here.[3] In July 1942, the gas chambers were installed and the people were poisoned by the different gases or asphyxiated when the chamber was turned into a vacuum and all the air was sucked out.[4]

Huge transports are shipped in steadily and the Hitlerite murderers can no longer "dispose of" them quickly enough. During this time, a special structure is built containing twelve gas chambers[5] where from 6,000 to 7,000 people could be forced in at one time. The number of Jews exterminated in Treblinka before the uprising and the destruction of the death camp is over 3 million.[6] Himmler, who was a steady "guest" at Treblinka, personally supervised his henchmen.[7] On his advice, the bodies were carried out and burned on pyres to extinguish every last trace of them. The ash was collected to fertilize the neighboring fields.

We were divided into two labor battalions. The first numbered 700 men and worked at unloading people from the trains, sorting out the clothes and valuables. The second group of 300 people were the ones who carried the dead out of the gas chambers and burned them on the pyres. We were interned in two separate barracks, cut off one from the other by barbed wire.

During this whole time, there were very many individual acts of revenge by Jews who refused to take any more: the time the young Jew from Warsaw, after seeing his wife and child pushed into the gas chamber, attacked the SS man Max Bilo with a knife and stabbed him to death. From that day on, these SS units were named after that Hitlerite murderer. The plaque calling for revenge, which hung over their barracks, and the general slaughter the SS then started in retaliation, didn't intimidate us in the least—just the opposite: it aroused us and incited us to battle, to avenge ourselves and our people. The death of the young man from Warsaw became our rallying cry. The will to revenge, which lived in us, grew stronger all the time and took concrete shape. Especially when the Warsaw surgeon, Dr. Chorążycki, joined us. He worked at the camp dispensary where the Germans played their last evil hoax on the miserable victims before sending them into the gas chambers.[8] He seemed like a very remote, formal person, making his rounds in a white coat and a Red Cross band just like he had once in his clinic, acting like he didn't care at all. But a warm Jewish heart beat under that uniform, and the burning desire for revenge.

After the hellish experiences of the day, the initiators of the uprising would meet at night on their wooden bunks to discuss our plans, with an eye, first of all, to getting hold of the right explosives and arms. Among them was Dr. Chorążycki, whom I just mentioned, the former Jewish officer of the Czech army, Captain Zela, Kurland of Warsaw, and Lubling of Silesia. After the first steps were taken, a few more were coopted, like Monyek, "*Kapo*" of the "*Hoyfyidn,*"[9] from Warsaw, Zaltsberg the furrier from Kielce, and a twenty-two-year-old, Marcus from Warsaw. There were two ways of getting weapons: from the outside or on the inside—stealing them from the German and Ukrainian SS men. Attempts were made to take down the exact plan of the camp arsenal which was located at the very center of the SS barracks—they were all sitting right on this powder keg.

Only Germans were allowed in the area and there could be no thought of getting inside directly. Many plans were drawn up to dig a tunnel underground. But this might expose us to terrible danger and it was almost impossible to accomplish under those severe circumstances. It was decided to make a passkey, though, at any cost. This was an almost impossible obstacle because no one could get near the arsenal, let alone check its iron doors. But there was no other choice than waiting for the right moment. But to our surprise, in a very short time, the right opportunity presented itself. A defect was discovered in the arsenal lock. The Germans had to call on Jewish locksmiths. But they took such precautions that they forced all the work to be done in the locksmith workshops under their continuous watch. But a locksmith succeeded in pressing a mold of the key in shoe wax when the German guard looked the other way for a moment. A few days later, the leaders of the planned revolt got the finished key. It was guarded like a holy object. We awaited the right moment anxiously. Some colleagues took it on themselves to buy guns from the outside. Dr. Chorążycki succeeds in making contact with a Ukrainian guard who agrees—for money, of course—to get hold of some light arms. Several of these transactions are made, but a tragedy puts an end to the purchases as well as to the life of Dr. Chorążycki. One time, when the doctor had an especially large sum of money on him for the guard, SS man Müller came to the clinic on an inspection. He was the head of the groundskeepers and had noticed the large bundle of notes sticking out of the doctor's coat as he was walking to the dispensary. He runs quickly to Franz the "Doll"[10] and tells him everything. The "Doll" rushes over to Dr. Chorążycki with his vicious guard dog, "Hari," and screams at him,

"You have money!" He suspected him immediately of planning an escape from the camp. Chorążycki knew what the consequences would be, grabbed a surgical knife, and sprang at the "Doll." But the "Doll" fell under him and heaved Chorążycki off. Chorążycki then jumped straight through the window. He knew what kind of tortures were awaiting him and how this could endanger the conspiracy. He grabbed out the large potion of poison most of our colleagues carried with them. The SS men call on doctors to keep him alive so he can be subjected to torture, but it did them no good.

This was the end of the initiator of the uprising. His death didn't interrupt our work but inspired us even more, setting an example of sacrifice for our ideal. After Chorążycki's death, the leadership was rightly assumed by Captain Zela, the Jewish former officer in the Czech army. The presence of a military expert helped us carry out our very complex undertaking in those dreaded moments of resignation, when many had already lost hope the uprising would ever really start. Then, unexpectedly, Captain Zela was transferred into the second camp, the "death camp."[11] Now plans had to be sent across to him and he worked on decisions, no matter the risk. Effective command was taken over by Engineer Galewski of Łódź.[12] He also served as the "inmate commandant,"[13] and had revealed to us his commitment to our cause. He had many good qualities like humaneness and self-control, and we considered ourselves fortunate to work with him. The uprising had been planned for April of 1943—while Dr. Chorążycki was still alive.

During this month, the transports with the last Jews of the Warsaw Ghetto Uprising arrived. They were tortured mercilessly. Most of the train cars are full of dead ghetto fighters[14] who were trapped, beaten, then jammed into the wagons. The few survivors told us of the Warsaw Ghetto Uprising. These new people weren't like the inert, broken inmates who'd arrived till now. They didn't carry tears in their eyes, but pocketfuls of explosives. We got many weapons from them.[15]

The leadership was waiting for the best moment to start the revolt. There were a group of workers in camp who were made to do domestic assignments and polish the boots for the SS. They were called the "Hoyfyidn." They were able to maneuver more freely through the camp. They had a lot of chances to get near the arsenal. The leaders started to recruit them and put them under the command of Monyek the "Kapo," a young Jew from Warsaw. He could do anything. Their mission was to "liberate" 100 grenades on the day of the uprising. When the time came, they carried it out to the letter. Marcus the boot polisher and seventeen-year-old Jacek managed to lift several grenades from the arsenal and go undetected. The fourteen-year-old Zaltsberg, the son of the Kielce furrier I mentioned before, was especially good at this. He took an armload of military tunics—supposedly to have them pressed—and filled the pockets with grenades. Unfortunately, the grenades had no pins and the uprising was postponed at the last minute.

This was when the last survivors of Węgrów got here. Dr. Leichert[16] joined us. He was picked out of the Węgrów transport as the medic to replace Dr. Chorążycki. He was drawn completely into our ongoing work and quickly became an active member of the battle-staff. A Czech national also started working with us. He was Rudolf Masaryk, a close relation to the late Czech president.[17] He didn't want to be separated from his Jewish wife and had joined her and the common fate of all Jews, coming to Treblinka. He was selected for the labor brigades. He himself stood by while his pregnant wife was driven into the gas chamber. Masaryk became one of our most active conspirators. I should also mention the driver-mechanic, Rudek-Obranicki of Plotzk, who worked in the SS garages. Those structures became the focus for our operation. The arms were stock-piled there. Tense months passed in anticipation—we stared death in the face ten times a day, and had to witness further German atrocities. Hundreds of thousands of men, women, children, and old people were stripped naked and paraded every day in endless columns into the *"Judenstaat,"* as the Germans sardonically called the building with the twelve gas chambers, which was topped with a tall *mugen duvid.* Franz the "Doll" screamed his diatribes at us every day: "As long as one Jew remains alive on the face of the earth, the gas chamber will never rest!"

Our passion for revenge knows no bounds now. Those driven into the gas chambers demand that we avenge them.

Finally, our dream is realized. Engineer Galewski, the inmate "commandant," gives the signal for the uprising to begin. The date set was August 2, 1943, 5:15 P.M.

The plan at the outset was eluding the main "dogcatchers," then executing them; disarming the guards; cutting telephone lines; burning down and destroying all the apparatus of the "death factory"; and bringing the killing to a halt forever. We were also to liberate the "Polish" camp[18] two kilometers away where many Jews were imprisoned, and join with them to form a huge partisan force.

Monday morning, everyone in camp is tense beyond endurance. The leaders assign special units to see to it that the daily work is carried out routinely, to avoid any suspicion. The combat group is divided up into platoons. When the signal is given, every unit must man its position. We report to the afternoon *Appel* as if nothing is going on. Then, Commandant Galewski announces that work will let off an hour earlier because *Schaarführer* Kitner is departing for Malkin to bathe in the Bug. He winks: another kind of "bath" is being gotten ready for him! At around two in the afternoon, the guns are handed out.

Our people have spent the day sifting through the SS compound and stealing weapons under their noses. They bring out pistols and rifles—even a huge machine gun—and carry it all into the garages. The hardest thing will be to break into the arsenal. We were in luck— the arsenal was being cleaned out that day, garbage was being carried out. This disguised our maneuver to a great extent, but we kept getting interrupted by the supplies adjutant, SS man Müller, until he left off duty and went to sleep right inside the stockpile.

Sudowicz[19] of the groundskeepers breaks in on Müller to inform him that an urgent earth-moving operation must be undertaken immediately "to insure the geological distribution of the tension" or some such thing. At the same time, Marcus and Zaltsberg are dragging out an endless procession of carpets into the arsenal passageway and start dusting them out by beating and flapping them with all the strength they have. All the dust drove the SS guards away from the entrance. In the bat of an eyelash, seventeen-year-old Jacek from Gdansk slips in, darts to the window, cuts out the pane with a diamond, and passes me the rifles and grenades through the opening. They're carted off immediately to the garages and the dispensary. Działosinski of Kalisz worked with me on this. This time, the grenades were all capped with pins.

We're all so exhilarated, almost approaching ecstasy. We get the leadership to move the start of the operation up an hour—to 4:15. At 3:30, men are dispatched to the garages and dispensary to get the guns. Anyone getting a gun must give the password "Death," to which he's answered: "Life!" "Death-life! Death-life!": the cadence of a hot, impassioned battle cry as our hands clutch the rifles, pistols, and grenades we've hungered for so long.

Almost immediately afterwards—the murderers are attacked! The telephone lines are cut. The guard towers set ablaze,[20] the barracks, too—all with benzine. The benzine pumps in front of the garage are lit by Rudek and explode. Captain Zela hacks up two guards with an axe and breaks into our camp where he assumes overall command again. The garages are defended by a German armored assault vehicle which Rudek has commandeerd and is using as a tank barricade. His firing rips apart *Sturmbannführer* Seidler[21] and other Hitlerite mad dogs. We, groundskeepers, storm the arsenal. The arms are passed around among the group. There are now around 200 of us who are fully armed, the others attack with axes, picks, and spades.

Commander Zela issued quick, new instructions. We're overcome with the rage of vengeance. No one thinks of his own life. We free still more guns. The heavy machine gun we've gotten is unstoppable. Rudolf Masaryk mans it and turns it on the "dove tower."[22] He's spitting fire at the Ukrainian barracks and at the Germans. His cries are heard: "This is for my wife! And for my child, who never saw the world!! And this, scum, for humiliated and grieving humanity!!!"

The mock train depot with its macabre signs, "Białystok-Wołkowysk," "Ticket Office," "Rest Lounge," and so on, is burned to the ground. The barracks named for the murderer Max Bilo go up in flames. The perimeter fences are cut through and the posts uprooted with cries of "Hurrah!"—the gas chambers are burned down, and then the "bath"!

German reinforcements are called in from all directions as the shooting rocks the entire region and the flames rise higher and higher. SS, MP's, and field gendarmes pour in from Malkin, *Luftwaffe* personnel are rushed in from the nearby airstrip at Kosów, and even elite SS commando forces from Warsaw are sent to take up positions in the camp. A major battle develops. Captain Zela leads the assault and rallies all our forces forward, until he's cut down by a Hitlerite bullet in the thick of the fighting.

Night is falling. Our ranks are thinning out. Ammunition's in short supply. The Germans are reinforced with wave after wave of men and matériel. But our revolt has succeeded 100 percent. The entire camp is in flames and completely destroyed. The hangmen are no more. They all got their punishment. We got rid of about 200 Germans and Ukrainian Fascists.[23] The order is now given to break out of the siege any way possible and regroup in the surrounding forests. The majority of our combatants are cut down in this attempt. Only individuals[24] break through, and most are then later murdered by the Polish assassins.

(The veracity of this testimony is confirmed by A. Gurevitch, secretary of the Culture Committee, Eschwege.[25] [Stamp of above.]

Eyewitness Testimony 48. Uprising in the Sobibór Death Camp

B.F. Born in Warsaw in 1928; lived in Łódź from 1935. Recorded by Blumeh Vasser in Warsaw in 1945. The witness talks about the war's outbreak in Łódź, the death of his father while fleeing to Warsaw, the ordeals of the orphaned children and his widowed mother in the Warsaw Ghetto, his escape together with an older brother to Turobin, Lublin District, where he was caught in the *aktsye* in Turobin of May 10, 1942. The death march took them to Krasnystaw, from where they were transported to Sobibór. He testifies further.

After traveling on the train for a few hours, we suddenly stopped—we'd arrived in Sobibór. A platform on both sides of the tracks in the middle of a forest, with a tower ahead of us covered by barbed wire and vines through which the tracks led deeper into the woods.

Eighteen carloads are brought into the camp, and when the eighteen wagons are emptied, they're rolled back out and another eighteen are sent in. In the beginning, there are no signs on the tower. Only much later did they put up: "SS *Sonderkommando—Juden Übersiedlungslager.*"[1]

After our train moved in, the doors were thrown open and armed Germans and Ukrainians, cracking whips, drove us out of the wagons. We had bloody welts all over our bodies. The day we came to Sobibór was May fifth in the year '42. We were led through a second tower to an assembly point which was ringed by barbed-wire fences, with posts on the wire perimeters capped by some sort of metal hoods. They split us up here—men to one side and women and children to the other. Soon, SS squads came in and led the women with the children away. Where they were being taken to we didn't know, but off in the distance we heard screams of people being beaten and stripped and then we heard the rumblings of motors being started. It was the women and children being killed. We could sense in the air that, locked up like this between the wires, we'd be slaughtered right here. Night fell and we fell into a panic. We'd been told that in Bełżec, people were burned alive in pits. We wouldn't believe this while we were in the ghetto, but here, when we saw a fire in the distance, we were sure they were burning people. We were overcome with fear and started saying our *viduyim.*

It was a nightmare. The Ukrainians beat us and wouldn't let us out to relieve ourselves. People evacuated on the spot. Later, they told us they wouldn't do anything to us, that the women had only been taken off to work. In the morning, SS men came and selected craftsmen and artisans to work as shoemakers, carpenters, locksmiths. I felt they'd let these people live. I also wanted to join these *baleymlukhe,* but I'd never been a worker and was afraid that if they ordered me to saw off a small piece of wood even, I'd bungle it and then would be worse off. So I sat and wondered—what can I do? Then the SS man pointed out all the healthy young men and ordered them to step forward, so I jumped up and squeezed in among these towering youths and sturdy craftsmen. I pleaded with my uncle to come with me, but he wouldn't move and I went alone. He was afraid, and something in my heart told me he wouldn't survive anyway. It took a long time to carry out this *selektsye.* We were led through still another tower, again to an assembly area, but there were no barracks here yet, only lean-tos and frames. The others were immediately sent away and we never saw them again.

There were thirty men in our group. They divided us up right away. Some were used to sort our belongings. The bundles were lying in ditches surrounded by wires and vines, with the same metal-hooded perimeter posts. The whole camp looked like this. I was taken into the second group and set to work digging a latrine. I never held a shovel in my life and a German who guarded us at work noticed my "skill" and let fly such a blow over my head that he nearly split my skull. That was when I learned how to work.

We worked from daybreak till nine, then they gave us breakfast. Bread and fingerbowls of fat was all we got and afterwards, they put us to work till late evening. As night fell, we were all lined up and an SS man informed us nothing would happen to us if we behaved well. If we didn't—they'd "make us a gift" of a bullet to the head. For the time being, they say, we work here, and in a week they'll take us to where the women are working. They've already reached their destination and we'll be able to correspond with them soon. Their belongings which are still lying in the ditch were left behind because they were given new work clothes at the labor site, so we could go ahead and help ourselves to their coats and cover ourselves up and even sleep in the work shacks nearby. Then, simply because he had the urge, he picked two men out—one who had stomach pains and the other who just wasn't to his liking—and led them off into the woods where he shot them. Most of the time, the men returned from work beaten, bloodied, and injured all over the body. We knew what was in store for us now and everyone just limped off to go to sleep. The SS man who ranted at us was *Schaarführer* Steubel.

There were three camps. The first contained all the artisans. The second, all the barbers, clothes-sorters, and the train *Kommando* who helped at pulling the people off the trains. In the third camp were those who worked the gas chambers and the burial brigades, the ones who dug up layer after layer of earth, dumped the bodies in, and spread lye over them. They could only be burned after a time. The people were marched naked from the second camp through connecting passageways of barbed wire into the "bath." From there, the way led further into the woods and to the pits.

This is what the system of going into the "bath" was like: As soon as a train with a transport of people arrived, everyone was either pulled off violently or made to jump. They were all forced to march into that sealed area. Later, the people were led off in groups of thousands, sometimes groups of hundreds.[2] An SS man, *Oberschaar-führer* Michen,[3] addressed them, saying since there was a war on, everyone had to work and they were about to be transported somewhere else for labor. They'd be well taken care of. Children and the old wouldn't have to work, but wouldn't lack food either. So great attention must be paid to cleanliness and we had to take a bath first. Those from the West would always applaud at this point. Later, when the Polish Jews arrived, they knew all this ended in death and screamed and made an uproar. So he said to them: "*Ruhe*,[4] I know you long for death already, but you won't be obliged so easily. First, you must work." And he kept punishing them and demoralizing them like this.

Inside the first barrack, they had their coats, jackets, and pants taken off and in the second barrack, had to strip down completely nude. They were told in that first speech that they wouldn't need any towel or soap—they'd find all that in the bath. All this led to them being brought naked into the third barrack near the bath. There was a special cell there where they were kept on arranged benches, guarded by Germans. Not a sound was permitted. Twenty barbers cut off the women's hair. When the women came in naked and saw the men there, they pulled back, but the Germans dragged them and beat them forward. They had to sit naked. I was one of the barbers. To shave someone's head lasted half a minute. We held the long hair out from the head and snipped it off all along the scalp so that "stairs" were left—tufts of hair sticking out from the scalp. The foreign Jews didn't suspect anything, they were just sorry about losing their hair. The Germans said it didn't matter—in half a year, the hair'd grow back. But on the other side, the Polish Jews screamed and wouldn't let us cut their hair, and they were beaten and tortured. From there, they went straight through a corridor into a chamber. . . .

I was in the camp eighteen months already. The next day, a transport of Czech Jews was brought to the camp. They came at three in the morning and we were chased out of the bunks in the dead of night. We hauled the bundles off the train, running between two rows of Ukrainians who did nothing but beat us savagely. We worked like this without stop until ten the next night because there was so much cargo. Well-off Jews with all their valuables. They were brought here in first-class compartments.

That evening, SS man Paul[5] harangued us as usual. He says he has to have five men for the *Lazarett*. What's a *Lazarett*? Well, a *Lazarett* is a place you don't have to work, you can sleep without interruption and don't have to bear any more burdens. But the real *Lazarett*, which means field hospital, was a small structure with a cross and icon of Jesus inside—probably from before the war—and there was a pit there where he'd lower people down and shoot them. This was his own *Lazarett*. The people he got to bury the dead there didn't come back either—they were dragged off to the third camp and burned there. Every day, that monster had to have from three to five Jews in his *Lazarett* and he'd pick them out himself or just ask, "*Ja*, well, who's sick today? Who doesn't want to work anymore?" Or he just grabbed them at random. If he hated someone, he simply pointed his finger at them and said, "*Komm, komm,* you look like you don't want to work anymore," and then led them away. There were times when some Jews had heard before what the

Lazarett meant, and they came forward to die voluntarily, because this life had driven them mad with despair. Victims succumbed like this every day. At the beginning of the work we did, we had 250 men. A month later, around eighty of us were left. Death came in many ways: sometimes by shooting, sometimes being bludgeoned to death with clubs. Some committed suicide. There were times we got up in the barrack in the morning, and before our eyes, saw several Jews hanging from the rafters.

The most cruel death was at the jaws of Paul's dog, "Bari." Paul would yell at him: "Bari! Be my deputy!" and the dog tore people into pieces and devoured them. As soon as he got his jaws on you, there was no way out. He snapped you around, whirling you and tearing at you so long, till there was nothing left for his jaw to clamp down on. The dog bit me twice and I have a scar on my leg. Two holes, where there was once matter. I also have a scar on my right cheek where I got slashed with the whip. The cheek was split open completely, the right ear torn up, and I was thrown down against the wires and got a brain concussion.

Wagner[6]—he was the worst murderer—broke a shovel over my head. My face was completely disfigured. The eyes were pulp. No matter on which side I tried to lie down, I couldn't. I stayed up whole nights and howled and wept in pain. They tortured us unbelievably. I looked like death itself. Everyone said I was a candidate for the *Lazarett* because, in the beginning, I was never completely conscious. I was young, so they kept beating me. We had to keep working like this for two weeks without stop, because what seemed like an endless number of transports were arriving then from Czechoslovakia, Austria, and Germany and afterwards, from Poland. Later, we got rid of the dog, "Bari." We were so relieved, because the one sent to organize Treblinka,[7] also took Wagner the murderer[8] along.

After we labored several months, new transports arrived from Holland, France, and isolated ones from different camps and we were sent to the trains again. There was a "guest" who also arrived by train—not by plane like he usually did—with an entourage of thirty men. The whole camp was surrounded by field gendarmes. He came unexpectedly—if we'd known, some of us would have fallen, but we'd have taken some of them down with us. He was of medium height and wore spectacles. If he were caught today, he'd surely deny ever having been in Sobibór. I was still working near there when they arrived, but we were immediately driven off.

I want to tell you something that is unknown about Himmler till now. It's this: Just before his arrival, 300 women were detained for two days and stuffed like cattle. When the telephone rang announcing Himmler was about to come, they were quickly herded into a "bath" to help him visualize the extermination process. That hangman Himmler climbed to the roof, peering down through a small ceiling opening upon his "sacred work": the annihilation of Jewish women, Jewish mothers, and defenseless Jewish children.

At the same time, a transport of Jews arrived from Biała Podlaska and we were ordered to load thirty traincars with matériel for Germany. Since there was much too much work, and there were only eighty of us, another 100 men were added on from the just-arrived transport. We eighty were addressed as the "tried and true" Jews and because of this, would be given slightly less work today. To distinguish and separate us from the other Jews, we were given fedoras and assigned a special lane on the left to run along while carrying the bundles. The others, though, had to run bareheaded down the right line, under enormous packs, between two rows of Ukrainians and Germans. But to describe how those poor Jews were tortured is impossible—I just can't do it. . . . Some had nets wrapped around their heads and sand was funneled down their mouths. Others were shackled in chains and yanked forward like dogs on all fours. Several were hung outright on the train platform and two Jews slashed their own wrists with razor blades. All were then beaten, prodded, tortured, and right after work they were all shot because there was no point "running the bath" for such a small number of Jews. We had to wear the fedoras for a couple of months. It was forbidden to remove them. They humiliated us with the vilest curses: "sloppails," "asses," "blöde Hunde," "verfluchtes Volk.". . .[9]

In the year '43, our group kept growing till it reached 600 people— 120 women and 480 men.

Paul the murderer fell bewitched of a Czech Jewish girl. She cleaned up in his barrack and his attitude to us now became less sadistic. The other Germans realized this. One time, they waited till he left for the day, then came and shot the girl. When he got back, they teased him: "Well, Paul, where's your Jewish girl now?" He was so enraged, he persecuted us even more than before. He'd stand by the barrack door through which we hauled the packs, with a hatchet in his hand, and whenever the urge took him, he just swung away till he hacked someone down in a pool of blood. When the new latrines were dug and he came upon some impurity, he threatened all of us with execution. Once, he walked into the latrine area and saw two Jews stooping over the ditch, but there was a pile nearby so he dragged the two Jews over and made them eat it. They fell into a swoon, begging to be shot instead. But he wouldn't call back his order. They had to keep eating and then heaved up for the rest of the day.

After the death of his favorite dienst,[10] he showed us what he was really made of. The same day, he had found a mouse. There was a storehouse for clothing and there was no shortage of mice. When he saw the mouse, he ordered a number to be caught, then he made some men tie up their pant bottoms and forced the mice into their shirts. The screaming was unbearable. He forbade them to make a sound, or even move, making everyone stand *auf Achtung*.[11] They begged to be killed quickly. It was no use, he got his perverse pleasure from this and the other Germans and Ukrainians held their sides to keep from splitting with laughter. I only prayed he wouldn't call me over to the mice.

Once, he ordered a Jew over fifty to crawl like a dog and imitate all a dog's actions, making him tug at everyone's pants with his teeth, run after them and bite them. Wherever we walked, he had to run after us on all fours and tear at our pants, pounce on us and bark. When we were marched from the labor sites and forced to sing, he had to run alongside and bark, and he was whipped, to keep this up all day long.

They assigned the worst SS elements to the camp we were in—the hardened criminals. One time, I was getting up in the morning, and I feel my head spinning. I take my temperature and find I've got 38 degrees Celsius. But I had to go out for labor, because if I didn't, I'd be marched off to the *Lazarett* in an instant. I gathered all my strength and went off to the labor site. The next day, I can't even hold a saw. This was the time a Ukrainian stood guard over us, not a German, and since he had no order to kill us directly he had to ask permission. I used this moment to drop to the ground and take a breath. The Ukrainian saw me, though, and jumped over to me yelling: "Ha! You're sick! You get shot immediately!" and he cocked the trigger of his gun. Luckily, the midday break was sounded, and we were marched back to the barracks.

I had nothing to eat all this time—it was a "slack" period, no transports with extra rations. All I got were moldy noodles and everything I put in my mouth, I threw up. I had to report to the *Appel,* it was unthinkable not to. I felt I would go under at any moment because I had 40 degrees temperature and couldn't keep on my feet anymore from the hunger and fever. I had spotted typhus. I pleaded: "*Yidn,* brothers, save me! If you don't—they shoot me today!" We had a Jewish *Kommandant*[12] named Moyshe, but we weren't permitted to call him Moyshe—we got fifty lashes if we did. We addressed him as "*General Gouverneur.*" He wasn't a bad sort and got another youth to replace me at cleaning the barracks so I was left unguarded by the Germans and could afford to sit down for a while. Whenever a German entered, I made motions like I was working but couldn't really make out a word being said to me. Whenever I had to get up for the *Appel,* I blacked out. I was just lucky I had some color in my face from the fever. Once, I felt I was dying of dehydration so I got hold of some lighter fluid, lit it, and cooked up a bit of tea over the fire. Suddenly, the German, Wagner, breaks in and yells: "What?! You don't work, and drink tea yet?!" He tells me to go outside and let down my pants, then he whips me hard. And since I wasn't dead yet, he tells me to carry in a bench, lie down over it, and he lashes out another fifty strokes. By now, I was absolutely insensate. Blood was oozing, but I felt a kind of relief—maybe because he started my body juices flowing with the beating.

At nightfall, the group comes back from the site, and seeing me and hearing I'd been whipped, they are amazed. No one can understand how I was able to survive. I myself couldn't imagine what strength it was kept me going. I wasn't completely conscious and didn't realize what was going on around me. No one helped me. Occasionally, someone gave me a lump of sugar—this was all the food I had for fourteen days. At night, I was delirious. I crawled up and down the bunks raving incoherently and had no idea what was happening. In the morning, I still had to report to the *Appel*.

One time, I felt I was at the end of my strength and didn't consider the risk or danger, but just lay down and two other youths promised to keep watch and warn me if a German came near. This way, I'd be able to get up on my feet at once. That same day, two other youths were taking a nap—but they were two good carpenters and the Germans ignored it if they tried to rest. They had typhoid fever and tried to control themselves and remain active, but they couldn't push themselves any more and were told to lie down in the bunks above mine. My two friends were distracted and missed the two Germans, Hans Wagner[13] and Steubel, who stormed in past them and threw the two carpenters out of their bunks, chasing them outside. They hadn't seen me. I didn't make a sound and thought to myself: "It'd be easier to die than to get up." They asked if there were any others ill and my friends answered no. They just went about their cold-blooded business and led away the two young carpenters and shot them.

I couldn't understand it. So many of the sick and infirm had been killed off during this time, and they had missed me. At night, as we're lining up, I stumble out late and the German calls me over and demands to know why?! But I can't make out what he wants, and I laugh in delirium or from temporary insanity. Unbelievably, the German goes berserk too and guffaws like a madman and pushes me back into the rows. No one could comprehend this miracle. I couldn't walk anymore. I was dragged along by the others. At night, I'd have visions: "*Oy*, what a sight when they shoot me, I can see it, just let it be one moment after that now, just one moment after that." My friend who sleeps alongside me tries to arouse me: "You're fine, fine! Hold on just one more day and it'll pass!" It's the sixth day by now, and I really have kept myself going, really tried, really wanted to

live and survive these fourteen days that seemed like a year. I looked
like a skeleton. At work, every rib stuck out. Only later, when I got
a little better, did people realize that there must be something wrong
with me, that I must be sick.

And we carried on the regular work of sorting the transports and
enlarging the small factory so the work of swallowing up even larger
transports would go faster. The old and sputtering machines were
improved, new efficient ones installed. One day, while I was sorting
away the valuables, a German came up, an SS man named Weit—
he composed "ditties" about the Jews—and wants to practice his aim
on us. Weit called over Moyshe the *"General Gouverneur,"* who
wore a red hat with a ribbon band and a *mugen duvid,* epaulets with
stars on them, and he had a whip. He was forced to use it—if he
didn't put it to constant use he'd be strapped down and whipped,
to be shown the proper way of punishing the Jews. All *"Komman-
danten"* had whips. Then that deranged tyrant put a cup on Moyshe's
head and shot it off from a distance. He called me over next and
placed the cup on my head to shoot it off. I could see this would be
my end—I could hardly make out what was happening. He aimed
from far away and shot off the cup. Then he ordered another soldier
to shoot, too. He wouldn't do it—why waste a bullet? Better put it
straight through my head. At that instant, a transport pulled in from
Majdanek. Complete skeletons, not even human in appearance,
planted in clogs and wrapped in striped rags. But just then the
machine broke down and they had to face their own death all night
and into the following day. They had to stay out under the stars
locked inside the fenced-in perimeter. In the morning, the "bath" was
prepared and they all got out of their clothes so routinely as if what
could be more natural? After everyone was led away—about 4,000
people—22 dead bodies lay in place, the ones who couldn't survive
this one last night. There were some lying there who were still wheezing. In a world that was normal, they might still have been saved,
but here they were only thrown onto the corpses.

Steubel now approached our group and selected out about twenty
men, including me. He ranted at us and ordered us to strip. We
thought this was the end, but he tried to convince us not to be afraid;
on the contrary, he wished to spare us disease, contamination and
infection brought by these "POW's." Their clothes had to be disposed
of, he made us to understand, and the dead had to be carted away,
so it would be more sanitary if we did it in the nude. And we did just
like he said. We slaved like this till four in the morning. The work
we did was clearing away the clothes and dragging the corpses off to
the railroad tracks. They were then loaded into cars and taken away
to be incinerated. We didn't witness this last phase of the "work."
We dragged them by a leg tucked under our arm and running at a

fast pace. I turn around—no one's looking—I rest a bit. Suddenly, I'm startled—the "corpse" sits up and asks: "Is it far?" Seeing that he's still alive, I stand him up and lead him by the arm. He collapsed twice. A German caught us and began beating me. There was nothing I could do but put down this live person and drag him along by one foot. . . .

Sometimes, naked women hid out under the garbage, under rags. One time, I was about to sort through the rags when I take a look and see a woman lying among them. What do I do? I can't pull the rags away because a German will spot her immediately, so I went off to another pile of rags, but it didn't work—she was found out. She was led off and clubbed to death.

Another time, after one of the disinfections,[14] we found a child, one and a half years old, among the rags. But a Ukrainian immediately ordered me to take the child to the garbage pit, where he said: "*Ach*, a waste of a bullet!" and took a garbage shovel and split open the baby into pieces. The child hardly let out a whimper.

Often, mothers bore children during the night. Whenever found, the babies were thrown straight into the garbage pits or were torn apart down the middle by their legs, or just flung up and shot in the air or wherever they landed. They made no fuss over children. Finally, the women rebelled. While stripping, they would scream out and attack the Germans, clawing at them and yelling, "You've lost the war anyway! Your death will be a lot crueller than ours! We're defenseless, we have to go to our death—but your women and children will be burned alive!!!" And they screeched and wailed.

The Germans couldn't stand it and shot anyone they could. There were so many of these victims. It quieted down for a while, but soon, the screams started up again. They took out all their money and currency and tore the notes into shreds with such defiance and hate in their faces, that all of them were pushed away at once to be shot. They left behind them a sea of scraps of 100-*zloty* and 50-*zloty* notes. Feet sank into the money like into feathers, and this enraged the Germans who cursed: "*Verfluchte Juden!*"

While we cut their hair, we stole some conversation with the women—as long as no German was watching, of course. They asked, "Tell us, can you? Will this death be painless? Does it last long?"

They asked us how we were still able to work for "them" while everyone else was dead. We answered, "You have it better. You're going to die soon—but we have to keep working, getting beaten all the time, till we're finally exterminated, too."

Many told us where they hid their gold and jewels so that we could save ourselves, and they begged us to take revenge against the murderers. They couldn't part with their children—if to die, then together, together till the last moment. While we cut their hair, they clutched their children to their bodies to be together like this till the end. And many women wouldn't let their hair be cut! They were shot at and beaten but it was no use. They sat down and refused to move, not letting the barbers cut their hair, and refusing to walk on into the "bath." They were either shot on the spot, or such a hail of blows rained down on them that they were driven live into the furnaces. . . .

Many times, we planned dropping poison into the soup kettles so we'd die—but what would it have accomplished? We wanted to achieve a death that would take some of "them" along with us. But some of us must survive so the world would learn of us. There were countless times we planned rebelling and sabotaging the work. Enough! But then what? They'd shoot us and get others. It was senseless. We had to do something which would really change things and hit at them: arson, assassinations. As long as one person survived to tell the world! We thought up and planned many things, but there are different kinds of people, and our own brothers betrayed us and blocked all our attempts. At night, we stayed up to scheme, scheme, keeping watch against our own flesh and blood. Everyone had another plan. There was talk, talk, when all of a sudden a German would enter and want to know what we'd just been discussing. We decided beforehand, that anyone caught during these sessions would answer we were discussing the midday meal, the cooking preparations for tomorrow, food.

During this time, a transport of well-to-do, assimilated Jews was sent in from Holland. Now, the "production line" ran very smoothly, the machine worked perfectly. Seventy people were selected from among the group for labor. The healthiest-looking and best-dressed Jews. Of course, after just one day, their appearance changed—and they lost their former look for good, adjusting to their new one as if they'd always worn it. All their poise and bearing was lost immediately, their dignity not long after. There was this sea captain among them—I don't remember his name—in his forties. He turned out to be a fine person, and we didn't hesitate letting him in on our plans. We felt—and he agreed—that every day spent in the camp was wasted, we just couldn't stay any longer, we had to face either death or life—if falling, then destroying the camp with us. We started working together right from the start. He helped us, talking to the Ukrainians—he and a Polish Jew from Tishevits,[15] Yosif Pelts. He and Yosif worked mostly at carpentry assignments, although he'd never been a carpenter, and he even supervised Yosif, who was a master builder.

We made some contact with the Ukrainians. There were a few Ukrainians who also realized that they would be put to death in the end, and they also wanted to escape. But we still had to bribe them with large sums of money and we let some of them in on our plans. We sent them notes and they replied through the Jewish cooks who worked for them in the kitchen, and this was how we drew up the plan. One of the original members of this activist cell, Laybl Felhendler of Zhulkivke,[16] is still alive.

One time, the Germans found out about our plans through a Ukrainian informer, and they were even told the Dutch Jew, the sea captain, was a co-conspirator. He was summoned and they told him, if he wished to remain alive, he would divulge the numbers of the organizers and those trying to escape.

He refused and said only, "I alone wish to escape. I alone want to destroy the barracks."

Beatings and tortures were no use. His only reply was: "Just me wants all of this. Just me and me . . ."

They shouted at him that if he didn't tell which of the Jews were involved, then all the Jews—a group of seventy people—would be taken out and killed. But he didn't as much as hint to them that only Polish Jews were involved in this. His only answer was: "I won't talk. It won't do you any good. Whatever happens, it's my fault alone!"

Then, by order of *Oberschaarführer* Frenzel,[17] this is what was done: The seventy Jews were lined up along with the ship captain, led into the third camp, and were all exterminated. According to accounts we got, they were first tortured unimaginably. We couldn't find out exactly because it's impossible to talk with the people in the third camp, all they got out was one word—all of them went to the "beam." What this means for sure we don't know to this day—maybe it means hanging, because this is what was done to us many times. We were all shaken and dispirited. We saw what became of our plans and the tragic results they caused. There was also an incident in the third camp where two men and a woman joined a Ukrainian, and the four of them broke out of camp. When the Germans found out the next day, they attacked the inmates wildly and slaughtered over 150 people. We were informed of this by the Jewish *"Kommandant"* who used to come to us to get food. He was worse than a German. He was later killed, too.

Another time again, a tunnel leading out beyond the wires was discovered. It was an unbelievable accomplishment. It would have taken just one more week to finish this huge tunnel. They used to carry the earth out in their pants which were knotted at the bottoms, and dump it out along the way to the labor site. Right at the last minute, the Jewish *"Kommandant," yimakh shemoy,* found out about it and gave them all away. As soon as the Germans were informed, they massacred another 200 people in the third camp, so that everything we tried was betrayed, every attempt failed. The Ukrainians themselves sometimes said they were sorry we failed: "Ach, wouldn't it be great for us if one fine day, we get up in the morning and find the whole camp empty."

From that time on, there were constant inspections and searches.

They checked all the barracks and fences to make sure there were no holes or tunnels. We had to face the hardest kind of obstacles. But again we started wondering, "How do we get out? What do we do to save ourselves and tell the world?"

Our most active member was Yosif Pelts of Tishevits—he was in his forties. A few days earlier, he told me he'd been a community activist in his *shtetl,* and he was planning some kind of action here, too. The obstacles in his camp were especially difficult. There were only skilled workers in this first camp. Life was sometimes tolerable for them because the Germans needed their work—they were good tailors or could make good shoes for the wives and children of the SS. Not all of them wanted to destroy the camp and sacrifice their lives, and they protested when Yosif Pelts started telling them his plans. They argued that they had another three or four weeks to live and he even wants to deprive them of this, and things like that. Yosif Pelts had no dependents, and he disappeared one morning with another friend from Hrubieszów or Krylow.[18]

Some days earlier, he had put on a pair of good boots, taken a scissor and a plier with him to work, and—"*vayivrakh!*"—he had cut through the wires. It happened on a rainy night and the guards fell asleep, so he succeeded in escaping. He did it when there were still no mines planted there, because later, the whole perimeter of the camp was mined. The next day, Moyshe "*Kommandant*" ran to tell the Germans that two were missing from the first barrack. We were fortunate, because the *Oberschaarführer* wasn't there, only the *Unterschaarführer,* who was less sadistic and selected ten men, instead of hundreds, to be shot. We could bear the loss of ten men when we thought of the millions who'd been killed, and our feeling for revenge was strong enough so we didn't hold it against Pelts that he'd escaped and brought about the shooting of ten men. A few of the ten Jews were ashen-faced, but the others carried themselves with pride and even smiled to us as they pleaded and demanded only that we take revenge. They were joined by a Dutch woman who had fallen in love with a Polish Jew, and her son also walked with her. Their lives were cheap to the killers. All of them were led away and shot. More victims of our plans and actions.

Yosif Pelts was a good man. Later, when they were nearing his *shtetl,* Tishevits, the Poles blocked their path and murdered them. The Germans tried to rob us of our will to escape, so they said those two had definitely been caught by the guards and killed.

A young man from Warsaw, Moyshe Toyber, was ready to sacrifice himself to save the group. It was decided to set all the storehouses on fire, and while everything burned and the Germans were working at putting out the flames, everyone would take advantage of the uproar and commotion and escape. Everything was made ready—we got hold of two bottles of benzine and Moyshe Toyber was lying at this moment among the things in the storehouse, waiting for midnight. In the evening, we told all the people in the first barrack to get ready to escape, that we'd give them our plan. As soon as they heard this talk they started screaming: "What's wrong with you?! We have barely a few weeks left to live and you're ready to steal these last minutes from us, too?!" They ran off and dragged Moyshe out of there and kept him from lighting the fuse in the bottles. We were stopped again.

Now this Moyshe *"Kommandant"*—I already mentioned him— could also be pretty decent to us.[19] He was partly mad, but he had a "Jewish heart." When the atmosphere was relaxed and the Germans were preoccupied with their own things, he really gave us trouble, but whenever we lost hope and there was talk that as early as tomorrow, we'd all be taken away and shot, he'd become as tolerant as could be expected from him. He decided then to escape with us—about twenty people. When we found this out, some of the men started sleeping in their clothes to be ready at any moment to escape with him. He saw that this group was now too large, so he put it off for another day. A German Jew learned of all this and informed the *Unterschaarführer* that Moyshe *"Kommandant"* was behind it. The German immediately summoned Moyshe *"Kommandant"* along with three others—Moyshe Toyber, who'd been prevented from setting the storehouse on fire, was one of these—and shot them all.

There was a separate group of forty people among us—twenty Polish Jews and twenty Dutch Jews—who worked outside the camp in the forest chopping down trees. The Polish Jews were from Iżbica, near Lublin. They'd formed themselves into a resistance unit there and planned an escape. They were often sent from the forest under an escort of Ukrainians into a village to get water. Yosl Kop was an amazing man. Even before Sobibór, he had two Germans "on his conscience," and as soon as he walked into the camp he said: "I won't be here long." Now, as he was going for water, he kept his word. He decapitated one Ukrainian with an axe, grabbed his rifle, and they all escaped. After waiting a long time for the group to return, guards were sent to find out what had happened. A courier was sent back right away with the news that the Ukrainian had been found dead—the body in one spot and the head in another—and they knew, of course, that the Jews had done this and escaped. Then everyone was ordered to drop their tools and stop working. The people were lined up and led along a narrow path near the barracks. They were certain they were being led off to die. Along the way, they made up a plan. One of them was very heroic and was ready to fall victim in order to save the others. He told them he would break away to the left and when the Germans went after him, everyone should scatter off to the right, and that's what happened. As soon as the Germans started chasing the one who ran left, shooting at him, his group broke away and ran right. The Germans turned and fired at them and hit four. Most of them managed to escape, though. But the Dutch Jews stood frozen to one spot and wouldn't move. They showed they were "good patriots." Everything was chaos. The Germans stopped chasing the escapees and surrounded those who had stayed and marched them off at gunpoint, afraid they would all run, too. Then they forced them to kneel down and crawl to the barracks on their bellies.

Once inside the barracks, a search was started and all pocketknives and other things were taken from them. They were searched for guns and ordered to hold their hands locked behind their necks. The Germans rounded us up and led out the whole barrack to the spot where the "criminals" were lined up. We were also sure they were taking us away to die. We agreed among ourselves that once they led us to the third barrack, we'd throw ourselves at them, but they brought us to the place where the others had been sat down in columns, hands behind their backs. They made us form a circle around them, and then the *Oberschaarführer* started his harangue that because of what happened, the Jews would be shot, and right before our eyes, ten Jews from Poland were pushed forward and shot. Like those before them, their last words to us were also: "Avenge us!!"

The Dutch Jews were given the explanation that such actions had to be taken because only they, the Dutch Jews, had remained in place. And these were the last people of an entire transport that had immediately been sent to their deaths. They treated the Jews from Holland better, making them feel they were worth more than the Polish Jews.

That night, there was a head count, the barracks were sealed, barbed wire was hung over the windows, and a guard was positioned at the door. From that time on, the Jews from Poland were prevented from leaving the camp for work. The camp was reinforced with still more wire—electrified—mines and obstacles were dug into the earth, and we were warned that anyone found with a knife or razor blade would be shot. We were all kept under tight security but we shaped small knives and razor blades into long knives and razors, anyway. In the last few days, searches happened all the time, and one of us was found with a weapon and shot.

Around the first of October, a transport arrived with prisoners from Minsk in Russia. Fifty of them were transferred to the camp we were in for labor. They were fine young men. They weren't like the Dutch, German, or French Jews. They were our loyal brothers. We made contact with them right away and formed a unit. We held strategy sessions and other discussions. There was a lieutenant[20] among them and some were from Warsaw. They sent us ten boys to help peel potatoes and that was where we formulated the exact plans for the uprising. We also decided on the date. But the plan was aborted at that time because a mob of special German inspectors and observers swarmed into camp and we had to change the plan to the fourteenth of October, at four in the afternoon, when the Ukrainians were off at their recreation and the barracks, which were unguarded then, could be stormed and the rifles taken out.

Men were assigned to all the barracks and labor sites and told which tasks to perform on the final day. No foreign and Dutch Jews were involved. On the last day, about 330 Jews and some Polish and one French *Kapo* knew about the plans. They swore secrecy and created diversions for those people who could have found out about the uprising and sabotaged it.

At exactly four P.M., *Untersturmführer* Neumann came to the tailors to have a uniform measured. He was received very warmly, told to sit down, and from behind, his head was split into two pieces with an axe and the halves were swept under the bunks. I should tell you that for the two weeks before this, the masons were advised to sharpen the spades and chisels well, and on the day of the uprising, everyone was armed with a sharp knife or hatchet under their coat.

At the exact same time, *Oberschaarführer* Greshits, a Ukrainian, arrived at the shoemaker workshop, and in a second, he was turned into a corpse. Any German caught by the Jews was assassinated. If they came into the barrack to force us off to the labor sites, we thought to ourselves: "*Briederke,*[21] this won't take long—you'll be dead in no time." We let them into the barracks and they never left again.

I ran from battle station to battle station as a courier, informing the units of our progress. We broke into the German compound and took all their arms, then headed for the administration office. *Schaarführer* Beckmann was at his desk. He knew right away something was up because he'd just come from our barrack and found no one there, not even the *Oberschaarführer,* so he went straight back to the administration office, where we cut him off. He reached for his revolver but there wasn't a chance—all of us jumped him without guns and beat him dead because we didn't want to shoot. The longer we kept things quiet the better off we'd be. It was hard to keep him down because he jerked around in wild death spasms.

The time was getting close now and the laborers started returning from the work sites. They didn't know what was going on. The six men who'd been inside the administration office ran in front of them with their bloodied hands and shirts and rallied them to sing the German song, *Wester Wald.* When everyone was already assembled inside the camp and we were getting ready to attack the arsenal, *Zugwachmann* Rel—how many times he'd beaten me!—suddenly appeared and realized something was happening when he saw the cut wires. The electricity and telephones were all put out of order by one of us who had access to the generators and smashed them. Rel asked us nervously: "*Was gibt es neues?*"[22] He just happened to be walking right in front of me, so I raised my axe and, along with two friends, chopped him up into little pieces.

Now everyone knew what was about to happen and a deafening cheer went up, shouts of "*Vperyod!*" "*Vorverts!*" "*Foros!*" Our targets were now ahead of us, not behind us—the arms stockpiles! We stormed the arsenal, killed two Germans where they stood, and brought out the guns. All this time, we could see nothing but bullet after bullet ripping at us from all sides—from the guard towers, from the Germans and the *Volksdeutsche* and the 300 Ukrainians who were shooting at us from all around, especially from the fourth camp. They were soon reinforced by another 150 Ukrainians who assaulted us with heavy automatic weapon fire. We returned fire with the few guns we had. But we didn't keep static positions—we ran from station to station shooting in all directions, and defying the risk, broke out of camp. We were still at the wire perimeter when a youth beside me took a bullet and was left hanging on the wires. I was using a rifle I had gotten from the stockpile and kept on running. There were explosions all around—the mines went off, the bullets struck and flashed everywhere we went. The sound of men being torn to pieces, bullets shattering, and mines detonating thundered all through the area. Later, all we could do was laugh as we heard the rattling of the machine guns trailing off behind us. The shooting kept up all night and we got farther and farther away from the camp. We threw off everything along the way.

Today, when I see those things in my mind, I rejoice—my heart can't contain my pride! We washed our hands in the blood of the biggest murderers of our people! It was worth it to be killed yourself just to have seen it—as long as we were out of Sobibór! I still have nightmares today of Sobibór: how they're going to shoot me and I'm pleading with them, "Let me work! Just don't shoot me!"

Afterwards, the Germans could hardly find the remains of those we'd killed because we'd stuffed the body parts in among all the rags. The remnants were thrown into sixteen coffins and buried in Chełm. We were later informed about all of this in great detail. The camp existed for a few more months only, and then Sobibór was totally liquidated.[23]

During the first ten minutes, we killed nine Germans.

After we ran several hours and were far from the camp by now, we counted ourselves up because everyone had run off in a different direction. There were twenty-four in our group. We kissed and embraced and couldn't believe we were really outside the camp. We walked all night through the forest and found a good spot in a gorge grown over with thicket, and that's where we rested. We didn't eat all day because what we'd accomplished put us into such a state that we were all flushed from exhilaration and our blood was feverish and made us tremble. We couldn't eat a bite and there was nothing to eat in the forest anyway. Someone had a piece of bread, a lump of sugar, so we shared it later.

In the early dawn, German planes were already circling the forest, trying to locate us, dropping charges and trying to flush us out with bombs, but we just laughed at them, because it was impossible to see us. Then, gendarmes from Lublin County and the area around us were alerted and brought in to find us.

Night fell and we started walking, but without a clear direction. We didn't know where we were going. We wanted to be as far from the camp as possible, or even across the Bug. Without a compass, we circled back up into the mountain forests of Sobibór again. When we came to a spot we recognized, a shock charged through us—what! back in hell!? So we started running again. We circled and circled like this for six days and once, almost fell onto the barbed wire of Sobibór all over again.

After walking this way for a long time, we finally came into a village called Uchon.[24] We went to a peasant for something to eat and they told us we shouldn't go left because there was a checkpoint there, but to head right. Then the person leading us made a blunder and headed left. We had no special leaders. We ran straight into the Germans and they all fired at us. We had three rifles, one pistol, grenades, and we shot back and managed, with luck, to escape unharmed. The Germans thought they'd been attacked by a band of partisans so they stayed frozen in their positions, afraid to move after us, only firing into the forest blindly, and we got away.

We wandered without food and drink for three more days. No matter which goyim we met, they always told us the Germans had just caught and shot this one or that one from Sobibór, and the life went out of us—what meaning was there left? We wanted to join the partisans but they wouldn't take us.

On the third day, we're sitting like this, binding our wounds, when we see an armed Gentile suddenly come out into the clearing. We could see he wasn't German so we relaxed—as long as he wasn't German. We decided to talk things over with him. He comes near us and starts speaking. He questions us and decides to take us on into his group. Then he asked us if we were hungry and said he'd bring back some food.

He did like he said. He left and came back with a whole gang of armed shgutsim and gave us some bread. We're sitting around and eating and they're asking us if we have guns, gold. They tell us to hand over our guns. This is how it's done, they tell us, and later, they'd hand out guns to everyone. We knew it was wrong, but gave up the few light weapons we had just to have done with it. Now, many more of them start coming. They load the guns and—they start shooting at us point-blank! We're trapped! We have nothing to return fire with and it ends in tragedy. Came out of Sobibór to be gunned down by the likes of these! We throw ourselves down on our stomachs and try to crawl, stumble and run off. Bullets hit. Friends fall. We dig and lunge ahead on our stomachs. We can't raise our heads because they spray bullets over us, but we finally managed to put a little distance between us and them.

I look around. There are only three of us left: a friend from the Minsk transport—Shimin Rozenfeld—Avrum Raz from Tishevits, and me. Maybe someone else managed to survive, but I don't know. Where we were, there were only three. We were completely shaken by this tragedy, stumbling and running farther, though we had no strength left. We had the choice of either commiting suicide by hanging ourselves in the forest, or foraging through these woods for food. And you know we would have been mad to go to the *goyim* for food. Who could trust them now—because if the Poles were capable of murdering us this way, what other horrors might they commit? We tried nourishing ourselves on the wild mushrooms and turnips.

We were approaching Tishevits. Raz knew some peasants there and that's where we were heading. But before we got there, we were stopped by a peasant who agreed to give us food. We paid them with a five-ruble note and went on. Then a second peasant stopped us, but when he found out who we were and from where we came, he did the same as the first peasant. He told us he'd even let us stay in the barn for a few days, but that evening, he showed us a message which said the gendarmes would be there in the morning for potatoes and he got scared, so we left. As long as we had some bread, we weren't too worried.

We walk on. Our goal is to reach the Savin Forest,[25] where we heard it was safe because of the partisans. Some peasants pointed out the way. Once we got there, we marched the length and breadth of the forest and didn't find a soul. We headed towards Chełm. We enter the Chełm forest. We hear a great commotion in the villages nearby. We thought we were in Reyvits.[26] Raz said we should run from there because of all the military traffic. We heard a train whistle blowing, a pump beating. All this caused nothing but panic in us. We felt like trapped animals, wild with frenzy from being lost. Suddenly, we see a pot of beans hanging from a tree. This must mean there's someone in the forest or someone has just left! We move on. We come upon half-buried bottles of water. A new sign that there were people just here. We walk on and look around and then find Duvid Sertchuk of Chełm. We're overjoyed at this sudden meeting.

He tells us there are another five Jews here from Sobibór. He takes us to them. A pot is on the boil and Yuzek, Duvid's brother, sits at the head of the group, stirring the pot. He sees us—Jews from Sobibór! We kiss and embrace everyone. We get a large bowl of food. Yuzek, our "protector," tells us we can calm ourselves. "We'll survive all this," he says. And we've been sitting here for ten months already and continue to survive.

Eyewitness Testimony 49. A Jewish Combatant in the Polish Warsaw Uprising

S.Y.L. Born in Łódź in 1923; lived there. Recorded in Polish by Mikhl Zylberberg in London in 1954. The witness, together with his parents, was deported to Cracow in December 1939. In June 1940 he went to Warsaw and was later put into the Warsaw Ghetto. His father was shot on the street at the start of 1942 and in that year he crossed over to the "Aryan" side with his mother. He was assisted by Polish friends and found shelter there. Posing as a Pole, he worked in a private Polish firm until the outbreak of the uprising in August 1944. He now continues.

Once, an SS officer came into the office. He was completely drunk and tried to amuse the employees. Suddenly, he switched the topic to Jews, and said that many of them were hiding on the "Aryan" side. He looked long into one face, then another, and pointed his finger at a young Pole, calling him *"Jude!"* Everyone started when he said the word *"Jude"*—it was the most terrifying thing at that time, something that meant certain death or maybe even worse than death. The officer suddenly came straight up to my desk and yelled into my face, "You're a real Polak—blond hair, blue eyes, you're a real beauty you are, just like an Aryan's supposed to look!"

He started badgering me to admit the other one, the Pole, was really a Jew. It was only when the manager intervened and assured him he would never take the risk of harboring Jews in his business, that the German seemed convinced there were no Jews here.

When the uprising broke out in August 1944, I volunteered immediately and was assigned to one of the AK[1] detachments. I was one of the many Jews who took part in the fighting and no one ever had the slightest suspicion I was a Jew. I, myself, sometimes stopped giving it thought.

One episode has etched itself into my memory. This was toward the end of October,[2] when it was clear to everyone that the outcome of the uprising would be the rout of the Polish side. I was on watch a few dozen meters from the German line. A Polish officer appears, completely overcome by alcohol, and starts cursing the Jews: "The Jews are responsible for the fate of this uprising, too!" Of course, he didn't suspect me. He said Jews organized the uprising, and he cursed the American and English Jews who were "responsible for the defeat of Poland!" He claimed he could tell these "heroes" by their "fat hands" and "pointed ears." All this time, I didn't say a word. I was only glad that, in this dark autumn night, he couldn't see my hands and ears.

This was the last night of battle. In the morning, the uprising was officially called off, and the Polish army capitulated. I decided to keep on pretending I was Polish, so I'd be taken prisoner along with the uprising army. Most of these Polish prisoners were vicious anti-Semites. They ridiculed the heroic Jewish Ghetto Uprising and cursed the Jews Hitler was murdering right under their eyes.

Eyewitness Testimony 50. Jewish Participants in the Polish Uprising

S.S. Born in Radom in 1898; was a supervisor in the Communication Institutes of Warsaw. Recorded by Hersh Vasser in Warsaw in November 1947.

During the August Uprising of 1944, I was serving in the medical corps of the *Armia Krajowa* in the Old City all along the front lines up to Theater Square. On September 2, 1944, I was assigned along with two other medical workers to the hospital on Długa Street to treat three seriously wounded combatants who had gone through hell making their way through the sewers to the city center. All at once, while I was standing in front of the entrance to Długa 21, I could see the turret of a German tank visible from around the corner on Bankowa Street. The Germans were calling on the populace to surrender, threatening to burn and level all the buildings now if they didn't. Fear and desperation drove all the people who were left here—the women, the old people, and youths—to hang out a white flag. The women and children were gathered together and led away and the rest of us, including myself, were shoved off to the square in front of the former Pasaż Simonsa. After some time, the young people were selected out—what happened to them I don't know—and six of us were marched off to Krasinski Square by way of the Krasinski Gardens. While we were walking through the gardens, I saw a group of six priests and twenty Jews there. The Jews were talking among themselves, mostly in Yiddish, some in Hungarian. The Polish rebels spoke in awe of the exploits and support by Jews during the uprising. These Jews, thirty to forty years old, who'd gotten out of the ghetto— most likely from the prison on Gęsia—showed only contempt for the Germans, and with serenity facing their fate of life or death.[1]

We were put to work on Krasinski Square from where I could see the Germans bombard the building at Długa 7, putting to death the wounded soldiers inside. Later, we were brought to Leszno Street. At one point, they ordered two of us to carry wood into the building at Żelazna 89 and to the German kitchen at Leszno 75. Across the way from us at Leszno 75, a unit of nineteen Jewish combatants was assembled and led off by fours into the courtyard at Żelazna 89, where the highest ranking Gestapo officer shot them in the back of the head, killing them instantly. After the nineteen Jews were executed, a second unit of twenty Jews, among whom was a seventy-year-old woman, was brought there. I noticed that this special group of Jews made no show of resistance before they were executed, nor did I ever see this by any Poles who were disarmed. As I passed the building at Żelazna 89, I could see trails of smoke rising upward—the bodies of the forty-one Jewish combatants were being burned. I have to add that each time a group of four was led off to die, they were first brought into one of the shops on Żelazna corner Leszno, where they were interrogated. I couldn't make out what was being demanded of them, but they gave no reply.

I give this eyewitness testimony in clear conscience. I have hidden nothing.

Eyewitness Testimony 51. A Jewish "Nazi"

B.A. Fragments from a longer testimony she recorded with B.K. in 1946.

I first met Shmiel Riefazen in 1940 to '41 in Wilno at Kibbutz Akiva.[1] Shmiel Riefazen, born in 1920 in the Poyzn[2] District of a father who was a *shoykhet,* impressed everyone as a quiet, modest, and intelligent youth. After finishing the *gymnazye,* he came to Wilno to join a kibbutz.

In 1940,[3] when the German-Soviet war broke out, I returned quickly to my hometown of Mir. Riefazen and I were separated and he stayed on in Wilno. On the fourteenth of November, 1941, a few days after the *aktsye* against the Jews in Mir, I was walking to work with my friend Leybl Dreslin. Coming toward us was the chief of the Mir gendarmerie and he was walking arm in arm with a Byelorussian policeman. I recognized the policeman immediately as Riefazen. As soon as he saw me, he let go of the chief's arm and bent down as if trying to straighten his boot. The police *Kommandant* kept on walking and Riefazen blurted out, "B——! I'll come see you later!"

My friend who was walking beside me wanted to know what this policeman had wanted with me. I answered that I hadn't heard a thing. . . .

After the first *aktsye* against the Jews of Mir, the police intensified their terrorizing of the Jews with unimaginable cruelty. In the middle of the night, the police broke into Jewish homes, plundered them, humiliated us, forced the girls to strip naked and dance for them, to roll around and sing, and then they raped them.

On November 14, 1941, at eleven at night, someone banged loudly at the door. We had to open up. Into the room stalks Riefazen the gendarme and demands to see our documents. We were all trembling in fear. Riefazen started yelling and intimidating us. Then, after he checked everyone else's identity, he throws a quick glance over my papers in which my picture shows me smiling broadly. He starts yelling like a maniac, just like the Germans did, about how had I the nerve to laugh here, that I was laughing at the German authorities, and he went on and on like this. The crying and pleas of my mother and family that the photo was taken before the war did nothing to appease him. He told me to get dressed and to come with him. He followed me out of our home with his automatic trained on me. As soon as we had walked some distance from the house—it was midnight by now—we fell into each other's arms. Riefazen cried like a little child. Once we were clear of the city, this is what Riefazen told me:

After the Germans took Wilno, he blotted out the name "Szmuel" from his Soviet passport and wrote in "Oswald," and instead of the nationality being "*Yevrey*," he changed it to "*Polak*." He left his family name the same. Then he quickly got out of Wilno and stayed in a small village for two months with a Pole. After that, he traveled to stay with the Pole's brother in the village of Turec, Baranowicze area.

In Turec, he became the janitor of the *shiel*. While the *Kreiskommandant* of the Mir militia was staying there, they became acquainted. He was a Byelorussian named Sarafinovitch and the mass murderer of the entire region. "Oswald" was passing himself off as a *Volksdeutsche* and Sarafinovitch, who took a great liking to "Oswald," invited him to come to Mir as his private German-language tutor.

A short time later, German gendarmes were dispatched to Mir. Until then, there'd only been Byelorussians. "Oswald" got on friendly terms with the head of the gendarmes, who took him on as interpreter.

The head of the gendarmes grew very fond of "Oswald" and trusted him completely. He treated him like his son. . . .

That time I first met "Oswald," he was interpreter and liaison man for the head of the gendarmes.

"Oswald" told me that the purpose of his life was to help the Jews and save them. He'd been offered a commission in Baranowicze, but since all his past friends were here, he'd decided to stay.

We used to meet every few days inside the burned-out ruins of the *Mirer Yeshive*.[4] "Oswald" promised me he'd let me know beforehand about every act of persecution and all the deportations planned against the Jews. And he did—he informed us of every "visit" the Gestapo intended paying, every time they were going to descend on us to rape and other things. I informed the chairman of the *Judenrat*, Borekh Shulman, that a Polish acquaintance had promised to let me know whenever there was danger threatening the Jews.

Our continued meeting in the *Mirer Yeshive* became dangerous and we'd surely be found out in the end, so we decided to meet through two couriers: Hersh Piernikov, who was a courier for the municipality, and Fanye Shmushkovitch, who was put to work cleaning at command headquarters. . . .

In December of 1941, a roundup of the Communists in Mir was planned. The Police were supposed to surround the town and they decided to include the Jews by causing a panic among them and shooting them down as they tried to run away.

"Oswald" found out about this too late and had no way of getting the information to me on time. He got right on his horse and rode through town looking for his courier. When he spotted him, he dismounted and started yelling at him, "Hey *Żyd!* Come here, fix my saddle!"

When Piernikov leaned forward toward the saddle, "Oswald" told him that tomorrow, none of the Jews should run away or leave their homes because this way they wouldn't be threatened directly by the roundup. . . .

It wasn't only us "Oswald" helped by his warnings; he kept up steady contacts with the priest, and warned the Polish townspeople of retributions and provocations by the authorities. He aided the Gentiles and showed them how to avoid these persecutions.

"Oswald" also helped the Russian prisoners-of-war every chance he had. He created the conditions for a group of forty prisoners to escape while they were being led to the Horodzej train station to be loaded onto a transport. "Oswald" made out a report that the prisoners were so hungry and exhausted, only three policemen were needed to guard them. While they were passing through the woods, the prisoners broke away and escaped. . . .

These prisoners-of-war would talk among themselves and say that "Oswald" was on their side, that he was a "*Vostotchnik*."[5] Poles said he wasn't a *Volksdeutsche* but a Pole. The Jews didn't know what to make of him and just considered him a provocateur.

A Jewish blacksmith, Volf Mikosay, a "man of few precautions," was inside a peasant's hut at that time and said straight out that a time was coming when the Jews would tear the Germans' guts out. A gendarme was seated behind a partition and quickly hauled Mikosay off to the gendarmerie.

"Oswald" was supposed to bring the charges at the inquest. He told the chief it was the peasant who had tried comforting the Jew, who was bemoaning his bitter fate, by telling him a time was coming when the Jews would tear the Germans' guts out. The gendarme had simply used the pretext of the blacksmith being Jewish to haul him in. The chief of police now scolded the policeman and ordered a protocol drawn up that would indict the peasant. "Oswald" was able to have the whole matter dropped. . . .

In the winter of 1942, "Oswald" warned the *Yidnrat* that final preparations were being made to exterminate the Jews in the countryside.

Benye Simonovitch made a deal with the peasant Chudoba for a pistol. Chudoba then went to the police and informed them about it. "Oswald" made out the indictment. The police gave Chudoba a pistol he was to take into the ghetto on Sunday. As the transaction was being made, gendarmes and police would storm into the ghetto and use this as an excuse for a mass roundup.

"Oswald" rode into the ghetto on a bicycle—he was extremely agitated. . . . He called me out of the ghetto, ordered the gates locked and allowed no one in, because something horrible was about to happen. Chudoba knocked on the gates but without success. The gendarmes also kept knocking but weren't let in till much later. The provocation failed.

There were many incidents like this. "Oswald" had to warn the ghetto repeatedly against provocations, treachery, tribute, blackmail. . . .

In May of 1942, we were all deported from the ghetto and locked up inside a castle of the nobility. During this time, "Oswald" had advanced in the ranks. He was appointed *Ortskommandant* and a few weeks later, *Kreiskommandant.*

"Oswald" was extremely well liked. He distinguished himself among his Byelorussian peers by his intelligence. The conditions of the Jews improved. Ignoring the decree about the liquidation of the ghetto, the Jews wandered freely around town and bought food at the marketplace. The *Judenrat* started suspecting "Oswald." How was it possible, they asked, that a German *Kommandant* treated the Jews so well without taking a bribe?

My friends and I started trying to convince "Oswald" to accept some kind of gift. He wouldn't hear of it.

On my own initiative, I informed the *Judenrat* "Oswald" was demanding a watch. When I offered it to him, he got angry. I stuffed the watch into his pocket. He pulled it out, threw it into a pond, and said, "Now tell them, I took a bribe."

In June 1942, we heard rumors that Jews were being deported from the surrounding towns and villages. The police tightened their surveillance over us. Contacts with "Oswald" were interrupted. From time to time, when he rode his bike into the ghetto, panic would break out. Everyone tried to hide the food they were carrying or smuggling, and in their fright, it all tumbled out of their hands.

"Oswald" came to the *besmedresh* often. It was inside someone's home and used also for *davenen*. One time, he walked up to a man sitting before the *gemoreh*. The Jew went white with terror and tried hiding the seyfer. "Oswald" looked at me and said, "B——, I can't keep this charade up any longer.". . .

At the end of June 1942, "Oswald" told me the massacre of the Mir Jews could no longer be delayed and we should organize a resistance. He said he'd deliver us guns personally. We set up an underground resistance organization which numbered sixty young people.

We took everyone we trusted into the organization no matter what party they belonged to. The members were divided up into cells of five.

We planned to mount the resistance during the *aktsye*. "Oswald" was supposed to join us at the last minute, bringing along machine guns.

We knew beforehand exactly how the *aktsye* was going to be carried out, where the Germans would be heavily concentrated. Osher Kokh was to hurl the first grenade at the Germans. This would be the signal for all of us to fire. During the battle and commotion, the people of the ghetto would flee and those who came out alive, were to regroup in the Włodzierów Forest.

Every few days, "Oswald" brought new arms into the ghetto. And each night, a guard made up of members of the organization waited by the gates for "Oswald" to hand the guns over to them.

"Oswald" brought eleven rifles, eight revolvers, ten grenades, and several thousand rounds of ammunition into the ghetto. Our gun detail was supposed to stockpile the arms at their own responsibility.

By the end of July 1942, "Oswald" already knew for certain that on Wednesday, August 13, 1942, the *aktsye* in Mir would begin. "Oswald" even informed us of the exact location where the mass graves were being dug.

In July of 1942, "Oswald" had participated in raids against the partisans. He knew almost exactly how many of them there were, and more or less, which trails they used.

After endless strategy sessions, we finally changed our whole plan. "Oswald" felt there'd be fewer victims if all the Jews broke out before the *aktsye*.

We decided that on August 9, 1942, at six in the evening, "Oswald" would take the police out in four buses on a raid against the partisans.

That same night, the armed youths in the ghetto would break out and follow "Oswald's" tracks into the woods. There would be absolutely no police in the *shtetl* that night, and this would be the best and maybe only chance to leave the ghetto.

"Oswald" was to return from the raid by another route on Monday morning, the tenth of August, at eleven A.M. He figured that until the police realized the full extent of what happened, and until they managed to inform him, it would be nightfall. The Jews would by then have had all night and the following day to leave the ghetto and escape.

"Oswald" foresaw that on Monday at seven P.M he would have to surround the ghetto.

We agreed that "Oswald" would be informed as soon as we met up with the partisans. Then, he was supposed to go out on a raid and purposely fall into an ambush we'd set. A few days before August 8, Mekhl Pisetsner, a member of the *Judenrat* who shared a room with me, found a rifle in the attic. The *Judenrat* was afraid that this was a provocation and called me to a meeting. They asked me outright if we had any guns. I replied yes. They started yelling—how dare I take upon myself responsibility for the lives of all the people in the ghetto?! I assured them the guns weren't hidden inside the ghetto. The members of the *Judenrat* wanted to make sure the person who was supplying us with guns wasn't trying to provoke an *aktsye*. I answered that I had complete faith in that person. The members of the *Judenrat* asked me to at least tell one of them where the guns were hidden, that this would satisfy them and make them calm. They picked Tsaleh Charne for this. I told him we knew for sure that the *aktsye* in Mir would start any day, that we were organized, and that on a certain night, we were planning an escape from the ghetto and then all the others would be able to follow because there'd be no police in the town that day. I also told him we buried the guns in the *besoylim* outside the ghetto. I misled him on purpose, because the guns were really still inside the ghetto.

Tsaleh Charne asked us to take him into our group. . . .

On Sunday, August 9, at six in the evening, as planned, "Oswald" drove them away for the raid. That same night, sixty armed and 150 unarmed Jews left the ghetto. We headed for the Mironisko woods. Just as "Oswald" had warned, at seven P.M on Monday, the ghetto was sealed off and 500 Jews were locked up inside.

By Tuesday morning, the police already knew the escaped Jews were armed. During the night of Monday to Tuesday, we took our revenge on the peasant Chudoba, the traitor with the pistol.

On Tuesday, the chief of gendarmes came into the ghetto, assembled all the people, and tried persuading them with deceitful logic that there was no reason to run, there was absolutely no threat hanging over the ghetto. The graves were all ready. The Jews believed this German. Rumors were spread that the Jews who escaped drowned or were killed, and here this German was proposing a way to stay alive!

A Jew named Stanislavski worked with the horses at the gendarmerie. The chief promised to let him live and give him special privileges if he informed him from where the Jews had gotten the guns, and who told them about the planned roundup. Stanislavski, believing he could save himself through this betrayal, agreed to the *Kommandant*'s conditions. He told him he heard say "Oswald" had given the guns to the Jews and had planned their dispersal with them. . . .

The *Kommandant* summoned "Oswald" and asked him for his gun. He informed him of the charges against him. The chief spoke to "Oswald" with compassion, like a father: "I know you're soft-hearted and you pity the Jews. You warned them and showed them how to escape. But why did you give them guns, knowing the guns would be turned on you?"

"Who told you all this?" "Oswald" suddenly asked the chief.

"A Jew from the ghetto."

Tears welled up in "Oswald's" eyes and he said, "I did what I had to—I'm a Jew!"

The *Kommandant* almost dropped out of his chair. There was dead silence. After a moment, he sprang up and screamed, "What am I supposed to do to you for this?!"

"Oswald" answered, "Give me the gun and I'll shoot myself." The chief paced the room nervously. "Why didn't you come to me about this first? You're a child! Why didn't you deny it? I'd certainly have believed you rather than that Jew!"

Oswald: "I had to do it. I couldn't keep this joke up any longer."

The chief let "Oswald" make out his own report and he would take it to Baranowicze tomorrow to have the matter considered.

"Oswald" was put under house arrest in the *Kommandant*'s home and was guarded by a gendarme.

The same day, the eleventh of August, 1942, at seven in the evening, "Oswald" broke through the window and escaped. They went after him right away. The bullets missed him. He hid out in the wheat fields. At night, he stole into a convent and hid there for a year and four months. When the nuns were ordered to vacate the town in two hours, they dressed him in a nun's habit and took him along through the town like this. Not being allowed to stay with the nuns any longer, "Oswald" headed into the forest to look for the partisans. In the village of Rubieżewicze, "Oswald" ran into the Ponamarenko Battalion of the Lenin Brigade. He was taken to headquarters where he was condemned to be shot as a German *Kommandant*.

The Jewish partisans heard about it and went immediately to see the staff commander of the local partisan movement, Tchnernishov—*nom de guerre* "Platon"—and explained "Oswald's" entire history. "Platon" called off the death sentence and ordered "Oswald" inducted into a unit.

"Oswald's" time in the convent effected his mind and behavior. He became very spiritual. He kept to himself in the partisan unit and acted like an ascetic—never accepted clothes or shoes and walked around barefoot and in tattered sackcloths.

"Oswald" told us about his miraculous escape and the last exchange with the German *Kommandant* after he joined us in the forest.

After the war, he spent some time in a monastery in Cracow.[6]

Eyewitness Testimony 52. Jews in the Slovakian Resistance

K.K.H. Born in Olomouc, Moravia, Czechoslovakia, in 1924; lived there. Recorded by Dr. Kurt Weigel in Vienna in July 1947. After describing the conditions in his hometown when Slovakia became a satellite to Hitler, the witness continues.

In July, I was deported to the *Sammellager* at Zilina.[1] Fortunately, they stopped sending out further transports from the camp for four weeks, and during this time, I decided to escape. Three people from our camp were inducted into a labor battalion of from 500 to 600 men who were kept watch over by six overseers of the "Hlinka Guard."[2] I had informed my parents of my plan through a contact, and escaped. It took me a week to reach them.

The same day I got back, I took a train to Pressburg.[3] The first thing I did was to report to a construction firm where I was employed as a Jewish assistant and got my work permit because of this. During this time, through the aid of a Slovak from Zilina who I learned was a Communist Party member, I made contact with the central committee of the Zionist Organization, which operated in Bratislava illegally. This was the end of 1942. We started putting together a plan for issuing forged documents. This was the time the deportations had slowed down, and we had a limited time to plan our actions.

I borrowed all the "Aryan" papers a Slovak acquaintance of mine had, and we brought him in on the conspiracy. We modeled all the personal documents we issued after these papers. At the same time, we heard that a liaison man for the Czech Resistance Movement was forging documents for the members who crossed into Slovakia. I was then introduced to a former Czech officer who was on the general staff of the Resistance Movement. The Resistance also had the cooperation of an aid to the Bratislava police commissioner who got us police seals impossible to duplicate. This was when I became the liaison man between the Zionist Organization and the Czech Resistance Movement.

In the remaining time, we worked without stop at producing documents and we finished up papers for many people who were in danger.

No further transports were sent out until the start of September 1944, and we could work in relative peace. All this time, I was in constant contact with my parents. September 1944, was when the Slovak Uprising broke out. In the first days of the Uprising, I spent a week in Zilina as a courier, then left for the mountains near Srečno, five kilometers from Zilina, where I was told a Resistance unit was operating. From there, I was sent back to Bratislava to continue my work with the Resistance intelligence unit.

This was some of the work I did for the Resistance: I received bulletins in an envelope from a courier and passed them on to a second contact. These Slovaks knew I was a Jew. Both my parents' papers and my own were made out for "Aryans." I was legally registered with the police, but my personal profile folder was lifted from the files by our contact, so now the authorities knew nothing of my whereabouts or existence.

Another part of my work, and the most important for me, was the issuing of forged documents which saved between 1,000 and 1,500 Jews who were hidden in bunkers.

There were twelve of us young Jews assigned to live in separate sections of Bratislava. But we spent most days in my flat. Besides us, there were four other people, including a girl, who worked in the external affairs unit of the Resistance. We issued almost every forged document used at that time. . . . [A detailed description of the forgery process follows.] They were distributed by our couriers to Jews who were in danger. We received the addresses of these people through M. Dounan, the Swiss representative of the International Red Cross in Bratislava. The commander-in-chief of the whole group, Dr. Reves,[4] took the finished documents from us and followed up on them. I personally never met the recipients of the documents. My work consisted of forging the original signatures and filling out the rest of the document. We used to get 1,000 Czech *kroner* a month to carry out the work.

It's been estimated that 1,000 people were saved from deportation thanks to our operation. Of all our couriers, three were shot and the girl was deported to Theresienstadt.

On April 4, 1945, we were liberated by the Russian army after a battle which lasted forty-eight hours.

[The witness has given me photographs of eight of his personal forged documents.—K.W.]

Eyewitness Testimony 53. Working in the Belgian Resistance

A.F. Born in Częstochowa, Poland, in 1898; emigrated to Belgium in 1920. Recorded by Yankiv Fishman in New York in 1954. The witness talks about the first decrees against the Jews of Belgium and the deportations in August 1942, when he lost his wife and children. He now speaks of this.

My wife was still stubborn and believed the Jews were safe. She had never seen Jews being rounded up and sent to concentration camps. In this sense, things went on as before. But I myself also didn't foresee the *Khorbn* like other Polish Jews. When the tragedy happened in August 1942, while the Jews were being caught in the streets and Jewish families were dragged out of their homes and taken to the camps inside Belgium itself to be transported later in closely watched trains to Poland, to Oświęcim,[1] just then I got a heart attack and was taken to the hospital. Because I was incapacitated, I begged my wife to take the children and find a hiding place somewhere. She put it off from day to day. This shattered me. I couldn't do anything for my family anymore. All I could do was tell them, beg them to be prepared for danger. It was no use. Four weeks after I was put in the hospital, my family was led away and interned in the transit-camp of Malines. After spending a few days there, they were taken to Oświęcim and killed.

When they no longer came to see me in the hospital, I knew tragedy had struck. I couldn't remain still. I wanted to return to the house. My condition only got worse this way and the doctor wouldn't let me leave the hospital yet. I remained hospitalized for another two long weeks. When I got back to my flat, I found it was empty. My family gone. All I found were their pictures.

I immediately went underground. I changed my name. Not A—— F—— anymore, but Charles Bayeury. I was drawn into working for the underground by the well-known editor, Marcel Gaspar Jacob. We knew each other well. I stayed in Liége, but, of course, in another flat and in another quarter of town. I grew a beard, typically French, and dressed differently from before. All that time, no one recognized me.

The aim of the group was—and we carried this out—to aid Jewish families in hiding. We got new passports for them and "Aryan" documents. We placed the old people in local old-age homes. And the orphans we put in orphanages. The Gentile townspeople helped us 90 percent of the times we asked them to. We were financed mostly by individuals—Jews and non-Jews—who gave us larger sums, and we also got money from robberies, expropriations, and ambushes. We stormed the post office a few times and got away with huge sums. Altogether, we confiscated and collected millions and millions of francs. We overran the office that issued food-ration cards for the people. In no case did anyone ever dare put up resistance. Once, we liberated sixty Russian POW's from a German camp. This was an amazing operation. I was part of it. Some of us dressed up as German officers. The prisoners were called out of a coal mine. Our disguised "Germans" presented authorization documents to the mines administration which called for the release of the Russian prisoners into our custody. They were handed over to us in an instant. And here they were being led through the town as free men. We hid them in a safe place. We got them a change of clothes and food for as long as the war lasted.

We rescued Allied parachutists who were shot down and prevented their falling into German hands. I participated in the rescue of four American fliers. It was hard for me to make myself understood. They spoke no French and none of us knew English. We watched the German fighter planes attack the American bombers. In the end, the American planes were shot down. The four young "boyes" hid in the middle of the field, scared to death. If they were found, they'd be shot for sure. A couple of minutes too late, and the Germans would have seen them and captured them. We were able to hide them out. We brought them clothes and food. They couldn't stop thanking us. I have the names of those four boys somewhere in my archives. After being in America for three and a half years, I still haven't gotten around to looking them up. It's very hard for someone like me to live in this country.

In January 1943, the Germans found out there were forty Jewish children in the children's home. The Germans used special methods against these Jewish orphans. Instead of grabbing them up or attacking them and kidnapping them as they usually did, they first sent round an announcement to the home's administration on this matter. We contacted the most respected and famous personalities—Gentiles—and urged them to protest. Word finally reached the old Queen and she made known her opposition to the Germans. The decree was called off. This children's home was located in Wiesenberg. My present wife was one of the directors there. She had informed me immediately when the German death notice arrived.

Germans caught me many times. But I was never suspected of being a Jew—all they tried to prove was that I was a member of the Underground. They surrounded me in the streets at gunpoint, frisked me for weapons or documents from the Underground. Never found any. The civilian secret police searched my flat many times. Interrogated me—who was I and what did I do? I knew every time they were whistling in the dark, that they didn't have any proof against me—all they had were suspicions. It lasted about an hour each time, and they always left my flat in ruins.

At the end of January 1943, the Germans put their plan against the French Jews into operation. They worked at lightning speed. After they issued the decree that all French Jews must liquidate their businesses, the final deportation of the French Jews began. Very few of them went into hiding. Practically all of them were led off to Oświęcim. The French Jews were completely overwhelmed and never considered hiding from the Germans for an instant.[2] According to reports we received from Oświęcim, the Polish Jews there had greater endurance than the French Jews from Belgium. By percent, more Polish Jews survived Oświęcim.

The group I belonged to in the Underground wasn't soft when it came to killing collaborationists who couldn't outdo themselves exposing Jews and handing them over to the Germans. Anyone betraying the Jews was paid 1,000 *francs* by the Germans.

In October 1944, the Americans occupied Belgium. The Germans retreated. There was dancing in the streets. Jews who had hidden for so long came out of their holes. But two months later, in December, the Germans started their counteroffensive on Belgium. Everyone fell into a panic. The despair was beyond words. For many reasons, it was now impossible to return to those hideouts, but hysteria was the main factor. It was heart-wrenching to see the Jews wandering the streets, crying and wringing their hands. There were even isolated instances of suicide. To our great fortune, this didn't last long. The American army delivered the death blow to Germany. The Germans were now completely annihilated. The Germans were no more. The Belgians celebrated in ecstasy. Captured Germans were paraded through the streets. Throngs of Jews drove them from behind as to a funeral.

Eyewitness Testimony 54. The Jewish Doctors of the Yugoslav Partisans

A.B. Born in Karlovac, Yugoslavia. Survived together with his family in the ranks of the Yugoslav partisans. Recorded in German by Kurt Weigel in Vienna in 1955. The witness tells of the attacks against Yugoslavian Jews, who were herded into labor camps. Exceptions were made for Jewish doctors and pharmacists (his father was a doctor), and he describes their escape to the partisans and the part they played in the battles against the Nazi Occupation Forces. He then continues.

In September 1944, our whole family, all that was left—my parents, my brother, and I—escaped and joined the partisans. With us was a renegade German corporal whose wife—she was Greek—urged him to get away together with us. The corporal was my father's patient and through him, we made contact with the partisans. My father immediately took over direction of the field hospital, and my brother and I were sent to Jajce, where there was a large military camp. I underwent an officers training course there, working first as a radio-telegraph operator, then heading a communications post.

The partisans worked closely with the Americans and English. During all of my activity with the partisans, hundreds of Germans were taken prisoner and done away with. As an officer, I wasn't obliged to participate in these executions. I doubt, though, that I could kill an unarmed man.

There were few Jews in the partisan ranks since it was almost impossible for the Jews locked up inside the camps to escape. But since the doctors and pharmacists hadn't been interned inside the camps directly, they were able, after a while, to make their way to the partisans. This was why almost the entire medical corps of the Yugoslav partisans was made up of Jews. Distinctions weren't made openly between Jews and non-Jews for the most part, and Tito's attitude to the Jews was officially favorable. . . .

[The witness recounts an episode involving American fliers who'd parachuted from their burning airplanes into the area of the partisan airstrip, "Sanski Mast," and how he and his group rescued them.—K.W.]

I took part in many campaigns and was decorated. Toward the end of the war, fierce battles raged everywhere, and the Germans suffered enormous losses. Many were taken prisoner. Those who were known arch-criminals were executed summarily. The others were held hostage and later exchanged because we usually got back ten partisans for one of them. The whole time I was with the partisans, I never heard from my parents and brother. I became extremely anxious about them because I'd seen what the Germans did with captured partisans. My brother's father-in-law was hanged in the year 1943 while imprisoned as a hostage.

On May 1, 1945, I became ill with spotted typhus and was sent to the hospital at Daurka Luka. It turned out that the director of the hospital was my father! This was the greatest moment of my life, seeing my father, who I didn't know was dead or alive. I stayed in the hospital for one and a half months and then went back to the front at Bosnia. The battles against the remnants of the "Ustasha"[1] dragged on till the beginning of 1946.

In December 1945, I was demobilized and returned to Banja Luka where I found my brother once again.

Eyewitness Testimony 55. Children in the Forest

Y.L. Born in Bielica, Lida County, Poland, in 1933. Recorded by A. Yerushalmi in Tel Aviv, 1947. The young witness, who was nine to eleven years old during the events described, tells of the suffering of the Jews of Bielica. He was present during both the massacre of his hometown and the slaughter of the Jews of Zhetl (Zdzięciół). He goes on.

After that, a second massacre took place. I was separated from my parents, my brothers and sisters. I saw them no more. . . . My mother and two younger brothers and a smaller sister fell into the hands of the police. My father and another brother hid somewhere else. My grandfather and me lay in the cellar of our house. Suddenly, my grandfather went crazy and started screaming. One of the women in the cellar wanted to smother him. There was a big tumult. A Christian woman heard us and ran to tell the police. We knew we were doomed and broke out and scattered in different directions. I ran into the outhouse, crouched down into the waste, and stayed there all day. In the evening someone came up to the door and tried to pull it open. I held the door shut tight and didn't let him in. He was a Jew. . . . The Germans ran up, spun him around, and shot him right in front of the outhouse.

Late at night, we came out. There was me, nine years old, Yankiv Baron, nine years old, Sureh, his youngest sister, eleven years old, and a grown girl who broke away from us later. We ran past the guards and got on the road, heading toward the forest. Along the way, near Lipiczanska Puszcza,[1] I left the group for a while and a gendarme caught me. He sat me on the bars of his bike and drove me into the village where the police were. I begged the policeman the whole way to let me go, but it did no good. Then I yanked at the handlebars and the gendarme fell off and smashed his head. I ran back out of the village into the cornfields, then I found the road and joined up with the boy and his young sister again. Along the way, we were stopped by a *shaygitsl* who threatened he'd turn us in. He demanded [inaudible]. . . . I wanted to strangle him and throw him into the ditch, but the little girl gave up her shoes without complaining.

I went into a village where I found another boy. The two of us walked on to Dworzec.[2] As we came near the *besoylim,* we saw Germans digging up graves there. They were saying something about looking for gold. I went inside the ghetto. I was given food there. They put me into the orphanage. I stayed there three months. I found my twelve-year-old brother in Dworzec. During all this time, my father had been in the woods. He heard my brother and me were alive. He sent over a man who took us back to him.

The forest we were in was at Lipiczanska Puszcza. We stayed together as a family group. There were large partisan units all around us and they didn't bother us. There were fifty people in our families unit, including five children. We would get food from peasants we knew. A teacher, Lazar Meir, used to take care of the children. He was also able to buy guns for the group. One time, he left for the Lida Ghetto and came back with five Jews.

In the winter of 1943, fifteen other Jews and two children came to us. After that, still more and more people joined us. In the summer of 1943, the White Poles[3] of the AKa attacked us. They captured a Jewish partisan of the Orliansk Brigade, Duvid-Hershl Meykl,[4] a man of about fifty-five, and they murdered him.

For the time being, we had to cross into the Letaiskoje Boloto Forest[5] from the Lipiczanska Puszcza. But the Germans came after us and attacked us here, too. They captured Basye Kraynovitch and her brother-in-law and shot them down with machine guns. From that time on, we didn't roam freely through the woods anymore, but sent scouts ahead.

Once, Kolodko, the village chieftain of Zaczepice, informed on us. We found out about it. We went to him, supposedly on a "courtesy call," and shot him dead. We avenged ourselves like this against five peasants who informed on us.

We were able to get a machine gun. Jewish partisans joined us and took up positions here. They were Elyuhi Bumel,[6] Yitskhik Kovenski,[7] and others.

In the summer of 1944, the forests were put under siege by 32,000 Germans and Ukrainians. Partisan units pulled back. We hid out in deep bunkers. The starvation during that time was horrible. We used to get a few beans a day to eat. This went on for fourteen days. There was room for five people in our bunker—fourteen people lay down there during the siege. As a camouflage, we dragged two dead horses over to cover the entrance. When the Germans moved through with their hounds, the dogs bolted back from the stench. But we suffered terribly from those worm-eaten carcasses. The worms crawled all over us and we choked on the stink of death. We fainted from the putrid air.

Another time, we heard cavalry riding past followed by infantry. We thought they were Germans. We crawled out and started to run. My father was the only one to stay behind in the bunker. The "Germans" got him out and wanted to know who he was and what he was doing here. He told them he was part of a partisan family unit. All they did was yell at him for keeping a fire lit, then they left. They were partisans like us.

Later, we moved to another part of the forest. We were led there by a member of our group, Yankl Mołczadzki, who knew the whole region well. We waded through a swamp up to our necks. Some of us drowned. Mołczadzki got us on a sand bank surrounded by water. We dug a bunker there. Afterwards, we made contact with Davidov's group which was made up only of Jews. They had a wireless over which they passed on information to the Russian command post. One time, a long German convoy was passing through our part of the woods. Davidov's radio operator gave their positions to headquarters and the Russian planes smashed every single vehicle and wiped out the whole transport.

Davidov's group had corn, and we got some to grind up with knives, and baked bread down in the bunkers the withdrawing partisans left behind.

Once, the Ukrainians went right past us. We hid in the bulrushes and they lost our tracks.

One time, while we were lying in the bunker, the air circulation was cut off so we had to lift up the top a bit. In an instant, two Ukrainians ran up and looked in under the lid. One of them even reached down and grabbed up a package belonging to a woman inside, but they didn't see all the people stretched out and packed so tight against each other down in the bunker because it was so dark. One of them even said: "Akh, shame I don't have a grenade on me, or a mine—I could have blown up this bunker!"

The children would wander around outside the bunker. Once, two boys—Yosif and Srulik, aged seven and eight—and two little girls, aged four and five, fell into the hands of the Ukrainians. They shot the little girls dead right away and took the boys in to the village gendarmes. The boys pleaded with the police to let them go. At that moment, grown-ups from our group passed by, and the boys started shouting: "See?! There go the adults!" The Ukrainians let go of the children and chased the grown-ups. The children got away and ran down into the bunker. Malke Shmulovitch[8] fell into the Ukrainians' hands. They led her into the village, cut out strips of her flesh and poured salt into her wounds. She betrayed no one, though, and died heroically.

This is the way we suffered for such a long time. We always had knives ready at our sides, to take our own lives if we fell into the hands of the Ukrainians.

One day, Captain "*Severny*" Avreyml Shereshevski came to see us to tell us the good news that the Red Army was near. I was the first one he met. I ran to tell the glad news to my people. I searched for them all day and finally found them. When I told them the joyous news they simply came back to life.

Eyewitness Testimony 56. A Bunker under the Ruins of Warsaw

F.I. Born in Przemyśl, Galicia, in 1913; lived in Stanisławów. Recorded by Mikhl Zylberberg in London in 1955. The witness talks briefly about her experiences in Stanisławów during the Soviet Occupation. When the Germans invaded the town, she overheard the plans being made for the annihilation of the Jews of Stanisławów in October 1941. She talks about her work in a photo lab in the city, and continues.

My employer on the "Aryan" side, *Pan* Pogorzelski, talked me and my sister-in-law into running away from Stanisławów. When we finally agreed, he himself went to his sister in Warsaw and took care of all the papers, finding us a roof over our heads. I had a sister in Lemberg,[1] and I decided to go there first. I contacted my sister, who sent me a go-between—a Pole. He was supposed to take my sister-in-law and me to Lemberg, and from there, to Warsaw.

We both left for Lemberg with our guide. I went inside the ghetto to my family, and my sister-in-law got ready to leave immediately with the guide for Warsaw. At the train station, the guide took all her money and turned her over to a Ukrainian gendarme. She bribed him with everything she had left on her body and escaped into the ghetto.

We were in the Lemberg Ghetto for a month and survived two *aktsyes*. The conditions deteriorated critically and we decided to try to get to Warsaw. At our request, *Pan* Pogorzelski traveled to Lemberg and agreed, though he'd be risking his life, to come with us to Warsaw. The police detained my sister-in-law at the train station again. She "didn't look right." By a miracle, she was able to buy her freedom this time, too, but *Pan* Pogorzelski got scared and refused to go with us.

We both rode in one compartment, but acted as if we didn't know each other. We got into Warsaw without any trouble. As we were leaving the station, a Polish policeman detained us, then took us to Police Headquarters. We were questioned by two Polish police interrogators. One of them wanted to finish, but the other was determined to destroy us. They examined each of us in minute religious matters, and went over all our documents. They spoke only Yiddish during all of this, and even sang some Yiddish songs. Then they started arguing: the first one wanted to let us go and the other to turn us over to the Germans.

We were finally freed after two hours of interrogation and the commissioner instructed a policeman to escort us to a carriage. This was winter, 1942 to 1943.

We got to *Pan* Pogorzelski's sister, Dr. Maria Jurewicz, without anyone stopping us. We stayed in her house for three months, unregistered, and without proper identification. Dr. Maria Jurewicz herself was put in danger because of her work for the Polish Underground. But she risked it and hid us for all this time and wouldn't accept money. She was good to us and helped us keep our courage. Her flat was on Zolibórz Street.

Three months later, *Pani* Jurewicz came to the conclusion it was disastrous [for us] to stay in her house and we were forced to leave. We knew *Pani* Czesława Dorożynska from Stanisławów—she'd decided to resettle in Warsaw earlier. *Pan* Pogorzelski forwarded our money and the woman used it to rent a flat in Bielany,[2] letting us stay there for a few months on the further income we provided. But soon the flat was "burned."[3] *Pani* Jurewicz told us to get in touch with Dr. Helena Radlinska, the well-known professor and community activist.[4]

Pani Radlinska was a Jew who was hiding in a convent and she helped many other Jews. First, she turned me down. When I told her I was the daughter of Professor M—— R——'s[5] brother, she changed her mind and sent me as a servant girl to Professor Wiktor Wąsik, without revealing my nationality.

My sister-in-law contacted *Pani* Dorożynska's—the one I just mentioned—brother. He was a laborer who put up and saved many Jews in his home. He was called Edward.

Edward constructed a bunker in his walk-in flat on Hoża Street, which opened up on the sewers. He also fixed up a special stove that could roll on wheels from the flat to the bunker entrance, with an electric apparatus lit inside that made it look as if a fire were burning. There were ten Jews inside this hideout until the Bor-Komorowski Uprising broke out.

I worked at Professor Wąsik's till the outbreak of the uprising in 1944.[6] Thinking I was a servant girl, he and his family treated me with the usual cruelty. And I have to tell you that their attitude to Jews was repulsive. Once, during a reception at the professor's with many people present, people of the professional intelligentsia, they all toasted, with hurrahs, the extermination of the Jews of Poland. This special reception was called the day the final annihilation of the Warsaw Ghetto took place.

In the summer of 1944, I was so weak and exhausted from working at Professor Wąsik's, I had to stop. I was given a release from a doctor for a month and spent that time in the bunker at Edward's flat on Hoża Street, together with the ten Jews.

I was inside the bunker with the ten people till the start of the uprising. When the fighting began, we left the hideout and appeared in the street openly.

The Poles were extremely hostile to the Jews who participated in the uprising. One of the people in our group, *Frand* Sukharevitch, the most active member, who used to provide us with all our essentials, was hated by the Polish neighbors and they threatened to denounce him as a Jew. Sukharevitch had been inside Treblinka and escaped, killing the Ukrainian guard while at labor in the forest. A religious Jew with a long beard, he was active in the vicinity of Hoża, and though he resisted along with everyone else, he was threatened and denounced. But because of this situation, he was always shadowed by a bodyguard, who was assigned to him by the area commander, an active member of the *PPS*.[7]

When the Polish populace of Warsaw was given the order to evacuate the city,[8] we decided to stay behind in the ruins. We found a shell of a building on Wspólna Street, whose cellar was still intact. We walled up and blocked the entrance to one of these basement rooms. We thought we'd only be down there a few days because the Russians were still camped in Praga.

We left the cellar in secret and took many precautions to bring down a few bottles of water, and we also bought two sacks of flour and a sack of sugar from the *"Armia Krajowa."* These were all the stocks we were able to get and we took them down to the cellar. There were ten people inside. Soon we were joined by three Jews who'd been freed when the *AKa* broke into Pawiak Prison on the first day of the uprising. One of them was from the group of Greek Jews the Germans brought from Auschwitz to clear away the rubble of the Warsaw Ghetto.[9] A young Polish woman who preferred to stay among the ruins rather than leave the city also came down to the cellar. By now, there were fourteen of us. It was so crowded in that hole that when one group sat, the other had to stand. We fed on lumps of sugar, kernels of wheat, and drank the fetid water. At night, we crawled out for a few moments.

One night, from out of nowhere, Sukharevitch's friend appears, a Warsaw Jew who'd seen us descend into the bunker. He was part of a group of eighteen Jews who were staying in another cellar and he tried to get us to unite with them. Right away, we started knocking down a wall to make the hideout bigger. We scavenged through other cellars, collecting whatever we could: quilts, rugs, sheets, dishes, and most important, more food supplies.

In a few days, four basements were fixed up and linked by a corridor and a kitchen. The whole bunker was piled over on every side with rubble. The only exit was through a slim tunnel we covered every morning with rubble, and swept clear in the evening. Inside, the bunker looked even luxurious. Every wall was covered with expensive tapestries. The sheets were changed every week and we burned the dirty ones. We did the same with our underwear and clothes.

It was hard to solve the problem of getting water for thirty-two people. But we were able to do this, too. Some members found a fire-fighting hose and a well which was about seventy-five meters from us. Every third night, water was drawn straight from the well through the hose and dropped into our pitchers.

I took care of the maintenance and was helped by three women. We also did the cooking, baking fresh bread and cakes, and the meals weren't bad. Every night, two of us kept watch by the tunnel while two others crawled out. They were armed with two revolvers. During the day, everyone slept, and our "normal" life only began at night.

The group of eighteen, who had arrived afterwards, was made up of common people who used physical force to get what they wanted. There were young couples among them, two fathers with young sons and four unmarried men.

During our stay in the bunker, we had all kinds of experiences. This is what happened once:

A German patrol stopped to rest over our bunker and lit a fire. They spent a few hours sitting there, then left and didn't put out the flames. The smoke started seeping down into the cellar, and since we couldn't leave during the day, everyone started choking. We had to wait till night to stumble outside and put out the fire. The flames had spread and burned out the ground floor—which was the ceiling of the bunker—so badly, that the boards couldn't support another footstep. It was about to cave in any minute and the Germans would have fallen through into the bunker together with their fire. All the men started work right away to reinforce the ceiling with beams pulled out from under the ruins.

On another night, Sukharevitch came upon someone else again, this time a woman with a five-year-old child, who were lying in the ruins not far from our bunker. It turned out the woman had been wandering around through the ruins for weeks and found nowhere to hide. We took them in with us. They stayed down here even though the second group, which had come in later, objected.

And still another time, we ran into a very religious Jew and a *mishimed* staying together. They'd also been wandering over the ruins. They found a bunker, but the Germans uncovered it and they only got away at the last minute. We took them in with us, but this time, a violent argument broke out. The violent people refused to keep them. They even talked about taking them outside to be shot. After a long quarrel, they finally agreed to let them stay with us.

Not far from where we were, there was a second Jewish bunker and when they discovered ours, they attacked us and it almost came to bloodshed. To this day, I have no idea what made them do it, but in the end, they realized their mistake and we united.

One of the three Jews had tuberculosis and fell very ill. He started spitting up blood and the people around him were in danger of infection. He was treated as in a hospital, especially by the Polish woman. But he died, tragically. We had to carry the corpse out of the bunker right away because it was stifling hot inside. There was almost no air and we burned carbide lamps all the time. It got even worse when we couldn't take him out during the day when it was too dangerous. But ignoring the risk, two of our people quickly carried the corpse out into the next building, and buried him under the rubble as fast as they could. By nighttime, when we went out for the real burial, rigor mortis and frost had already stiffened the body. All of us without exception were there when we buried him in another cellar. It was all done in the traditional way. Candles were lit and we shared the few *sidirim*. We said the appropriate prayers and "*Kaddish.*"

Not long after this, we had a second funeral. The father-in-law of the dead man couldn't stop mourning for his wife who died in Treblinka. He let out the most heart-rending laments. Now, after the death of the person nearest to him, he broke down completely and committed suicide by hanging. It took us a few days before we found him. All that time, we were scared to death the Germans had captured him.

One night, while we were roaming through the rubble, we came upon two Jews with long beards. They were Duvid Guzik of the "Joint" and *Khaver* Bernard of the "Bund."[10] They had been staying with a group of Jews in a bunker. When the Germans uncovered the cellar, the people inside tried to run away in all different directions. Both of them were totally demoralized, starving, covered with hoarfrost, filthy and soiled. We took them back down with us and kept them here for almost a month, till Liberation.

Of the women with us, two were pregnant, but luckily, they gave birth after Liberation. Their husbands were always by their sides down in the bunker.

Our people often ran into Polish marauders who pillaged the cellars at night. We convinced them we were a remnant of the *AKa* that was hiding in the ruins. We made a deal with them and they provided us with fresh meat every few days—the only basic food we were missing. The distribution of the meat was controlled by the violent group, who tried to frighten the rest of us away.

For a month, a silence hung over everything as if we were in a cemetery. This made us tense, nervous, and anxious all the time. We had absolutely no idea what was going on in the world. Finally, for several nights without stop, we heard heavy artillery barrages. This gave us hope. It felt as if something were happening, something would change. We couldn't stop arguing among ourselves in the bunker. Our "enforcers" even thought of ways to keep all the valu-

ables we'd gotten for themselves. But most of us only thought of surviving these last few days.

On the final night, we were out near the corner of Hoża and Marszałkowska and suddenly saw a whole group of Germans running
away from us. The entire area was lit up by burning buildings and
we could make all of them out clearly. The longer we stood there, the
faster they ran. We knew now that the end was near.

We still stayed in the bunker. After the Russians had been inside
the city for a day, we finally found out from the Jews in another
bunker that it was safe to stay outside. As soon as we came out to the
light of day after so many months, all we could see was yellow. Our
skin was all sallow and even the whites of our eyes were completely
yellow.

The Russians found out about us. They showed us off to the press
and the photographers right away. They took down the details of the
life we'd led. In these first days, two more bunkers were uncovered
near us. Inside one of them, everyone had been shot dead. In the
second, all the people had died of starvation. These Jews didn't have
the courage to go out and look for food for themselves.

Soon, our group broke up. Everyone went their own way.

Eyewitness Testimony 57. Clearing the Rubble of the Warsaw Ghetto

L.H. Born in Wąwolnica, Lublin County, in 1907; lived in Mysłowice,
Silesia. Recorded by Yankiv Fishman in New York in 1954. The wit-
ness describes the first three days of the war in Mysłowice and the
Sammellghetto in Mądrzejów,[1] near Katowice where he was sent
afterwards. He is talking now of the *Aussiedlung* of the Mądrzejów
Ghetto to Auschwitz.

They were about to deport me. I knew from before that Oświęcim
was only the preparation for the next step. . . . But first, we'd have to
be made into "loyal" slaves.

A huge number of Jews are gathered in one place. I'm among them.
No one knew what it was all about. Names are called out. Also my
name. Everyone called out, stands off to the side. No one knows what
all this is leading to. One thousand names are called out. Now they're
leading us to the train. We're crammed into freight cars and the train
pulls out. We arrived in Warsaw. This was the beginning of January
1944. They led us through the streets of the city, over mountains of
rubble, through huge, gaping craters. I couldn't recognize this city
anymore, couldn't tell which street I was passing. And I lived in

Warsaw for years. But as soon as we were led inside the military prison, I knew we were on Zamenhofa and I could visualize Gęsia over there, and a little further down—Nalewki. The entire time we marched through these streets of rubble, I hardly saw a soul. The stench was indescribable. A total wilderness. There were Jews in our group from all over Europe, but not one was from Congress Poland. I was from Silesia. Not one from Warsaw or Łódź. We figured it was because the Germans were afraid the Jews of Warsaw or Łódź would immediately make contact with the Polish populace. We were brought inside the military prison. While the ghetto still stood, this had been where the *Yidnrat* and all the Jewish agencies were housed. Now it was a camp—a concentration camp. We met Jews here who'd been slaving in the area for months. Most had been sent here from Oświęcim but there were a lot from other camps, too. There were about 8,000 of us altogether.

We worked at dismantling the bombed-out buildings still standing, brick by brick, window by window, and also hauling away the rubble where nothing was salvageable. It was the most painful and deadening work. The Germans watched over me to make sure I didn't so much as chip a brick—this could have finished me. They cursed us, humiliated us, and beat us. We had to demolish it all intact! Civilian Polish workers were there, too. They did the mechanical work and fixed the machines when they broke down. They were very patriotic and hated the Germans. All of them were involved in some kind of conspiracy or underground work. They told me all the news from the front and the situation in Poland.

We did another kind of work which was much worse. We had to scavenge through the skeletons of buildings and rubble to find valuables for the Germans. All over these collapsing empty ruins we came upon dead Jews and severed limbs. We found merchandise and instruments, tools and books—so many Jewish books. We had to carry it out and clear it all away so the Germans could make good use of it. I even "earned" a little doing this. Sometimes I'd smuggle something out and barter it to the Poles for a bit of food. This labor "front" was too enormous for the Germans to be able to guard us closely all the time. Besides food, I needed a shirt and I got this from the Poles, too.

This area was a concentration camp though there weren't any crematoria here. The reason for the camp was mainly to annihilate us. First of all, there was the inhuman labor. And second, hardly any food—a lump of bread and a mouthful of coffee once a day—and this way they were sure we'd collapse dead. And third, by not giving us shirts, they planned for the lice and filth to cause epidemics and disease. We were constantly beaten to death for no reason at all. The sick and exhausted were sent off to Oświęcim to be burned. Hundreds of men dropped dead in their tracks every day from the worms. I mean this. Swarms of maggots crawled all over the victims' bodies and the Germans, who always boasted about their cleanliness, just stopped resisting when the lice attacked their own bodies. They'd done all this on purpose. Hundreds of people fell unconscious every day from typhus. In the first few months, these victims were packed into trains and sent to Oświęcim to be cremated. Later on, they were just left where they dropped without any medical treatment. This landscape was from a nightmare. Men lost their minds. Some became like vegetables. Before I was brought inside this hell of Warsaw, 3,000 Jews had died here. I was told this by those who were still here before I came.

In March 1944, the Germans interrupted the labor of scavenging through the charred ruins for valuables. They were in a hurry, these Germans. They started blowing up and smashing all the ruins. The work I, and thousands upon thousands like me, did was clearing away the mountains of sand and stones that were left now. The work was a torture. No food was handed out now and I was still in the shirt I wore when they brought me here. The rubble was heaved onto huge loading trucks and carted off somewhere on the outskirts of Warsaw. Only hired Poles were allowed to work at this operation. We had to level all the cleared-out areas completely so there would be no obstacles to the eye. We tidied up the destruction of Warsaw.

June was the first time I was sent to Powązki,[2] to a public bath, to bathe. And this was after I got typhus. They rationed me my first shirt here at the bath. In July, the Germans set up a bath inside the camp itself. We thought this meant the regime was getting better—but we were wrong. The bath was built so the contagious diseases, passed on from the excrement and maggots, wouldn't infect them.

They drove us without letup at the labor sites so we'd work at the greatest speed. They wanted to remove every last sign of the way they'd devastated Warsaw. High commissions of Nazis came through all the time for inspections, always enraged when signs of their cruelty still stood. They screamed how their past was still visible and they blamed it on us, so we were made to work there round the clock—much more than the fourteen-hour days we did till now—and all the time faster, faster. They beat and prodded us with clubs and whips.

Most of the work was over in August—the end of August. The Germans were in terror of the Russians, still camped in Praga. They could have marched in whenever they wanted. But we were still kept on here. They were afraid to let us loose over Warsaw. And since there was no work left to be done now inside the city, they thought up tortures for us as only these lunatics and degenerates could. Every night, they made us dig graves inside the camp. We usually dug two large trenches a night. All the while, we were thinking of what they were about to do to us. Then, in the morning, they ordered us to refill the pits. We even had to smooth them down on top with powdered rubble and the Germans just laughed like hyenas.

At the end of September 1944, they led all of us onto a square. They set fire to the underground level of the camp. This is when they burned the infirmary. There were continuous executions. The Germans were now shooting to death the last few hundred sick men and burned the clinic with all the dead inside together.

We were marched out of the camp at three in the morning, in the dead of night, and led away from Warsaw. We walked like this for five days on end. Not a bite of food all that time. At night, we sucked on grass from the fields. We ripped out every kind of weed and tried to keep ourselves alive this way. When we came to a river, the inmates would bend down to drink and the Germans shot them dead at water's edge. Many people tumbled into the water and were shot again. Red currents swirled all through the river.

There were now about 4,000 of us. We were all that had survived of the over 10,000 men who were shipped to the camp in Warsaw during the year 1943, all that had stayed alive were the 4,000 of us.

They loaded us into freight cars. One hundred and twenty jammed into each car. They beat us and rammed us into the walls of the wagons to make more room. They were sending us back to Oświęcim. . . .

Eyewitness Testimony 58. Building the V-1

Y.F. Born in Piotrków, Poland, in 1923; lived there. Recorded by Yankiv Fishman in New York in 1954. The witness tells of his ordeals working in the Bełżec labor camp in 1940. He escaped from the camp with a resistance group made up of his countrymen and they continued their work back in Piotrków together with the help of the *Yidnrat*. He was caught and made to work at the local glass factory. During the *Aussiedlung* of Piotrków, he was to be deported to the munitions works at Pionki. He continues.

When the sixteen members of the *Yidnrat* and its institutions were arrested and shot a few weeks later,[1] the Jews of Piotrków lost all hope and sank into despair. All of us were expecting the worst now. Our terror and panic grew from hour to hour.

The first *Aussiedlung*, which meant the liquidation of the Piotrków Jewish community, was started in October 1942. Twenty-five thousand Jews were transported to Treblinka, and of them, almost no one survived. A thousand people were shot dead in the streets during the *Aussiedlung*. As the Jews were driven from one place to another over the years, then finally herded into Piotrków, their number had grown to 25,000. During the years '39 to '42, masses of Jews had fled to Piotrków from the provinces.[2] The *Aussiedlung* went on for ten full days. Those of us who worked at the "Kara" Glass Factory were locked up inside. We had to sleep in the building during the night. We couldn't find out what was happening in the city. The day after the catastrophe, they let us out of the building to sleep at home, and as we walked through the city, we saw nothing but total desolation before our eyes. There wasn't a Jew left behind in Piotrków—my mother and all her children were gone. We just dropped to the ground and rocked back and forth, wailing over the tragedy. A small ghetto had been left for those who were kept inside the "Kara" and "Akapa."[3] About 1,000 people. No more.

In September 1943, 150 people were removed from the glass factory. I was part of this transport along with my father. My brother was left inside the factory with another 350 people. We were shipped to Pionki, which is in the Radom District. There were 5,000 Jews imprisoned in the camp at Pionki. Of these 5,000, 1,500 of us were made to work in the gunpowder factory. The factory was built deep in the woods. We were guarded by Ukrainians. This had been a gunpowder plant from before the war, too. There were explosions and fires every day. The gunpowder was produced from cotton, paper, [inaudible], and whiskey. During the time I was here—three months —twenty-five Jewish women were burned to death. My father also worked here. There was food, sometimes. They started letting us remove a liter of whiskey when the work was over. We sold it inside the camp. It's true.

Most of the victims of the explosions were Jews. The Germans made us work without any kind of safety precautions at all. The rest of the Jews in camp, the 3,500, worked at unloading freight trains and other slave labor. After working here for three months, my father and I were led into a just-cleared, sealed-off area in the forest. Sixteen men and twenty-four women were brought here. This was a top-secret area. We were completely cut off from the outside world here—like in a concentration camp. This is where we built the V-1 missiles. We had injuries all over our bodies from the work—we were constantly burned, slashed, and maimed. We performed acts of sabotage all the time. One time, the Germans caught three Jews who tried to blow up the plant and shot them. I don't know exactly what they did or if there was any proof, but these murderers didn't need any reasons to execute them.

This was the situation till July 1944. The Russian army was attacking. The whole complex was liquidated and we were all shipped away to different camps. My father and me were taken to Oświęcim. We were only inside Oświęcim one day. They shipped us on to Sosnowiec. We were made to work in an oil-drum factory here. This is what they made here before the war, too. There were about 500 Jews working here, together with another 300 Russian prisoners-of-war. The factory was situated outside the city. The SS were the guards here, and controlled us. They beat us and shot and hanged us. Many of us escaped, but almost all were then captured and hanged. The people could see the Germans were *"in dreyrd,"* that the war was ending, and they just lost all patience.

In December 1944, my father and I were sent to Mauthausen in a huge transport. The Germans had crowded together thousands of Jews, Russians, and all other nationalities here. We—my father and I—worked at the Messerschmidt Airplane Factory. The factory was built back up in the mountains. We estimated that there must have been around 100,000[4] slaves here.

We're bombed all the time by Allied planes. There were a few small concrete structures for shelters. That was all there was for a mass of 10,000 people. The Germans scattered like poisoned rats. The huge mass of people panicked and everyone rushed toward the small enclosures, and this was how a large number were trampled to death and smothered every time. I practically never saw my father at Mauthausen. We didn't work on the same shift.

On May 5, 1945, the Americans entered the camp, led by a brass band playing march music. In a panic, I ran around looking for my father but couldn't find him. I ran into the administration office, which was now taken over by Americans. They checked the camp records. They told me my father died here just a few days ago. But they wouldn't tell me how. Maybe the reason wasn't put down in the files. I felt deathly ill. I was swollen all over. I was kept in the hospital five months. I left for Italy. I was brought to Italy by the soldiers of the Jewish Brigade.[5] This was just before the Russians overran Mauthausen.

In 1946, I was brought to Germany when they found me a place in Feldafing. I married a girl there in 1947 who also worked in Pionki at the V-1 missile plant. That same year, we were brought to America.

After Liberation, I found out my brother had survived and was in London. He escaped while we were being deported from the glass factory in Piotrków and had spent all those years till Liberation in the forests. We started writing letters and he finally agreed to come to America. He was given citizenship and supports himself in New York.

Eyewitness Testimony 59. The Death March

E.G. Born in Šeduva, Lithuania, in 1922; interned in Kaunas, Stutthof, and other concentration camps during the Occupation. Recorded by Yankiv Fishman in New York in 1954. The witness recounts her ordeals in the Kaunas (Slobodka) Ghetto and the adjoining concentration camp. She then continues.

I was now past exhaustion and the rags just hung from my body. I come back into Kovne.[1] To the ghetto. Every day, there was a new *aktsye*. Against different groups. Especially against the kids. There were also separate ones against old people and separate ones against the sick. I was only inside the Kovne Ghetto a few days this time. I'm marched off to the train station with a large group of Jews. We're supposed to be deported to Latvia. I had heard before this that the camps in Latvia were death camps. I had no positive information, just as I had no sure idea where they were taking me now, but I hid in the train station anyway. It was better to stay behind here alone than to be in Latvia. I crawled behind the tall parterre curtains there and crouched, hunched over, till the group was sent away and the guards split up. I walked back into the ghetto. It was almost impossible to get inside now. Almost anybody I met could have informed the Germans I'd escaped from the transport. I lied my way in and walked through the gates, telling them I fainted at the station and was sent back because of this. It worked.

The *aktsyes* in the ghetto were so complete, that by August 1944,[2] only about 7,000 people were left alive. Right at the beginning, in 1941, the Lithuanians slaughtered 30,000 Jews. From that time till now, 23,000 other Jews were murdered or deported. Of the 60,000 Jews who'd been driven into the cramped Kovne Ghetto, no more than these 7,000 were now left alive.

Now, in August 1944, they're sending the rest of us to Stutthof. The Kovne Ghetto is empty. All of us knew what Stutthof meant— that's where Jewish bones are turned to soap. What could we do now? I couldn't believe it when these killers gave out ordinary food for the trip—bread and butter—to deceive us. All my things were taken from me in Stutthof and I was handed the striped camp uniform. Two Jews from Kovne, Luria and Margolies, got special protection working for the Germans. They looked as if they were all dressed up for a wedding. It was a miracle I only stayed here three and a half weeks. I was sent to a *Feldlager* close to Stutthof. They kept us in tents. But even this was better than being in Stutthof. There was more food here than in Stutthof. As long as you're out in the fields, there's always grass to keep you from starving to death. You find corn sometimes or stumble on a potato or a turnip. I worked in fields that covered a whole region, and stretched over many villages. They were managed by German peasants. The inmate *Älteste* was a Jewish girl from Germany—she was about twenty-five. Her name was Lea-Aris. She was really a fine person. And this was incredible, because the *Sturmbannführer* was a savage murderer. If it weren't for this girl, many of us would have been killed right in the fields. We worked those fields eight straight months. There were 500 of us there—all women.

Now they're taking us to a spot further from the front. They march us on foot during the days and we spend the nights in stables. We starved gradually. We knew they were retreating deeper into Germany. They were terrified the Russians would reach us any moment. On the seventh day, I finally escaped with four other girls. We ran back from where we came. We stopped into a peasant woman's cottage and told her and her son a tale—that we were Lithuanians and our overseer had run away. They believed us and even acted sympathetic. They let us stay there four weeks. They left out food for us. A neighbor of theirs, a Pole, also sent over food. And suddenly—this was just two days before Liberation—we're all arrested. We girls, the peasant woman, and her son, and the Pole and a couple of other people. They did this because we disobeyed the order for everyone to evacuate the countryside when the front had opened up here. None of us even heard the order. They put us "Lithuanians" in prison.

We were inside the jail twenty-four hours. We were then taken under an escort of German gendarmes into the next village. They also added a Lithuanian *shaygets* to the group and he proved right away what he was made of. He told them as soon as he saw us that we were lying, that we were really Jews. The Russians were so close. We tried to convince the escort we were Lithuanians by acting like them and got the guards' attention away from that criminal until we couldn't keep it up any more and had to offer some "proof" we were right. They finally left him behind somewhere and took us into a village with great formality, handing us over to the mayor as "Lithuanian girls." The mayor, a very old German, received us well. He wrote us out a pass to let us stay with a peasant. He was completely submissive to us and told us in great "piety" that it was God's will that this unfortunate war end now. The peasant also tried to make a good impression on us. He brought in a bucket of water for us to wash in and then got us some food. He asked us what kind of girls we were. "Lithuanians," we said right away. He told us—and acted as if he had no regrets—that the Russian army was positioned just outside the area. He told us not to leave the house until the Russians saw all of us together. He was almost hysterical about this and we had to calm him down and agree. He was overcome with relief. His wife, his boys, and daughter—complete peasants—couldn't do enough for us now. They pushed steaming bowlfuls of hot food under our noses. The peasant woman and her daughters gave us their better clothes to wear instead of the rags we had on. They kept this up for eight days. Then, Russian patrols came in. The army was taking control of the village. We declared openly we were Jews. This happened February 20, 1945. We spent the rest of that day with the peasants. It was pathetic how he begged us to stay by his side. But we left, thanking the peasant and his family for their help.

We traveled to Thorn.[3] We met some other girls from our *Feldlager* here. We were received by a Jew. He brought us to the Red Cross. They make us nurses here. What relief! I'm dressed like an immaculate nurse here. I sleep in a regular bed. I can eat my own food. Liberation.

I worked in the hospital four months. The work was hard, but my girl friends and I felt lucky. Where was there left to go? I knew the tragic fate of my whole family, of the whole *shtetl* of Shadovo. But we had to stop working in the end. There was still a world outside and we had to go to it. Our work releases were handed to us. We took the train to Łódź. We know Jews are starting to appear in Łódź —the ones left from the camps. We thought we might be able to get back to Lite[4] from here.

In Łódź, I broke down in tears when I saw all the Jews who had struggled to survive the war. I was sure there wasn't a Jew left alive in the world. I was introduced to my future husband in Łódź. We fell in love. We were married in the year 1946. A half-year after our wedding, we traveled through Austria and stayed for a while in Linz. In 1949, we were brought to America. Three and a half years ago, my Khanele was born.

Eyewitness Testimony 60. Belated Revenge

R.F. Born in Będzin, Poland, in 1924; lived there. Recorded by Yankiv Fishman in Tel Aviv (?) in 1954.

. . . . The first *Aussiedlung* was in 1942.[1] During the raid, the Germans shot anyone they found in the street and fired blindly into the buildings. Stacks of murdered Jews started piling up on the sidewalks. Since my father-in-law was on the *Judenrat,* he knew this was the start of a much more tragic plan. He had seen signs of it already. And suddenly, by a strange miracle, a German who'd just been sent here from Germany with his family, dragged us into his house. I can't tell you how this friendship between my father and this German started. Drescht is his name. He was completely devoted to us. Didn't want to act as the other Germans were. He kept us in his house till the *Aussiedlung* was over. But now we expected the worst and knew we'd be deported in the end.

Oh yes. A year earlier—mid-1941—my father was arrested as a *"zakładnik."*[2] The *Kehileh* ransomed the fifteen "hostages" from imprisonment for ten pounds of gold and fifteen pounds of silver.

On August 1, 1943, we were expecting a new *aktsye*. For week after week, the merciless German terror against the Jews in the city had been increasing every day. We were scared to step out into the street. The German *Kommandant* Mitschko and his German assistant, Dörflen, walked through the streets all day and shot Jews for sport as if they were shooting birds. The Jews of the city built bunkers and hid in them. We were also hidden inside a bunker. We stayed in that one bunker for seventeen straight days. There was no food left. My brother and my father-in-law left the bunker to try to find some produce. But the Germans pulled up, uncovered the hideout, and dragged us all away. That same day, we were transported to Sosnovits. Why we didn't try to hide this time at Drescht's, I don't know. We were put inside the labor camp at Sosnovits. There were about 5,000 other Jews here. I was put to work sorting the stolen Jewish belongings. Everything was sent to Germany—both scraps and valuables. Then there was a big *selektsye*. My sister Regine, my brother, and I hid inside the barracks till the tragedy was over. My father and mother and my sister who'd already been given away in marriage, together with her husband and our youngest sister, were sent off to Oświęcim. My father was forty-nine then, my mother forty-two, the married sister twenty-four, her husband was thirty-three, and the youngest sister was only fifteen.

The three of us now stayed together. Regine was our protector. She was like our mother to us. She was tall, blonde, and very beautiful. We were in the camp till December—for three months after the *Aussiedlung* of our family. Then the Germans transported us along with a large group of Jews to Oświęcim. When we got to Oświęcim, we found out our family had been exterminated as soon as they arrived. We were also put into a kind of "quarantine" in Oświęcim. They started getting us ready. Our heads were shaved and numbers were scraped into our arms. At this point, our brother Duvid was taken away from us. We lost him. We have no word about his fate. I kept close to Regine like a child at its mother's apron. Now there were only the two of us. A *Kapo*, this German female called "Bloody Mary," beat us up all the time because we didn't give up the gold we had hidden here. It was no use talking to her. She was a beast. She fell into ecstasy when she lashed us with her belt.

After six weeks in Oświęcim, we were sent into Birkenau, right next to Oświęcim. We were able to survive here. Both of us worked in the munitions factory. A few weeks later, we were secretly handed a short note from our brother, from Duvid! He wrote that he was in Birkenau, but we couldn't meet him. After a time, we ran into him while they were marching the different battalions off to the labor sites. We stayed with him for about two minutes. We all of us couldn't stop crying.

We worked twelve hours a day locked up inside the factory. There was almost no food. Typhus raged rampant among the girls. There was a woman at the factory who had contacts in the underground "cells" and they were in touch with a partisan unit outside the camp. Some other girls and myself, we brought out small amounts of ammunition and gave them to the woman every day. Hössler,[3] the *Kommandant* of the women's camp, found out about it. I was arrested together with fourteen other girls. I was thrown into a dark dungeon. The other girls were also down there. Hössler soon came down with two other Germans. They ordered us to strip off our clothes. We were flogged across our bare bodies with whips. Blood poured from our torn flesh. We blacked out. When we came to, we tried to crawl up from the dungeon. I could barely get up. Four of the girls were then publicly hanged on the *Appelplatz*. Two of them were from Bendien: *Froh* Shapirshtayn, thirty-two years old, and *Froh* Estushe Gertler, thirty years old. Shapirshtayn cried out, "Oh, how you Germans have lost this war!" The Germans there kicked her in the groin for this.[4]

At the end of 1944, they sent us out of Birkenau.[5] The talk was that the Russians were here. The Allies started bombing just outside the camp. Germans were killed. Houses right outside the death camp fence burned down! They forced us on a march that lasted six days. All of us went on foot. The Germans just kept shooting into the group all along the way. Whoever was near them was finished—they were sure to be shot. Bullets streaked by over our heads. We were even bombed along this road, too. Our girls died from the Allied bombs. Could the Allied pilots have mistaken us for Nazis? The only small consolation we got were the German corpses scattered among our own.

We got to Chorzów in Upper Silesia. We stopped here for no more than two days, then had to get back on the march. And they kept pushing us, faster and faster. Soon, we were in Ravensbrück. We were kept here three weeks. Besides being tortured all the time by the German male and female SS, we were beaten and terrorized here by Russian and Ukrainian girls—prisoners like us. They were nothing but "boot-lickers." That's why the Germans made them overseers. They were often worse animals than the SS women. After three weeks, we were moved out of there, again on foot. We dragged ourselves on with our last bit of strength. Girls dropped dead from total exhaustion. The German killers shot those who were still trying to crawl along the ground. We reached the outskirts of Leipzig and were thrown into some crumbling barracks. We could at least rest here. There was even a spoon given out with the food. And the little food we got here was still more than we got till now, which was nothing.

It was March 1945 by now, and we were evacuated. They brought us to Dachau. An SS woman told me that anything could happen now—it would soon be the end. There weren't any young Germans here anymore, male or female. They just vanished. The camp *Kommandant* was an old German man. He addressed us and said that when peace came, we should surrender to the Americans, not the Russians. But while he was giving this political talk, we were starving to death. The camp personnel got their rations from the airlift. For us—nothing. If we stole a few potatoes, we were beaten almost to death. This happened to me so many times.

Then, all of a sudden, I spotted that old German of ours in camp, the one from Bendien, Drescht. The one who had hidden our family in his home. He had on the inmate "stripes." "What happened to you?" I asked. He told me the "swines" had condemned him to five years hard labor because he was for the Jews. I was glad to see him.

Liberation came soon. The Russian soldiers were here. They fell on us girls like wild men. They couldn't keep their hands off. I knew immediately what would stop them. I told them we were *"Yevreyki."* They looked at us as if we were from another world, then they started mocking us and jeering at us, those anti-Semites. They said Jews were cowards and had put up no resistance during the war and other lies like that.

An order came and the Russians were led off somewhere. I left for Feldafing. When I got there, I suddenly saw my brother Duvid from a distance. I swooned. He cried like a little child and held me and kissed me and wouldn't let me go for a long time. Our happiness knew no limit. In Feldafing, I met a young man, a *katzetler*. We became friends. We were married here. There was a big crowd at our wedding. Even that good German, Drescht, was among the guests.

From Feldafing, we left for Munich.

In 1948, I had two chance meetings when I was able to take revenge. Walking in the street, I ran into Dörflen, the assistant to the German *Kommandant* in Bendien, Mitschko. They used to shoot Jews every day just for the sport, for the "pleasure" it gave them. I stopped him. Germans closed in on us and *katzetler* came running. I explained to everyone who this was—he was a murderer! He acted like a sissy, like he wouldn't hurt a fly, and whined that he'd never even been in Bendien. The other Germans protected him, defending his lies. They threatened to get even if we didn't leave him alone. A couple of the *katzetler* started slapping that filth around, but the

Germans were screaming: "Get your bloody hands off!" Police came after a while. Some months later, I got a letter from the Nürnberg Tribunal asking me to appear as a witness in the proceedings against Dörflen. I traveled to Nürnberg. I was at the trial. The first step was to identify Dörflen from among ten Germans who were paraded before me. I pointed to him at once. I even told the court I remembered Dörflen was lame. The court checked his leg and proved I was telling the truth. Then Dörflen, that cold-blooded killer, broke down crying and whimpering that it wasn't his fault. I don't know the court's decision. The verdict was given later and I didn't wait around for it. I went back to Munich.

The second meeting was also in Munich. I was walking in the street with my husband when I saw "Bloody Mary" coming toward us. She looked like a slut. This was the *Kapo* in Oświęcim who beat up my sister Regine and me every day so we'd give up the gold we had hidden in camp. German men and women ran up from all sides and tried to save the woman. My husband and our friends held on to her while I ran to get a policeman. I came back with an officer. He took down my name and address. I was called as a witness at the trial. "Bloody Mary" was brought into the courtroom from her cell. I told the court what she had done to me and my sister, who had died so tragically in Birkenau. The judges lowered their heads. "Bloody Mary" was so crazed in the court, she screamed at the top of her voice with all her hate how she wished she had managed to choke me, too. The chief judge of the tribunal banged his gavel hard and told her to shut up. I got some satisfaction from this. This she-beast was condemned to seven years in prison.

Eyewitness Testimony 61. A "Voyage of the Damned"

D.H.S. Born in Łódź in [inaudible]. Recorded by Dovid Botwinik in Montreal in 1955. In August 1944, the witness was deported from the Łódź Ghetto to Auschwitz together with her family and, two weeks later, was transported to Stutthof. During an *Appel*, she was kicked in the groin by an SS woman, collapsed, and was dragged off to the infirmary. She became infected with typhus there. She continues her account.

With God's help, I lived through this sickness and started recovering, but just then—on April 20, 1945—Stutthof was bombarded from the air and ground. The bombing went on day and night.

It was said the Russians were now only eighteen kilometers from Stutthof. Eight days before, the camp *Kommandant* ran away and left three or four Ukrainians in his place with big dogs, and they were now terrorizing the camp. The Stutthof camp was enormous and from one end to the other it was burning down from the air attacks. Countless numbers of *Katzetler* were killed by the bombs. I myself was lucky, because a bomb hit our ward and three-quarters of the sick were killed or wounded. The day after, the last survivors were herded together—the Germans said they were transporting us out—and we were marched off on foot for a whole day and night.

There were now only 3,000 of us left alive—just Jewish women. A fourth of this group collapsed and couldn't go on. Wagons were also brought along, loaded with casualties from the infirmary. They pushed us without stop. And we were driven like this until we got to the harbor. I think it was Danzig. There were ships everywhere. The sea was red all around from the fires which burned out of control.

They packed us inside a cargo ship which had just been bombed and was all hollowed out. We were swimming in stinking waste, either because of the fire or from animals. The odor was so bad, it was almost impossible to stay conscious down in the hold.

While they were loading us into the ship, we saw about six, seven, or maybe ten male inmates standing there. From where they'd come, I don't know. But we knew what kind they were right away. These were Ukrainian murderers dressed in round, red Russian fur caps who burned people in the crematoria. They were put on board and appointed by the SS to be *Kapos* over us. They beat us and hounded us to death. Once the ship was a few hours on its course and out in the middle of the sea, the SS started an *aktsye,* and the inmates who were wounded lightly from the bombing at Stutthof, who would have survived, were selected out to be thrown live into the water. Almost half of all the people on board were thrown in. The Ukrainians did this. Oy! the people's screams! Oy! those people yelling! I'll never be able to forget it. They were all women from Kovne[1] and Łódź and all of them were only wounded lightly.

We sailed and sailed and went into ports many times. Which, I can't remember. But no port would let us stay because there was a yellow flag flying from the top, meaning the ship was supposed to be carrying people with contagious diseases on board. Besides the two main SS men and the Ukrainians, there was also this captain on board, dressed in a white uniform, and the sailors, dressed in regular military uniforms.

At every port, the captain declared he was carrying women refugees and asked permission to unload them. But he got the same answer everywhere: *"Scheiss mit den Häftlingen! Sie schmeissen in Wasser hinein!"*[2]

At one port, they did agree to let us land. We thought we were saved. Can you imagine it? After so many days without food? We were filthy, the lice were feeding on us. We were ordered off the ship. The SS pulled up, along with captains of other ships anchored in the harbor, to gawk at us and they ordered us to line up to find out what kind of "material" we were. They looked us up and down—they had to get drunk to do it. They stumbled and fell on their backs and screamed with laughter: "*Cha, Cha, Cha, Cha, Cha!*" And we just stood there and pleaded: "*Gnediger Herr, nemt ints of, mier haben Hunger, nemt ints of!*"[3] But it was no use. We were pushed back into the ship and sailed on.

Alongside one port, some German soldiers threw two or three bucketsful of crusts and moldy bread onto the deck and down into the hold. We almost killed each other scrambling for it.

The whole time we were on the ship, for all the eleven days, all I drank was the salty sea water. I had found a cup that once belonged to other inmates. I tore off a piece from my dress, made it into a long strip, tied one end to the cup, and brought up some water from the sea. Three or four days before Liberation, the captain announced: "Today you'll be getting sweet water." Oy! What celebration there was! What joy! I was sure I'd be the first to get the sweet water since I had the cup. But when the captain saw it, he threw it into the sea. I cried so hard then—even more than when they killed my parents.

On the fifth day of our endless floating on the sea, we were bombed for the first time. Five of us were killed. Right beside me, a piece of shrapnel shattered the head of a woman from our convoy, a blonde— I can still see her. During this first bombing, the whole ship was blasted full of gaping holes—even more than before. We lay in the hold. The SS and Ukrainians also jumped down there and lay among us during the bombing. Besides the people who were killed, there were many wounded.

The second bombing happened a day later. This time, many more people were killed—shattered skulls, shattered shrapnel.

A day before Liberation—on May third early in the morning—the ship was attacked a third time. The bombs destroyed the engine room and the whole ship went up in flames. Everyone was screaming! The last shouts of many were: "*Shma Yisruel!*" The blood just flowed all over our bodies. The ship started taking on water. We were down below and not everyone managed to clamber up to the deck—many more would have survived if they could have reached it. I was able to pull myself up to the deck. A piece of shrapnel shot into the back of my head—I still have the scar—and the blood washed all over me. The captain and two sailors were also wounded. The ship slowly started to sink. The water swirled all around the deck. I and the other women were hanging from the ropes which were fastened from the top of the mast, or the smokestack—how can anyone describe this? We were out in the middle of the sea. Four or five sailors crawled into some rubber tubes and jumped into the water because they thought they saw rescue ships in the distance and started swimming in that direction. After some time, a rescue launch pulled alongside us. The deck of the ship could no longer be seen below us.

Everyone who could, tried to swing themselves into the boat or grab on to the sides and climb on board. The German sailors screamed and beat us back: "*Wir können nicht so viel hereinnehmen!*"[4]

The screams, the pleading, the dead, and the half-dead—oh help me! Only fifteen of the women were let on board the boat. I was among them. Besides us, they took on the wounded captain and both the wounded and ablebodied sailors from the ship. The wounded sailors later lay in the same English hospital they treated me in.

Each was jealous when they took someone else aboard and not them. A mother and a daughter who weren't let on board yelled to the high heavens and in the end, just as the boat was pulling away, they threw themselves—right before my eyes—into the sea and drowned. What happened to the rest of the women I don't know, because the rescue launch sped away. Of the 2,000 women who had been on the ship then, only thirty-three people survived. Of those, I know seven. Every year, as I've heard, they place a wreath on the boat. It's still anchored in Kiel to this day—in the harbor.

We sailed the whole night of May 3–4 from out at sea toward the shore. We kept hearing deafening bombardments along the way and fantastic explosions lighting up the horizon. We saw countless numbers of burning ships and huge cargo steamers packed full of people everywhere we passed. The soldier convoys were all on fire and the Germans were jumping into the burning waters. It was all one huge conflagration.

We women were trembling and the sailors repeated over and over: "Everyone keep order! Everyone keep order! They mustn't see who we are!" and they ordered us to stretch out on the bottom.

They also had a radio receiver on the boat. One sailor—he was young, a German with a conscience—tried to cheer us up: "Don't worry. The war's over. I also have a wife and a child. They're going to free all of us. The radio said so. Just be calm."

On the morning of May fourth, we docked in the harbor at Kiel. The entire port was in flames. The whole city was burning. At the docks, we could already make out German civilians with the *Militz* armbands. But they still refused to let us on shore. Suddenly, a captain drove up and gave orders: "Let them off! Let them off! *Heraus! Heraus!*" They stood over us with whips, screaming: "*Schnell heraus!*[5] *Schnell heraus!*" There was a bombed-out building on the other side of the port and we ran inside.

Three or four hours later, tanks rolled in with Englishmen inside. The *Militz* crawled out of their hiding places a while later and told the English: "Over there you'll find Jewish refugees we rescued from the *Kazeten.*"

The English treated us really well. They kissed us and tried to give us new hope and said to us: "Just you wait, luvs. We won't be a moment and we'll get us all some food!"

The English boarded us on a ship and three hours later, they had brought us to Friedrichshof. In the beginning, we wouldn't let them take us on board the ship—we were still terrified, still couldn't believe they were really Englishmen, and not SS who were trying to deceive us again.

In Friedrichshof, we were quartered in an army camp. I was then transferred into a field hospital together with the other wounded women and placed under treatment. Many of the women breathed their last here. When I entered the field hospital, I weighed twenty-eight and a half kilos.[6]

Eyewitness Testimony 62. Łódź-Auschwitz-Dachau

P.H. Recorded by Duvid Rom as a deposition for the Canadian Jewish Congress in Montreal in February 1946.

I was born in Poland in the city of Łódź. I'm fifteen years old now. At the age of nine, I was locked up inside the ghetto together with my family. We suffered hunger and misery. People swelled up and died. In 1943,[1] the Germans took away all the children to the age of ten. I had a younger brother who was seven. We hid together with him, lying in an attic without food or drink. In a week, there was a new *aktsye* and the German SS charged into all the buildings looking for weak and emaciated people. I lay hidden along with my family and counted the shots. My father, like all the other men, had to go down into the courtyard for the *selektsye* and try to save the women and children this way. Can you imagine our heartbreak as our own *tahte* stands out in the courtyard about to be shot or deported any second? We were ecstatic when we saw our father and husband again, though he came back with the news the Germans had sent away children and shot their mothers. In the end, we survived even these days filled with terror and were saved for a short while. But there was one thing which kept us alive and gave us courage, and this is that we were all together. I couldn't value as a young child what it means to have a family of a father and mother. I only really appreciate it now that it's too late, when I'm left all alone, with no one.

In the middle of 1944, we were transported to Auschwitz. How painful was this day in my life—as we were getting off the trains, the Germans tore the wives away from their husbands and the mothers from their children. These heart-piercing cries and not being able to say goodbye! The people just went limp. I was torn between my parents. My mother sent me across to my father and my father sent me back to my mother. My mother had my little brother by her side and she said through her red, tear-filled eyes, "Go. Be with your father."

This was her intuition—that the worst would happen to me if I didn't go with him. I was almost left all alone among this vast group of crying people. In a second, a Jew who worked at unloading the bundles from the train ran over to me and said I'd be better off going with my father, with the grown-up men. After looking all over, I finally found my father again as he stood with his head bowed, crying like all the others. I took a place in line next to my father, in front of the German officer who was selecting the healthy men out from among the weak ones. He sent away all the other people and all the children to be burned. I was very flushed from crying and packed around with a lot of clothes, so the officer thought I looked fit, and I went up to him and declared boldly that I was seventeen. He looked me over and sent me off behind my father. Two days after coming to Auschwitz, I was given thin clothes and sent away with my father to the labor camp at Kaufbeuren.

We were 600 men. On the first morning, we were sent out to the sites. My father worked in the forest for two days and caught pneumonia. I tried to muster all my strength for this work and was beaten hard all the time. After eight days, my father got better but he was still too weak for the labor gangs. They put him in the infirmary—which was very bad. He died in two days. I was left all alone, without anyone or any hope for tomorrow. The number of dead grew from day to day. Of 600 Jews, only 320 were left. The camp went on operating for another week, and by then, the last exhausted remnant of 125 people were transferred to Dachau. I looked like a corpse, with no strength left at all. We were put into the infirmary, but forty other people had died in the train on the way there—they couldn't have held out for another moment. Since I was the youngest here, the others gave me more food and I only started coming back to life after two long weeks. The doctor, who was French, felt sorry for me and didn't discharge me from the infirmary right away. He gave me light work to do inside the clinic. On April 25, all the Jews were packed into a transport that was headed for the Tyrol. This doctor tried to save me and write out a false diagnosis which confined me to bed, though I was already better. Both of us risked our lives doing this. But luckily, they crossed me off the transport list and I stayed behind in the infirmary.

On April 28, the Americans walked in. Thousands of people "rose from the dead" to come out on the grounds and stare at the liberators. The SS were marched past us with their hands stuck high in the air. I reacted coldly to all these signs of liberation—I had no reason to be glad. I fell into complete apathy. I watched the people sing and dance with joy and they seemed to me as if they'd lost their minds. I looked at myself and couldn't recognize who I was. I lost all sense of what had happened to me. After a long time, I began to understand. I was left all alone, without help and protection, without a living soul I could call my own. There were time I regretted having been left alive among these last survivors and handful of Jews. This was how the two months at Dachau passed. Many people died and many recovered. From Dachau, I was sent to a Jewish camp—Feldafing. I felt more at home here among my own brothers. The Jewish "Joint" did all it could to help. In a short while, I was sent to Heidelberg where, with the aid of the "Joint," I was put into the school for Jewish children. I only live today for the words my father said to me on his deathbed: "I'm already forty-three—I won't be able to survive this hell. But you—you're young, see to it our name isn't torn out from the pages of the world."

This keeps alive my spirit and I live with the hope for a better tomorrow.

GLOSSARY

"Adonoy yinukem domoy" (Heb.)—"May God avenge his shed blood."

Aktsye (Yid.)—Operation of deporting Jews to the death camps, or of killing them on the spot.

Älteste der Juden (Yid.)—Chairman of the Jewish Council.

Amkho (Yid.)—Jews as opposed to Gentiles.

Amtskommissar (Ger.)—Local high official, chief.

Appel (Ger.)—Callup.

Appelplatz (Ger.)—The camp square where callups were conducted.

Arbeitsamt (Ger.)—Labor office.

Arbeitsschein (Ger.)—Work permit.

Ashmedai (Yid.)—Devil.

"Ashre yoshvey veysekhu." (Heb.)—"Happy are they that dwell in Thy house" (Psalms 84:5).

Ausseidlung (Ger.)—Transfer of population; a euphemism for the deportation of Jews to the death camps.

Aybershter (Yid.)—God. (He who is above.)

Baley-mlukhe (Yid.)—Artisan.

Baley-tshive (Yid.)—Repentants.

Banderovsti—The extremist group of OUN (Organization of Ukrainian Nationalists) in Galicia under the leadership of Stepan Bandera, son of a Ukrainian priest, active before WW II.

Besmedresh (Yid.)—Prayer and study house.

Besoylim (Yid.)—Cemetery.

Blockälteste (Ger.)—Inmate head of barracks in concentration camp.

Blockschreiber (Ger.)—Barracks clerk in concentration camp, in charge of the evidence of the inmates.

Blokowa, Blokowy (Pol.)—Woman or man supervisor of barracks in concentration camp.

Brikhah (Heb.)—Underground smuggling out Jews to Palestine.

Bund—Jewish labor movement, founded in Tsarist Russia in 1897.

Davenen (Yid.)—Praying.

Daytshe (Yid.)—German.

Deka—Approximately 2.8 ounces.

D-Lager, Dulag, Durchgangslager (Ger.)—Transit camp.

Erev (Heb.)—The eve of Sabbath or holiday.

Eretz Yisrael, Erits Yisruel (Heb., Yid.)Land of Israel.

Feldlager (Ger.)—Field camp.
Folkshul (Yid.)—Public school.
Froh (Yid.)—Mrs.

"Gdzie jest Żydowka?" (Pol.)—"Where is the Jewess?"
Gemine (Yid.)—Jewish community board.
Gemoreh (Yid.)—Talmud.
Gemures (Yid.)—Volumes of the Talmud.
Gildn (Yid.)—*Zloty*, Polish coin.
Goy, goyeh, goyim (Yid.)—Masculine, feminine, and plural of
    Gentile.
Gymnazye (Yid.)—High school.

Häftling (Ger.)—Camp inmate.
Halb-Jude (Ger.)—Jew of mixed blood, specifically a person with at
    least one Jewish grandparent.
Hashem yisburekh (Heb.)—God, blessed be His name.
"Heraus!" (Ger.)—"Out!"
Hoyfyidn (Yid.)—Court Jews serving the rulers.

Judenrat (Ger.)—Jewish council appointed by the German authori-
    ties.
Judenjagd (Ger.)—Chasing of Jews.
Judenreferent (Ger.)—Official in charge of Jewish affairs.
Judenrein (Ger.)—Free, clean of Jews, used to denote areas from
    which Jews had been deported or killed off.
Judenvernichtungsbrigade (Ger.)—Brigade for annihilation of Jews.

Kaddish (Heb.)—Prayer said by a mourner; by extension, a male
    heir.
Kahle (Yid.)—Bride.
Kameraden (Ger.)—Friends.
Kanzilarieschreiber (Yid.)—Office clerk.
Kapo (Ger.)—Inmate supervisor in concentration camp.
Katzetler, katzetnik (Yid.)—Inmate of concentration camp.
Kehileh (Yid.)—Jewish community. Also used to denote the board of
    the community management.
Kennkarte (Ger.)—Identification card.
Khanike (Yid.)—Chanukah, the Festival of Lights.
Khazn, khzunim (Yid.)—Cantor, cantors.
Khol-hamoyed Paysekh (Yid.)—Days between the first and last days
    of Passover.
Khorbn (Yid.)—Holocaust.
Khsidim (Yid.)—Hasidic Jews.
Khzunes (Yid.)—Jewish liturgical music.

Kidushin (Heb.)—Wedding ceremony.
Kishefmakherin (Yid.)—Witch.
Klei koydesh (Yid.)—Officials carrying out religious functions.
Kloizn (Yid.)—Prayer houses.
Kol Nidre (Heb.)—Solemn prayer for Yom Kippur eve.
Komisarz (Pol.)—Police official.
Kommando (Ger.)—Unit of workers.
Kommandoführer (Ger.)—Head of a military or police unit for a special task; foreman of workers.
Kreishauptmann (Ger.)—County chief.
Kreiskommandant (Ger.)—Chief of county police.
Kuchälteste (Ger.)—Chief cook.
Kücher (Ger.)—Cook.
Kultusgemeinde (Ger.)—Jewish community.

Lag Boymer (Heb.)—Jewish spring holiday.
Lagerdirektor, Lagerführer (Ger.)—Concentration camp commandant.
Landesrat (Ger.)—County chief.
Landslayt, landsman (Yid.)—Countrymen, countryman.
Lausige (Ger.)—Dirty.
Lebensschein (Ger.)—Work permit, which extends the right to live.
Luftgaukommando (Ger.)—Air force detachment work unit.
Luftwaffe (Ger.)—Air force.

Makherin (Yid.)—Female speculator.
Mameh (Yid.)—Mother.
Mezuzes (Yid.)—Parchment scriptural scrolls affixed to doorpost of Jewish houses.
Mikve (Yid.)—Ritual bath.
Militz (Yid.)—Militia.
Minyen (Yid.)—Quorum of ten men for liturgical purposes.
Mishimed (Yid).)—Convert.
Mischling (Ger.)—Mongrel.
Mugen duvid (Yid.)—Star of David.

Nebenkommando (Ger.)—Affiliated work unit.

Oberschaarführer (Ger.)—Rank in SS hierarchy.
Obersturmführer (Ger.)—First lieutenant of SS.
"Oleyhu hashulem" (Heb.)—"May she rest in peace."
Ordnungsdienst (Ger.)—Jewish ghetto police.
Ortskommandant (Ger.)—Chief of local police.
"Oshamnu, bogadnu" (Heb.)—First words of confession of sins.

Pani, Panie (Pol.)—Mrs., Mr.
"Partizaner gayen" (Yid.)—"Partisans are marching."
Payes (Yid.)—Side curls.
Payrik (Yid.)—Chapter.
Paysekh (Yid.)—Passover.
"Podyom!" (Rus.)—"Move!"
Poyle Zion (Heb.)—Zionist Workers Party.
Präses—Chairman of council.

Rasn kvurim (Yid.)—To pray on graves.
"Ratuystsye!" (Rus.)—"Help!"
"Raus!" (Ger.)—"Get out!"
Reichsdeutsche (Ger.)—Ethnic German.
Reiterzugpolizei (Ger.)—Police cavalry.

Salo (Rus.)—Lard.
Schaarführer (Ger.)—Lower ranks in the SS hierarchy.
Schutzpolizei (Ger.)—Regular German police.
Sejm (Pol.)—Parliament.
Selektsye (Yid.)—Selection of Jews for death or forced labor.
Seyfer (Heb.)—Book; plural *sfurim*.
Shabbes (Yid.)—Sabbath.
Shabbes tzu nacht (Yid.)—Sabbath evening.
Shames (Yid.)—Sexton.
Shaygets (Yid.)—Gentile boy; plural *shgutsim*.
Shiel (Yid.)—Synagogue.
Shkhite (Heb.)—Massacre.
Shma Yisruel (Heb.)—Beginning of Jewish confession of faith.
Shoykhet (Yid.)—Ritual slaughterer.
Shtetl (Yid.)—A town in Eastern Europe with a large number (even a majority) of Jewish inhabitants.
Shtibl (Yid.)—Hasidic prayer room.
Shvues (Yid.)—Pentecost.
Sidirim (Yid.)—Prayerbooks.
Sifre toyre (Yid.)—Scrolls of the Torah.
Slęzak (Pol.)—Native of Silesia.
Sochnut (Heb.)—Agency; Jewish Agency for Palestine.
Sonderführer (Ger.)—Head of a Sonderkommando.
Sonderkommando (Ger.)—A police (or SS) commando for a special task.
"Stoi!" (Rus.)—"Stop!"
Stubdienste (Ger.)—Chambermaid.
Sturmbannführer (Ger.)—Lower ranks in the SS hierarchy.
Sztubowa (Pol.)—Supervisor of inmates in a single room.
Szwab (Pol.)—German.

Talis, talaysim (Heb.)—Prayer shawls.
Tahte, tata (Yid.)—Papa.
Tfilin (Heb.)—Phylacteries.
Tilim (Heb.)—Psalms.
Tilimlekh (Yid.)—Booklets of Psalms.
Toller (Yid.)—Dollars.
Toyre (Yid.)—Torah.
Transportenblock (Ger.)—Barrack of inmates destined for transportation.

Uhrl (Heb.)—Gentile.
Umschlagplatz (Ger.)—Place for loading Jews into trains for death camps.
Unterschaarführer (Ger.)—Lower rank in SS hierarchy.

Verboten (Ger.)—Forbidden.
"Verfluchte Juden" (Ger.)—"Cursed Jews."
Viduyim (Heb.)—Confessions before death.
Viertel Jude (Ger.)—See *Halb-Jude.*
Volksdeutsche (Ger.)—German minority groups long settled in other European countries.
"Voruzhye!" (Rus.)—"To arms!"
"Vorverts!" (Yid.)—"Forward!"
"Vperyod!" (Rus.)—"Forward!"

Wehrmacht (Ger.)—German armed forces.
Werkschutzkommando (Ger.)—Factory guard.

Yevrey, yevreyki (Rus.)—Jew, jewesses.
Yidishe (Yid.)—Jewish.
Yidn (Yid.)—Jews.
Yidnrat (Yid.)—*Judenrat.*
"Yimakh shemoy" (Heb.)—"May his name be erased."
Yontev (Yid.)—Holiday.
Yurtsat (Yid.)—Anniversary of death.

Zakładnik (Pol.)—Hostage.
Zayn libn numen (Yid.)—Euphemism for God.
Zeilappel (Ger.)—Callup for counting of camp inmates.
Ziel und Spiel (Ger.)—Aiming at people as a game.
Zugwachmann (Ger.)—Camp guard.
Zulage (Ger.)—Additional food ration.
Zyd, żydówka (Pol.)—Jew, jewess.

NOTES

Part One

1. Quoted in *Unity in Dispersion: A History of the World Jewish Congress* (New York: 1948), p. 109. Joseph Tenenbaum, "The Anti-Nazi Boycott Movement in the United States," *Yad Vashem Studies on the European Jewish Catastrophe and Resistance*, vol. III (Jerusalem: Yad Vashem, 1959), gives a somewhat more positive evaluation of the duration and effectiveness of the boycott movement.

2. Isaiah Trunk, *Judenrat: The Jewish Councils in Eastern Europe Under Nazi Occupation* (New York: Macmillan Publishing Co., 1972), pp. 372–73.

3. *Pinkas Zamoshch* (Memorial book of Zamosc), ed. by a Committee, (Buenos Aires: 1957), p. 951.

4. Trunk, *Judenrat.* loc. cit.

5. *Zygelboym Bukh* (New York: Unser Tsait, 1948), pp. 110–11. cf. Sara Erlichman, *Beyedey Tmayim* (Tel Aviv: 1975), p. 19, (Hebrew).

6. The food ration for a Jew contained approximately 300 calories per day.

7. *The Chronicle of the Łódź Ghetto* (YIVO Archives), (Polish).

8. Ella Lingens (Reiner), *Prisoners of War* (London: 1948), p. 142.

9. Nathan Eck, *Wanderings on the Roads of Death* (Jerusalem: Yad Vashem, 1960), p. 37, (Hebrew).

10. Elie A. Cohen, *Human Behavior in the Concentration Camp* (New York: W. W. Norton and Co., 1953), pp. 158–64.

11. Eck, op. cit., p. 130.

12. Cohen, op. cit., p. 167.

13. Emanuel, Ringelblum, *Ksovim fun Geto, 1942–1943* (Warsaw: Yiddish Bukh, 1963), vol. II, pp. 266–67, (Yiddish).

14. Peretz, Opoczynski, *Reshimot* (Tel Aviv: Ghetto Fighters House, Hakibutz Hameuchad, 1970) pp. 141–45 (Hebrew). Translation in Lucy Dawidowicz, *Holocaust Reader* (New York: 1976) pp. 199–201.

15. *Bleter far Geshikhte* (Warsaw: Jewish Historical Institute, 1948), vol. I, no. 2, p. 116.

16. Ibid., p. 119.

17. Ibid., pp. 112–13.

18. Ibid., vol. I, nos. 3–4, pp. 192–93.

19. Ibid., p. 197.

20. Shimon Huberband, *Kidush Hashem* (Tel Aviv: Zkhor, 1969), p. 85, (Hebrew).

21. Ibid., pp. 89–91, 103, 110–11.

22. See Part Two: Eyewitness Testimony No. 8.

23. Isaiah Trunk, *Lodzher Geto* (New York: Yad Vashem and YIVO, 1962), p. 411.

24. ———, *Judenrat: The Jewish Councils in Eastern Europe under Nazi Occupation* (New York: Macmillan, 1972), pp. 194–95.

25. Ibid.

26. Victor Frankl, *Man's Search for Meaning* (New York: Beacon Press, 1964), p. 33.

27. *Bleter far Geshikhte*, vol. I., nos. 3–4, pp. 101–2.

28. Trunk, *Lodzher Geto*, p. 410.

29. Sh. Glube, "Di Din Toyre," in *Fun letstn khurbn* (Munich: Central Historical Committee of Liberated Jews in the American Zone, 1947), No. 6, pp. 44–47, (Yiddish).

30. *Bleter far Geshikhte*, vol. I, no. 2, p. 112.

31. M. Litvin and M. Lerman, eds., *Dos bukh fun Lublin*, (Paris: Lubliner Komitet, 1952), pp. 503–8.

32. Trunk, *Judenrat*, p. 201, and *Geshtaltn un gesheenishn* (Buenos Aires: 1962), pp. 187–88, 229–30, (Yiddish). *Maladie de Famine: Recherches cliniques executées dans la Ghetto de Varsovie en 1942* (Warsaw: A.y.D.C., 1946).

33. *Bleter far Geshikhte*, vol. I, no. 2, p. 117.

34. M. Tenenboym-Tamaroff, *Dapim min hadleyka* (Tel Aviv: Hakibutz Hameuchad, 1948), p. 118, (Hebrew).

35. In Warsaw, during the night of April 17, 1942, the Gestapo dragged over fifty persons from their homes (mainly activists in the ghetto underground) and shot them in the streets.

36. Ringelblum, op cit., vol. I, pp. 353–54.

37. Sholem Grajek, "*Yitonut hamakhteret begeto*" in *Encyclopedia shel galuyot* (Tel Aviv: Khenat Entsiklopedia, 1953), vol. I, pp. 675–76, (Hebrew).

38. Liber Brener, *Vidersthand und umkum in chenstokhover geto* (Warsaw: 1951), pp. 54–55. Yisrael Gutman, *The Jews of Warsaw, 1939–1943: Ghetto Underground Uprising* (Warsaw: 1977), pp. 179–85, (Hebrew).

39. Trunk, *Lodzher Geto*, pp. 380, 407.

40. Trunk, *Judenrat*, p. 539.

41. Herman Kruk, *Togbukh fun vilner geto* (New York: YIVO, 1961), p. 356, (Yiddish).

42. *In di yorn fun yiddishn khurbn* (New York: Unser Tsait, 1948), pp. 64, 140.

43. Ringelblum, op. cit., vol. I, p. 354; Y. Gutman, op. cit., p. 179.

44. Trunk, *Lodzher Geto*, pp. 469–70.

45. Ibid., p. 386.

46. Philip Friedman, "Ukrainian-Jewish Relations During the Nazi Occupation," *YIVO Annual for Social Studies* (New York: 1958/59), vol. XII, pp. 278–79.

47. YIVO Archives, Berlin Collection, doc. Occ Eb. β.

48. Friedman, op. cit., pp. 287–94

49. YIVO, Berlin Collection, doc. Occ E3a-14, p. 5.

50. Ibid., doc. Occ E3-30, p. 9.

51. Ibid., doc. Occ E3–30.

52. YIVO Archives, Eyewitness testimony of a former inhabitant of Goniądz.

53. Memo of the Lublin *Judenrat* to the *Landrat* of October 10, 1939. Photocopy in the Archives of Ghetto Fighters House, in the kibbutz of the same name, Israel.

54. *In di yorn fun yiddishn khurbn* (New York: Unset Tsait, 1948), pp. 18, 62.

55. Melekh Neistadt, *Khurbn un oyfshtand fun di yidn in Varshe* (Tel Aviv: Vaad Hagola shel Hahistadrut Haklalit, Yiddisher Natsionaler Arbeter Verband in Amerika, 1948), vol. I, p. 129, (Yiddish).

56. Haim Lazar-Litayi, *Metsuda shel Varsha* (Tel Aviv: Mekhon Zhábotynski, 1963), pp. 87–100, (Hebrew).

57. London Archives of *Studjum Polski Podziemnej*, Radiogram No. 347, January 4, 1943, file no. 4.

58. Ibid., file no. 4.

59. Ibid., An item in *Robotnik* (underground organ of the Polish Socialist Party) of April 3, 1944, concerning the murder of eight Jews and a Pole who had hidden them. See also Part II, Eyewitness Testimony 48.

60. Ibid., "Materials received in London from the Delegate of the (Underground) Government"; report of Berezowski (code name of Dr. Leon Feiner) to the representative of the Bund in London of November 15, 1943, in *In di yorn fun yiddishn khurbn* (New York: Unser Tsait, 1948), p. 113.

61. Letter in the Archives of Yad Vashem, Israel (copy).

62. Archives of *Studjum Polski Podziemnej,* file no. 4, Report of the *Rada Pomocy Żydom* of October 23, 1943.

63. Ibid., file no. 4, Sentences of the underground court for persecuting Jews.

64. See, for instance, Mark Dworzecky's *Yerushelaim dlite in kamf un umkum* (Paris: Yiddisher Folksferband in Frankraych, Yiddisher Natsionaler Arbeter Verband in Amerika, 1948), pp. 53–55, (Yiddish).

65. Trunk, *Judenrat,* pp. 413–20; Ringelblum, op. cit., vol. II, 42–44.

66. Ringelblum, vol. II, p. 330.

67. Ibid., p. 22.

68. *Trials of War Criminals Before the Nuremberg Military Tribunals* (Washington, D.C.: U.S. Government Printing Office), vol. VI, p. 426.

69. Reszo Kasztner, *Der Bericht des juedischen Rettungs-Komitees aus Budapest, 1942–1945* (Basel: Vaad Hatsala, 1946), p. 35.

70. *Trials of the Major War Criminals Before the International Military Tribunal* (Washington, D.C.: U.S. Government Printing Office, 1949, Blue Series), vol. XXVII, pp. 4–8.

71. *Nazi Conspiracy and Aggression* (Washington, D.C.: U.S. Government Printing Office, 1946–1948), vol. V, pp. 700 ff.

72. Eyewitness Testimony No. 8 in Part II.

73. *Bleter far Geshikhte,* vol. IV, no. 2, 1951, p. 199.

74. *Institut für Zeitgeschichte* (Munich), doc. FB85/2.

75. *Jewish Resistance During the Holocaust. Proceedings of the Conference On Manifestations of Jewish Resistance* (Jerusalem: Yad Vashem, April 7–11, 1968), p. 473; cf. Ringelblum, op. cit., vol. II, p. 11.

76. Quoted in B. Mark's *Powstanie w getcie Warszawskim* (Warsaw: Yiddish Bukh, 1963), pp. 302–3, (Polish).

77. Copy of the Report of Jürgen Stroop, Chief of the SS and Police in the District of Warsaw, to the Higher SS and Police Chief in the General Government, YIVO Archives; Report of SS General Fritz Katzmann, doc. L-018, *IMT,* Blue Series, vol. XXXVII, pp. 391–431.

78. Isaiah Trunk, *"Mikhtavim myshnot hashoa." Yediyot bet lokhamey hagetaot* (Israel: April 1957), nos. 1–2, pp. 22–29, (Hebrew).

79. *Commandant of Auschwitz: The Autobiography of Rudolf Hoess* (London: Weidenfeld and Nicolson, 1959), pp. 165–67.

80. *Jewish Resistance During the Holocaust,* p. 475.

81. Answers to a questionnaire, YIVO Archives, nos. 611, 618, and 623.

82. Trunk, *"Mikhtavim,"* p. 25.

Part Two

All place names appear in the forms used within the geopolitical boundaries of September 1, 1939.

Eyewitness Testimony 1

1. Tykocin, Białystok District. Dvokeh is unidentified; probably a nearby village.

2. "You can't get away without some penalty."

3. "Why has only this small crowd assembled here and no more?"

4. "Within half an hour, everyone must assemble here! If not, the *Judenrat* gets shot on the spot!"

5. German-Yiddish: "I'm the famous shoemaker. Don't I make good shoes and good boots for the Germans?!"

6. "Enough already!"

7. Unclear which is his true name, Okan or Kogan.

Eyewitness Testimony 2

1. Some rabbis took as their moral credo the famous dictum of the Rambam (Maimonides, 1135–1204), that if one Jew is demanded by the enemy in order to spare the whole community, then the whole community must submit to the punishment rather than sacrifice the one individual.

2. DP camp in Germany.

3. Jadow—Warsaw district.

4. Urle—a summer resort in Warsaw district.

Eyewitness Testimony 3

1. Unidentified.

2. In Lwów County.

3. Unidentified; probably work camp outside Lwów.

4. Yiddish (and German) name for Lwów.

5. Labor camp on Yanowska Street in Lwów.

6. Unidentified.

Eyewitness Testimony 4

1. The first group of Jews from Poland and other occupied countries who were permitted to leave Europe as part of an exchange for German citizens living in Allied countries arrived in Ankara, Turkey, after many ordeals on November 16, 1942. Among them were thirty-one former citi-

zens of Poland who were now citizens of Palestine; thirteen of them were from Radom. See Ḥaim Barlas, *Hatzala biyemei shoa* ("Rescue during the Holocaust") (Jerusalem: Kibutz Hameuchad, 1975), p. 152.

2. Unidentified.

Eyewitness Testimony 5

1. In Stanislawów District, not far from Bursztyn.

2. He means the *Kreishauptmann* of Rohatyn County in Stanislawów District.

3. This date is impossible because as the witness himself states, this was the day he arrived at the peasant Shkurlak's hut in the Witan woods.

4. All in Stanislawów District.

5. This is, of course, a subjective explanation for the lull in the deportations.

Eyewitness Testimony 6

1. The final *aktsye* in the liquidation of the Grodno Ghetto took place in August 1943.

Eyewitness Testimony 7

1. Yiddish for Bałuty, also the broader name for the slum sections of Łódź where the Jewish folk masses were concentrated before the war and inside the ghetto.

2. Shoes made from plant husks were produced here.

3. The curfew for the September *aktsye*, from the fifth to the twelfth, 1942.

4. *Amtsleiter*, chief of the *Gettoverwaltung*. Tried and executed for war crimes in Poland in 1946.

Eyewitness Testimony 8

1. Yiddish for Siemiatycze.

2. Dr. Fritz Todt was in charge of German frontier fortifications during the war, and was appointed *Delegatgeneral* for all construction projects under the "Four Year Plan."

Eyewitness Testimony 9

1. The *Judenrat*.

2. In Polish, Zaborowo, Leszno County. The camp was run by the *Wasserwirtschaftsamt* of Wartheland.

3. An urban labor camp in the city of Poznań.

4. See Yishaye Trunk, "*Yidishe arbetslagern in varteland*," *Bleter far geshikhte* I: 1 (1948), 156, 164 (Yiddish).

5. During the liquidation of the Warta Ghetto on August 24–25, 1942, some of the healthy and ablebodied people were sent to the Łódź Ghetto.

6. Yiddish for Polish *działki*. Empty lots in the Łódź Ghetto that hadn't been utilized by the Germans were leased by the *Judenrat* to individuals for growing food.

7. The number of Gypsies whom the Germans began deporting to Auschwitz in February 1943 from every part of Europe reached several thousand. They were kept in Block BIIe in Birkenau. Their extermination in the Auschwitz gas chambers started in the spring of 1944. See Ota Kraus and Erich Kulka, *The Death Factory: Documents on Auschwitz* (Elmsford: Pergamon Press, 1966), pp. 185–86.

8. Unidentified. Waldenburg was an extension camp of the *Konzentrationslager* Gross-Rosen.

9. Another branch of *KZ* Gross-Rosen.

10. He survived and is active.

Eyewitness Testimony 10

1. Altogether, four "transports" from Prague arrived in the Łódź Ghetto: on October 18, a group of 1,000 people; on October 22, 1,186 people, on October 27, 1,063; and on November 1, 1,000 —4,249 Jews in all.

2. The Germans changed the Polish place names in the incorporated territories.

3. It was Max Hertz, a Jew from Cologne. He had managed to reach a train station in the suburbs after escaping from the ghetto. While he was buying a ticket, the *mogen david* patch fell out of his pocket. The cashier saw it and had him arrested.

4. These were the transports of Jews from Hungary.

5. This was a slave-labor camp for the concern of Bernsdorf et Co. in Dresden. It was an *Aussenkommando* of *KZ* Flossenburg.

6. "Hold on. It won't be too much longer."

7. "Ladies, we're free."

Eyewitness Testimony 11

1. Pravenishek in Yiddish. Not far from Kaunas.

2. Yiddish for Kaunas.

3. Deportations to the concentration camp in Riga from the Kaunas Ghetto took place on February 6 and October 20–22, 1942.

4. The testimony is inexact. The shooting took place October 31, 1942, and not twelve but forty-two Jewish policemen were executed. See Max Kaufman, *Die Vernichtung der Juden Lettlands* (Munich: 1947), pp. 170–180.

5. Town outside of Kaunas.

Eyewitness Testimony 13

1. Media Equipmant Installation, which produced different apparatuses for civilian and military communications purposes.

2. August 1942.

3. The remaining Jews of the Cracow Ghetto were expelled to Płaszów and other camps on March 13–14, 1943.

4. Płaszów was a suburb of Cracow, which was turned into a large concentration camp complex. The civilian populace of the area also worked in its many plants.

5. At various times, this man was known or suspected to have been an informer-agent for the Gestapo, a ghetto policeman, and a collaborator. He was appointed commander of the camp guards, and when he learned of the plans for the liquidation of the camp, he and his family and associates tried to bribe the Germans to let them escape. There were also reports of his having tried to save Jews in some instances. The SS deceived him and had him and all his dependents shot on the last day of the liquidation of Płaszów.

6. Amon Leopold Goeth, the *Lagerkommandant* of Płaszów, was condemned to death by a Polish tribunal and executed September 13, 1946. See *Proces Ludobójcy Amona Goetha przed Najwyższym Trybunałem Narodowym* (Warsaw: Central Jewish Historical Commission, 1947), p. 493.

Eyewitness Testimony 14

1. Skarżysko Kamienna (Skarzhisk in Yiddish), in Radom County, Kielce District. Between August 1942 and July 1944, almost 8,000 Jews were forced through this labor camp. It functioned mostly as a munitions works.

2. The *Aussenkommando* (annex camp) of Ravensbrück.

Eyewitness Testimony 15

1. There is no corroborating information about a separate *aktsye* against Jewish women.

2. After the first *aktsye* in March of 1942, the wives of the laborers who had been exempt from death on the basis of their temporary usefulness received a card with the letter H—*Haushalt* or "Domestic"—which also reprieved them from death for the time being.

3. The name Rokeach doesn't appear among the listed members of the *Judenrat*. He was an employee, apparently.

4. Psalms 145: 1.

Eyewitness Testimony 16

1. "There are Jews here!"

2. "Where's the Jewess?"

3. Code word for the Gestapo.

4. An error; it should be August.

5. Outside Warsaw.

6. An extension of the Buchenwald Concentration Camp in Lower Saxony.

Eyewitness Testimony 17

1. Unidentified.

2. Rymanów, Krasno, Dukła, and Sanok are in the Lwów District; Jasło and Żmygród, in the Cracow District.

3. Near Sanok.

4. A rural settlement not far from Sanok.

Eyewitness Testimony 18

1. In Brzeżany County, Tarnopol District.

2. In Tarnopol District.

3. Towns not far from Stanisławów.

4. Village near Stanisławów.

5. After the withdrawal of the Red Army, the Jews, who were identified with the Bolsheviks, were accused of having slaughtered large numbers of Ukrainian arrestees in the prisons, and this libel was used as a pretext for murderous pogroms against them.

6. "What do you want, dog?!"

7. "Away, dogs! *We're* here to do the beating!"

8. This number is probably exaggerated. Various sources give the number of murdered Jews at between 8,000 (Josef Kermisz, *Akcje i Wysiedlenia* [Łódź, Centralua Żydowska, 1946], p. viii) and 12,000 (*Arim viyimahot beyisrael*, V (Jerusalem: Romisja Historyczna, 1952), p. 395. The massacre took place on October 12, 1941.

9. This number, too, is also estimated to be smaller in other sources.

10. The witness seems to be in error with regard to the chronology of events. The operations against the Jews, which included the burning of the ghetto in March and the execution of the Jewish workers in the "Rudolf Mill" in June or July, took place in 1942.

11. This is probably incorrect. The death transports were sent to Bełżec at that time.

12. The liquidation of the Jewish hospital took place on the first day of Rosh Hashanah, 1943. See *Arim viyimahot beyisrael* V, p. 400.

13. "No crying!"

14. Acronym of the Polish name of the Organization of Worker's Universities.

15. Today retired.

16. The witness has apparently confused the names: Wilhelmshaven is near Bremen and not Berlin. Perhaps she meant Wilhelmsdorf.

17. *Allgemeine Elektrizität Gesellschaft.*

Eyewitness Testimony 19

1. Eastern Galicia.

2. Yiddish for Sarny, in Volhynia.

3. July 13, 1942.

4. See Mark Dvorzecki, *Yirusholayim delite in kamf un umkum* (Paris, 1948), p. 201, and Layb Garfunkel, *Kovna hayehudit biḥurbana* (Jerusalem, 1954), p. 130.

5. Yiddish for Seliszcze.

6. "Little daughter of mine."

Eyewitness Testimony 20

1. She later perished in Auschwitz.

2. Elsnig was a branch of *KZ* Buchenwald.

3. Unidentified; perhaps she means OPEJ—*Oeuvre de Protection des Enfants Juifs.*

Eyewitness Testimony 21

1. The *aktsye* took place during the days of October 22–24, 1942.

2. "May God avenge his blood."

3. In Opatów County, Kielce District.

4. In Upper Silesia.

5. A large industrial complex of the I.G. Farben company which was set up in Monowice, eight kilometers from Auschwitz, in the autumn of 1942 for the manufacture of synthetic gasoline and imitation rubber. See Ota Kraus and Erich Kulka, *The Death Factory*, pp. 18–24.

6. In Lower Silesia; now in Poland.

Eyewitness Testimony 22

1. Yiddish for Radów (?) and Szydlowiec.

Eyewitness Testimony 23

1. An error. Deportation of approximately 6,000 Jews from Łódź to the Government General took place from the fourteenth to the seventeenth of December, 1939.

2. Probably Heniek Zimmerman, mentioned in the eyewitness testimony of M. Sh. titled "Jewish Partisans in the Lublin-Bychowo Region" in *Dos bukh fun lublin* (Lublin Memorial Book, Paris, 1952), pp. 550–51.

3. A hamlet eighteen kilometers from Lublin; part of the incorporated village of Piotrków.

4. Unidentified.

5. In Lublin County; part of the incorporated village of Zembożyce.

Eyewitness Testimony 24

1. This "voluntary, self-imposed" exile from Auschwitz to Lublin, has been documented nowhere else until now.

2. Between the ninth and fifteenth of April.

3. Yiddish for Będzin, Sosnowiec, and Chrzanów.

4. Until 1918, Oświęcim (Auschwitz) was under Austrian administration as part of Western Galicia and Będzin was part of Czarist Congress Poland.

5. Polish name Brzéziny Śląskie in Silesia.

6. Brand *Arbeitslager* in the Aachen Region.

7. A slave-labor camp for Jews not far from Breslau, which was started at the beginning of 1941 and operated until March 1944.

8. In Cracow County.

9. The witness is referring to the thousands of loaves of bread laced with cyanide that the camp command had allegedly prepared for the inmates at the very end. It was only because of a last-minute admission by a German doctor that a mass poisoning in Bergen-Belsen was thwarted.

Eyewitness Testimony 25

1. A street bordering the Jewish and "Aryan" sectors of the city.

2. A suburb of Warsaw lying close to the Vistula River.

3. Janów County, Lublin District.

4. A Polish coalition committee with Jewish representation founded in the fall of 1942 to secure the safety of Jews crossing to the "Aryan" side. Code name ŻEGOTA, "Rada Pomocy Żydom" in Polish. It was active in Warsaw and had liaison men in the provinces.

5. From July 22 until the end of September, 1942, during which approximately 300,000 Jews were deported to their deaths in Treblinka.

Eyewitness Testimony 26

1. Wilhelm Hoffmann was the owner of this undergarment factory. During the summer *Aussiedlung* of 1942, he was allotted 500 Jewish workers who were given the so-called *Lebensschein*.

2. Yiddish name for the *Judenrat* (from the Polish *Gmina*); also applied to the prewar Jewish *Kehileh* and transferred to the Warsaw Council, as several members, the building, and some of the functions remained intact.

3. In Radzymin County, Warsaw District.

4. A town near Warsaw.

Eyewitness Testimony 27

1. Yiddish for Częstochowa. There were four labor camps in Częstochowa: (1) HASAG Pelzer (HASAG is an acronym for *Hugo Schneider Arbeitsgesellschaft*), (2) HASAG *Apparatenbau* (Equipment), (3) HASAG Warta, and (4) HASAG Częstochowianka, which worked thousands of Jews to death.

2. An extension camp of *Mittelbau,* the concentration camp lying between Buchenwald and Bergen-Belsen.

Eyewitness Testimony 28

1. Chairman of the *Zentrale* of the Jewish Councils in Eastern Upper Silesia.

2. Auschwitz.

3. This behavior has not been attested to in any other source.

4. "Not when you want, but when I want!"

Eyewitness Testimony 29

1. A village in Końskie County, Kielce District, where a labor camp was set up.

Eyewitness Testimony 30

1. Yiddish for Kanzleischreiber.

2. Ujazd, Kielce District.

3. Białystok District.

4. Yiddish for Sadowna, Volhynia District.

5. Near Warsaw.

6. Jürgen Stroop, SS *Brigadenführer,* in charge of the suppression of the Warsaw Ghetto Uprising in April–May 1943. He was tried by a Polish court in 1951, condemned, and executed.

7. Lublin District.

8. A mistake. The name was Rastatt, in Baden, Germany.

9. Cracow District.

10. Cracow District.

11. Near Cracow.

12. "Caps on! Caps off!"

Eyewitness Testimony 31

1. Yiddish for Kanzleischreiber.

2. An emaciated, lifeless inmate on the verge of death. In Auschwitz, the name for these people was "Muzulman."

Eyewitness Testimony 32

1. The last stages of the liquidation of the Tarnopol Ghetto happened in May 1943. From July 1941 until that time, six *aktsyes* had occurred; during the first, almost 5,000 people were shot on the spot.

2. Rokita, a Ukrainian, was arrested after the war, tried in Warsaw, and executed.

3. Should be Katzmann. Fritz Katzmann, SS- and *Polizeiführer,* came from the Radom District to the Galician District in 1942 and led the extermination process against the Jews of Galicia.

4. SS-*Untersturmfuhrer* Hildebrand was Katzmann's most active assistant.

Eyewitness Testimony 33

1. Yiddish for Świerzeń.

2. "Zhukovtsy" was the name of the Jewish unit in the partisan brigade named after Chapayev (Soviet partisan leader during the Civil War) which belonged to the "Union of Partisans" under the leadership of Major-General Kapustyn. It was organized in Kopyl County, Minsk District.

3. See Eyewitness Testimony 41.

4. Compare Eyewitness Testimony 41.

5. Thirty kilometers from Świerzeń Nowy.

6. Unidentified.

Eyewitness Testimony 34

1. Gendarme.

2. Town hall.

3. Marshal.

4. Police headquarters.

5. The mister—right, and the lady—left.

6. Countryside.

7. Corn.

8. My God (Yiddish).

9. Why are you bothering him?

10. "I'm a Jew."

11. "German! German!"

12. "I'll take it."

13. The British army.

14. "In remembrance of the meeting of two countrymen in Froli."

15. "You go. A car's coming for me."

Eyewitness Testimony 37

1. Railroad.

2. Berlin Jewish Community Board. Until its liquidation, central body representing Berlin Jews.

3. Major action.

Eyewitness Testimony 38

1. She has confused the names—possibly for psychological reasons, as the reader might deduce further on.

2. A prominent, extended family.

3. Yiddish for Drohobycz.

4. In Upper Silesia.

Eyewitness Testimony 39

1. Yiddish for Zdzięcioł, Nowogródek District.

Eyewitness Testimony 40

1. This was the *aktsye* against the children up to the age of ten, and the sick and old people, which was carried out between September 5 and 12, 1942.

2. A Bundist economic enterprise founded before the war.

3. This account of a separate *aktsye* against the sick in 1944 hasn't been verified by any other source. Such an operation took place on Sept. 1, 1942.

4. "I Want to Go Home."

5. Auschwitz.

6. "Leave your baggage!"

7. "Daddy! Daddy!"

8. He is mistaken; the war ended May 8, 1945.

9. Unidentified.

10. "Come out!"

11. "Comrades."

Eyewitness Testimony 41

1. He was a member of the Bundist youth movement, *Tsukunft*. Compare Eyewitness Testimony 33.

2. Another version of this note was published by Josef Reich, who says he was its co-author, in his book *Vald in flamen* ("Forest in Flames," Buenos Aires: Yidbukh, 1954), pp. 97–98. There is much complementary and parallel information in this book about this particular Eyewitness Testimony.

3. Yiddish for Stołpce.

4. Świerzeń Nowy.

5. "Today the world is born!"—popular saying from prayer for Rosh Hashana.

6. At the former boundary line between Poland and the USSR.

7. "Comrade Commander, request permission to report—sixty men."

8. "Mission accomplished."

9. Rodyanov was an officer in the Soviet army who withdrew during the general retreat, was surrounded by the Germans in Minsk, and voluntarily surrendered himself and his entire command to be held captive in a labor camp. He started collaborating with the occupation forces in combatting the partisans but eventually turned against his German captors and brought his people over to Zheleznyak's partisan brigade, having previously overrun several German garrisons.

10. "Sing something, something Hasidic, and knock us out!"

11. "Sing something Hasidic!"

12. "What do we need this Third Unit for?!"

13. Unidentified.

14. Reich gives his name as Ananchiko (*Vald in flamen*, p. 279). He is called Anichenko in the book about Jewish partisans by Moyshe Kaganovitch, *Di milkhome fun yidishe partizaner in mizrekh-eyrope* (Buenos Aires: *Tsentral farband fun poylishe yidin in Argentina,* 1956), vol. I, p. 351.

15. "This is a commander's weapon."

16. "Jewboys without guns."

17. Commissar Donayev was the leader of the Russian partisan unit, *"Boyevoy!"* Shtors is the name of a Bolshevik combatant during the Civil War. General Ponamorenko was chief of staff of the Byelorussian partisan movement.

18. Oyzer Maza, provisions officer for the Jewish Zhukovtsy unit.

Eyewitness Testimony 42

1. Russian for Hitler.

2. He means Praga, the suburb of Warsaw on the right bank of the Vistula.

Eyewitness Testimony 44

1. The attack was carried out in August 1942 by the partisan battalion named "Stalin" near the village of Naliboki. Ninteen of the *Einsatzgruppe* troops were killed, among them the chief of the Baranowicze *Sicherheitsdienst*. See Kaganovitch, *Di milkhome . . . .* , p. 392.

2. August 4, 1942.

3. For more about this successful tunnel-escape, see Kaganovitch, *Di Milkhome . . .* , pp. 214–15. The date of the escape is given there as September 26, 1943, and the number of inmates who got away through the tunnel as 233. According to this source, only about 150 of them reached the woods. The others, including Berl Yoselovitch, were killed in the German pursuit after the breakout.

Eyewitness Testimony 45

1. After the summer deportations of July–September 1942, the Germans left behind only about 35,000 legal laborers, but in reality, a few tens of thousands of Jews still remained, those who hadn't been uncovered in their bunkers and hideouts, the so-called *"vilde,"* wild ones, who had no legal status in the ghetto. Over time, most of them managed to get counted among the German labor gang and become legitimized this way.

2. Gepner headed the Provisions Department (*Zaklad Zaopatrywania*) of the Warsaw *Judenrat*. In the bunker with him at Franciszkanska 30 were the *"vilde"* battle groups, the unaffiliated armed combatants, who put up a resistance alongside the *Żydowska Organizacja Bojowa* (Jewish Combatant Organization). See Yosif Kermish, *Mered geto varsha be'eynei haoyev* ("The Warsaw Ghetto Rebellion as Seen by the Enemy," Tel Aviv: Yad Vashem, 1959), with map of Warsaw Ghetto.

3. The brush workshops were situated on Swiętojerska Street, on the block between numbers 30 and 34. Fierce battles raged there from the twentieth to the twenty-first of April. A mine previously planted by the combatants exploded under the route of the marching Germans and left behind scores of German dead and wounded. The entire brush works region was flattened and pulverized by German artillery during the day of April 21.

Eyewitness Testimony 46

1. Yiddish for Poniatowa, a Jewish labor camp in the Lublin district.

2. The executions in Poniatowa labor camp went on from the third to the fifth of November, 1943.

3. Most of the ghetto police and their families were deported to Treblinka on September 21, 1942, in the general deportation. They were no longer needed.

4. "It's all over. We're going to Mother."

5. A well-known doctor, a heart specialist.

6. Hessenthal (Schwäbisch-Hall county).

7. Annex camp of the concentration camp at Dachau.

Eyewitness Testimony 47

1. Yiddish for Siedlce-Małkinia.

2. Częstochowa.

3. An official inquest in Treblinka estimated the number of Jews exterminated there at a minimum of 731,600, but made a point of adding that the number is clearly far higher. See *Biuletyn Głownej Komisji Badania Zbrodni Hitlerowskich w Polsce* ("Bulletin of the Main Commission for Investigation of German [Hitlerite] Crimes in Poland"), vol. I (Warsaw, 1946), p. 142. Hereafter, *BGKBZH*.

4. This last method has not been attested to anywhere else.

5. From the end of July 1942, one building with two gas chambers inside was used to exterminate the Jews. At the start of autumn, 1942, a second larger building with ten gas chambers on both sides of a passageway was completed and its death mechanisms activated.

6. See above, Note 3.

7. Himmler visited the camp during the spring months of 1943. The names of twenty-one SS men who serviced the death chambers especially for him are known. *BGKBZH*, vol. I, p. 138.

8. This is where Jewish laborers needed by the Germans were treated. Jewish doctors lived and worked there.

9. So called after the "Court Jews" of the Middle Ages, who culled special favor with the feudal rulers, often serving in primary leadership capacities. In the camp, they were the "privileged domestics."

10. *"Di lyalke"* in Yiddish. Sardonic name assigned by the Jews in Treblinka to Kurt Franz from Thüringen, vice-*Kommandant* of the camp.

11. This was the second, smaller part of the camp where the gas chambers and mass graves were located side by side.

12. In the Eyewitness Testimony of another survivor (No. 64 in the YIVO collection), he was said to be from Warsaw.

13. He was actually the *Lagerälteste* or *Oberkapo*.

14. This description seems improbable. It hasn't been corroborated by any other source. The people he mentions were probably not actual ghetto

combatants, who had already been killed for the most part, but Jews who'd been drawn out of their bunkers, or who'd been forced out of hiding in the conflagration of the ghetto.

15. This also seems improbable and hasn't been verified anywhere else.

16. Not mentioned in any other source, though in the Eyewitness Testimony of Shimon Goldberg reprinted in Nahman Blumental, *Dokumenty i Materialy z Czasow Okupacji Niemeckiej*, vol. I—*"Obozy"* (Łódź, 1946), p. 180, a Dr. Rybak is mentioned.

17. Also mentioned in Eyewitness Testimony 64 of the YIVO collection, but without referring to his relation to the former Czech president.

18. This camp, which was a labor camp for Jews and a penal camp for Poles, was constructed in the summer of 1941 and sanctioned by the decree of the Warsaw District Governor, Fischer, of October 15, 1941. Its official name was SS *und Polizeiführerarbeitslager* Treblinka. *BGKBZH*, vol. III (1947), pp. 109–10.

19. Engineer Sudowicz, an agronomist. In Warsaw, he headed the Society for the Promotion of Agriculture Among Jews, known by its initials in Polish as TOPOROL.

20. No other source mentions this. The fact that the Ukrainians fired from the guard towers seems to indicate they weren't burned down.

21. Kurt Seidel, from Berlin; oversaw the paving work.

22. A small watchtower in the so-called "Tiergarten," where pigeons also nested.

23. The number is exaggerated.

24. At least eighteen known people of those who survived the Treblinka Uprising lived to see the end of the war.

25. DP camp in what is now East Germany.

Eyewitness Testimony 48

1. "SS Command for Special Tasks—Resettlement Camp for Jews."

2. An official inquest determined that the five gas chambers could hold over 500 victims at a time. *BGKBZH*, vol. III (1947), p. 54. The name of the camp is not mentioned in the official inquest.

3. Probably Michael Hermann. *Ibid.*, p. 52.

4. "Quiet."

5. Apparently Paul Intner. *BGKBZH*, vol. III, p. 52.

6. Gustav Wagner. *Ibid;* recently identified in Brazil and arrested. Poland, Germany and Israel declared his extradition.

7. Franz Stengel, *Kommandant* of Treblinka from the summer of 1942 to August 1943. In 1970 was arrested in Brazil and extradited to West Germany, where he was tried and died in prison before sentencing in 1971.

8. The witness apparently forgot during the interview that he'd stated Bari's master was Paul Intner of the SS.

9. "Mad dogs, cursed people."

10. Servant.

11. At attention.

12. Meaning *Älteste* or *Kapo*.

13. Should be Gustav, unless there was another SS man named Hans Wagner in camp.

14. Of the clothes.

15. Tyszowce, in Zamość County.

16. Żółkiewka, Krasnystaw County, Lublin District. He was chairman of the Jewish Council in Żółkiewka. Murdered in the Kielce Pogrom of July 1946.

17. Karl Frenzel.

18. In Lublin District.

19. Here the witness contradicts what he said earlier about this person.

20. Alexander Pechorski of Minsk. See A. Pechorski, *Der oyfshtand in Sobibór* ("The Uprising in Sobibór, Moscow, 1946).

21. "Hey, good brother!"

22. "What's new?"

23. The camp was liquidated in November 1943. All installations, apparatus, and equipment were removed, the buildings were blown up, and the debris was hauled away by train. Part of the grounds were planted over with a sapling grove.

24. Probably Uchanie in Hrubieszów County.

25. Between Chełm and Sobibór.

26. Rejowiec, not far from Chełm.

Eyewitness Testimony 49

1. *Armia Krajowa*—Polish underground army, or Home Army.

2. He means in September 1944, when the uprising was defeated.

Eyewitness Testimony 50

1. A group of twenty-two rescued Jewish combatants fought alongside the AL (*Armia Ludowa*—People's Army) in the Polish Uprising of August 1944. Among the participants in the battles were also Greek and Hungarian Jews who were brought in to clear the Warsaw Ghetto rubble before being freed from Pawiak Prison by Polish combatants. The witness was mistaken with regard to the name of the prison.

Eyewitness Testimony 51

1. Zionist youth training colony in Vilna for settlement in Palestine.

2. Yiddish for Poznań.

3. 1941 is meant.

4. Centuries-old Yeshiva which was one of the first targets for Nazi destruction.

5. A forced exile from the East.

6. He lives today as an Israeli citizen in a Carmelite community near Haifa and is called "Brother Daniel." He regards himself as a Jew.

Eyewitness Testimony 52

1. Zilina, in Slovakia, was used as a concentration area for the transports of Jews who were deported to Poland.

2. Pro-Nazi police contingents, named after the head of the Slovakian "Autonomist Party."

3. Bratislava.

4. Dr. Georg Reves, a Jewish youth leader in Slovakia who was active for a time in the rescue of Polish Jews in the Polish-Slovakian border zone and the Jewish "Center" in Bratislava. See Yirmiya (Oscar) Noiman, *Bitsel hamavet* (Tel Aviv: M. Newman, 1958), pp. 153, 257.

Eyewitness Testimony 53

1. Auschwitz.

2. An obvious misstatement. Of the 300,000 French Jews then, 85,000 perished, the great majority in the gas chambers of Auschwitz.

Eyewitness Testimony 54

1. A Croat nationalist terrorist organization that collaborated with the Nazi occupiers under Ante Pavelić.

Eyewitness Testimony 55

1. In Wołożyn County.

2. Nowogródek County.

3. Right-wing anti-Semites.

4. Meykl, who was from Bielica, escaped into the forest from the Zdzięciół Ghetto in August 1942. He led a Jewish unit of the "Borba" battalion, "Lenin" brigade. The family units were also under his protection. He was killed in the village of Zaczepice. See *Sefer hapartizanim*, vol. II (Tel Aviv), p. 732.

5. Unidentified.

6. Should be Busel. There were two Zdzięcioł partisans in the "Borba" battalion named Busel, Yosif and Yisrul, both killed while mining convoy roads. *Sefer hapartizanim,* vol. II, p. 678.

7. Should be Zelig Kovenski of Zdzięcioł, formerly of another Jewish unit and transferred to the "Borba" battalion in 1943. He fought in the Soviet army after Liberation and was killed in Białystok in July 1944. Elyuhi Kovenski was a partisan in the Molczadż Forest who was killed in an attempt to break out of an enemy encirclement. *Ibid.* p. 756.

8. Another account of her death—she was killed in June 1944 during the encirclement—is given in *Sefer hapartizanim,* vol. II, p. 777. She was active in the battalion as a nurse.

Eyewitness Testimony 56

1. Lwów.

2. Warsaw vicinity.

3. Betrayed by informers.

4. She was a professor of natural science in the Polish Free College of Arts and Science, "Wszechnica," in Warsaw.

5. A well-known professor of medicine at Warsaw University.

6. Contradicts what the witness says later.

7. *Polska Partia Socjalistyczna*—Polish Socialist Party.

8. In the beginning of September, after the capitulation of the rebels.

9. Compare Eyewitness Testimony 58.

10. See Bernard Goldstein, *The Stars Bear Witness* (New York: Viking Press, 1949), pp. 254–73. "Joint" is short for Joint Distribution Committee. "*Khaver*" means "Comrade."

Eyewitness Testimony 57

1. Not far from Sosnowiec.

2. A suburb of Warsaw on the left bank of the Vistula.

Eyewitness Testimony 58

1. The *Judenrat,* whose leading members were prewar Bundist representatives on the *Kehile,* was involved in underground activities of the Bund in the Government General. In July 1941, a Polish underground courier, Maria Szczęsna, was arrested while carrying illegal publications and the names of underground activists, also of Bundists. In a short while, four *Judenrat* members were arrested. One of them surrendered to the

German authorities voluntarily in solidarity with his arrested comrades. They were sent to Auschwitz, and soon a telegram arrived that they all "died." Isaiah Trunk, *Judenrat* (New York: Macmillan, 1972), pp. 463–64.

2. Or they were expelled there from other towns and cities, mainly from Wartheland and Zichenau district.

3. Annex factory.

4. Number exaggerated upward. He himself says immediately afterwards that the number was 10,000.

5. A force of Jewish soldiers from Palestine that fought with the Allies in Europe in the late stages of the war. They participated in the rescue and transfer of Jews to Palestine.

Eyewitness Testimony 59

1. Kaunas.

2. Should be July 1944. The final day in the liquidation of the Kaunas Ghetto by conflagration was July 15, 1944.

3. Toruń, Pomorze District, western Poland.

4. Yiddish for Lithuania.

Eyewitness Testimony 60

1. There were two *Aussiedlungen* in 1942: June second and August twelfth.

2. Polish for hostage.

3. Franz Hössler, *Kommandant* of Birkenau.

4. These events were in connection with the uprising of the Jewish *Sonderkommando* in Auschwitz on October 7, 1944. The two other women were from Warsaw. They were hanged in the first days of January 1945. See Raaya Kagen, *Nashim bilishkot hagehenom* ("Women in the Chambers of Hell," Tel Aviv: Merḥavia Press, 1947), pp. 228–29, 235–36. On the mutiny of the *Sonderkommando* see: Oto Kraus, Erich Kulka, *The Factory of Death* (London: Corgi Books, 1964).

5. The evacuation of the inmates from the Auschwitz-Birkenau camps was begun in October 1944 and ended in the forced march of January 18, 1945. Since the witness was present at the hanging of the four girls, which took place at the start of 1945, she must have been taken out of the camp in January 1945 at the earliest.

Eyewitness Testimony 61

1. Kaunas.

2. "Shit on the inmates! Throw them into the water!"

3. Yiddish-German: "Kind sir, take us on, we're hungry, take us on!"

4. "We can't take so many on!"

5. "Out quickly!"

6. About 63 pounds.

Eyewitness Testimony 62

1. Should be September 1942.

Index of Places

Index of Persons, Organizations and Ethnic Groups

Adamowicz, Irena, 47
Akiba, Bnei, 36
American fliers, 299, 301
American Jewish Committee, 7
American Jewish Congress, 7
American Jewish Joint Distribution Committee (A.J.D.C.; the "Joint"), 33, 163, 328
Americans, 106, 121, 122, 140, 166, 187, 203, 214, 217, 233, 262, 300, 315, 328
Ananchenko, partisan commander, 243
Anders, Gen. Wladyslaw, 49
Arbeitsamt, 140
Aris, Lea, 317
Armia Krajowa (AK; Home Army), 47, 48, 287, 288, 303, 307, 309. *See also* ZWZ (Union for Armed Struggle)
Atlas, Dr. Yechiel, 228
Auerswald, Heinz, 17
Austrians, 106
Aznberg, Mendl-Duvid, 192

Bandera, Stepan, 38, 43
Banderovtsi, 116, 226, 251
BBC, 51
Beckmann, *Schaarführer*, 283
Bernard, *Khaver*, 309
Belgian Underground, 298–300
Belgians, 218
Berliner Jüdische Gemeinde (Berlin Jewish Community), 219
Berman, 242
Bezręki, Borys, partisan leader, 228
Bialik, Hayyim, 37, 92
Biebow, Hans, *Amtsleiter of Łódź Ghetto*, 97, 103, 229–30, 231
Bilo, Max, 263, 268

Birnboim, Shmiel, 80
Bloch, Chaim, 19
Blockälteste (*Blokowa*), 24, 109, 110, 162–63, 200, 202, 204
Blokowa. See Blockälteste
"Bloody Mary," 319, 322
B'nai B'rith Anti-Defamation League, 7
Bor-Komorowski Uprising, 306
Brandkommandos (conflagration squads), 55
Brikhah, 116
British Army, 216, 325–26
Bruno, *Lagerälteste*, "Killer from Poznan," 200
Bumel, Elyuhi, 303
Bund, 33, 34, 36, 37, 46, 47, 49, 71, 229, 230
Byeloruskaya Narodnaya Respublika, 43
Byelorussian police, 236, 237, 253, 254
Byelorussians, 40–43, 210, 228, 229, 241, 242, 253, 290. *See also* White Russians
"Bystry." *See* Iwinski, Maj. Henryk

Canadians, 128
Catholic Front for a New Poland, 49
Catholics, 11
Chapayewtsy, Soviet partisan unit, 208, 245
Charne, Tsaleh, 294
Chilewicz, head of Jewish camp police in Płaszów, 118
Chorążycki, Dr., 263–65
Chudoba, 292, 294
Communists, 33, 46, 47, 291
Coughlin, Father Charles E., 7